CONTACT WITH THE OTHER WORLD

CONTACT WITH THE OTHER WORLD

THE LATEST EVIDENCE AS TO COMMUNICATION WITH THE DEAD

by

JAMES H. HYSLOP, Ph.D., LL.D

GYAN

Published by

GYAN

Gyan Publishing House
5, Ansari Road
Daryaganj, New Delhi-110002
Phone: 011-47034999, 9811692060
E-mail: books@gyanbooks.com

Distribution Network
gyanbooks.com
India, USA, Canada, UK, Australia, France

ISBN : 978-81-212-6028-2 (PB)
First Published, 1919

2nd Impression 2021

Printed at: Gyan Press, Delhi.

Contact with the Other World
Author: James H. Hyslop

CONTACT WITH THE OTHER WORLD

THE LATEST EVIDENCE AS TO COMMUNICATION WITH THE DEAD

BY

JAMES H. HYSLOP, PH.D., LL.D

FORMERLY PROFESSOR OF LOGIC AND ETHICS IN COLUMBIA UNIVERSITY

1919

CONTENTS

PART I
HISTORICAL

PART II
PRELIMINARY PROBLEMS

PART III
EVIDENCE OF SURVIVAL

PART IV
MISCELLANEOUS QUESTIONS

CONTENTS

ILLUSTRATIONS

PART I

HISTORICAL

CONTACT WITH THE OTHER WORLD

CHAPTER I

INTRODUCTION

SOME years ago a well-known college president thought to put an end to psychic research with the public by calling it a return to fetishism. He has lived long enough to learn that calling names does not refute facts, and we no longer need to apologize for the subject. When the work of investigation was first organized, no man's reputation was safe unless he joined in with the persiflage of the Philistine or the skepticism of the scientific world generally. It is easy to understand the accusation that psychic research is connected with fetishism, for its fundamental interest is in a doctrine that had its origin in what is known as animism, which is the spiritualism of savages, among whom it even took the form of regarding inorganic objects as animate. But the attempt to throttle investigation by invoking the contempt heaped on primitive minds was hasty and ill advised. Those who think it dignified to study folk-lore certainly cannot consider it undignified to pursue inquiries into the real causes of animism. But culture always has its antagonisms, and none is stronger than that which exists in the intellectual classes against ideas supposed to be wholly barbaric. That feeling I myself at one time shared, but I did not purpose to ignore facts in the opinions that I might hold. Prejudice had to be overcome in the face of what was indisputable, or so wide-spread as to demand explanation. Primitive minds may have been wrong in their theories, but they seem to have had facts which require consideration, even though we go no further than fraud or hysteria to account for them; and to find these facts is to discover their kinship with those of modern times.

But true psychic research took its origin not from any sympathy with the ideas of savages nor from any consciousness that the two stages of culture are connected. It was a very concrete set of incidents that exacted of fair-minded men the examination of the facts. Even the types of phenomena did not present themselves clearly at the outset. The most prominent were those claiming to embody some form of communication with the dead; but types of unusual phenomena were soon found that could lay no claim to this character, and as they seemed less clearly to contravene the accepted laws of nature, they offered a ground for compromise between orthodox science and the claims of the supernatural. Among such phenomena were telepathy or mind-reading, dousing, hypnosis, suggestion, muscle-reading, and perhaps a few others. They opened a field for discussion that made the consideration of spiritualism unnecessary, at least for the time, since they were possibly susceptible of (natural) explanation.

It was a mistake of scientific skepticism to invoke any preconceived ideas about the explanation of things in order to eliminate the consideration of psychic phenomena. The question of fact, not of explanation, is the first concern of science. In selecting his course, however, the skeptic exposed himself to all the reactions which follow the proof of what he doubts or denies; and we are to-day reaping the harvest of his imprudence. The public is running off into every imaginable philosophy and religion, because of the trust of believer and skeptic alike in religious and philosophic traditions. Sympathy would have given the skeptic the leadership in a course in which he has been outrun; he now appears as the hindrance to knowledge instead of its supporter. A man should never be required to choose between doubt and belief. He should be able to intermingle both in due proportions. The spirit of open-mindedness and impartiality is to the intellectual world what brotherhood is to the ethical world. Woe betide the man who does not see this elementary truth, for he is sure to fall into one dogmatism or the other.

The facts that led to the conception of psychic research were a set of phenomena which, at least superficially, appeared to be inexplicable by the ordinary theories of science. They were taboo to normal psychology and psychologists, for no scientific man was prepared to reinstate the traditional idea of the supernatural. The opposition between the natural and the supernatural was so fixed that it was necessary to avoid misunderstanding of the latter term in order to pacify the orthodox psychologist. Hence the terms "psychic research" and "psychic phenomena" were chosen to denominate a border-land set of phenomena that might possibly be resolved into recognized types of events which, though unusual, would not necessitate a revision of orthodox beliefs. Abnormal psychology had come to accept many extraordinary things, but only as exhibitions of acute sensibility or as phenomena of coincidence. It was therefore necessary to make one's peace with this attitude and not to rush off prematurely into the regions of the miraculous. Psychic research thus became a compromise offered by one school of recognized scientists to another in the hope that some means might be found to extend tolerance to certain persistent facts that would not disappear at the command of conjurer or skeptic. The three types of phenomena which gave most offense were telepathy, apparitions, and mediumship. Hypnotism had won recognition, though only after meeting opposition hardly less bitter than that which these more inexplicable facts encountered. Muscle-reading and phenomena due to hyperæsthesia, or acute sensibility, lay on the border-land, and offered to the conservative mind a natural explanation of the facts to which they were relevant. Fraud, coincidence, and suggestion were explanations which further limited or refuted the claims of the supernormal and the supernatural.

For this reason psychic research appropriated for its territory all phenomena that might be explained by hyperæsthesia, whether visual, auditory, or tactual: the nature and limits of guessing and chance coincidence; hypnotism; hallucinations, whether subjective or veridical; apparitions, whether visual or auditory; mediumistic phenomena of all types; the physical phenomena of spiritualism, including raps or knockings, table-tippings, and telekinesis, or the movement of physical objects without contact, as well as the so-called materializations of common fame.

Not all of these are of equal value in the study of the problem which came easily to the front; namely, the problem of the existence of discarnate spirits. The theory of spirit agency had been advanced from time immemorial to cover the whole field; but it was the first task of investigators to discriminate among the phenomena and to determine their evidential values. For instance, neither telepathic coincidences nor the movement of objects without physical contact is in itself evidence of spirit agencies. The field had to be mapped out for scientific scrutiny on the basis that many people were not discriminating in the explanation of the facts. Only apparitions and mediumistic phenomena presented any immediately apparent evidence for discarnate spirits. The others, however they might ultimately be explained, offered no manifest evidence for such a hypothesis. But all of them were related at least as unusual phenomena hitherto not explained by ordinary causes, and so constituted a group of facts that had been disregarded by orthodox science. Psychic research simply claimed the field as a new country, possibly like the old, but not superficially so. It challenged science to apply its methods to the facts and, if possible, to reduce them to some sort of natural order.

In all ages the discovery of any new fact which is either not easily or not at all reducible to the normal has excited speculations of all kinds. The discovery of galvanic electricity roused all Europe to an interest in metaphysics; even Humboldt wrote a book, which he afterward regretted, that proclaimed magnetic forces to be the basis of cosmic causality. The discovery of radium started a revolution in science, though by this time scientists usually took discoveries of the kind more cautiously. But any new fact alters the perspective of previous knowledge, even when it does not revolutionize it. Psychic research was well adapted to rouse curiosity on the subject of the supersensible. Even telepathy so threatened the stability of materialism that skepticism was irreconcilably opposed to it, though telepathy did not involve spirit agencies. But phenomena that even looked like evidence in favor of spirits excited the most rabid skepticism, because they seemed to threaten all the conquests of physical science over the supernatural. Their recognition seemed to affect the laboriously built fabric of natural science as well as to offer hope and consolation to the human mind. No one objected to the latter, but the sacred structure of physical science must not be touched by hands soiled by the supernatural. Consequently, the interest of two opposing parties was strongly aroused by the claims in behalf of the supernormal in so far as these seemed to open the way into a transcendental world, one of support, because of an emotional satisfaction, and the other of hostility, because of the disturbance to the materialism of many years.

It was at least impossible to evade the discussion of the doctrine of spiritualism in the face of its claims. No matter what our decision about telepathy, dousing, telekinesis, and hypnotism, the apparent meaning of apparitions and mediumistic phenomena required further consideration; and whether we believed or disbelieved in the spiritistic interpretation, we had to face the issue. The practical and ethical interests of man concentrated attention on this one question and subordinated all others, no matter how vigorously was urged the need of cool scientific investigation. Spiritualism, therefore, gained prominence, and in the course of time challenged any defender of materialistic science to meet it in the arena. Skepticism was asked to consider evidence, and to offer some practical and desirable alternative to death without resurrection or survival. Skepticism was handicapped in such a debate. It might insist on natural laws, but it was always menaced by the prospect of contending with human needs, which have as much influence in determining many beliefs as any of the rigid standards of evidence that will have nothing to do with the ethical ideals of man.

The importance of a belief in survival after death depends partly on the conditions of the age and partly on the conceptions we have of that life. There have been ages in which the idea of immortality exercised little influence on the ethical and social life, and there have been ages and races in which it was central, determining even political institutions. In all cases its value depends on the existing state of knowledge and on belief in many other things. If man's moral nature is rightly developed without the belief in immortality, proof will be more an intellectual than an ethical concern; but in an age when the affections are highly developed, and the intellect has adopted conceptions which virtually nullify the influence of the affections, it will be a matter of some importance to learn whether nature is as careful of personality as it is of atoms and matter. We may play the part of Stoics in this respect when we have no grounds for belief, but Stoicism itself is in most cases a tribute to that which it concedes cannot be obtained. Few natures can live a purely Stoical life. The most ethical impulses are not cast in that mold; and we welcome that attitude only when it conforms to what the affections teach, though it has given up the beliefs that fostered them. It is true that we have to submit if we do not have evidence for either faith or knowledge; but the loss will not be compensated by Stoicism, and most people will seek for light beyond a horizon which seems to hide the future from us. At least there is something to be said for the hope that consciousness may be prolonged beyond the grave. It is as natural and rational as the impulse toward self-preservation.

The necessity of discussing the existence of spirits at various points in this work makes it important here at the outset to dispel certain illusions about that term. It is probable that in earlier writings I did not sufficiently allow for these illusions. But here I shall not permit readers to indulge them without taking the responsibility for them. Nearly all the difficulties of most people, except scientific psychologists, in the matter of believing in spirits depend on their conception of the term. In the ancient discussions about idolatry, and, in fact, during the whole period of controversy with materialism, the believers in spirits assumed and kept in the forefront of the argument the fact that spirits represented supersensible realities beyond the field of sensory perception. Even when they conceived them as quasi-material, they did not forget their inaccessibility to sensation. But when the exigencies of that controversy passed away and materialism again took the helm, there was a return, largely unconscious, perhaps, to the conception of spirits as quasi-material or as representable in the forms of sensation. When the church relaxed its hostility to idolatry, it permitted the introduction of art into its temples and started the materialism which gradually undermined its foundations. In modern times esthetic needs and lack of logical thinking resulted in conveying to men's minds the idea that spirits could be represented in the forms of sense perception. The physical phenomena of spiritualism, especially those of materialization, taught men to think of spirits as sensory forms of some kind; and with sensation as the standard of reality, most people take imagination and newspaper representation as indicating what scientific spiritists believe when they say they believe in spirits. It is this inexcusable error which has to be dispelled.

In the present work, as in all that I have written on the subject, as I have often explained in former discussions, the term spirit means nothing more than *the stream of consciousness or personality* with which we are familiar in every human being. Whether it is accompanied by what is called the "spiritual body" of St. Paul, the "astral body" of the theosophists, or the "ethereal organism" of the Greek materialists and many scientific spiritualists of to-day, is irrelevant to the question, and is not assumed in this work or in any other published work of mine. It may be true that we have "spiritual bodies" not perceptible to sense and only occasionally accessible to supernormal functions of the mind, when conditions are favorable. I am neither upholding nor denying such a view. It is simply no part of the scientific problem before us. Even if one assumes this spiritual body, one does not necessarily accept the spiritistic theory of the mind. What we want to know is whether that spiritual body is conscious or not, and conscious with the same memory that the person had when living his earthly life. If the spiritual body has no memory of the past, if *the stream of consciousness or personalty* does not survive with it, there is little interest in the fact of survival either as a spiritual body or in the form of reincarnation. The interesting and important thing is the survival of *personal identity,* which consists wholly in the stream of consciousness with its memory of the past, and not in any spiritual body, no matter how necessary this latter may be to the survival of the mental stream itself.

The existence of spirit in this discussion means the existence and survival of this stream of consciousness or personality in independence of the physical organism, regardless of *how* it survives. How such a thing is possible is another and separate problem, unaffected by the evidence of the fact of survival. Personal identity is not accessible to sense perception. It is as transcendental as atoms, ether waves, ions, electrons, and other supersensible realities of physical science, if there are such. The problem of spiritism is the collection of evidence to show that consciousness continues after death; its difficulty lies wholly in the strength of the hypothesis that consciousness is a function of the brain and requires some such structure for its existence. Indeed, the sensory and materialistic conception of it is so strong that many people say to me that they do not see how consciousness can survive without a brain. They are so fixed in the modern theory that consciousness is a mere function or phenomenon of the brain that they cannot conceive of this as an unproved hypothesis. When one makes sense perception the criterion of truth, it is natural to make this assumption, especially when all normal experience shows the constant association of consciousness with a physical organism and reveals no traces of it when the body is dissolved. But the absence of evidence for survival is not evidence of the absence of it; hence only normal experience favors materialism. Supernormal experience, if proved, suggests a very different interpretation; it brings us in contact with the supersensible. In normal life, consciousness in all its forms is a supersensible reality, even when we suppose it to be wholly dependent on the physical organism. In asking people to believe in spirits we ask them only to suspend the dogmatic assurance that materialism has said the last word on the problem; simply to be as skeptical about materialism as they are about spiritism. They may then be in a position to discover the illusions which have affected all their thinking on this subject. If they simply try to understand what psychic research is aiming at, and so disregard the question of a spiritual body; the quasi-material conception of the soul, as not the primary question, and acknowledge that we are only trying to ascertain if personal consciousness survives as a *fact,* and not *how* it survives, they will find the problem very much simplified.

Consequently, in this work and in all the publications of the Society for Psychical Research the term " spirit " stands for *the personal stream of consciousness,* whatever else it may ultimately be proved to imply or require; and all the facts bearing on the issue must be conceived as evidence, not necessarily as attesting the nature, or any sensible conception, of spirit.

CHAPTER II

PSYCHIC PHENOMENA IN ANTIQUITY

IF it had not been for our present knowledge of psychic phenomena, no matter what the explanation of them, we should be unable to make intelligible most of the stories that have come down to us from ancient times. But present knowledge makes it easy to understand their meaning. Even savages were conversant with psychic phenomena, in the form of superstitions. Savage, no less than civilized imaginations, went far beyond the facts in their efforts to explain them, went so far that science has ever been disposed to cite these imaginings as proof of feeble intellectuality, as superstitions which it has been the achievement of civilization to overthrow. Tylor's "Primitive Culture," Herbert Spencer's works, Frazer's "Belief in Immortality among Savages" and many similar works, as well as the legends of folk-lore, bear testimony to the existence of psychic phenomena in the earliest times, even though we make due allowance for magic, fraud, hysteria, and morbid conditions. Dreams and sorcery seem to have been the chief forms of manifestation. In dreams the savage mind seemed to find evidence of survival, and in sorcery and magical rites it seemed to find means to invoke the aid of the dead or to propitiate their anger. The study of savage beliefs will some day be deemed as important as it is interesting in this respect, but only as throwing light upon the history of psychic phenomena. In all ages these phenomena participate in the character and preconceptions of the people affected by them. Their form is influenced and shaped by the preconceptions of normal experience. Moreover, savages assumed a reality in their experiences which the modern psychic researcher does not assume. They interpreted occurrences according to superficial appearance; but we have learned from the distinction between subjective and veridical hallucinations that these may have a genuine import even when they are only quasi-material.

This is particularly true of apparitions and voices. The significant fact regarding savages is that identical ideas of the soul arose among tribes that had never had any communication with one another, tribes as far separated as the Australians, the New-Zealanders, the South Sea Islanders, the Africans, and the North American Indians. Tradition cannot account for these similarities, but similar experiences can explain them.

But we cannot dwell here upon savage customs. They are only the antecedents that help to explain the deviations and survivals of certain ideas and customs in more civilized times. Perhaps we should not know the significance of these primitive customs, were it not for the survival of savages on the boundaries of civilization. But when they are once known, much becomes intelligible that could not easily, if at all, be otherwise unraveled. The more civilized periods arose out of the earlier conditions and were characterized by a revolt against them, which embodied itself now in a philosophy and now in some form of purified religion.

A more interesting period is that which followed savage times, in which the superstitions of earlier people were partly outgrown. The ancestor-worship of China and Japan is the oldest survival of animism, which is the belief of primitive races. As culture advanced, this worship took various forms. The more intelligent classes dropped the ideas of the more ignorant and substituted respect for the memory of ancestors in place of fear of their influence as spirits. But there were other and rival beliefs. When Buddhism and Confucianism arose, the former denying the existence of spirits and the latter admitting their existence, but disregarding their importance, ancestor-worship underwent modifications. Brahminism, the philosophic upholder of immortality, substituted a supersensible conception of the soul for the quasi-material idea of earlier times. But Buddhism directly attacked Brahminism, and, by denying all survival, including personal immortality as the Brahmins understood it, tended to uproot ancestor-worship. Confucius admitted that spirits exist; but his system was primarily concerned with secular ethics and laid no stress on the doctrine of survival. In political and social problems, all of these religions compromised with animism and made concessions to it. To-day we have every conceivable form of belief among the Oriental races. Ancestor-worship, in most cases simply the spiritualism of the East, survives as the exponent of immortality. Its influence is evident in the widely extended belief of the Chinese in demoniac possession.

Judaism in its early period, when it attacked idolatry, was in essence an assault on fetishism or animism. The pure theism of Moses marked an advance in a more philosophic conception of the world, and represented the same intellectual movement as that of Xenophanes and the Eleatics in Greece. In fact, it was more or less synchronous with the rise of Buddhism and other religions in the Orient, and at one period was contemporary with the intellectual development of Greek philosophy. In calling the worship which preceded theism " idolatry," modern minds, if ignorant of the meaning of animism, would mistake the nature of the movement. Animism had various forms, from the most superstitious type to an advanced stage of spiritualism, as represented in mediumship. Its most objectionable form was fetishism. A more familiar form is represented in incidents like that of the Witch of Endor, and, among the common people, in the general recognition of mediumistic phenomena, which it was to the interest of the state religion to persecute. The intellectuals of the age opposed the lower types of belief in the interest of a purer religion or ethics and even identified themselves with what we should now regard as the scientific spirit. Judaistic theism recognized the idea of God as absolute unchangeableness, while fetishism made Him or other discarnate realities altogether capricious and unmoral. In making the Divine unchangeable, the intellectuals identified God with natural law. It was only the later emergence of Christianity, with its appeal to the supernatural, which reinstated the animistic conception of the Divine. Had religion held to the notion of natural law, it might have escaped the consequences of its identification of the Divine with the irregular and capricious. The elder Judaism was virtually identical with the movement of Xenophanes in Greece, in so far as the conception of God was concerned, and represented philosophy *versus* superstition.

The origin of Christianity was associated with psychic phenomena to a marked degree. The story of the transfiguration, and the appearance of Moses and Elias on the mount is a conspicuous instance. It does not make any difference whether it be true or not; it was told, and modern psychic research has made it entirely credible, even though we give it no other import than that of an hallucination, objective or veridical. Furthermore, there is the story of Christ and the woman at the well; and that of Christ walking on the water, which is not regarded as a physical miracle in the New Testament, for it is not his physical body, but his spirit — the revised version says *apparition* — that is represented as walking on the water. We have the story of the disciples on the way to Emmaus after Christ's crucifixion; the story of St. Paul's vision on the way to Damascus, when he thought he saw his Lord after the crucifixion; the speaking with tongues on the day of Pentecost; the miracles of healing, which have been repeated a thousand times since that period, in more or less striking manner; and lastly the story of the resurrection, which investigation shows was connected with the phenomena of apparitions. The very term is the same as that used for such phenomena by Homer, Herodotus, Æschylus, and Sophocles. Many theologians have held this view independently of and even previous to psychic research. In addition, we have the "spiritual body" doctrine of St. Paul and the remarkable classification of the types of mediumship, or "spiritual gifts," described by him in the twelfth, thirteenth, and fourteenth chapters of First Corinthians; the fifteenth chapter of the same book developed his doctrine of the "spiritual body" and the resurrection.

What followed among the early Christian fathers, especially among the Greek philosophers who accepted Christianity, proves this genesis of Christianity in psychic phenomena. I shall have occasion to refer to them a little later. But the controversy about the resurrection between the Pharisees and the Sadducees, before the story was told of Christ, indubitably proves that Christianity simply followed the common beliefs of the age and had no antagonist except materialism and orthodox institutions interested in preserving the political fabric at the time. Those familiar with the whole field of psychic phenomena can easily recognize them in the various incidents of real or alleged spiritual healing narrated in the New Testament. Suggestion, trance, mediumship, and telepathy are apparent in the record; were it as perfect as later records are, we might discover still more evidence of this affiliation.

Greek philosophy, like all similar movements in the Orient and Palestine, was a protest against the polytheism of the preceding period, with a remote relation to fetishism and animism. When it arose, it seems to have been unaware of fetishism, the worship of "stocks and stones," against which Judaism was directed. Polytheism had succeeded Fetishism, which was either forgotten or ignored without being seriously considered. But the interest in monotheism on the one hand, and in scientific tendencies on the other, evoked an attack by the materialists on polytheism and incidentally on all theistic conceptions. In its inception the movement coincided with the same tendency at that time in other countries.

But the earlier philosophers did not wholly escape the influence of animism. Even the Ionian materialists, or physicists, as they are usually called, admitted the existence of souls; and the materialists like Empedocles and Democritus frankly admitted the existence of souls and their survival, one of them even avowing reincarnation. But they did not admit these agencies into causal relations with the cosmos or man. They initiated that conception of the divine which terminated in the more distinctly avowed and logical doctrine of the Epicureans, namely, that the gods, though they exist, have no causal relation to the physical world. They substituted what may be called *material* causes for *efficient* causes in the explanation of the cosmos. The elements or atoms were held to be the constituent material of things, explaining what things are, their qualitative, though not their temporal, origin.

Later thinkers had to compromise with the idea of creative or efficient causes, which Socrates, Anaxagoras, Plato, and Aristotle to some extent acknowledged. In so far as they did so, they either bordered on the recognition of the spiritual, which the physicists and materialists excluded from their explanation of the universe; or they openly avowed this spiritual intervention. But even the earlier thinkers, supposed by most historians of philosophy to have had nothing to do with modern spiritualistic ideas, admitted them in many details, from which students of psychic research can easily reconstruct the whole doctrine. For these thinkers excluded spiritistic ideas only from the interpretation of nature; spiritual realities were held to exist side by side with material phenomena. In this acknowledgment we find the dualism of Greek thought, from which it never escaped until materialism totally denied the existence of spirit of any kind.

Plato was familiar with the popular view and embodied it in his celebrated narrative about the destiny of the soul after death; but he distinctly asserted that this story was mythical. His doctrine of immortality was conceived after the analogy of our conservation of energy. He believed in reincarnation, or transmigration of souls, and often expressed himself as if the conception were the same as that of some modern believers; but he did not assume the survival of personal identity. This theory is what connects his view with our notion of the conservation of energy, by which the form of matter in one condition is not retained in another. He was careful to repudiate the popular ideas and to maintain transmigration as a philosophical doctrine, though it is probable that, just after the death of Socrates, his emotional interest influenced him to hold to personal survival. But when he came to test it by his philosophic doctrine, he adopted a view which is not consistent with personal survival.

Aristotle also believed in immortality, but he carefully distinguished between the immortality of the "rational" soul and that of the "animal" soul. He denied the latter. But he was generally so reticent about what he meant that his real doctrine is a matter of conjecture. He believed in premonitory dreams and tried to explain them away in some natural manner, but confessed that he was not sure of success. He was probably familiar with the popular spiritualism; and, if so, we may surmise that his "animal" soul was the "spiritual body" assumed by him and others to be the basis of vital phenomena, but not of consciousness; in this case the "rational" soul would be simply the stream of consciousness, self-consciousness, which survived in some way that he could not intelligibly represent. But he was not interested in the doctrine and probably referred to it only because philosophy could not escape its consideration. Since he had to leave Athens to escape persecution, he probably veiled his own agnostic views in the distinction mentioned; it may have meant no more than Plato's transmigration, though possibly evoking less hostility.

The Stoics believed in some form of immortality, perhaps adopting the view of Aristotle, though they did not always regard it as an essential belief either for explaining the world or for establishing a basis for ethics. The Epicureans admitted the existence of the soul, or "ethereal organism," "spiritual body" of St. Paul, but they denied that it survived death. They were perfectly familiar with the popular spiritualism, but rejected all its beliefs except the doctrine of an "ethereal organism," which they rather inconsistently held to be a fine form of matter, since they affirmed at the same time the indestructibility of matter and the perishability of the soul. Perhaps they preserved consistency by conceiving the "ethereal organism" as complex and assuming that all complex organisms at some time dissolved or perished.

This brief outline of Greek ideas shows throughout a thread of animism or primitive spiritualism. The attempt to explain change inevitably introduced the idea of efficient causes; and with these the popular mind, relying on oracles, who were the Greek mediums, fraudulent or otherwise, and on apparitions (*anastasis*, the Greek term for resurrection), felt secure in defending survival after death. But the philosophic mind, which always opposes the interpretations of naïve realism, could protect itself only by an agnostic or hostile attitude toward the doctrines that had their origin in the earlier form of animism. The spiritualistic interpretation of man's destiny survived side by side with these philosophic views. The two doctrines were combined in Neo-Platonism, whose chief followers tried to reconcile philosophic with popular ideas. Whether they succeeded or not it is not necessary to inquire. What we know of Plotinus and his followers shows that they took seriously the phenomena which had given rise to the popular doctrine, and tried to explain them in accordance with the abstruse idealistic metaphysics of the time and of later Christianity.

There was a period between Epicureanism and Christianity in

which the traces of philosophic and scientific thought were almost lost. No men of special historic note have survived in the records of their contemporaries. Antiquarians might pick up stray evidence of both philosophy and psychic phenomena in that interval, but it was Christianity that precipitated a return to the consideration of the facts. Philosophy had gone to seed. The intellectuals had rejected facts as superstition and had wallowed in speculation and imagination until respectable orthodoxy could do nothing else. The common people again, as usual, raised the issue by an appeal to facts, and occasioned a revival of interest in the popular ideas which Greek philosophy had repudiated just as Old Testament Judaism had rejected animism. This revival manifested itself in Neo-Platonism. Its founder was Ammonius Saccas and its chief representatives Plotinus, Porphyry, and Jamblichus. These men lived in the second and into the third century after Christ. The historians of philosophy say little or nothing about their mysticism, and give an account only of their conclusions, which have no meaning apart from the facts that determined them. The Neo-Platonists were well versed in all the practices of spiritualism; indeed one modern author of great learning maintains that they knew more about it and were in this respect more rational than the moderns, such as Judge Edmunds, Andrew Jackson Davis and their followers. Plotinus went into trances, about which little or no information is given us by the orthodox historians of philosophy. Jamblichus gives minute accounts of the forms of psychic phenomena, especially phantasms and materializations, which he, more rational than modern spiritualists, identifies with apparitions. Apollonius of Tyana was more or less an adept in the subject, though, despite acknowledged good traits of character, he passed among skeptics as an impostor. No doubt some of these men did not report their facts in such a way as to escape the skepticism roused by methods of deception, which existed then as they do today. But the *ensemble* of incidents reported by men of intelligence created a presumption that where there was so much smoke there must have been some fire. This is evident in the essay of Plutarch on "The Cessation of the Oracles." Many of the stories bear the marks of imperfect observation; for this, and for fraud,

Plutarch allows. From his account, any one familiar with proved modern psychic phenomena can recognize, after proper discounts, the existence of the same phenomena then as to-day.

The author of "The Apocatastasis," a classical scholar in one of the American colleges, who went over the whole subject thoroughly, calls attention to the trial of Apuleius for "witchcraft" before a Roman judge on account of his experiments with an epileptic boy. Isodorus, the philosopher, describes a woman who poured water into a glass vessel and therein beheld phantasms representing future events; this is an instance of crystal gazing.

The author just quoted, after canvassing the whole of antiquity upon the subject, summarizes the phenomena in the following manner:

"The methods of intercourse between the two worlds and of prying into futurity were by means of oracles, omens, dreams, the lot, astrology, magical divination (the ancient mesmerism), aided by magical statues, tripods, rings, spheres, water, mirrors; and necromancy proper, or the evocation of and direct conversation with the spirits of the dead."

He then catalogues all the types of phenomena in relation to modern records. It is a remarkable list.

"Physical

Lights, both fixed and moved.
Halo, encircling the medium.
Spectra, luminous, or otherwise visible.
Self-visible spirits.
Sounds, cries, voices in the air, trumpets, speaking spectres (materializations), musical intonations, musical instruments played.

"Physiological

Trance.
Magnetic sleep.
Magnetic insensibility.

"Psychological or Physico-psychological.

Spirit speaking, spirit writing.

Speaking unknown languages ('speaking with tongues,' echolalia).
Answering mental questions.
Clairvoyance, in relation to both time and space.
Magnetization, by the eye, the hand, music, or water.
Spirits answering questions through mediums or without mediums."

The author might have added to this list the reading of the contents of sealed letters, of which he reports a case or two.

It matters not whether the phenomena were genuine or not. Some of them represent types of occurrences which have good credentials in modern times, though others remain to be proved. Certain physical phenomena still have to prove their claims, but many of the mental type, though they belong to abnormal psychology, have their genuineness established.

The same author quotes from Plutarch a remarkable statement which shows not only critical acumen on the part of that intelligent Roman, but also a distinct anticipation of the theory of interfusion of the minds of the medium and the spirit in the delivery of messages. It occurs in the account of his observations in connection with the Pythian oracle:

> "If the verses of the Pythia are inferior to those of Homer, we need not suppose that Apollo is the author of them. He merely gives the impulse whereby each prophetess is moved according to her peculiar disposition. For if the responses were to be given by writing instead of speaking, I do not think the letters (*grammata*) supposed to be written by the god would be found fault with because they lacked the caligraphy of royal epistles; — for the voice, the intonation, the diction, and the metre, are not the god's but the woman's. He only causes visions and supplies light to the soul in relation to the future."

There is evidence in modern investigations that a foreign stimulus is always present to give rise to subconscious recollections and interpretations and that the phenomena are not always, if they are ever, pure invention by the psychic. There is the intermingling of two minds. Transmission of thought is not merely the process of delivering messages verbatim; it is never free from subconscious modification by the medium through which it comes. In the passage from Plutarch we have an observation which is confirmed by modern experiment.

Plutarch lived in the first century of the Christian era; his work on this subject therefore coincided with, and may have been influenced by, the new interest created by Christianity in psychic phenomena. But from this time on, the subject was more or less confined, so far as favorable notice of the facts is concerned, to the Christian Fathers. The rising conflict between paganism and the new creed tended to discredit the oracles, one side opposing them because they did not favor Christianity, and the other unable to defend them from the philosophic point of view. Christianity had control of the situation for the long period of its domination; the works of the Fathers are full of stories of the continuance of miracles, though on the whole they rapidly declined in number after the crucifixion, or at least after the end of the first century. On the whole neither this period nor that of the Greek and Roman oracles can be quoted except as evidence that better accredited phenomena in modern times had their antecedents in antiquity; and if we do not reject them as wholly idle tales, it will be because we have proved the existence of the super-normal in the present age.

CHAPTER III

MODERN SPIRITUALISM

IT is a curious fact that most investigators connected with the English society for Psychical Research have associated modern spiritualism with the Fox sisters almost exclusively, though conceding, with Mr. Andrew Lang, that it has its roots far back in the earliest history of man. There is little excuse for this narrowness of view, though there is no doubt that the Fox sisters gave the subject a popular vogue which it did not have until their experiences excited attention.

Modern spiritualism really originated in the work of Swedenborg. The phenomena of Swedenborg were not physical, as were many of those alleged by the Fox sisters. They were of the mental type, consisting of visions with his own interpretation of them — illustrations of the type now called pictographic. While such phenomena have been casually reported in literature ever since the time of the Christian fathers, these reports were given little credence until similar reports by Swedenborg made them seem more credible. He was a man of good education and creditable probity, who never exploited his powers as did the charlatans of the Middle Ages. He was born in 1688 and died in 1772. These dates placed him before the time of the great revolution in philosophic thought brought about by Immanuel Kant. He was educated at the University of Upsala and became a civil engineer. He made himself famous in almost every department of science, and even anticipated Kant and Laplace, according to Grieve, in the nebular hypothesis. He also suggested a flying-machine and produced a model which he knew, and said, would not work, but which he thought would suggest the principles on which such a machine might be constructed. His inventions in other fields were numerous and successful. But we hear less of them than of his philosophical works in the sphere of religion and real or alleged supernormal psychology. When he was in London he claimed to have obtained by supernormal means information of a fire in Copenhagen. There was reported of him also the clairvoyant discovery of a lost paper, which strongly impressed Kant. But his "revelations" appealed to more minds than did these trivial supernormal phenomena. These revelations purported to come from discarnate spirits, to reveal the nature of the next life, and to give instruction on all religious matters of importance to human kind. Swedenborg's works abound with evidence that much of his material was influenced by his own mind and its stores of reading, though his diary records the experiences in a form more free from interpretation. The impressiveness of his work affected Immanuel Kant in his early life sufficiently to induce him to write his "Dreams of a Ghost Seer" (*"Traüme eines Geistesschers"*), in which he weighed the speculative arguments for and against spirit communication, leaving the question unsettled. Some writers see in this work an ironical treatment of the problem; but there are too many statements seriously recognizing the possible validity of spiritistic claims to justify such a judgment except to men who are wholly unfamiliar with the evidence for the subnormal. Kant, however, ceased to have interest in the subject, though it was later revived, as the works of Hegel and Schopenhauer show. Both of these philosophers became convinced of the existence of the phenomena; but their attitude toward this subject is disregarded in most discussions of their philosophic systems.

Scientific materialism arose as a consequence of the renaissance of science which began with Copernicus. Men had a new interest in nature and the physical universe. They had long been fed on tradition and speculative metaphysics, and the reactions, as shown, both in skepticism and the revival of materialistic tendencies, is apparent in the agnosticism of Kant and in all subsequent philosophy. Swedenborg made an attempt to counteract this materialistic trend of things, though he, perhaps, did not feel the impulse of the materialistic movement so strongly as did many others who had followed in the wake of Cartesian thought. Whether they felt this trend or not, however, believers in immortality were supplied by the method of Swedenborg with scientific evidence. This method was an appeal to facts and to communication with the dead for evidence of another life, and it even went so far as to map out that life. Whether Swedenborg adequately met the demands of scientific method is another matter. There is no doubt that too much was made to depend on his mere probity and his authority as a scientific man and that his system soon developed into the same kind of dogmatism as that of Christian theology. The experiment of continued communication with the dead was not kept up, except as it was practised by people who had abandoned the orthodoxies of both philosophy and religion. Despite its defects, however, the method of Swedenborg represents the right conception of the problem. Materialism and skepticism acknowledged nothing but normal experience for regulating the beliefs of mankind; and that experience does not attest survival. It may stimulate hope and faith, but these sources of belief give no such assurance as the scientific mind requires. With the new criterion of truth set up by scientific investigation, came an increased demand for better evidence for survival than natural science on the one hand and religion on the other were capable of supplying. Swedenborg anticipated the method by which this evidence can be obtained; but his followers, like Christian theologians, settled down on the authority of their master and regarded spiritual revelation as closed. Scientific experiment and investigation had to wait another century for recognition, except as the problem was kept alive by sporadic instances of mediumship and other phenomena outside the limits of science, philosophy, theology and even Swedenborgianism. These instances found favor mostly among the common people, but they were ridiculed by the respectable adherents of other beliefs. Events may have justified this attitude of mind on the part of the educated; at any rate these occurrences occasioned no such interest as did the movement initiated by the Fox sisters.

The interest in spiritualism after the time of Swedenborg was kept alive by the performances of Mesmer and by the investigators who followed him. Among German authorities of note who investigated the subject, Jung Stilling, a man of university education and standing, is the most important. Contemporary with him were

Keiser, Wienholt, Fischer, Kluge, and Baron von Reichenbach; the last, a scientific man of some attainments, experimented and wrote much upon the subject. We cannot go into any notice of his work, and refer to it only to indicate that the phenomena would not have received so much attention, had they been merely sporadic. This attention was centered on mesmerism or animal magnetism, now called hypnotism, an artificial method of inducing trance, which often resulted in supernormal manifestations and mediumistic phenomena. Among the most noted of the somnambules of the period was Frederika Hauffe, called, from her birthplace, the Seer of Prevorst. The poet and physician Kerner published a life of her after her death, which was prior to 1829. Kerner had also another case of which he published some account; but there is no space to discuss these cases. They illustrate the usual phenomena, however explained, and were no doubt accompanied by hysteria, the usual concomitant of such manifestations, but they are of interest as demonstrating that the modern movement began outside of America, and long before 1848.

Swedenborg aroused some interest in France, but he had no sectarian following there of any special note. It was Mesmer who created the interest manifested there. His performances in Paris soon after he moved there in 1878 excited great interest, and resulted, as did somnambulism in Germany, in the revival of supernormal phenomena transcending hypnosis. Deleuze was the chief representative of the movement in this period, but he suspended his judgment on spiritistic phenomena. He was interested in the naturalistic interpretation of somnambulism and clairvoyance, though conceding that there were facts which required further investigation. He had some controversy on the subject with one Billot, who defended the spiritistic theory. Cahagnet aroused some interest, but, as he had no scientific training, his work was without authority; he seemed to have experimented much in various directions and accepted the spiritistic theory. The materialistic tendencies of France, however, after the expulsion of the Huguenots by Louis XIV, created an atmosphere of skepticism about everything supernatural or savoring of spirits, so that the first inclination of all inquirers was toward what they were pleased to call "naturalistic" explanations. Hence spiritualism made little or no progress until long after 1848.

In England mesmerism aroused some interest. Elliotson and Esdaille successfully practised it and also met with supernormal experiences. Another student of mesmerism was Braid, but he encountered few, if any, supernormal phenomena. On the whole, spiritualism, at least in so far as public and literary notice are concerned, made little headway in England until after the episode of the Fox sisters.

Though the phenomena are very old, as we have seen in the foregoing account, it was the rappings of the Fox sisters that created a world-wide interest in the facts. The manifestations were accompanied by no mesmeric nor hypnotic phenomena. America knew and cared little about mesmerism in the scientific sense. It was chiefly occupied in the organization of a new social and political system, and in the accumulation of wealth. Spiritual interests were confined largely to the orthodox in religion. Consequently, scientific and skeptical people were not fired with interest in the immortality of the soul. The movement broke out in a simple agricultural community, wholly unacquainted with the philosophic and scientific problems of Europe. It boldly proclaimed itself as spiritualism — a word whose history is honorable, but whose meaning has degenerated into a term of contempt — with a creed based on certain physical phenomena said to have originated in the presence of the Fox children.

These phenomena began in Hydesville, New York. The history of the occurrences is well told in the work of Mrs. Underhill, a sister of the two chief mediums concerned. Her account is a good one and there is no reason to question it, though we may not fully share her enthusiastic interest in the events. She, with many others, thought that they betokened the rise of a new religion, unaware that they only repeated phenomena associated with the early history of Christianity. The enthusiasm was natural; for these people felt that they had found proof, to take the place of the uncertainties of faith. I am convinced that the abuse which has been heaped upon the movement has obscured the value of some of the phenomena — value not necessarily as supernormal occurrences, but as cases of interest to abnormal psychology. It was the confession of Margaret Fox that deprived the movement of both its scientific and its religious interest. She confessed to making the raps with her toe joints. It mattered not that there were other and mental phenomena which were well-attested, and that there was testimony that raps had occurred in localities where action of the toe joints could not be effective. The confession of fraud sufficed to rob the case forever of scientific interest.

Other forces also contributed to nullify the importance of the phenomena. A religion dependent on raps and on proved defects in moral character was not likely long to survive. It would have been wiser to leave the significance of the facts to science and to allow religion to obtain its credentials from ethical and spiritual ideals of another type. But the consolation obtained from alleged proof where only faith had previously existed was too much for uneducated people to withstand, and their emotional reaction discolored the facts. The confession of fraud left no room for apologies; no intelligent person could afterwards feel or express an interest in the phenomena. The spiritualists who endeavored to defend their protégés only weakened their cause and brought it into deserved contempt. There can be no doubt in the mind of the present writer that the phenomena of the Fox sisters never received their deserved investigation; but the spiritualists did not take a course that would invite the interest of intelligent people. They succeeded only in giving the word spiritualism a meaning that has made it almost impossible to use it in a favorable sense among respectable people.

It is worth remarking, however, that all important movements of the kind have originated among common people. The intellectuals have never originated an important ethical or spiritual reform. They have supported art and refinement, but have never founded a religion which rules over the destinies of civilization. Such a religion has always originated among the common people, who have no prejudices against nature nor in favor of æsthetics as the first condition of truth or virtue. This is the excuse for the interest shown in the Fox phenomena. They were intelligible to common understandings, though they did not conform to the more refined conceptions of educated people. It is true that even the actuality of the raps and physical phenomena reported in the case have no bearing on the explanation that aroused enthusiasm and gave consolation. But physical phenomena, like the alleged miracles of Christ, have always attracted the untutored mind; one can therefore understand the interest excited by the movement even when one does not share it. The spiritualists have never made a sustained effort to attract the attention of scientific men to their phenomena or their religion. Their performances are little better than vaudeville and their religion, as an organized affair, little better than a cloak to protect them against the invasions of the police. Recent developments have somewhat modified this situation, but many followers are interested in neither ethics nor religion, but only in a show. Christ deplored the fact that his followers cared more for his miracles than for his ethical teachings; and mankind have ever since justified this rebuke. If spiritualism had organized ethics and practical life and laid less stress on its phenomena, it might long ago have won the world's respect. All religions are judged by their external appearances; if they are vulgar in their appearances and have no redeeming features in ethical and spiritual life, they will not attract the intellectuals.

But the spiritualist movement was restored to a measure of respectability by Judge Edmunds and Andrew Jackson Davis. Judge Edmunds was a lawyer of sufficient ability to become one of the judges in the supreme court of New York State. His first psychic experiences came through his own daughter; they were private and never exploited as were those of the Fox sisters. His two volumes have great interest for psychology, whatever explanation we give to his data; but he made the mistake of laying little or no stress on supernormal phenomena, giving the prominence to alleged communications from Francis Bacon and Emmanuel Swedenborg. He offered no proof that these philosophic and other revelations came from the source ascribed to them. The same criticism holds true of the work of Andrew Jackson Davis. Both his defenders and his opponents misjudged the facts: his defenders exaggerated Davis's ignorance and his critics exaggerated his knowledge. His work has at least great psychological interest, but his investigation of facts never pursued a method that would lead to convincing interpretations.

The author of the "Apocatastasis," mentioned above,[1] took the right view of the facts. He thought it probable that the phenomena were spiritistic, but he insisted that this conclusion was not a basis for accepting the teachings which the communications contained. He drew the important distinction between the *origin* and the *validity* of the contents of the communications. It is one thing to prove that a statement comes from a spirit, but it is another and very different thing to prove that it is true and valid. This distinction is constantly forgotten. A man may exhibit supernormal faculties, but these do not give him insight into reality. Moreover, he may get messages from spirits; but the ability of a spirit to send a message does not guarantee veracity of the sender, any more than the conversation of your neighbor over a telephone assures you of the correctness of his statements. The value of a statement is not determined by its source. It was the mistake of the admirers of Judge Edmunds and Andrew Jackson Davis—a mistake shared by these men themselves—to assume that the evidence that spirits were back of the phenomena furnished also a reason for belief in the contents of the messages. Ignorance, impersonation, confusion of messages, as well as the coloring given by the medium, offer objections to the passive acceptance of messages as true. These facts should have been realized by all who were connected with the cases. It was perhaps pardonable that few or none saw the difficulties involved, because Christian thought, in its whole history, had been based on vindication of the source of teaching as a sufficient criterion of its validity. It required later reflection on the consequences of evolution to discover that the value of facts is established by function, not origin.

It would be interesting to follow in detail the history of modern spiritualism through all its vicissitudes, but this would require more than one volume. I have devoted attention to it merely to emphasize the fact that its origin is not recent, but that its phenomena are as old as the human race. Only the scientific investigation of it is modern. This investigation would not have been undertaken,

[1] "Proceedings" English S. P. R., Vol. I., p. 106.

had not Christianity, like paganism, begun to show signs of decay, and had not the triumphs of physical science weakened the faith of mankind and developed an exclusive interest in physical life. Whatever faults the spiritual customs of Christianity had, they always kept alive the serious view of nature and human life, and saved civilization from debauchery in the period following the break up of paganism. That was achievement enough; but had it adjusted itself to the advances of science, it might have held the reins of power still longer.

CHAPTER IV

THE SOCIETIES FOR PSYCHICAL RESEARCH

PSYCHIC phenomena finally excited such a world-wide interest that they compelled the attention of scientific men. The phenomena might possibly have remained unnoticed much longer, had it not been for their occurrence in respectable families, sometimes to men and women of intelligence and training. But interest even among intelligent people continued for some time without being strong enough to organize any effort to apply scientific methods to an investigation of the facts. At last, however, a few men concluded that it was the scandal of science that the allegations of centuries had not been taken up and investigated. The persistence of the phenomena, and of the claims for the supernormal, was a perpetual challenge to science; at last this challenge was accepted.

John Addington Symonds states in his letters, with a half-sneer at the folly of it, that Professor Sidgwick of Cambridge University was investigating mediums as early as 1867 with the hope of finding evidence of survival after death. This date was fifteen years before the organization of the Society for Psychical Research.

The experiences of the Reverend W. Stainton Moses were among the chief incentives to the formation of the society. These experiences were confirmed by other sporadic, remarkable incidents among intelligent people, such as Lord Brougham, Cotter Morison, Andrew Lang, and Sir William Crookes. The Reverend Stainton Moses had been educated at Oxford University and was for a long time a clergyman of the Church of England; but during his intercourse with some skeptical members of his own congregation he was persuaded by them to investigate spiritualism. He found nothing at first; but he finally developed automatic writing himself, and became convinced by it that the claims of the spiritualist were correct. His unquestioned integrity left intelligent people no choice but to investigate the matter. He was personally known to Professor Sidgwick, Mr. Myers, Edmund Gurney, and others of the same standing. With his case and others challenging science, the men just named organized, in 1882, the English Society for Psychical Research, and obtained the coöperation of other prominent men. Prof. (now Sir) William F. Barrett, however, was probably the chief instigator in the matter. He had independently and individually been investigating the phenomena, especially those of mind-reading, or telepathy, for years, and had brought the matter to the attention of the British Association for the Advancement of Science, which would have nothing to do with it. He continued to urge the subject among scientific men, however, until he saw the fruit of his interest and work in the organization of the Society. He was himself one of the vice-presidents in the organization, Professor Henry Sidgwick being the president. Professor Balfour Stewart was also one of the vice-presidents. With them were associated Arthur James Balfour, M. P., Richard Hutton, and the Honorable Roden Noël. The council of the Society was composed of Frederick W. H. Myers, Edmund Gurney, Frank Podmore, Charles C. Massey, and others not so well-known in America. These names guaranteed a scientific treatment of the subject.

Before this time the Philosophic Society had investigated the phenomena and published a favorable report on them; but its report had not been received by the scientific world with the respect it deserved. The present Society, however, had more than a temporary interest in the subject and was determined to pursue the investigation until some light was thrown upon the phenomena. Sir William F. Barrett read the first paper on *Thought Reading* at the first meeting of the Society, and Professor Sidgwick read his presidential address. A draft of the purposes of the Society was published as a circular; the objects of study included phenomena purporting to represent the influence of "one mind on another apart from any generally recognized mode of perception" (afterward called telepathy), hypnotism, clairvoyance, the experiments of Reichenbach, apparitions, haunted houses, the physical phenomena of spiritualism, and the collection of existing materials bearing on the history of these subjects. This was an extensive program, but it has been carried on now for more than thirty-five years. The publications of the Society have consisted of a *Journal* issued monthly and a volume of "Proceedings" issued annually, often in parts distributed through the year.

In 1884, two years after the organization of the English Society, an American Society was formed, with Mr. N. D. C. Hodges as secretary. Professor Simon Newcomb was its first president. Its vice-presidents were Professor, now President, G. Stanley Hall of Clark University, Professor George S. Fullerton of the University of Pennsylvania, Professor Edward C. Pickering of the Harvard College Observatory, Dr. Henry P. Bowditch of the Harvard Medical School, and Dr. Charles S. Minot of the Harvard Medical School.

At the sixth meeting of the Society, on January 11, 1887, Dr. Richard Hodgson of London, England, was elected secretary. The Society had on its membership list a large number of scientific men. It issued annual reports which, in the course of five years, made a volume. But by this time membership fell off and interest declined, perhaps because the public did not find the expected progress made. The American Society was therefore abandoned and reorganized as an American branch of the English Society. Dr. Richard Hodgson was continued as its Secretary and remained in that office until his death in 1905.

A year before the death of Dr. Hodgson, the present author, having resigned his position in Columbia University to recover his health, resolved to organize an independent American Society, with the object of finally merging the American branch with it when the financial support of the work justified it. It was determined not to compete in any way with either the English Society or its American branch. The plan was to make Dr. Hodgson its secretary, as he had expressed his willingness to merge the branch with the new American Society. To effect this merger, effort was concentrated on raising the sum of $25,000 as a fund to guarantee preliminary organization. Just as this money was secured, Dr. Hodgson died. The present author refused to organize the new society on his own responsibility alone, conditioning it on either the coöperation of the English body or the dissolution of the American branch. The latter alternative was adopted by the English Society and the new American Society was organized with Dr. James H. Hyslop as its Secretary. This was in May, 1906. Its publications did not begin until January, 1907.

There are organizations of some sort in both France and Italy under the auspices of scientific men, but their constitutions are not known to the present author. The Psychological Institute in Paris was founded to include psychical research in its field of inquiry.

These societies are intended to give scientific character and respectability to the investigation of unusual phenomena bearing on the problems of mind and its survival of bodily death. The prejudice against spiritualism was so strong at the outset that its objects had either to be disguised or ignored. Telepathy, dousing, hypnotism and various phenomena which present no superficial evidence of the intervention of discarnate spirits received the first attention. After the supernormal in some form had been proved, the credentials of spiritualism came under notice. In the course of the work, most of the leading members who have conducted personal investigations have become convinced that man survives bodily death; but it has been regarded as not always good policy to avow the conviction with any missionary zeal. Hence conviction on the point appears to the public to be less strong than it actually is. There are enough questions still unanswered to suggest caution on the subject, especially on aspects of it as yet wholly uninvestigated. But the existence of supernormal phenomena has been so well established by the work of the several groups of investigators that men are fast coming to acknowledge that the subject can no longer be evaded or ridiculed as it was at the outset. Psychic research may now be regarded as having proved its right to a place among the investigations of science.

As its first work, the Society undertook experiments on telepathy or thought transference with some success. But some doubt was ultimately cast on two series of the experiments, those with the McCreery sisters and those between a Mr. Blackburn and a Mr.

Smith. The McCreery sisters confessed that they had used signals in certain experiments, a circumstance which gave the skeptic opportunity to decry the whole work. But the experimenters soon showed that they had attached no value to any experiments save those in which signalling was impossible. The girls insisted also that they had not used a code in those instances which had seemed most impressive. In the other case, as Mr. Blackburn was proved to be a liar or at least wholly untrustworthy as a witness, even in his own confession of fraud, his testimony even in the latter case could not be accepted at its face value. There were additional and better results on which to base the claims of telepathy; something of the kind seems certainly to be a tenable hypothesis. It is true that since its origin, the meaning of the term has been enlarged to cover many and various processes; consequently all the claims made regarding it have been viewed with suspicion.

Telepathy, in its original meaning, was limited to the transference of present states of consciousness; but, for the sake of combatting the evidence for the existence of discarnate spirits, the definition was extended to include subconscious acquisition of memories from others, by a selective process on the part of the person who received the thoughts thus transmitted. No scientific evidence for this theory has been advanced, though there are coincidences which might well suggest it.

This, however, is not the place for discussing in detail the meaning of telepathy. Strictly speaking, the term denotes the transmission of thought from one mind to another independently of the recognized channels of sense, or, as the present writer prefers to define it, in order not to suggest any known process, telepathy is a coincidence between the thoughts of two minds, which cannot be explained by chance or normal sense-perception. The facts which it includes are not evidence of the existence of discarnate spirits. This definition leaves undetermined the nature of the process and the directness of transmission.

Not all of these qualifications were made in the first stages of the investigation; but they were usually implied. It was the object of the Society to ascertain whether there were any supernormal phenomena that would not excite the antagonism which spiritualists always evoked by their claims. It was apparent that the proof of anything like telepathy would involve the possibility of communications with the dead, given the actual survival of personal consciousness. This method of approach made the hypothesis appear less objectionable to the scientific skeptic.

In the course of several years of investigation, two types of phenomena, with perhaps a third, made something like telepathy seem plausible. These were *spontaneous* coincidences between two persons' thoughts and *experimental* coincidences, in which the conditions of the result could be regulated and the phenomena repeated more or less at will. The third type consisted of apparitions; since these naturally suggested the agency of spirits, believers in telepathy were interested in attempting to prove the adequacy of that process as an explanation.

I shall give a few illustrations of the phenomena. I adduce them, not as a scientific proof of thought transference, but only as illustrations of the kind of cases which were for many years collected, and which, whatever the explanation, very frequently occur.

In "Phantasms of the Living," the authors record the following incident. It is partly experimental and partly spontaneous. A gentleman willed that a lady who lived at some distance from him should leave the part of that house in which she was at the time, should go to her bedroom, and should remove a portrait from her dressing-table. When the gentleman next saw her, she told him that, at the time in question, she had felt strongly impelled to go up to her room and remove something from her dressing-table. She did remove an article, though it was not the portrait. In this case, the man's act was experimental; the lady's act, since she did not know that the experiment was being made, was spontaneous.

The following, in the form of a dream by the percipient, is spontaneous on both sides:

"I dreamt I was looking out of a window, when I saw father driving a Spids sledge, followed in another by my brother. They had to pass a cross-roads, on which another traveller was driving very fast, also in a sledge with one horse. Father seemed to drive on without observing the other fellow, who would without fail have driven over father if he had not made his horse rear, so that

I saw my father drive under the hoofs of the horse. Every moment I expected the horse to fall down and crush him. I called out 'Father! Father!' and woke in great fright. The next morning my father and brother returned. I said to him, 'I am so glad to see you arrive quite safely, as I had such a dreadful dream about you last night.' My brother said, 'You could not have been in greater fright about him than I was,' and then related to me what had happened, which tallied exactly with my dream. My brother in his fright, when he saw the feet of the horse over father's head, called out, 'Oh, father, father!' "

Thousands of such coincidences have occurred, many of them under conditions and with confirmation that seem to prove the reality of telepathy. It is difficult to believe that they are due to chance.

But I am not concerned to prove anything by these incidents, which are only illustrations of what, if performed under proper conditions, would be regarded as proof of the supernormal transfer of mental states or pictures. The Society carried on experiments for a long time and in large numbers, besides recording as evidence spontaneous incidents as good as or better than that quoted. It felt justified in maintaining, despite the objections of a critical scientific world, that the existence of telepathy has been proved.

Of course, part of the difficulty in carrying conviction arose from the lack of an exact definition of telepathy or thought transference. If the Society had held to a negative conception of the term, assuming neither its value as an explanation nor the directness of transfer between the two minds, it might have aroused less criticism. But it and the public used the term as if it explained certain occurrences, and as if it necessarily implied direct transmission. We have no evidence to justify these conclusions; we proved only the existence of certain coincidences not due to chance nor to normal sense-perception, and not evidence of the discarnate. The controversy with the spiritualists, however, gave the term in relation to spiritistic theories a meaning that it should never have had.

Two other types of occurrence, however, made it necessary to ask whether spiritual beings exist: namely, apparitions and mediumistic phenomena. The Society then began to investigate phantasms or apparitions; the two volumes published on that subject, together with the volume entitled "A Census of Hallucinations,"[1] announced the unanimous conclusion of the committee that these apparitions were not due to chance. The committee regarded this conclusion as proved, regardless of the explanation, which many assumed to be telepathy. As the census was limited to phantasms of the living or of persons at the moment of death, the hypothesis had its plausibility. Apparitions of the dead were not considered in this report.

Mediumistic phenomena strengthened the case of the spiritualists. Soon after the announcement of the conclusions regarding telepathy and apparitions, the Society discovered Mrs. Piper, through Professor William James, who had reported on her phenomena as early as in 1885. In 1887, Dr. Richard Hodgson became acquainted with the case; in the course of eighteen years of work with Mrs. Piper he, together with some other members of the Society, became convinced of the spiritistic theory. After Mrs. Piper, Mrs. Verrall, Mrs. Holland and others exhibited the same type of phenomena. The American Society has investigated Mrs. Smead, Mrs. Quentin, Mrs. Chenoweth and a few others. There can be no doubt, whatever the explanation, that supernormal information has been obtained through them.

In the meantime other fields of inquiry were opened. The original Society unsuccessfully tried to repeat the experiments of Reichenbach. Sir William Barrett spent much time in investigating dousing, and issued two reports, in which he announced the conclusion that the finding of water by the divining-rod is possible. Hypnotic phenomena were to some extent investigated, particularly with a view to inducing conditions for proving telepathy; some remarkable experiments were performed by Edmund Gurney. In the course of thirty years of work, the Society collected an immense amount of data, which leaves the scientist no excuse for ignoring the immemorial claims of a supernormal element in human experience.

The American Society has been handicapped in its work by the need of funds and a laboratory for scientific work, and of coöperators in the field. It has succeeded in raising an endowment of

$160,000 for its work, but the income from this, together with membership fees, guarantees only its publications and the running expenses of its office. It has made no experiments in telepathy, and has had only limited opportunity to investigate spontaneous phenomena. But it has managed to do some work in the mediumistic field, and maintains its "Journal" and "Proceedings" with such material as it can secure from personal reports and the experiments with a few psychics. It has not yet exercised any such influence over the public as has the English Society. Academic and scientific support, probably on account of the avowed spiritistic sympathies of its secretary, has been weak.

The work, however, is well established, and probably in the future will not be neglected. Enough has been accomplished to make scientific neglect of the problem inexcusable, although much work remains to be done, to overcome prejudices of our materialistic age. When the fact is commonly recognized that psychic research is concerned not with a metaphysical theory, but with the collection of facts which may establish a great truth, the bias of the scientific world will be overcome. The Societies have done much to further this progress; and it is probable that the immediate future will see the barriers of prejudice broken down, with the serious investigation of questions more far reaching than those in any field of physical science.

PART II

PRELIMINARY PROBLEMS

CHAPTER V

THE PROBLEM OF A FUTURE LIFE

MOST unsophisticated people have no difficulty in believing in a life after death, especially if they have been taught this belief in infancy. In that period of simple trust in their superiors, children will accept what they are taught, and in most instances, the beliefs adopted at that time remain stable. In many people the beliefs formed in childhood cannot be shaken; in others, if the old beliefs are destroyed, the change proves disastrous. The effect of the change, however, depends on the importance which the belief holds in the economy of the personal life. If it be the one belief that has organized all a man's hopes and ideals, any rude shock given it will demolish the whole fabric of character. The immortality of the soul is so central to the hopes of many people, especially of the uneducated, that they will cling to it against all odds and resist all argument to give it up. Taken in with the mother's milk, so to speak, and organizing about it all the fundamental interests of life, it will either resist argument of any kind or yield to it only with the surrender of human ideals.

There are many, of course, who can shift the pivot of interest to ideals of the present life. But they have some ability to think, and have sufficiently strong will to shake off the sense of dependence which characterizes the child. Many people remain children all their lives; it is they who suffer most from the shock of change of belief. But those who grow to independence of judgment may readily stand the shock of skepticism and do so whenever they can substitute another interest for the one that was lost. This class, however, represents the minority of the human race, and usually comprises its leaders. Some of them boldly adopt skepticism and its consequences. Others attempt to justify their primitive beliefs in the name of philosophy. The unsophisticated classes will follow one or another of these leaders according to their temperaments. If they cling to the interests which have centered about immortality, they accept that belief on faith, or authority. But if they are rebellious or conscious of the real difficulties in believing it, they doubt it or give it up.

The one consideration which determines the attitude of mind towards this and all other beliefs is the criterion of reality. To the unsophisticated mind this criterion is *sense-perception;* even when it believes in what transcends sensation, it tries to conceive this assumed reality as still like that of sense in all but constant accessibility to perception. This conception, of course, goes to show that the unsophisticated easily abandon their most natural standard of reality. But they cannot give a consistent account of their procedure; and are at the mercy of those who rigidly insist on sense-perception as the test of reality. It is characteristic of the scientific mind to accept this same criterion of truth; in this respect it is like the unsophisticated mind. But they differ in the greater tenacity with which the scientific mind consciously clings to the standard. It is true that scientific men also readily abandon this standard for one which acknowledges realities transcending sense-perception—for example, atoms, ions, electrons, ether; but these men differ from the unsophisticated in adopting the maxim that all *provable* truth rests upon sense-perception. To them provable truth is what they can make another person believe by reproducing in him sensations which compel belief. The unsophisticated mind has no such rigid standard of evidence. It accepts as *subjectively* true much that does not appeal to sense. If the mind can see the truth for itself it will not require proof in sensory processes; but if it cannot see the truth without external proof, such *objective* evidence requires sense-perception. Herein lies the whole difference between the unsophisticated and the scientific mind. For uncertainty, according to the scientific mind, attaches to every belief or statement which cannot vouch for itself in terms of sense-perception. It may be true, but it is not provable, unless represented in sense-pictures or experiences. Science may accept facts not directly represented in sensation, but they must be logically involved in what sensation attests. The final test for science is some sensation constant or easily produced, under proper conditions, which will enforce the conclusion. The unsophisticated mind, however, does not *consciously* abandon sense-perception as its standard of truth. It simply has not analyzed the processes which determine conviction.

There are many degrees between these two extremes. The half scientific and half unsophisticated mind will combine the standards of belief in all sorts of ways; and it is in this intermediate class that all the perplexities arise. The scientific mind that does not care for consequences, moral or otherwise, can accept without compunction or remorse the limits which sense-perception prescribes to belief. But ethical minds, less pugnacious and more sensitive, halt before accepting the guidance of skepticism, and struggle with might and main to save their ideals and beliefs from the corrosion of doubt.

I have stated the case with some care, allowing for the criticism always made against wide generalizations. It would be easier and perhaps would satisfy certain skeptical minds, if I asserted that the test of all truth is sense-perception as that is naïvely understood. Those who wish to perplex the naïve mind may make this contention feeling secure that unsophisticated persons will not contest it. But while it is true that the test of reality is always sense-perception, it is true with a qualification. This qualification is, that sensation is not so simple a matter as the skeptic would like us to believe. Besides simple or pure sensations there are other mental states, which we usually represent by the term *judgment*. This term was rendered necessary by the existence of illusions. While an illusion is in fact an error of judgment or inference, it is so closely connected with sense-perception that our normal habit is to represent sense-perception as needing correction by judgment. The meaning of sensation is therefore limited to the simple occurrence of reaction upon external stimulus through one of the sensory end-organs; so defined it is not a complete standard of truth at all, but the elemental datum which gives rise to knowledge. Processes of judgment on constant and variable sensory experiences enable us to ascertain the meaning of things much more accurately than do the separate sensations. The naïve, uncritical mind does not go beyond the most elementary use of judgment. It discovers few illusions and ignores those which it does discover. The critical scientific mind endeavors to find unity in a variable experience, as better evidence of truth than that found in unorganized experience.

In studying the question of a future life, the unsophisticated mind follows authority or its wishes, or, if it relies on experience at all, accepts what the more critical mind resolves into illusions and hallucinations. The primitive savage accepted dreams and apparitions as satisfactory proof of another life, thus relying on real or apparent sensory data. But when the critical or philosophical mind approached the problem, difficulties arose, which obliged the belief in a future life to seek refuge in some transcendental philosophy or be abandoned. In all countries where philosophic habits of mind arose, one of the first dogmas questioned was that of the immortality of the soul; with the growth of materialism the doubt thus raised was strengthened. Previous teaching had maintained that matter and spirit are two independent realities, and that spirit survives death. But philosophy distrusted the idea of two independent substances or realities, especially if one of them seemed to interfere with the fixed order of nature. There is no doubt that primitive believers in spirits thought them capricious and as mischievous as any power over nature might be. Those who observed certain regularities in the world, certain fixed laws, either had to deny any interference with them or to assign to spirit a place in the world which would make it seem ineffectual and unrelated to the causal series of events. With sense-perception as the criterion of truth, the critical mind had a tendency to accept matter as the fundamental reality of the world; if it conceded the existence of spirit at all, it did so, not in response to the evidence, but in order to avoid trouble. In accordance with its standard of belief, it usually denied the evidence or dogmatically asserted the non-existence of spirit; this is the position of both materialism and agnosticism. Agnosticism means that we have no basis for either a positive or a negative conclusion; it admits that we cannot know that spirit does not exist. This, in fact, is the only tenable position for any intelligent skeptic. It follows from his maintenance of sense-perception as the test of reality. The absence of sense-perception of spirit does not prove that spirit does not exist, if we define spirit as transcending sense-perception. Such absence merely shows that the belief lacks satisfactory evidence. But materialism denies the reality of spirit, on what it supposes to be satisfactory evidence that mental phenomena are but products of the brain. It is this theory, firmly rooted in many minds, that disturbs the belief in a future life.

Materialism has a long history and stands for two rather distinct conceptions. In the present age, it is the result of several sets of facts, which we can only briefly state. Materialism has two forms: *sensational* materialism and *philosophical* materialism. The first of these is opposed to *idealism* and the second to *spiritualism.* If spiritualism and idealism were identical there would be but one form of materialism; but they are far from identical, as every philosopher well knows. Most materialistic philosophers evade the real issue by contrasting materialism with idealism, and allow the layman to think that they are quite orthodox on the doctrine of immortality, though they are careful to leave their teaching on this point indefinite. This sensational materialism is founded on the naïve view of the world as presented to sense-perception. The idealist has become convinced that knowledge and reality are not adequately expressed in sense-experience; and as the material world is supposed to be represented by sense-perception (though the scientific view of the material world is not so expressed) the idealist calls that view of the world materialism which is more or less interchangeable with naïve realism: namely, the view that sensation rightly represents the nature world of matter and hence of reality. The idealist denies materialism thus conceived, by asserting that some sort of transcendental reality exists behind sensation.

But a man may be at the same time an idealist and a philosophical materialist. Philosophical materialism is based upon as supersensible a conception of matter as that maintained by any spiritualism or theism. Like idealism, it does not rely upon sense-perception as the test of truth. It regards the real nature of things as hidden from the senses. It bases the whole sensible world upon supersensible realities as its elements or cause. This philosophic materialism began at the time of Empedocles and Democritus and was developed by the Epicureans. The atoms which constitute the basis of the whole sensory world were regarded as supersensible: it was their combination in the various forms of things that affects the senses and explains the world as we know it in sense-perception. These earlier materialists, however, admitted the existence of souls, as fine material or "ethereal" organism. But some of them denied the survival of this ethereal organism, which corresponded to the astral body of the theosophists and the "spiritual body" of St. Paul. Christianity tried to prove by the story of the resurrection that this soul did not perish, though its theory of the bodily resurrection made the belief only more difficult and required a most elaborate philosophy to sustain it. The real conception of the resurrection at the time, at least among most intelligent people, as indicated in the New Testament, was that of apparitions, the visible appearance of the "spiritual body" after death. Christianity thus directly denied the materialist's view of death as the end of all. It did not deny the existence of atoms; it simply affirmed the survival and reappearance of the "spiritual body," which, for all practical purposes, was synonymous with the soul. The materialist was challenged either to abandon or to modify his theory.

In the course of time the materialist chose the latter course. He gave up the hypothesis of an ethereal organism as the source of consciousness, and connected consciousness directly with the body or brain as a collection of atoms. Consciousness thus became a function of a complex organism rather than a function of a spirit or soul; and, as all functions of the physical body perish, the same fate was held to await consciousness. This view seems to be satisfactorily upheld by normal experience. Mental states are accompanied by physical structure; when this structure is dissolved by death there are no traces, at least in normal experience, of the independent existence of consciousness. It was quite natural to infer that it does not survive. It is true that the conclusion is not absolutely assured, but if there is no evidence whatever on the contrary side, we have at least to confess total ignorance; and the certainty that all other functions of the organism perish will establish a strong probability that consciousness is no exception to the rule. Its survival can be proved only by showing that it is not a function similar to those that manifestly perish, or by bringing forward actual instances of such survival.

This outline of the situation created by modern materialism shows just how we have to attack the problem. We have to adduce evidence that consciousness is not a function of the physical body. We can no longer rely on the philosophical method, which was based on the theory that consciousness is a unique phenomenon, which cannot be reduced to mechanical equivalents, nor conceived as a by-product of the physical organism. It is true enough that consciousness has not beeen reduced to mechanical laws nor identified with any chain of physical events. But this failure is no proof that consciousness is not derived from physical phenomena. The burden of proof is thrown on the man who affirms that it is so derived, but the question is left open. Common sense could not believe that light and sound are vibrations, but science proved that they are, even though the senses do not directly reveal the fact. If, therefore, light and sound can be reduced to supersensible physical phenomena, may not consciousness be similarly explained? At any rate the philosopher could not dogmatize on the subject, and the nature of consciousness had to remain an open question; yet the philosophic proof for the existence of the soul depended on the assumption that we know enough of its nature to deny its physical character.

The whole problem was shifted over to science, which is occupied primarily with facts and only secondarily with the nature of reality. Philosophy tried to explain consciousness and to infer its survival from a theory of its nature. Science let its nature alone and tried to study its behavior. It is concerned primarily with evidence and secondarily with explanation, while philosophy in the past has been too much occupied with explanations and too little with evidence. Science begs no questions as to the nature of anything. It first ascertains the facts and then expresses the nature of a thing in accordance with those facts as its effects or manifestations. When the philosophic method of proving immortality broke down, there was nothing left but to apply to science for the solution. Philosophy, in all its development, had depended on science for its premises, though it was disposed to admit this dependence only very grudgingly, if at all. The success of science, however, in overthrowing many philosophic beliefs, and especially religious beliefs, gave that method the highest authority in the determination of truth. As it pronounced in favor of materialism, it aroused the most determined opposition of all who were interested in preserving such a belief as survival after death, whether they undertook to defend it by religion and faith or by philosophy. But there is no escape from the verdict of science; on it depends the proof or disproof of survival. Theology and philosophy are now discredited authorities; if science cannot ascertain facts to prove immortality the belief is negligible. We may still insist on hoping for survival, but our hope will not have the credentials that the present age requires for all its beliefs. In ages when wishes and hopes are accepted as adequate reasons for belief, faith may survive; but when the demand for assured evidence is made, science must take up the task of making a negative or an affirmative decision.

That task involves the question, whether individual consciousness can be isolated from its apparently fixed, but really temporary, connection with the body. The fact is, that science has never proved that we do not survive. It has but established a theory on which the doubt or denial seems natural. While it knows that, in normal experience, consciousness is associated with an organism and that, when the organism perishes, there seem to be no traces of this consciousness, it knows only that in normal experience it simply is without evidence for survival. It does not have proof of annihilation. Its theory is but a working hypothesis, one of great strength, it is true, and convincing in proportion to the neglect of phenomena which appear to suggest the survival of consciousness. Yet it has not demonstrated the destruction of consciousness. Nor is it easy to do so, while certain phenomena continue to throw doubt on the conclusions of materialism. The present strength of materialism is due entirely to its neglect of these phenomena. It has considered the facts which fit its theory and has disregarded all that are inconsistent with it; and now psychic research, employing the same scientific method, has become the Nemesis of materialism.

Psychic research endeavors to isolate an individual consciousness, or to ascertain facts which prove that isolation, by the same method that a chemist uses when he proves the existence of a new element.

The facts purporting to attest survival are apparitions and alleged communication with the dead. There are other supernormal phenomena of great interest, but they do not directly prove the existence of spirit, and perhaps would not even suggest it to critical minds. Apparitions and mediumistic phenomena, on the contrary, if their validity can be proved, certainly conform to the scientific demand for the isolation of an individual consciousness. They at least are the kind of phenomena which we might expect if spirits exist and can produce any effect in the physical world. They show that it is not necessary to decide the nature of consciousness before believing in survival, that we may prove or show to be probable the fact of survival, while leaving the nature of consciousness wholly unexamined. The result may give rise to a philosophy, but does not depend on it.

Before the adoption of the scientific method, men paid the penalty for being less thorough than the situation required. They exposed their belief to the corrosive influence of the doubt cast by further knowledge. We have arrived at a stage of culture in which the faiths of the past have lost their power. The triumphs of science have established the confidence of men in its practical value and in its ability to explain the universe. The intelligence of the world is on its side; and mankind must follow intelligence always, if it is to gain its ends. Evidence, proof, reason, fact instead of faith, hope and desire influence belief. Whatever value these latter have, rests on the basis of proved truth, not on imagination and arbitrary hopes originating in the emotions and the will.

The problem is, therefore, not to bolster up faith without science, but to establish the truth by science, so that faith will become either unnecessary or rational. The authority of the priesthood is lost. If it acknowledges the conclusions of science, it can regain its power, but only on that condition. The intelligent world no longer takes its *ipse dixit* as final, but asks for evidence, which science alone can furnish. Materialism also must no longer select for consideration only the phenomena which support its preconceived theories, based upon a partial view of nature. It must take into account the exceptional phenomena as well as the regular routine of experience. If it fails to do this, it is exposed to the same criticism that it has directed against faith. It is only another dogmatism to neglect the rare facts of nature, a dogmatism the less excusable because science professes to found its beliefs on facts and not on preconceptions. Even in physical science, the exceptional phenomena of nature have deeper significance than ordinary occurrences. The discovery of Roentgen rays was due to an accident. The discovery of argon was due to the observation of an anomaly in the behavior of nitrogen, the neglect of which would have resulted in a false conception of that element. It is, therefore, not beyond the function of science to study the unexplained phenomena of mind. They cannot be explained as merely abnormal events. Whatever place abnormality may have in them, there is a relation between some of them and events not known to the subject, which makes some new explanation imperative. The facts have to be explained, and they are not explained by the usual theories. To deny the facts is not to explain them. The question is: do they demonstrate the isolation of consciousness from the body?

Of course, to laymen, the problem does not seem so technical. They follow public opinion in their conception of the issues. In all ages, being unable to investigate or philosophize for themselves, they have relied on the intelligent members of the community to furnish them their science and their philosophy. They have accepted all ideas on authority. When the intelligent classes were priests and philosophers and believed in immortality, the laymen felt assured of the truth of the belief. But when these same classes of men doubt or deny it, the laymen either follow them into skepticism, or allow the belief to atrophy. They may not have the courage to deny it altogether, but they feel their inability to defend it except by sheer force of will or faith. Niceties of scientific method do not enter into their processes of fixing their beliefs. They simply seize the easiest way of deciding the question, either yielding to authority on one side or the other, or stubbornly standing by their emotional preferences.

But wishes and hopes cannot remove the doubts which critical minds thrust at us. We have to overcome emotional bias, or the belief which has exercised such a powerful influence on the past will decay as all inadequately supported doctrines have done. We must invoke the method which has destroyed so much, and insist that it shall do constructive instead of destructive work. It must take account of all the facts, instead of neglecting some in the interest of a theory which selects what it likes and lays more stress on the uniformities of nature than does nature herself. We must show that consciousness can actually be dissociated from matter, instead of inferring our conclusion from insufficient premises.

The isolation of an individual consciousness involves getting into some form of communication with discarnate personality, or demonstrating facts which indicate the influence of discarnate mind upon the animate or the inanimate world. It will not be enough to prove that the brain cannot altogether account for consciousness. We have to prove the survival of personal identity; that is, of a personal stream of consciousness with its memories of past earthly life. A soul might lose its identity or its self-consciousness and continue to exist like an atom, without manifesting the properties apparent in a previous combination or "incarnation." Hence we require to know whether it is the same mind that manifests itself after death as before. Facts which present (1) supernormal knowledge, due neither to chance nor to normal sense-perception, and (2) evidence of the personal identity or the personal memories of the deceased, are the data needed to prove the isolation of an individual consciousness from its physical organism.

CHAPTER VI

THE PROBLEMS OF EVIDENCE

THE present chapter is closely connected with the preceding, for the nature of the problem largely determines the nature of the evidence. But the problem has been so complicated by concern with religion and magic that these subjects are inevitably brought into the discussion; various problems of abnormal psychology are also involved. So many facts are erroneously claimed by unsophisticated minds to be proof of the intervention of spirits, that a very large field has to be canvassed in the search for evidential material.

Besides, the sifting of evidence is a very complex matter. A fact in relation to another fact may be evidence, but out of that relation the same fact might not be evidence at all. It is therefore necessary briefly to examine the law of evidence. Let me take some concrete illustrations.

A human body is found with a bullet hole in the head and a revolver lying near the body. If nothing is known about the person either suicide or murder may account for the situation. If the man is known to have been despondent, to have failed in business or some other project, or to have been generally disappointed with life, the suspicion of suicide becomes stronger, and anything like knowledge of a previous threat of it would weaken the hypothesis of murder. On the other hand, if the man is known to have been an upright person in the community, a religious man, successful in business, with a happy family and nothing to make him unhappy, the theory of suicide would be less tenable. Not the mere fact of death by a bullet wound decides the question, but other general facts in the person's life are included in the evidence.

Suppose, however, that we know nothing about the man and his life and have to seek evidence from other sources. If, then, we find that the revolver was purchased at a certain store, not by the victim, this discovery would provide circumstantial evidence that the man had not committed suicide. It would not constitute proof, as the victim might have secured the weapon after its purchase. Suppose, however, that finger prints on the weapon are those not of the victim but those of the purchaser. This fact would greatly strengthen the suspicion of murder. Only an alibi or proof that these same finger marks had been observed on the revolver before the man's death could remove that suspicion. If now we should discover boot tracks near the body, and these tracks could be identified with those of the purchaser of the weapon, we should have additional, though not conclusive, evidence of his guilt. If to this we could add evidence that he had previously threatened the man with death, had been a personal enemy, and had actually been in the vicinity at the time, the case would be very nearly established. The convergence of a large number of incidents, each of which alone might look like chance coincidence, would prove the deed. All the facts must consist with the hypothesis. Mere coincidence between two events does not prove a connection between them, though it may suggest a hypothesis. This coincidence must be associated with a number of others, all of which hang together. But the uneducated mind rests content with a single coincidence and in this way is led into all sorts of errors.

When it considers evidence for the existence of spirits the untrained mind has always been accustomed to appeal to every "wonderful" occurrence as proper evidence. It frequently regards any unusual fact as an incentive to apply explanations that do not fit. It is not merely the unusual character of a fact that gives it evidential interest or force. It must be unusual if it is to be evidence of a fact hitherto unknown, but it need not be any more unusual than the fact which it attests. This is perhaps a truism; but, because prejudiced people try to represent as miraculous or supernatural the facts which psychic research adduces as evidence of spirits, it is necessary to make clear two things: (1) that no one regards as supernatural the new discoveries constantly being made in physical science; (2) that the idea of spirits is no more strange than that of a new element in chemistry. They are but the continuation of the consciousness we formerly knew as embodied.

It was the work of the Society for Psychical Research to discriminate among the phenomena it was investigating. Its first task was to classify them and to distinguish between those relevant to the hypothesis of spirits and those that have no bearing on the subject. The spiritualists had classed together all unusual phenomena, physical and mental, claiming all of them as spiritistic.

Before we have any right to assert or suppose the existence of spirits, we must adduce facts that imply supernormal knowledge, and this supernormal knowledge must be such as could be obtained only by communication from the dead. The term normal is purely relative. We can best give its meaning by illustrations. For instance, we can normally see a house some miles distant, but we could not normally see a fly at the same distance. The term normal is relative to the conditions limiting the activity of our senses. The existence of the normal, as well as of the supernormal, has to be proved by evidence. Only because this proof is easily within the reach of every one, we forget the grounds on which it rests. The limits of the supernormal are also determined by evidence, not by definition. If a man in America should have an accurate vision of events in Europe, we should call his perception supernormal, whatever the process involved. Whether such a vision has actually occurred is only a matter of evidence; we cannot say that it is impossible.

But before we admit the existence of anything so unusual we require that the evidence be critically tested and that the facts be inexplicable by any known law. To call such a phenomenon as the vision of events in Europe clairvoyance, is to give the fact a name, not an explanation. If the claim to the vision could not be confirmed by testimony from some one else than the visionary, we should not regard it as proved. The veracity of the person might not be questioned, but some illusion or mistake of judgment might stand in the way of our accepting his statement. If the reporter and subject of the experience were a scientific man, the statement would have more weight than if he were an ignorant layman, simply because the scientific man has the habit of accurate observation and statement. But even then there would be the possibility of error unless his account could be confirmed by the testimony of others. If a scientific man were to relate such an experience in a detailed manner, before the objective facts could become known to him and those in his vicinity, corroboration by others would exempt him from the suspicion of error, illusion, or mendacity. The facts would then stand out as unusual, and perhaps as requiring a new law to explain them.

Conclusive evidence of an hypothesis must exclude every interpretation except the one supposed; it must conform to two conditions, one positive and the other negative. The exclusion of a given interpretation is negative evidence; the applicability of the hypothesis to the facts is positive evidence. Thus the exclusion of fraud would be negative evidence for spiritism, if that were the theory in question. But the fitness of the facts to prove the special theory concerned, say the survival of personal identity, would be positive evidence. If spirits are to be proved to exist, the facts must indicate the continued personal identity of deceased persons, must be verified by living people, and provably supernormal in their origin.

In estimating the alleged evidence for the existence of spirits we have first to eliminate the explanations grouped under the name of *fraud*. This may take the form of lying about the facts, or trickery in performing feats claimed to be of spirit origin. But we must be exact in our conception of fraud. Fraud is not the act performed, but the motive of the act. It implies the conscious purpose to deceive, whether by false statements or by acts calculated to lead one to form incorrect judgments as to the facts. If a man should make a false statement in his sleep, or in a trance, or under hypnosis, I should have no right to ascribe lying or fraud to him. He himself might be deceived by dreams, hallucinations, or illusions. Hence many actions and statements are exempt from the suspicion of fraud, for instance, all actions and statements during somnambulism, trance, hysteria (if of an automatic type), ordinary sleep, intoxication, insanity (if of the hallucinatory type), and similar abnormal mental conditions. We must have proof that the person is normally conscious in order to attribute fraud to him.

Moreover we must not confuse the deception of the observer with the purpose of the actor. The fraudulent person aims at deception by misrepresentation. The deception of the conjurer, on the other hand, is legitimate enough, because he does not claim any supernormal elements in his exhibitions. The observer lets himself be deceived by what the conjurer frankly avows is a trick. But the fraudulent person maintains that the apparent facts are real, despite his knowledge to the contrary. If the person is normal, his honesty may be judged by his acts; but if the subject is abnormal, the phenomena are in the domain of abnormal psychology, not of trickery.

We are concerned, however, solely with the cause and the explanation of experiences, not with the motive of the subject. That cause may be subjective or objective. If the experience has no discoverable sensory stimulus and yet coincides with some objective event out of the reach of normal sense-perception it is supernormal. Honesty has no importance in determining the nature of the phenomena. Only tests to exclude normal knowledge and sensation can decide whether the facts are supernormal or not. For this reason the scientist does not care whether he is dealing with frauds or not, if only he can determine the conditions under which the phenomena are produced. The fraudulent person, of course, will not usually, if ever, permit this sort of experiment. But if the dishonest subject will submit to scientific conditions we shall not enter into the consideration of character or motives. However, in the work of persuading the public it is important to be assured that the subject of experiment is honest, because the public wrongly assumes that phenomena are genuine if the subject is honest.

But we have not satisfied all the conditions of evidence for the supernormal merely by removing the fact or the relevance of fraud. We must reckon with the subconscious or subliminal functions of the mind. At one time subconscious mental activities were as yet undiscovered. We could not then reckon with subconscious action as an alternative to genuine supernormal experience. The choice lay between the fraudulent and the genuine in all normal persons. But the discovery that the mind has subconscious activities has completely altered the situation. We have all along known what we called "unconscious," by which we meant merely involuntary, actions, whose meaning we ourselves learned as they proceeded.

Here lies the border-land of the subconscious. Strictly speaking, subconscious or subliminal actions are those of which the subject is wholly unaware. Our thoughts and actions in sleep, hypnosis, or trance are illustrations. In our normal state, we have no recollection of them. The distinctive marks of subconscious activities are anæsthesia and amnesia, i. e., insensibility and inability to remember. In sleep, trance, somnambulism, hysteria and various forms of insanity these phenomena are constant. They show the continuance of mental action after normal sensibility or consciousness has been suppressed.

Now we may exclude fraud from the explanation of alleged supernormal phenomena and yet have subconscious action of the subject to reckon with in explaining them. If apparently supernormal phenomena can be explained by the resurrection of subconscious memories or the production of automatic actions the claims of supernormality must be abandoned. Suppose. for instance, that John Smith reported to us that he had seen the ghost of Mary Jones. Having established his honesty, we should then wish to know whether he knew that Mary Jones was dead. If he did, we might explain the circumstance as a casual hallucination or a dream. The operation of memory would suffice to explain it, or to classify it with known facts. If Mary Jones were found to be alive, the case would be strengthened. If Mary Jones had died without John Smith's knowledge, we might still consider the vision a chance coincidence. It would be more difficult to explain it thus, if we found that the apparition occurred very close to the time of death. The time element is always an important factor in eliminating chance; close correspondence of the experience with the event indicated by it strengthens the case. But the question of chance coincidence and guessing enters only after we have eliminated the subconscious.

Many visions and hallucinations are referable to the subconscious, because their content can be reduced to previous experiences. We cannot assume that there are supernormal dreams or visions until we have eliminated the influence of previous experience upon the contents of the incidents. Hence, until we can report dreams or visions of verifiable facts not previously known to the subject, we are obliged to suspect subconscious memory as a sufficient explanation.

We must remember, however, that the nature and limits of the subconscious have not been accurately determined. This is both an advantage and a difficulty to the defender of the supernormal. It is an advantage because it challenges the advocate of subconscious action to show whether the process has been proved to include cases of the kind in question. It is a disadvantage, however, because the defender of the subconscious as an explanation may insist that its unassigned limits permit him to suppose its power to be unlimited.

Scientific method, however, does not allow us to use the subconscious as an explanation beyond its proved capacities. We have no evidence that the subliminal, of its own power and apart from normal sensory stimuli, can acquire any knowledge. It has no known transcendental powers. It is a name for mental action below the threshold of consciousness, or above it, if you wish to include hyperæsthetic conditions, but it is always dependent on normal stimuli for its contents, unless the supernormal be at once granted as a fact. Its capacity is thus as limited as that of the normal mind, and it exhibits no functions other than those of the normal mind, even when real or alleged supernormal phenomena filter through it.

This limitation of subliminal activity is a restriction on the skeptic who wishes to apply it as a universal explanation. He must first show the relevance of the application, which depends on showing that the previous knowledge supplied the subject with the data for subliminal use; and his application must be strictly limited by the proved capacities and habits of the subconscious.

It is important to note that the subconscious may be the vehicle for the transmitting supernormal knowledge. It may be the medium beween the transcendental world, if there be such a thing, and the physical world, and so may respond to stimuli from both sources. This view of the subconscious makes it the medium or vehicle for the acquisition of supernormal knowledge; the only refuge of the skeptic is to deny the source of the contents claimed to be supernormal. If he proves that the contents have been subconsciously acquired from normal experience, he can disqualify the evidence for the supernormal. In fact it is contents that must furnish the evidence. No assumption or discussion of the powers of the subliminal will decide the matter. If the phenomena are not traceable to physical stimuli, their explanation must be sought in the transcendental. The conditions under which the facts occur can alone decide the question, not the assumed or proved functions of the mind, conscious or subconscious.

It will thus be seen that we have to define carefully what we mean by the subconscious before we employ it as an explanation of the alleged supernormal. The believer in the supernormal has to prove that the normal senses were not the source or vehicle of the facts. The conditions under which the phenomena occur will determine this. The appeal to the subconscious will be irrelevant unless previous normal experience accounts for the special facts which appear to be supernormal. If these facts are based on such experience the claims for the supernormal are vitiated.

All this is perhaps obvious to most people; but I thought it was necessary carefully to analyze the problem. We now have made it clear that when conscious fraud has been eliminated, we have still to test the claim of any alleged supernormal phenomenon, such as telepathy, clairvoyance, apparitions, mediumistic communications with the dead, and dousing, by their relation to the normal knowledge and process of the subject. All precautions must be taken to exclude these normal processes when we assert that we have a transcendental fact to be explained. Proximity in time or space of the subject to the fact supernormally known may raise doubts of its authenticity, though these can be settled by a number of conditions. But great distance in time and space and all the conditions that will exclude previous normal knowledge by the subject will make an appeal to subliminal memories of doubtful value. The use of strangers and the employment of controlled experiments will dislodge the doubts attachable to spontaneous phenomena, and will easily disprove the presumption of subconscious influences, especially when the facts are provably unknown by the subject.

But assume that we have eliminated the subconscious from the explanation of the facts. The exclusion of subconscious influences will not prove that each individual phenomenon is genuine. There are still the possibilities of chance coincidence, or guessing. This, however, can easily be eliminated by any intelligent person. Bring two strangers together, and record what happens. Let A be the psychic and B the sitter. If A, without knowing the person present, without questions, without even seeing the person, who may have come for the first time from the other side of the globe, should give the sitter's name, state that he was a diamond miner, that his father's name was Chelmsford and that both his father and mother were dead, that the mother had given him a special picture of a little church on the corner of the street opposite their home — if these incidents should occur under such circumstances, we should have facts that would at least appear to exclude chance and guessing. Indeed it is easy to eliminate the supposition of coincidence by repeating the experiments. They may be exposed, though hardly in the present supposed circumstances, to the suspicion of fraud and subconscious knowledge; but they are not explicable by chance coincidence or guessing. Nevertheless we have always to think of these possibilities in estimating the value of the facts purporting to be supernormal. Isolated instances of these facts may be explained by chance or guessing, but a large collective mass of them, such as have appeared in the publications of the Societies for Psychical Research, cannot be so explained.

The four objections previously mentioned are the four most usual objections to belief in supernormal experience. We may, perhaps, regard secondary personality as a fifth. But secondary or multiple personality is only an organized form of subconscious action. Ordinary subconscious actions are isolated and do not represent another person in their collective meaning. But the secondary personality presents all the appearance of a complete and different self. Illustrations of this are the Ansel Bourne, the Charles Brewin, the Sally Beauchamp, and the Wilson cases. I might add, too, the French cases, those of Lucie and Léonie. In them the person went into states resembling hypnosis, as completely separated from the normal personality as another human being would be. The normal self did not remember anything about the subnormal self, though in some cases the secondary personality was aware of the primary self as another person. In others the amnesia was complete on both sides. When any phenomena purporting to be spiritistic can be explained by dual or multiple personality, we have to exclude the hypothesis of spirits from the explanation. Other forms of the supernormal are not connected with secondary personality, or if connected with it, are not explicable by it. Many, perhaps most, cases of secondary personality have nothing to do with the question of the existence of spirits. Sometimes the claim is made of spirit agency; but if the contents of the subject's statements could be obtained by normal experience, the hypothesis of spirits is not legitimate. Any objection to spiritistic claims based on this form of phenomena is but an application of the explanation by subconscious influences, and we need to mention the fact only because it is not generally understood that dual personality is an example of the subconscious mind.

But we have not decided the case in behalf of the supernormal when we have excluded fraud, chance, and guessing, subconscious action, secondary personality, hysteria and forms of insanity. We do, however, establish the possibility of it when we have excluded them; its proof thereafter depends on the quantity and quality of positive evidence. The exclusion of alternative explanation is only negative evidence; the possession of certain facts relevant to the kind of process supposed is required for positive evidence.

We may indeed prove dousing, telepathy, clairvoyance, telekinesis, and perhaps some other forms of the supernormal without admitting the existence of the discarnate; these facts may even be used in opposing spiritistic theories, as in the case of telepathy, which has been invoked to displace spiritistic interpretations. So long as it is conceivably applicable to the phenomena, it will stand as an objection to the hypothesis of spirits. When coincidence between the thoughts of two persons can account for the facts without the assumption of the personal identity of the dead, the hypothesis of telepathy is an objection to the application of spiritistic explanations. Telepathy, therefore, has the force of an objection in certain cases. The facts taken as evidence for spirits must run the gauntlet of all the previous objections named, whether these objections take the form of normal or supernormal explanations. Spiritistic evidence consists of facts which can be explained only by the continued personal identity of deceased persons, involving memories possessed by the deceased person and transmitted to the living by supernormal means. That is, we cannot believe in the existence of spirits until they are able to prove their personal identity, their conscious memory, by transmitting facts of their terrestrial lives to the living by apparitions, mediums, telekinesis, or some other supernormal method.

The one best means of proving this personal identity is the transmission of facts, for these are least likely to be referable to normal channels of knowledge. The more trivial the better; that is, the more likely to characterize the one person whose identity is concerned. A single trivial incident will not suffice. There must be a number of them which articulate rightly and have had a psychological or other interest for the person claiming to communicate. If a man should enumerate the books he had written, the statement would have no value at all, as it would be obtainable from the normal knowledge of the psychic or person offering it as evidence. The man's important deeds or the conspicuous events of his life are worthless as evidence of his survival, unless you can prove they were not known to the psychic. It is more difficult to prove ignorance of these events than of private and trivial facts of his career. Trivial incidents are the best evidence of identity. The ridicule applied to the triviality of communications from the dead is therefore unjustified.

The reason why most people object to the triviality of the facts adduced is that they assume that these communications indicate the character of life in the spiritual world. But in proving the existence of spirits we are not concerned about their status or life in the transcendental world. We are not investigating that problem. We are trying to prove that spirits exist, not that they are wise or exalted in their intelligence; and the materialistic theory itself prescribes for us, as we have seen, the nature of the problem and of the evidence for its solution. We have long been taught that the next life is an idyllic one, a life which throws off the limitations of the present. This may be true or it may not be true. With that question we have no concern in the scientific problem of a spiritual existence. We are trying to ascertain whether consciousness survives, not whether it is transcendentally exalted in intelligence or placed in an ideal world. Materialism makes it necessary to prove the survival of personal identity as the condition of any spiritual existence at all. Nothing but trivial facts will prove this; they are not brought forward as evidence in any respect of the spirit's intelligence.

The popular objections to triviality in the evidence explains why so many run after revelations of the nature of the future life. They suppose that, if communication between the spiritual and the physical world is possible at all, all sorts of revelations and communications about it are accessible. But no revelation of such a world can be evidence of its existence, unless verifiable by methods which will show that it is trustworthy. Thousands accept such revelations as evidence and pay no attention to trivial facts in proof of identity or scientific methods of investigation and criticism. They are only preparing to be deceived. Verification is an important feature of evidence, and verification is possible only by the testimony of the living or by a vast system of cross references and repetitions of messages impossible now to carry out. In proving identity, especially if we wish to exclude telepathy from the explanation, we must not only have trivial facts of a supernormal kind and illustrative of personal identity, but they must be verified by living people. This connects the past personality with a present consciousness and readily verifies the statement of the psychic. But any fact which cannot be verified by a living person is not worth a penny as evidence. Revelations are not verifiable by individual testimony of living people and occupy no place whatever in the scientific problem as affecting the existence of spirits.

Telekinesis, or movement of physical objects without contact, is usually regarded as conclusive evidence of the existence of spirits; but, in reality, it is not evidence of it at all. Only mental phenomena will prove the existence of spirits. Physical phenomena unaccompanied by mental phenomena showing intelligence or personal identity are absolutely worthless as evidence. They may be very interesting phenomena, and they may arouse the lethargic physicist to revise some of his previous views, but they cannot be adduced in evidence of spirits until the existence of the latter has been otherwise proved and their association with telekinesis also proved.

This examination of evidential problems in general prepares the way for a consideration of the facts adduced in proof of the supernormal and of the existence of spirits. We have only been outlining problems here and showing how complicated are the conditions necessary to the admission of any supernormal experiences whatever and especially the existence of discarnate spirits — though I am inclined to think that it ought to be easier, in the light of the facts on record, to admit the existence of spirits than to admit the claims of telepathy. But with that question we have nothing to do at present. We have been concerned with determining the principles of evidence in any field and the special conditions which affect it in psychic research. We have excluded fraud, subconscious mental action, secondary personality, chance coincidence, guessing, hysteria and other kindred phenomena as explanations of the apparently supernormal; we have then excluded several types of the supernormal from the evidence for discarnate spirits. Positive evidence for the discarnate we have shown to be supernormal knowledge indicating the continued personal identity of the dead.

CHAPTER VII

HUMAN PERSONALITY

THERE are three distinct meanings for the term "personality," two of them general and popular and the third technical and philosophical. The *first* and most general meaning is that personality is the sum of the characteristics which make up physical and mental being. These include appearance, manners, habits, tastes and moral character. The *second* meaning emphasizes the characteristics that distinguish one person from another. The two meanings overlap or merge into each other, as the first considers all characteristics pertaining to the individual, without comparing him with others, while the second sees the same facts in relation to the outside world and fixes attention mainly upon the features that distinguish the subject from his fellows. This second meaning is equivalent to *individuality.* It represents a widely prevalent conception of the term.

But the *third* meaning is the most important, and is the only conception of any value to the psychic researcher and the philosopher or psychologist. This conception of personality is concerned only with mental characteristics; it makes no distinction between common and specific marks. In fact it connotes mental processes rather than fixed qualities. The capacity for having mental states, or the fact of having them, constitutes personality for the psychologist and the philosopher. *Personality is thus the stream of consciousness,* regardless of the question whether any special state is constant or casual, essential or unessential. Physical marks will have no place in this conception, unless they may serve as symbols of mental states. It abstracts from them and denotes only the stream of mental phenomena.

This third meaning is so radically different from the other two that it gives rise to perpetual misunderstandings between the philosopher and the public. These misunderstandings arise particularly in the discussion of survival after death. The layman, with his conception of personality, looks for physical phenomena of some kind to illustrate or prove it. Consequently, if interested in psychic phenomena at all, he prefers materialization, which best satisfies his conception of personality. He cannot take the point of view of the psychologist or the philosopher, who neglects these purely sensory characteristics, and fixes his attention on mental states as the proper conception of the personality which may survive. Materialization would supply the very characteristics which the layman fixes upon to represent personality. But precisely the fact that mental states are not presented to sense, leads the philosopher to conceive of immortality as possible.

If the layman's conception were correct the philosopher and psychologist would deny the possibility of survival with entire confidence, as a necessary implication of bodily dissolution. The day could be saved only by the doctrine of a "spiritual body," an "astral body," or an "ethereal organism," supposedly a replica of the physical organism in its spatial and other characteristics. These represent personality after the manner or analogy of the physical body. The real spirit may indeed have a transcendental bodily form; but the stream of consciousness remains the same whether there is any "spiritual body" or "ethereal organism" or not. This is the fundamental element in all conceptions of spiritual reality. It is not necessary to decide the question of a "spiritual body" or "ethereal organism" as the condition of believing in the existence of spirits. That is another and perhaps a secondary problem. What we need to know is, whether the stream of consciousness survives, whether the personal memory continues, not *how* it continues. The *fact* of survival is to be considered first and the *condition* of it afterwards.

We have to determine the survival of personality in the same way that we determine whether another person in the body is conscious. We are so accustomed to think that we have direct knowledge of other personalities, that we forget the exceedingly complicated nature of the process of ascertaining whether other people are conscious. That this process is the same as that of ascertaining the existence of discarnate spirits will be apparent from the following considerations:

1. I have *direct* knowledge of my own existence both bodily and mental. I reach knowledge of my body by sensation and of my mental states by *introspection*. In fact, introspection is at the basis of my consciousness of bodily as well as mental existence. In both cases my knowledge of my own existence is *direct* and is not a matter of inference from facts which are capable of various interpretations.

2. I have no *direct* knowledge of any other consciousness in the world than my own. I have knowledge of other bodies only through my interpretation of sensations, and I have no direct knowledge that consciousness inhabits those bodies. I have to ascertain that fact by inference from certain phenomena occurring in conjunction with those bodies; for instance, behavior that seems to indicate in others the same kind of mental states as those behind my own acts. I observe certain motor or muscular phenomena precisely like my own, and I infer the same cause for them.

3. Death is only slightly different from paralysis or catalepsy. It involves the permanent lapse of consciousness, so far as our normal observation is concerned. In time the body also ceases to function and is dissolved. The materialist assumes that personality or consciousness disappears with it and can never reappear. Believing, as he does, that personality is a function of the organism, he consistently assumes that it does not exist after the death of the body. But he does not know directly that this is a fact. He never saw personality, nor have any of us seen it, as we see our own bodies or the bodies of others; and the materialist assumes that the only way to know anything directly is through sense-perception. In catalepsy and paralysis personality or consciousness seems to have disappeared. The recovery of normal consciousness in such cases shows that there it suffered only a lapse; followed by the resumption of organic functions. But there is no such resumption of functions after death, and the materialist therefore concludes that consciousness has become non-existent, like digestion, circulation, secretion and other functions of the organism. These undoubtedly disappear never to reappear; and, if personality is a similar function of the body, it too must disappear. Since we have no direct knowledge of this personality in others, even in life, and since we

cannot from normal experience infer its continued existence after death, we have to fall back upon facts derived from abnormal conditions or processes different from sensory experience, if we are to infer its survival.

Now psychic research is occupied with the effort to find facts from which we can infer the survival of personality. So we have seen in the previous chapter, fraud, subconscious actions, chance coincidence, guessing, and telepathy must be excluded as explanations before we can accept this evidence for survival. Assuming that this exclusion has been effected in any case, as in veridical apparitions and test mediumistic phenomena, we can only infer that personality has continued to exist after death, as it existed in paralysis and catalepsy when we had supposed it destroyed. Death has interrupted its causal action in the world; therefore, unless at some point it can resume that causal action on or through the living, we should have to remain without scientific evidence for its continuance after death.

To summarize the argument: (1) We know personality or consciousness *directly* or introspectively only in ourselves. (2) We know the existence of personality or consciousness in others only *indirectly* or by inference from behavior manifested in some form of action. (3) Catalepsy and paralysis in some cases involve a disappearance of personality similar to that of death, but its reappearance shows that it was still present when it was supposed to be non-existent. (4) Death offers a situation only slightly different from that of catalepsy and paralysis. Consciousness ceases to function, and we should remain in total ignorance of its continued existence, unless we ascertain facts which necessitate the inference of its persistence.

It is the stream of consciousness that is of primary importance in the question of survival. There might be "spiritual bodies," "astral bodies," or "ethereal organisms" without personality; it only defers the real problem to assume or prove their existence. Ultimately we are driven to the discovery of facts which will prove the continuance of personality as a stream of consciousness, by the method here used — namely, the isolation of consciousness from the body or the production of facts from which an inference can be drawn that this personality has persisted beyond death and is not a function of the physical body.

If there is anything at all perplexing about personality, the perplexity lies in the consideration of " split personality," " alternations of personality," " secondary personality," " dual personality " or " multiple personality," all of which are interchangeable terms. In former times, the personality or soul was held to be an indivisible unit. In its early history the dogma of the immortality of the soul was based upon this unity. For so long as the soul was believed to be indivisible its survival was assured, under the doctrine of the imperishability of the atoms or elements. But if consciousness is after all divisible into several selves, the argument for its immortality from its unity falls to the ground.

I shall not undertake at this juncture to solve the problem. I am here only explaining the perplexity which the alternation of personality offers to those who have based their belief in survival upon the unity of consciousness. What we must do is to prove survival independently of the question whether personality is simple and indivisible or not. It might be as complex in a spiritual world as it is here. Metaphysics will not settle the matter. We must have argument based on proved facts, not on mere beliefs. The appeal to the unity of personality affected only those who were bred in the old metaphysics, before the establishment of scientific method. In any case the problem of survival after death must depend on the question of *fact,* not on the *nature* of personality as conceived by traditional metaphysics.

CHAPTER VIII

TELEPATHY

TELEPATHY is a process now very widely assumed as an alternative to the spiritistic hypothesis. It is more or less synonymous with " mind reading " or " thought transference," which were the expressions in use before the more technical term was coined and adopted. It would have had little or no recognition if it had not been useful in displacing the supposition of spirits in the interpretation of certain phenomena.

It was a group of spontaneous experiences, called " mind-reading," which attracted the attention of investigators. But most people used the expression to mean more than the facts justified. They assumed some supernormal ability to read the mind without the use of normal sense-perception and interpretation. That is, they made the phenomena more unusual and exceptional than they were, or at least more evidential than they actually were. The exhibitions of Cumberland and Bishop, as well as of persons imitating them, can be explained as muscle-reading. It is necessary to discriminate between unusually delicate sensations, and the imparting of knowledge without any sense-perception. Muscle-reading depends on detecting unconscious acts of a person by a performer, and any conditions of contact that make muscle-reading possible under the circumstances discredits the phenomena as evidence for anything more. Muscle-reading may be defined as the interpretation by the operator of unconscious muscular movements in the subject experimented on. It is evident therefore that phenomena referable to it are not evidence of any agency transcending sense-perception.

The term telepathy was coined to express exactly and technically this transmission of thought from one mind to another without sensory perception even of the hyperæsthetic type. Whether such transmission actually exists was yet to be proved; hence the term represented only an hypothesis, not a demonstrated fact. It was meant to exclude every form of sense-perception including the subconscious. It might be easy to exclude conscious sense-perception, even hyperæsthesia, but it was not so easy to exclude subliminal sensibility. There was abundant evidence that subconsciously perceived stimuli existed. But we had to suppose that even subliminal perceptions were excluded from anything called telepathy; and the stimulus must be mere thought on the part of the sender, or agent. As thought is not a physical stimulus, any reception of it by another person could be said to be a phenomenon not involving normal sense-perception or even the interpretation of unconscious sensory stimuli.

It is very important to take all these facts into account, because the term telepathy has been very widely used to denote a process that would explain much more than the phenomena which it was coined merely to describe. The founders of the English Society defined the term as the "transmission of thought independently of the recognized channels of sense." I have preferred to define telepathy as "coincidence, excluding normal sense-perception, between the thoughts of two minds." There is no essential difference between this definition and that by the English Society. The original founders of the Society probably did not intend that the term should imply or express a definite process of explanation; but the use of the term "transmission" and the assumption, at least for scientific cautiousness, that this "transmission" was a direct process between living minds and not in any way connected with the action of spirits, soon gave the term an implication which it did not originally have. All that we strictly know is that A's thought gets into the mind of B, without reference to the process by which this effect was brought about. We know only the fact of a coincidence inexplicable by chance or normal sense-perception. We have no reason to assume that it is a process exclusively between *living* people and not permitting the intervention of the dead, if the discarnate exist and can act on the living.

It thus became necessary to define very exactly the meaning of the term telepathy, absolutely excluding either the evidence or the action of the discarnate, or both, or else defining it with such breadth as to include any undiscovered process of transcendental action between minds of any kind, whether incarnate or discarnate. Only the former meaning of the term would bring it into rivalry with the spiritistic theory, while the latter would permit the employment of the term to describe the action of discarnate as well as incarnate minds. There has been a growing tendency among some of the members of the English Society to extend the meaning of the term so that it might include transmission of thoughts between the living and the dead and between different discarnate minds, without fully realizing that they have cut off the right to use the term as excluding spiritistic interpretations of any or all of the phenomena involving transcendental transmission of thought.

In its only proper meaning, telepathy is a term to name facts which are not evidence for the existence of spirits, and it *implies no explanation whatever of the facts so named.* The process, if we knew it, might include a relation between the incarnate and the discarnate, and between different discarnate minds, if such exist. But the term itself is only a name for facts whose explanation we do not know. The first object of the English Society was the estimation of evidence, not the application of explanatory hypotheses. Telepathy involves no assumption of any known or hypothetical process to explain the coincidences cited as evidence of a supernormal relation between two minds.

The phenomena cited to prove the existence of telepathy represent the thoughts of A and the simultaneous acquisition or perception of them by B. There are no doubt coincidences between A's thoughts yesterday or ten years ago and those of B to-day or five years ago. But such coincidences would be no evidence of telepathy. But there has been a very marked tendency, even among supposed scientific students and investigators, to extend the import of the term to include coincidences between what may be a mere subconscious memory of A and the present thought of B. This extension of the meaning of telepathy has been adopted as an explanation of apparent spirit communications; that is, the messages which seem to indicate continued personal existence of the dead are regarded as a selection from among the sitter's subconscious memories, on the part of the medium. But no evidence whatever has ever been produced to prove that B can select memories from the subconscious of A. There may be, as I think there are, some coincidences which look very like selection from the subconscious rather than the direct action of the agent upon the percipient; but these are too often complicated with associated incidents indicative of spirit agencies, to be disposed of as selective telepathy from the subconscious.

Mediumistic phenomena too often suggest the action of spirits, to be cited as direct evidence for telepathy. The possibility of telepathy is only a ground for disqualifying an incident as evidence for the existence of spirits; but the fact that it is a possible alternative explanation is no proof that is the correct explanation. The possibility of spirits and the fact that an incident is appropriate to illustrate the personal identity of a deceased person forbids using it as positive evidence for telepathy. One can only insist that one theory is as good as the other to account for the facts. The possibility of telepathy in the case may nullify the value of the fact as evidence for spirits, but it does not exclude the hypothetical explanation of the fact by spirits, if the incident involves a proved memory of a deceased person. But when facts arise which both indicate the continued personal identity of the dead and are not explicable by telepathy, the spiritistic theory must be conceded.

Of course, the believer in telepathy replies that the proof for spirits has not been given and that telepathy still has the right of preference as a theory. But in order to make telepathy applicable to the facts, its defenders have unwarrantably extended its meaning. At first it was limited to the present active states of the agent and the percipient; that is, the present thoughts of A were received by B. Then, in order to avoid the acceptance of spiritism, its opponents invented, but did not prove, a selective telepathy. The meaning of the term was altered and extended to mean the selection by B from the subconscious of A, of the facts necessary to impersonate the deceased C. This selective process has not in any case been proved. But even the hypothesis of such telepathy is excluded when facts are obtained which B does not know about C, but which are verifiable from the mind of D, who is not present Hence, when one finds an incident that excludes both ordinary telepathy with the normal consciousness and selective telepathy with the subliminal consciousness of the person present, one must either abandon telepathy as an explanation or extend the meaning of the term to include selection from the mind of the absent D.

This sort of telepathy has been supposed, but no evidence has been adduced for it, and I do not see how it would be possible to adduce such evidence. Every extension of the term beyond coincidences between the mental states of two persons is wholly without warrant. The introduction of the assumption that this coincidence is due to a direct transmission from one living mind to another has never been justified, and as there is no known process whatever associated with the coincidences, we are permitted to use the term only in a descriptive, not in an explanatory sense.

An hypothesis may indeed explain facts that are not in themselves evidence of that hypothesis, but only after adequate evidence has already been adduced for it. An hypothesis may thus be applied to facts that are consistent with it but are not convincing evidence of it; and then associated incidents, not directly explained by the main hypothesis, will come under it as due to subsidiary causes consistent with it. But telepathy explains nothing—certainly not those associated incidents which might be due to spiritistic causes, though not primary evidence of them. It is only a discriminating device in the estimation of the evidential problem and so serves to postpone the final judgment of the case. It has no relevance to those attendant phenomena which might naturally follow the influence of a transcendental agent, especially on the supposition that it retains its identity,— for example, constitutional habits of the mind and organism that are often imitated by a medium, sometimes described as physical impersonation of the discarnate person. Very often the best proof of identity comes from this phenomenon, which bears no relation to telepathy.

Let me summarize the position we have reached in the scientific investigation of unusual phenomena:

1. There are in human experience a large number of coincidences inexplicable by fraud, secondary personality or subconscious creation, chance, or guessing. This general statement covers the whole field of psychic research, including telekinesis, or the move

ment of physical objects without contact, if we slightly stretch the meaning of the term coincidence. It includes, regardless of explanation, apparently spiritistic as well as telepathic experiences, and the phenomena of dousing. Apparitions may be classed as either telepathic or spiritistic.

Some explanation of these coincidences must be made. The coincidences are so numerous and so well accredited that no hypothesis which does not go as far as telepathy can have any standing whatever. But telepathy, if applicable, must be used in an explanatory and theoretical, instead of in a descriptive, sense. If telepathy is supposed to have powers of infinite selection and of impersonation, it may be invoked to oppose spiritistic explanations. But without this extension of meaning, it is powerless to explain the facts.

The spiritualists, of course, at the outset applied the spiritistic hypothesis to the whole field, and were as negligent of the analysis of the problem as the telepathists. The telepathists, in their turn, showed the same carelessness, in attempting to explain everything mediumistic by telepathy. Neither party has fully realized the importance of subsidiary circumstances in the phenomena. The public assumes that spirits are beings that have all the apparent properties of a living person except visibility and tangibility. The scientific man simply thinks of them as personal streams of consciousness, whatever else they may turn out to be; and capable of initiating or causing events in the physical world in coöperation with all sorts of bodily conditions and perhaps transcendental influences other than themselves. The scientific spiritist recognizes different kinds of phenomena, and uses the term spirits only when he wishes it understood that they are the chief cause of the series of phenomena manifested. He may not know in the least how this cause operates; he simply treats the facts as evidence of the existence of spirits and their undefined causal relation to the phenomena, whatever other causes or complicating circumstances may be present.

2. The rigidly scientific man has not yet accepted telepathy of any kind, unless as a possible hypothesis, which has to be eliminated before the spiritistic theory can be admitted even as an hypothesis

But he well knows, when he concedes such a possibility, that it implies no explanation whatever of the facts. It merely classifies them as inexplicable and mysterious. The public seems not to regard them as mysterious at all, as it assumes that telepathy is a mere common-place, when in reality it involves considerations far more mysterious to scientific men than the spiritistic theory can possibly be.

3. The experimental evidence for telepathy, as presented in the publications of the English Society, is still under dispute by scientific men, and some of its best data have apparently been discredited. I myself am not convinced of anything more than coincidences excluding chance and guessing, though I am willing to concede the point for the sake of argument. But there are many striking incidents in the Piper phenomena which, though not evidence to the continued personal existence of deceased persons, are undoubtedly supernormal. Similar incidents occur in the work of Mrs. Chenoweth. Scientific men would have to go at least as far as the admission of telepathy, in order to escape the spiritistic theory in the explanation of them. Even if the experimental evidence of the English Society were nullified, these incidents would make out an experimental case for telepathy of some kind. But so many of them imply the continued personal identity of the dead that telepathy is by no means the obvious explanation of them.

4. Whatever real or alleged evidence there is for telepathy limits it to present active states of consciousness between agent and percipient. There is no scientific evidence for any of the following conceptions of it: (1) Telepathy as a process of selecting from the contents of the subconscious of any person in the presence of the percipient. (2) Telepathy as a process of selecting from the contents of the mind of some distant person by the percipient and constructing these acquired facts into a complete simulation of a given personality. (3) Telepathy as a process of selecting memories from any living people to impersonate the dead. (4) Telepathy as implying the transmission of the thoughts of all living people to all others individually, with the selection of the necessary facts for impersonation from the sitter present. (5) Telepathy as involving a *direct* process between agent and percipient. (6)

Telepathy as explanatory in any sense whatever, implying any known cause.

Such unsupported assumptions as these induce the scientific man to neglect the whole subject; but unless they can be sustained, there can be no appeal to telepathy as a rival of spiritistic hypotheses. There are facts which justify entertaining the possibility of telepathy as a precaution against haste in accepting the spiritistic theory, but it has no relevance when these facts are incompatible with it, or have been otherwise accounted for.

There is an interesting tendency of many minds to extend the application of telepathy until it coincides with the reading from other minds anything known by a living person. This is the *fourth* type mentioned before. It includes the conception also that even the memories or thoughts of some dead people could also be acquired in this way without the supposition that they were obtained from the dead. Thus as Mr. Smith, who is living, receives telepathically the thoughts of all living people he has received the thoughts of all dead people who were more or less contemporary with him but died previously, and hence with them the thoughts of all dead people, prior to his own existence, but contemporary with those dead from whom he received his telepathic impressions. This theory would involve access to the memories of all dead people whatsoever back to the origin of the human race, and perhaps the impressions and states of consciousness of all animate life!

While those who regard telepathy as operative on any fact known by the living are not conscious that they imply this extension of it, the assumption only awaits formulation to be recognized as virtually present. It means that no verifiable fact can be taken as evidence of the discarnate, and that we should have to accept unverifiable facts as data for proof! That is, if telepathy can reach all the thoughts of every living person, we could treat as evidence for spirits only facts outside its range — that is, facts not known by any living person, and such facts could not be verified. But according to the extension of telepathy just explained, there are no unknown facts whatever, as presumably the thoughts of all living people would have been telepathically impressed on every other living person and with them also all the thoughts of the dead who impressed their thoughts on some living person before their death.

Such telepathy needs no serious consideration. But it is the logical result of the unverified and unverifiable hypotheses with which even psychic researchers play ducks and drakes with scientific method. If the simplest form of telepathy is still a subject of doubt for scientific men, what becomes of such a stupendous hypothesis as the one just defined? No intelligent man is called upon to take account of such extended hypotheses until the evidence is produced that they are probably facts or reasonably supposable. Their magnitude itself tells in favor of the spiritistic theory, because the latter hypothesis is the simplest explanation of the facts as observed and recorded. The telepathy assumed is both infinite and finite: infinite by implication and finite by the evidence of the facts. The failures in experiments to read the present active states of the agent and the inability to verify any thoughts outside those states, in the opinion of science, is so finite that its very existence is doubted, while the extended hypothesis requires us to believe in its infinity without evidence! But the natural and pertinent selectiveness of characteristics relevant to the personal identity of deceased persons, and the absence of selectiveness relevant to the identity of living people; the mixed success and error in the facts obtained; the fact that a pictographic process explains so easily the mixture of success and error in many of the facts; the fragmentary character of the data, with confusion so easily explicable by misinterpretation of stimuli and the evident rapidity of the process; the difficulty in getting proper names, though this varies with the psychological constitution of the psychic; the frequently symbolic nature of the phenomena, showing intelligence in the selection of them, whereas telepathy is conceived after mechanical analogies; all these are so inconsistent with telepathy in any form in which it can be imagined, that no intelligent person who has critically examined and analyzed the facts would be tempted to use it as explanatory of the phenomena on record, though he might admit it as a convenient term for distinguishing between types of evidence for supernormal experience. As a name for the facts, with suspended judgment regarding explanation, it is tolerable;

but there can be no doubt that spirits *explain* certain facts, while telepathy explains nothing. At least as an hypothesis, therefore, the spiritistic theory has the priority and the burden of proof rests upon the telepathic theory.

CHAPTER IX

INSTANCES OF TELEPATHY AND SIMILAR PHENOMENA

WE have discussed the meaning of the term telepathy and its elastic applications without adducing any facts in evidence either of its existence or of its explanatory character; now it is time to ascertain what are the facts that have given rise to the conception. They will still further elucidate its meaning and especially will enable us to ascertain the extent to which it is relevant to psychic research. The facts divide themselves into three distinct types, neither of which furnishes evidence of the existence of discarnate spirits.

These types are: (1) the spontaneous type, (2) the experimental type, and (3) a mixture of the spontaneous and the experimental types. The spontaneous type has two forms: (a) coincidences between two persons' thoughts, without reference to death, and (b) coincidences connected with dying persons. In the mixed spontaneous and experimental type we shall find incidents referring to the dead, but not evidence for survival.

Under the heading of spontaneous incidents I wish to adduce a number of coincidences between the thoughts of living people, coincidences which bear no suggestion of discarnate intelligence. They are usually trivial matters which, though they are evidence of something unusual and possibly supernormal, cannot be in any way adduced as evidence of the existence of spirits.

I must premise the giving of incidents with the statement that I am not attempting to *prove* the existence of telepathy, but only to give illustrations of the kind of facts which have been used to prove it. While the incidents quoted will be partial proof of it, they will not suffice to establish so large a conclusion. If readers want scientific proof for telepathy, they must consult more elaborate records than can be quoted here. I can only select instances that cannot be explained as chance coincidence or normal sense-perception. Whether they suffice to prove what is usually understood by telepathy may be debated, but they do at least challenge skepticism to explain them.

The first incidents will be taken from a diary kept by a lady, who therein recounted her coincidental experiences. It covers one year's time and includes 164 instances. I can take only a few as illustrations, and the selection shall be limited to cases that are wholly without suggestion of a relation to the dead. Each incident might be treated as a chance coincidence, if taken alone; it is the collective significance of the whole number that is of interest, though I can illustrate what I mean only by quoting them, without passing judgment on their value as proof. The dates given in the diary are omitted.

"I was in the front sitting room and dared not go out of the room for the cold; my plants were awfully dry, and hearing E. [her niece] in the kitchen, I telepathed her to bring me in some water. She at once came with a jug full and asked if I would water the plants."

"My husband was sitting reading his newspaper and I lay on the couch thinking of the young men's concert which we are thinking of getting up and wishing he would give over reading, when he looked up from his paper and asked me a question about it. We had neither of us mentioned the subject before that day."

"I willed very hard that Mr. Duke should come here before 12 o'clock, just to prove I could bring him. He came just before the time. My husband was at home and I told him afterwards."

"This morning I was thinking of Mrs. T. B., and said how I should like her to come in; I wanted to speak to her. This was at 11.30 A. M., and in the afternoon she came, and I told her I was thinking of her in the morning, and she said she made up her mind to come while she was cleaning the kitchen up in the morning after 11 A. M."

"I am again feeling Mr. Duke will call. He did, before E. had finished dusting the room. I knew he would. To-night a rap came at the front door. I felt it was a poor woman named M., and I told Mr. S. it was and I would not see her, and it was her. I had no reason for thinking it was her, only I felt it."

"I expect to hear my Aunt Sarah is much worse or has passed away. I am thinking so much about her all day."

On the next day the lady records in her diary: "The feeling about Aunt is not so strong today."

Then again on the day following the note just mentioned the lady writes in her diary: "I shall hear from Mrs. Ph. to-day. I did. We had a letter saying Aunt passed away at quarter to six o'clock on Sunday, 27th."

This last date was the date of the first record in which the lady stated that she expected to hear that the Aunt was worse or had passed away.

"I felt Mr. Duke would come this morning, but he did not." On the next day the lady records: "Mr. Duke came. I knew he was coming quite well, and hurried E. to get my room done. He said he wanted to come yesterday, but was too busy, he could not bring it in."

"Mrs. T. B. several times in church this morning seemed as if she must get up and go out, and I willed most strongly she should not, and each time she half got up I looked hard at her and told her telepathically to sit down again, and she did."

"This afternoon I telepathed to Mr. B. asking why he did not ask Mr. T. instead of Mr. S. for a solo for the P. S. A. Mr. B. came in the evening, and said in the afternoon he very suddenly thought of Mr. T. and went at once to ask him if he would sing, and he promised."

"Mrs. B. promised her son H. should bring me some patterns from a shop in the town at dinner time, when he came out of school. He did not bring them, and again at tea-time they did not come, so I waited until half past five. Then I telepathed to her, 'You are forgetting my patterns, and the light will soon be gone, so that I shall not be able to see them.' H. came with them at 10 minutes past 6 o'clock, and said his mother forgot them until half past 5, when she said, 'Make haste or the light will be gone, and your auntie will not be able to see them.' When the rap came, I said, 'That is H. with the patterns.'"

"Mr. Duke telepathed to me at half past eleven this morning that he should come in to see me in the afternoon, because it was

Good Friday. He came in as I thought, and said at half past eleven he made up his mind he would look in in the afternoon, because of its being Good Friday next day."

"I telepathed very strongly to Mrs. J. to come in to see me for a *minute*. I wanted to speak to her most particularly. She came, saying: 'I can only stay a minute."

"Mr. Duke called this evening, and said last night I appeared to him three or four times, and he got quite vexed at me, because I kept waking him, but he did not seem to be able to get rid of me. The last time he saw me I was in bed, as if ill, my arm was above my head and I had on a turquoise *blue jacket*. This is very remarkable, because I always wear pink jackets, and had only the day before finished making myself a blue one, and tried it on to be sure it was all right. I need scarcely say Mr. Duke knew nothing whatever of this."

Mr. Duke confirms this incident in all respects, except that the lady did not "appear" to him, as her word might imply a phantasm of her.

But there are 164 such incidents and we need not quote further. I should note, however, that two of them are connected with situations suggestive of something else than telepathy between the living. One of them is a premonition afterward fulfilled and the other a death coincidence.

I next take an incident from the first volume of "Phantasms of the Living." It also involves a coincidence apparently without purpose.

"'BRANTWOOD, CONISTON, October 27, 1883.

"'I woke up with a start, feeling I had had a hard blow on my mouth, and with a distinct sense that I had been cut, and was bleeding under my upper lip, and seized my pocket handkerchief, and held it (in a little pushed lump) to the part, as I sat up in bed, and after a few seconds when I removed it, I was astonished not to see any blood, and only then realized it was impossible anything could have struck me there, as I lay fast asleep in bed, and so I thought it was only a dream!—but I looked at my watch, and saw it was seven, and finding Arthur, (my husband) was not in the room, I concluded (rightly) that he must have gone out on the lake for an early sail, as it was so fine.

"'I then fell asleep. At breakfast (half past nine), Arthur came in rather late, and I noticed he rather purposely sat farther away from me than usual, and every now and then put his pocket handkerchief furtively up to his lip, in the very way I had done. I said, "Arthur, why are you doing that?" and added a little anxiously, "I know you have hurt yourself! but I'll tell you why afterwards." He said, "Well, I was sailing, a sudden squall came, throwing the tiller suddenly around, and it struck me a bad blow in the mouth, under the upper lip, and it has been bleeding a good deal and won't stop." I then said, "Have you any idea what o'clock it was when it happened?" and he answered, "It must have been about seven."

"'I then told what happened to *me,* much to *his* surprise, and all who were with us at breakfast. It happened here about three years ago at Brantwood to me.

"'JOAN R. SEVERN.'

"In reply to inquiries Mrs. Severn writes: 'There was no doubt about my starting up in bed wide awake, as I stuffed my pocket handkerchief into my mouth, and held it pressed to my upper lip for some time before removing it "to see the blood,"—and was much surprised that there was none. Some little time afterwards I fell asleep again. I believe that when I got up, an hour afterwards, the impression was still vividly in my mind, and that as I was dressing I did look under my lip to see if there was any mark."

Another incident of a trivial sort is reported in the same volume by the Rev. P. H. Newnham, who has also reported many other coincidences.

"'January 26, 1885.

"'In March, 1861, I was living at Houghton, Hants. My wife was at the time confined to the house, by delicacy of the lungs. One day, walking through a lane, I found the first wild violets of the spring, and took them home to her.

"'Early in April I was attacked with a dangerous illness; and in June left the place. I never told my wife exactly where I found the violets, nor, for the reasons explained, did I ever walk with her past the place where they grew, for many years.

"'In November, 1873, we were staying with friends at Houghton; and myself and wife took a walk up the lane in question. As we passed by the place, the recollection of those early violets of twelve and a half years ago flashed upon my mind. At the usual interval of some twenty or thirty seconds my wife remarked, "It's very curious, but if it were not impossible, I should declare that I could smell violets in the hedge."

"I had not spoken, nor made any gesture or movement of any kind, to indicate what I was thinking of. Neither had my memory called up the perfume. All that I thought of was the exact locality on the hedge bank, my memory being exceedingly minute for locality."

"Mr. Newnham's residence at Houghton lasted only a few months, and with the help of a diary he can account for nearly every day's walking and work. "My impression is," he says, "that this was the first and only time that I explored this particular 'drive'; and I feel certain that Mrs. Newnham never saw the spot at all until November, 1873. The hedges had then been grubbed, and no violets grew there."

"Mrs. Newnham confirms the story; and, though it cannot be regarded as proof of telepathy, it, with other and more evidential experiences of Mr. and Mrs. Newnham, is of sufficient interest to justify investigation of the subject.

"The next instance is interesting, as it might have coincided with death, had the person involved in it died at the time. The circumstances which give the incident its value will also have to be told.

"'November, 1884.

"'When I was a child I had many remarkable experiences of a psychical nature, which I remember to have looked upon as ordinary and natural at the time.

"'On one occasion (I am unable to fix the date, but I must have been about ten years old) I was walking in a country lane at A., the place where my parents then resided. I was reading geometry as I walked along, a subject little likely to produce fancies or morbid phenomena of any kind, when, in a moment, I saw a bedroom known as the White Room in my home, and upon the floor lay my mother, to all appearance dead. The vision must have remained some minutes, during which time my real surroundings seemed to pale and die out; but as the vision faded, actual surroundings came back, at first dimly, and then clearly.

"'I could not doubt that what I had seen was real, so, instead of going home, I went at once to the house of our medical man and found him at home. He at once set out with me for my home, on the way putting questions I could not answer, as my mother was to all appearance well when I left home.

"'I led the doctor straight to the White Room, where we found my mother actually lying as in my vision. This was true even to minute details. She had been seized suddenly by an attack at the heart, and would soon have breathed her last but for the doctor's timely advent. I shall get my father and mother to read this and sign it.

"'JEANIE GWYNNE BETTANY.'"

"The father and mother signed the document and then the lady herself in response to inquiries made the following important statements.

"(1) I was in no anxiety about my mother at the time I saw the vision I described.

"(2) Something a little similar had once occurred to my mother. She had been out riding alone, and the horse brought her to our door hanging half off his back, in a faint. This was a long time before, and she never rode again. Heart disease had set in. She was not in *the habit* of fainting unless an attack of the heart was upon her. Between the attacks she looked and acted as if in health.

"(3) The occasion I describe was, I believe, the only one on which I saw a scene transported apparently into the actual field of vision, to the exclusion of objects and surroundings actually present.

"I have had other visions in which I have seen events happening as they *really were,* in another place, but I have been also conscious of *real* surroundings.

"(4) No one could tell whether my vision preceded the fact or not. My mother was supposed to be out. No one knew anything of my mother's being ill, till I took the doctor and my father, whom I had encountered at the door, to the room where I found my mother as I had seen her in my vision.

"(5) The doctor is dead. He has no living relation. No one in A. knew anything of these circumstances.

"(6) The White Room in which I saw my mother, and afterwards actually found her, was out of use. It was unlikely she should be there. She was found lying in the attitude in which I had seen her. I found a handkerchief with a lace border beside her on the floor. This I had distinctly noticed in my vision. There were other particulars of coincidence which I cannot put here."

Mrs. Bettany's father has given the following fuller account:—

"I distinctly remember being surprised by seeing my daughter, in company with the family doctor, outside the door of my residence; and I asked 'Who is ill?' She replied, 'Mamma.' She led the way at once to the 'White Room,' where we found my wife lying in a swoon on the floor. It was when I asked when she had been taken ill, that I found that it must have been after my daughter had left the house. None of the servants in the house knew anything of the sudden illness, which our doctor assured me would have been *fatal* had he not arrived when he did. My wife was quite well when I left her in the morning.

"S. G. Gwynne."

This incident is interesting: for we cannot suppose that the mother was the agent without assuming that she had subconsciously thought of her daughter, which she would be less likely to do than to think of her husband. It is a case so closely allied to those which purport to involve the intervention of the dead that it is well worth quoting here.

I next take, from the "Proceedings" of the American Society for Psychical Research, an incident which was partly experimental, but which also represents a spontaneous coincidence.

"January 15, 1907.

"I sat down to read proofs a moment ago, and in the sentence, 'I had hoped by the article to begin the task of crystallizing,' the syllable 'izing' beginning the next line, I read the word 'crystallizing' as 'crystal gazing' twice, and being puzzled by its irrelevance I looked a third time and found that it was a most distinct illusion. I had a few minutes — perhaps ten or fifteen — before been occupied with the subject of classifying crystal visions.

"Immediately I resolved to test my secretary and, taking the proofs around to her, asked her to read the sentence aloud, without saying what I wanted. At the same time, I willed that she should say 'crystal gazing' instead of 'crystallizing,' which she did twice. As soon as it was over she told me that just a second or two before I asked her to read the sentence, she saw an apparition of a crystal and thought of crystal gazing several times. She could not have seen or known what I was thinking about.

"James H. Hyslop."

Another instance shows the caprice and spontaneity that justifies classification with spontaneous cases.

"Brooklyn, N. Y., January 1, 1907.

"Dr. James H. Hyslop.

"Dear Sir: I send the following instance of telepathy as a very satisfactory demonstration.

"Mr. C. C. Rodgers went out to make a purchase for me. He ran quickly down from the third floor and I heard the front door close. At once there flashed into my consciousness, 'Go to my gray trousers.' The message seemed to carry its own impulse. I obeyed without hesitation, surprise or thought of its meaning. I walked to the wardrobe and my hand at once touched the bunch of keys in one of the pockets. Then I knew. I put my hand in the pocket, got the keys, went to the front window and waited his return. When he came in the gate I threw the keys down to him. He let himself in at the front door and came bounding up the stairs. 'You got my message,' he exclaimed. 'When I realized I had forgotten my keys, I sent you a message to go to my gray trousers and throw them down to me.' No comment can make this stronger.

"Frederika Cantwell."

The gentleman confirms the story. I quote another incident from the same source. It was reported by Professor H. Norman Gardiner, of Smith College, Northampton, Massachusetts.

"May 6, 1909.

"My father and brother are ardent hunters, you should know. Recently my brother trapped a muskrat, which quite oddly was alive when he got to the trap. At this season they usually drown very soon after being caught. My brother was alone and my father did not know where he had been. All he knew was the fact of his finding a muskrat alive in his trap and killing him. I established this fact by careful inquiry of both of them.

"The next morning father said that he had dreamed the night before that he was trapping muskrat, and that when he got to one trap it had a live rat in it. (So far the dream was merely the reproduction of what he had been told.) But he went on to say that the rat was some distance from the shore, and that he hunted around and found a very long beanpole and with that dispatched the rat. Then Walter said: 'I killed mine with a bean-pole.' 'Mine was sharpened at the end,' said my father. 'And so was mine,' said my brother.

"It will not occur to you how odd that was, because it is unlikely that you ever hunted muskrats much. If you had, one of the last images which you would call up would be cultivated fields and gardens. I asked Walter if he had told any one about using the bean-pole, and he said he had not. I then asked father if he ever in his life had done the same thing or in any way connected muskrats and bean gardens, and he could recall nothing to bring up the dream.

"It seems to be thought transference. In our family this is not strange My brother, sister and I all agree that we all of us, to some extent, read father's mind.

"(Mrs.) F——."

These suffice to illustrate spontaneous incidents which occur by the thousand. They may not have scientific cogency, but they suggest the need of experiment to decide the matter. There is not the slightest superficial indication of anything more than some connection between living minds in these phenomena; if they are supernormal, they do not suggest any third party as a link in the series. We turn to the next type.

The occurrence of spontaneous cases suggested experiment for deciding the question. In the other sciences, if experiment was possible, it was not necessary to depend upon spontaneous phenomena for proof. Experiments were tried with apparent success. Illustrations are in order.

I myself on one occasion made an experiment of some interest. I was investigating a professional claimant of telepathic powers, and was not satisfied with his performance, as it showed distinct evidences of the signal code and other methods of the conjurer. At last I selected a young man from those whom I had invited to witness the evening's experiment. He was an absolute stranger to the man whom I was investigating and came with another guest of mine. I blindfolded the young man and superintended the experiments myself. The young man sat about four feet in front of me, and I stood up with a writing pad in my hand in such a position that he could not see it.

I first drew a triangle with a circle in it, while we remained quiet. No word or signal was uttered. In a few moments the young man got a triangle with a circle in it. I then drew a circle with a triangle in it and in the triangle a plus mark or cross. In a few moments the young man got two sides of the triangle and the cross inside them. I then drew a pig and he soon got "a goat or a pig." This ended the experiment. I am sure that there was no collusion nor possible fraud.

In a series of experiments some years later I obtained interesting results of another kind. The subject was unable to reproduce drawings or to get words or ideas simply thought by the agent, but could find objects and put them in places intended by the agents. In other words, she could carry out motor impulses apparently suggested by telepathy. The thought to be conveyed to her was written down in a book and read silently by the persons acting as agents, while the lady was in another room at some distance. She was later admitted to the room for the experiment. Two stood behind her and touched hands, but did not touch the subject or percipient. The percipient stood a moment with eyes downcast, then went to the object thought of, picked it up, and put it in the intended spot. This performance was successfully repeated so often as to exclude explanation by chance, and only those who did not witness the phenomena could offer to explain them as the results of unconscious suggestions.

For instance, in one experiment it was willed that the subject should get a pocketbook out of a vase ten feet distant, and put it on the bookcase in another room. She promptly went to the vase and got the pocketbook, and on the second trial put it on the bookcase intended. In another experiment she was to get the keys which I had concealed in the sofa in the reception room, and put them on the piano. Both actions were promptly performed on the first trial. One hundred twenty-four similar experiments, most of them quite as complex as the examples mentioned, were performed with a success that strongly suggested supernormal knowledge. The results were published in the "Proceedings" of the American Society. They are the only results that I was ever able personally to obtain in support of any kind of telepathy.

Mr. Malcolm Guthrie and Mr. Birchall, members of the Liverpool Literary and Philosophical Society, published some good results in the English "Proceedings."[1] I can choose only a few

[1] "Proceedings," English S. P. R., Vol. I, p. 263.

illustrations from a very lengthy report. The operators and subjects of experiment were people in private life, and no professional interests were involved. In some of the experiments contact between the agent and the percipient was allowed, but in many of them this contact was not permitted, so that ordinary muscle-reading was excluded. The nature of the objects chosen, however, and the promptness of the answers, in the cases where contact was permitted, show conclusively that contact did not affect results. I shall choose some instances from the cases in which contact was not permitted.

The agent thought of a *half crown;* the percipient stated her impression: "Like a flat bottom — bright . . . no particular color." In the second experiment the *four of spades* was in the mind of the agent; the answer given was: "A card . . . four of clubs." She said afterwards that she did not know the difference between spades and clubs. In the third experiment the agent thought of an *egg;* the percipient said: "Looks remarkably like an egg." In the fourth *a penholder with thimble inverted on the end* was the object thought of and the answer was: 'A column, with something bell-shaped turned down on it." In the fifth experiment the agent thought of *a small gold ear-ring;* the percipient answered: "Round and bright . . . yellow . . . with loop to hang it by."

In a set of experiments in which contact was allowed, out of four attempts only one was successful — a result which tends to show that contact was not a condition of success. In another set of four experiments without contact the following were the results: In the first experiment, *Object:* A gold cross. *Result:* "It is yellow . . . it is a cross." In the second experiment, *Object:* A red ivory chess knight. *Result:* "It is red . . . broad at the bottom . . . then very narrow . . . then broad again at the top . . . it is a chessman." Asked to name the piece, percipient said she did not know the names of the pieces. In the third experiment, *Object:* A half crown held up by Mr. B., taken out of his pocket after he had placed the percipient with face to the wall and away from the agent. *Result:* "It is round . . . bright . . . no particular color . . . silver . . . it is a piece of money . . . larger than a shilling, but not as large as . . . " The percipient was unable to say more. In the fourth experiment, *Object*: A diamond of pink silk on black satin. *Result:* "Light pink . . . cannot make out the shape . . . seems moving about." The object was held somewhat unsteadily by Mr. G. In both these sets of experiments the successes certainly cannot be explained as chance.

There is no superficial evidence of spirits in these instances of telepathy. We may suspend judgment as to the explanation of them, but we cannot quote them in proof either of the existence of spirits or of their influence to produce the effects. For aught that we know, spirits may be instrumental in producing them; but the phenomena themselves bear no testimony to that effect.

Professor Barrett, now Sir William F. Barrett, reported a series of experiments for telepathy under good conditions, of which the illustrations appended explain themselves. The experiments were made without contact and represent drawings by the agent reproduced by the percipient. ("Proceedings," English S. P. R., Vol. II, pp. 207–215.)

I now come to a type of phenomenon in which a living person appears to another, when one of them is thinking of the other or even trying to impress him with the sense of his presence. I shall quote only a few cases in illustration. I take the first incident from Mr. Podmore's "Apparitions and Thought-Transference."

Rev. Clarence Godfrey resolved to make himself appear to a friend. Without acquainting his friend with his intention, he determined before going to sleep to "translate" himself "spiritually" into her room so that he could be seen. This effort was sustained for about eight minutes; he then went to sleep, but was awakened at about 3:40 A. M. with some consciousness of her presence. This was on November 15.

On the next day, November 16, he received an account from the lady, telling her experience, saying that at about 3:30 A. M. she had awakened with a start and had seen Mr. Godfrey standing near the window on the staircase. He had vanished in three or four seconds.

Mr. Godfrey tried a similar experiment a second time and succeeded. Herr Weserman, an official in the German Government, tried the experiment frequently with marked success. Dr. Funk reported to me a case which I investigated and recorded.

A lady who had been reading Hudson's book on psychic phenomena learned from it that she might be able to make herself appear to another; she resolved to try the experiment on her husband. She was at Derby, Connecticut, at the time of the experiment, and her husband was away on business. She did not know where he was, but thought he might be in New York, Schenectady, Syracuse or Buffalo. She went to sleep in Derby willing that she should appear to her husband, wake him, and kiss him on the forehead. On that night he awakened at about one o'clock and saw his wife standing at the foot of his bed. He asked what she was doing there, whereupon she walked round and kissed him on the forehead.

There are numerous spontaneous cases of the kind, more or less well authenticated, which the skeptical are the more ready to accept because they afford a refuge from the spiritistic hypothesis. They require as much authentication as other types of apparition, and, as they are less numerous than those of the dying and the dead, they are not as cogent evidence for the supernormal, though, when proved, they afford support for telepathy. I have sufficiently illustrated the type, which supports the definition of telepathy as a coincidence between the mental states of two living persons. They do not suggest spiritistic interpretations of any kind.

We come next to a type of phenomena which have been classified under telepathy because they do not, superficially at least, serve as evidence of discarnate spirits.

The two volumes on "Phantasms of the Living," most of which are in fact apparitions of the dying, and the "Census of Hallucinations," Volume X of the English "Proceedings," include hundreds of cases of this type. They are usually appearances of a dying person at the time of death or very near it. Everyone must concede that the circumstances cannot be explained as chance coincidence. Let me abbreviate two instances, which I quote from the "Census of Hallucinations."

"TICKHILL, YORKS, June 12, 1891.

"An aunt of mine, who died in England last November, 1890, appeared before me in Australia, and I knew before I received the letter of her death that she was dead. I took a note of it at the time and found on comparing notes that she appeared to me the day she died — date November 17th, 1890."

The next instance is also of interest because of the distance between those concerned.

"September, 1893.

"At the end of August of the year 1882, my father, mother, and sisters left home for our usual summer holiday. At the same time a young man whom we knew quite slightly (although he was our neighbor) started to Texas to learn farming, for which I felt sorry, because I was looking forward to paint well enough by my return to ask him to sit for the principal figure in a picture I was longing to do.

"We went to a cottage in Gloucestershire, where my sister and I shared the same room. About the fourteenth of September, 1882, my sister and I felt worried and distressed by hearing the death watch; it lasted a whole day and night. We got up earlier than usual the next morning, about six o'clock, to finish some birthday presents for our mother. As my sister and I were working and talking together, I looked up, and saw our young acquaintance standing in front of me and looking at us. I turned to my sister, she saw nothing; I looked again to where he stood, he had vanished. We agreed not to tell any one — and, although I wished to put it down in my diary (which I had not kept for some time), I was afraid to do so; I therefore made marks to remind myself.

"Some time afterwards we heard that our young acquaintance had either committed suicide or had been killed; he was found dead in the woods twenty-four hours after landing.

"On looking back to my diary, I found that my marks corresponded to the date of his death."

These two typical instances have been chosen because the circumstances make it difficult to account for them by any previous knowledge on the part of the percipient. The main point is, that the writers of the reports of these phenomena explain them by telepathy, with the idea that this explanation excludes the possibility of the action of spirits. The impression is always left that the incidents are evidence of telepathy between the living, which in reality they are not. They are in no respect evidence for telepathy so defined. Some of the recorded instances show that the dying person was thinking of the percipient at the time, but the majority of them exhibit no such fact; that such thought was present cannot be conjectured as probable, and then used as evidence. The possibility is sometimes emphasized that the range of telepathy may be extended so far as to shut out the appeal to such cases as evidence for the action of discarnate spirits. I quite agree that they cannot be used as evidence for the existence and action of spirits; but neither can they be quoted as evidence for telepathy of the type that excludes the action of spirits. The fact that the coincidence occurs more frequently in connection with dying than with living persons tends to show that death has something to do with causing the phenomena; and, though we may not be justified in invoking spirits to account for the facts, it is quite as legitimate to explain the phenomena by regarding the dying person as a free spirit at the time as by regarding him as a telepathic agent. In other words, the cases are not evidence on either side of the controversy. They are border-land phenomena explicable by either hypothesis and evidence of neither.

This last statement, however, is dependent on the narrow meaning of the term telepathy. In the use of it as a rival hypothesis to that of spirit agencies, the term implies a limitation to coincidences between living people and so assumes nothing about a similar process between the dead and the living.

The only argument for telepathy in apparitions of the dying is the presumption that the consciousness of the dying person is not yet dissociated from the body. There are affiliations between such phenomena and two other types, which are more clearly indicative of the existence of the discarnate: visions appearing to the dying, and apparitions of the dead. Neither of these types is evidence for telepathy, in any sense determined by experimental and spontaneous coincidences and apparitions of the dying. They represent apparent communication with the dead, and, at least to some extent, are evidence of it. Visions that represent apparitions of the dead, appearing to the dying, lack all the conditions for evidence of telepathy between the living, though connected with those *in articulo mortis* conditions associated with the apparition of the dying to the living. They are in fact a border-land type of apparitions of the dead, just as apparitions of the dying are the border-land phenomena between telepathy with the living and telepathy with the dead.

I need not illustrate phantasms of the dead or visions of the dying in this connection. It is quite apparent that neither of them can be

EXPERIMENTS IN TELEPATHY

ORIGINAL DRAWING.

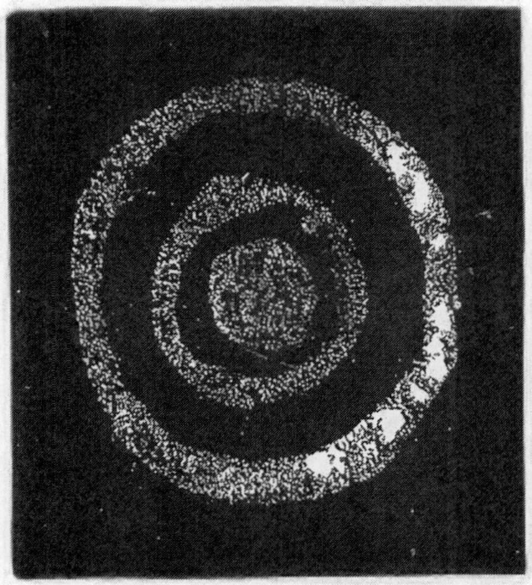

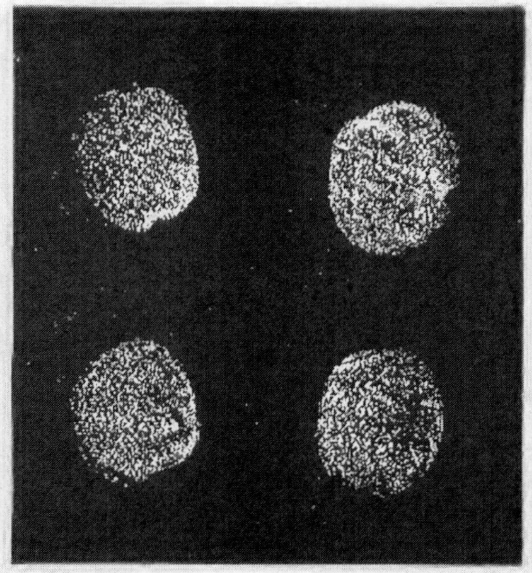

REPRODUCTION.

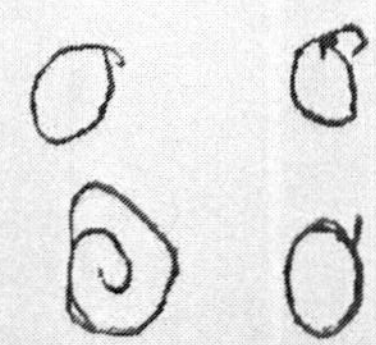

Experiment I

Experiment II

ORIGINAL DRAWING.

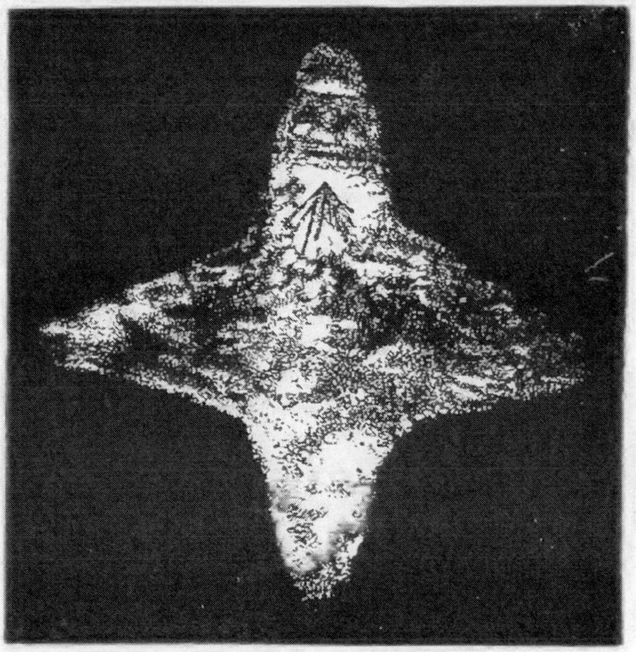

REPRODUCTION.

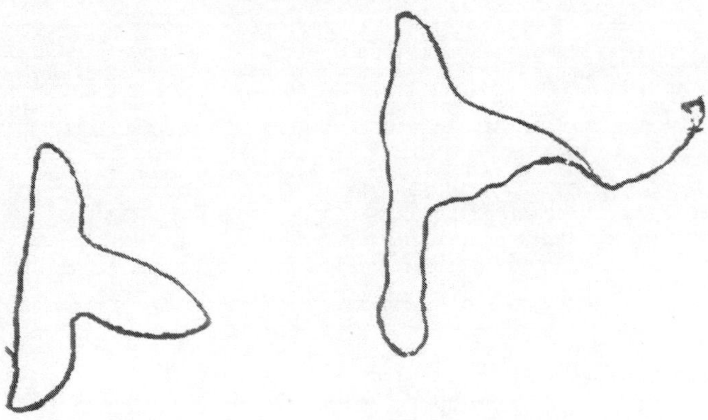

Experiment III

Original Drawing.

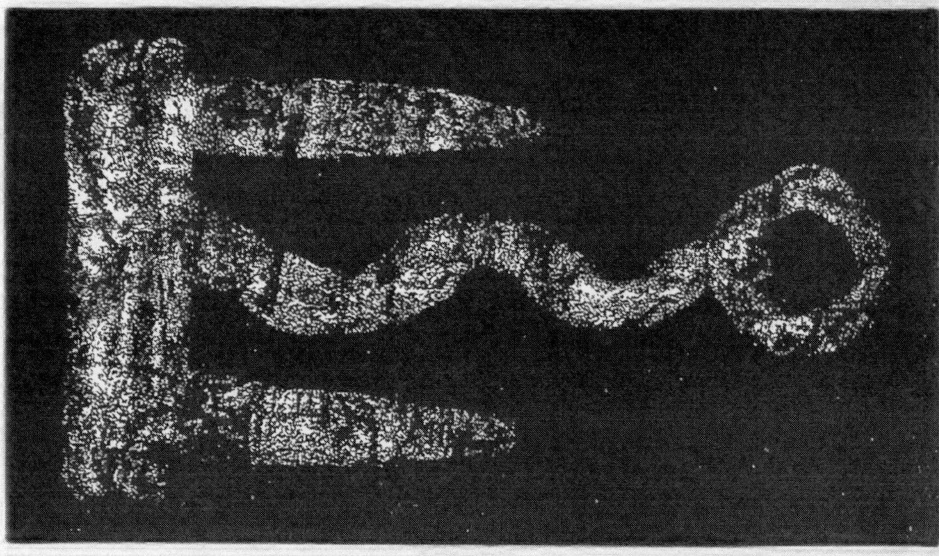

Reproduction.

Experiment IV

ORIGINAL DRAWING.

REPRODUCTION.

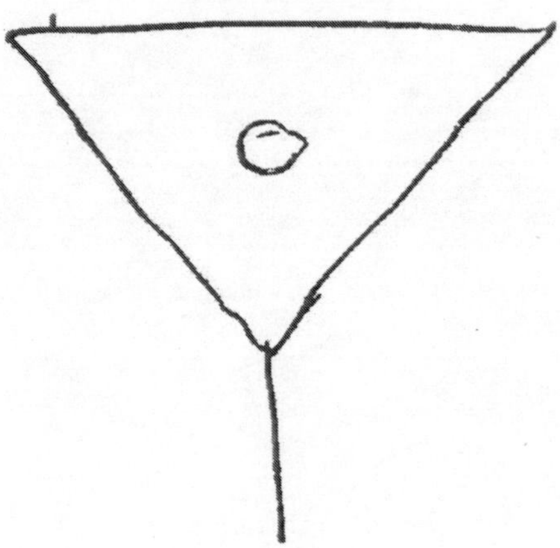

Experiment V

Original Drawing.

Reproduction.

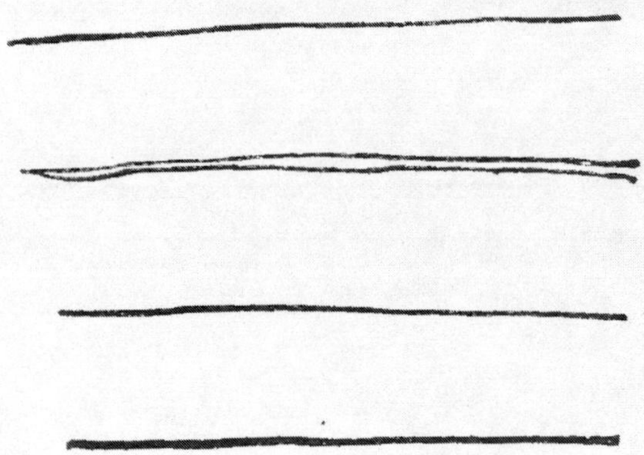

Experiment VI

Original Drawing.

Reproduction.

Experiment VII

ORIGINAL DRAWING.

REPRODUCTION.

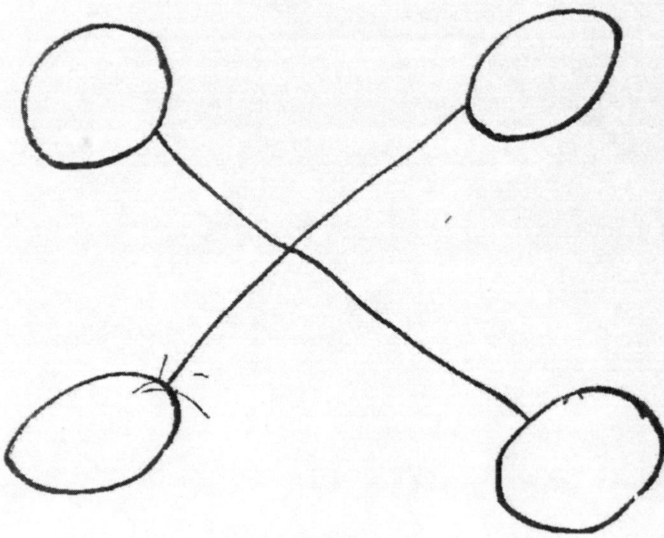

Experiment VIII

explained by telepathy between the living, except by stretching the meaning of the term beyond the evidence. If apparitions of the dead and visions of the dying are evidence of a telepathic process between the dead and the living, and so to that extent serve as evidence for the existence of spirits, the hypothesis of telepathy is abandoned, not as a fact but as an alternative to the spiritistic hypothesis. It may name a process of unknown nature, common to both incarnate and discarnate minds. I have no objections to such an employment of the term, but it nullifies the popular antithesis between telepathy and spiritism. It even involves the possibility that spirits may furnish the explanation of telepathy between the living. Mr. Myers saw this implication at the very outset of the investigations into telepathy. He perceived that any transcendental process of communication between the living involved such independence of normal sensory processes as to render the isolation of consciousness easily conceivable; the next step would be to regard telepathy as the manner of communication, at least in certain types of phenomena.

If the dead as well as the living may be telepathic agents, positive evidence alone is needed to show that discarnate spirits may intervene in telepathy between the living. In an address before the English Society, Professor Gilbert Murray, in order to suggest some known physiological or psychological condition that would make telepathy possible, proposed that telepathy between the living might be due to hyperæsthesia. But such an explanation would absurdly extend the limits of hyperæsthesia. We cannot apply tactual hyperæsthesia to perception at a distance of ten feet, nor visual hyperæsthesia to perception of a crow a thousand miles away. Nearly all the phenomena which believers in telepathy regard as evidence for the process are not explainable as hyperæsthesia.

It is evident that not all the phenomena outside of experimental and spontaneous coincidences between living people can be adduced as evidence for telepathy. They are at least open to other explanations. Telepathy itself explains nothing; it has no office beyond that of description and classification. So far as we know, the activity of spirits might explain telepathy itself, though for this explanation we should have to adduce evidence. Much will depend on the positive evidence for the existence of spirits. This evidence is confined to phenomena indicating the continued personal identity of the dead; so long as we limit the evidence for discarnate action to this type of occurrence, we cannot make the hypothesis of spirits explain either coincidences between the living, or any other phenomena not indicative of discarnate memory.

But if we once have sufficient evidence for the existence of spirits and also find evidence of their intervention in human affairs in phenomena that cannot possibly be explicable by telepathy, we may have reason to consider their intervention probable in the ordinary cases of telepathy. There is on record much evidence of this intervention; further evidence may show that intervention extends to the coincidences which have passed as telepathy between the living, which in the first stage of the investigation could not be considered direct evidence of discarnate intelligence.

In the experiments between Miss Miles and Miss Ramsden,[1] published as evidence for telepathy between the living, there were indications that the telepathy was effected by the intervention of the dead, or at least involved conditions associating the dead with the result. These indications were not apparent in the account of the facts published by the English Society. Nothing was there said about some other types of phenomena in which the agent and the percipient were concerned. Certain circumstances connected with the report of the results seemed unusual in telepathy between the living alone. I made inquiry of the ladies and found that only part of the story had been told. Miss Miles was an all-round psychic. She had had experiences in automatic writing, apparent telekinesis or the movement of objects without contact, apparitions, and dousing both by clairvoyance and by the use of the divining-rod. In addition she let drop in her correspondence with me, that she could always tell when her telepathy was successful *by the raps that she heard.* That is, she persisted in thinking of the object which Miss Ramsden was to perceive until she heard raps; she could then safely regard the experiment as a success. Now raps are not telepathic phenomena, but have altogether another association. These complications of the phenomena told decidedly against

[1] "Proceedings," English S. P. R., Vol. XXI, pp. 60–93.

telepathy between the living alone as an explanation, and the association or intervention of spirits had to be regarded as possible.

A paper read before the French Society narrated an experimental incident of some importance. It was translated for the "Journal" of the American Society for Psychical Research by Madame de Montalvo and published in Volume VIII (pp. 413–446). The incident of interest here is the following.

The gentleman who reported the circumstance had two subjects with whom he experimented. One of them went to the sea-shore without the knowledge of the other, and was spending some time there. Dr. Geley, the experimenter, was with the other in Paris, and tried clairvoyance one evening to ascertain if the subject in Paris could see the surroundings of the one at the sea-shore. He succeeded in getting descriptions of scenes and objects which he afterward verified. But accompanying his usual experiments with the lady were two visible lights. On this occasion there was but one light, which disappeared when the clairvoyance ceased. Now lights often develop into apparitions; at any rate, this association of lights with clairvoyance or telepathic phenomena is partial evidence for the intervention of spirits in them.

In communications through Mrs. Smead, the wife of an orthodox clergyman, Mr. Podmore, purporting to communicate, said that telepathy was always a message carried by spirits and that they could do it instantly. Mrs. Smead knew little of Mr. Podmore; there was no reason for her subconsciously putting this statement into the mouth of Mr. Podmore. He had always pressed telepathy between the living to explain all alleged spiritistic phenomena. Though it was not a proof of his identity to have this reversal of his opinion, it was not a natural view for Mrs. Smead to assign to him.

Apparently Mr. Myers took the same view of telepathy, as always involving the intervention of the discarnate. While my publication of the Miles-Ramsden experiments was going through the press, Mr. Myers purported to communicate through Mrs. Chenoweth, making a spontaneous allusion to telepathy and remarking that "it all depended on the carrier." Not wishing to mistake the meaning of this remark, I inquired what was meant by "the carrier"; and the answer was: "Telepathy is always a message carried by spirits."

Still better indications of spiritistic intervention in telepathy were given in communications from Mrs. Verrall soon after her death. She had believed when living that most of the incidents in the record of Mrs. Piper and in her own mediumship were explicable by telepathy between the living, and based her belief in spirits only on a few incidents which she thought could not be so explained. Mrs. Verrall died in July, 1916. In the following September she purported to communicate through Mrs. Chenoweth, who knew only that such a person had existed and had done automatic writing, and on the occasion of her first communications made an obscure reference to telepathy. The next day she spontaneously brought up the subject again, and said it was too early in her efforts to make clear her views on it. On the day following she again spontaneously referred to it in the following manner.

> "I said yesterday that I would write more about the telepathic theory as I now understand it. I am not as sure of the passage of thought through space as I was once, and I had begun to question the method by which thought was transferred to brains before I came here, but you will recall that I had some striking instances of what seemed telepathy tapping a reservoir of thought direct, and the necessity for an intervening spirit was uncalled for; but there were other instances when the message was transposed or translated and the interposition of another mind was unquestionably true. I tried many experiments and I think you must know about them.
>
> "I will say that I found more people involved in my work than I had known and there seemed more reason to believe that I was operated upon than that I operated — in other words, the automatic writing was less mine than I had supposed."

At the next sitting, a few days later, she again alluded to the process, and, speaking of having thought of it when living as a possible possession of all persons, significantly added:—

> "I am not yet convinced that this is my error, but I do know that we are companioned and aided by those who know the methods of the transference of thought."

Referring to the subject later, when mentioning a case that she had known before her death but that Mrs. Chenoweth did not know, a case of suddenly induced anæsthesia during an apparently normal state, she said: —

"It may be that these cases of anæsthesia were produced by contact with superior intelligence. That I am now investigating on this side. While one may not be conscious of such state of anæsthesia, it may still exist; and, if this be true, the spirit mediation theory is possible, even in these extreme cases where it seemed as if telepathy were proven beyond a doubt."

On the whole these statements are rather evidential, though other minds than her own may have contributed to the formal embodiment of the thought. But the statements distinctly affirm the possibility of the intervention of spirits in every form of telepathy. If that be conceded, we should explain away telepathy by spirits, rather than spirits by telepathy as the popular skepticism would do.

Since I wrote this work and while it is going through the press, I have been experimenting, by cross reference, with two cases where "telepathy" and the "malicious animal magnetism" of Christian Science would be the assumed explanation, and I have obtained evidence of spiritistic intervention in the phenomena.

We may revert to apparitions as corroborating such a view. I do not mean that all apparitions superficially indicate it; but there are instances too complicated to be explicable by the orthodox theory of telepathy. Some of the apparitions are premonitory of coming events, or indicative of approaching death; and premonitions are not telepathic. But even when not premonitory, many of them — for example, visions of the dying and apparitions of the dead — suggest the intervention of the dead as their most natural explanation. Some of them show complications too teleological for telepathy, which shows no evidence of purpose. For instance, I know of a subject who frequently had premonitions of coming deaths in the family. On one occasion she saw an apparition of her deceased sister, but immediately afterward she saw an apparition of her living aunt; in a few days her aunt died. The sister was apparently endeavoring to forewarn the subject of coming events. In another case, a lady saw an apparition of her living busband, but felt the presence of her deceased father; her husband died a few days later. On another occasion some months later the same subject saw an apparition of a heavy man walk through her door and fall down from drunkenness. At first she thought it was her father; but she later saw that it was the renter of her houses, who afterwards became the cause of her losing the income on which she lived. Her father came apparently to forecast some misfortune. The point is, that the apparitions of the living in these instances were caused by the dead.

The very nature of apparitions suggests an identity in this character that demands a single explanation. If the three classes require the same general explanation, that explanation must to some extent include the discarnate. Apparitions of the dead cannot be explained by telepathy between the living; even some apparitions of the living cannot easily be explained by telepathy without invoking the intervention of the dead. We may therefore be obliged to invoke the intervention of the discarnate to explain the three types of phenomena whose unity is indicated by their characteristics.

But I am not prepared strenuously to defend any such thesis. We have not the evidence to assert that all telepathic coincidences are due to the intervention of spirits. Nor indeed is it either necessary or desirable that we should insist on this point in our defence of a spiritistic theory. We could hardly expect supernormal phenomena to be limited to the intervention of the dead. Some supernormal phenomena might happen between the living alone. It is enough to extort the admission that telepathy may be the name for a process which is sometimes incarnate and sometimes discarnate. If we have souls, occasional instances of transcendental connection between the living would be likely to happen. Telepathy as a connection between minds without the intervention of sense-perception makes the existence of a soul so probable that we may well consider many instances of the supernormal as due to its activity in this life; on the other hand, we may connect discarnate spirits with many other phenomena than the intercommunication between two worlds.

The lesson to be learned from the fact of telepathy, though no explanation of it has been found, is that normal sense-perception is not our only source of knowledge. Materialism must stand or fall with the evidence for the limitation of knowledge to sense-perception; and telepathy, if it applies to information acquired at great distances, is a complete refutation of that theory. If we do not accept the large body of evidence for the existence of spirits, we are obliged to substitute for that view the theory of telepathy, which is in itself a guarantee of a transcendental world of some kind, since it implies that the brain is not the sole condition of consciousness.

CHAPTER X

THE PROCESS OF COMMUNICATING

THE popular terms for the method of communicating with the dead are automatic writing, raps, table-tipping, planchette writing, spelling by the ouija board, impressions, and the more technical terms of clairvoyance and clairaudience. All but the last two take their names from the physical instruments or the physical means employed in the work. The last two are names for peculiar phenomena in vision and hearing, which will be more fully described a little later.

Automatic writing is distinguished from ordinary writing only in being unconscious or involuntary. Only certain tests, such as trance or anæsthesia, or the testimony of a trustworthy subject, will decide whether a person is writing automatically. Many people suppose that automatic writing is always the act of some foreign intelligence, but it is not necessarily so. It may always be the unconscious act of the subject himself, even though we suppose that the instigating cause is foreign. Popularly, however, it is assumed to be due to the direct action of spirits, and even some scientific men maintain that, if spirits are connected with it at all, they are the direct cause of it. The matter, however, is not so simple as it seems, as we shall have occasion to see later. The factor that makes it appear to be the direct act of foreign intelligence is the exclusion of normal consciousness and intention. We naturally assume that anything not done by ourselves voluntarily is not done by ourselves at all, and if our ego were defined by our conscious and voluntary acts, as the Cartesian philosophy would have us believe, this view would be correct. But since the time of Descartes we have learned that there is a whole territory of unconscious actions instigated, at least apparently, by unconscious processes of the mind. These acts may not be due to spirits at all. The subconscious is presumed to lie between the fields of spirit agency and the normally conscious and voluntary actions of the mind. Whether in this region mental states and acts may be originated without foreign stimulus is debatable, but in the absence of evidence for this instigation we have to assume that subconscious acts explain the facts, especially when the knowledge manifested or action performed is entirely within the range of normal acquisition. But if information not normally acquired is conveyed by this automatic writing the subconscious certainly cannot be more than the vehicle or medium of its transmission. It is this foreign origin that gives the impression of direct control by spirits and so leads to the supposed significance of automatic writing.

But the psychic researcher is interested in automatic writing primarily as a supernormal phenomenon, whatever the source of the information conveyed by it. The process is probably very complex, as even normal writing is; but it involves at least one more factor than normal writing — that the stimulus to it may be not internal but external to the organism. Whenever it is connected with supernormal knowledge, we have to invoke foreign agency as at least one factor in the explanation. What goes on between the original impulse from foreign intelligence and the final act of writing we may not know any more than we know what goes on between the initial volition to write and the actual motion of the muscles of the hand.

The methods of table-tipping, the planchette and the ouija board are only modifications of automatic writing. Many people suppose that there is some mystery or virtue about the ouija, which enables it to spell out messages from other minds. They do not reflect that the same process is involved in all the methods named. The muscular system of the operators is in action in each of them in the same way. The instrument or means of expression has nothing to do with the result, when the human organism must intervene in the phenomena. There is no mysterious power in the ouija, the planchette, or the table, any more than there is in the pencil. They are all agents or media, as they are in normal action of the same kind. The actual evidence for the supernormal lies, not in the action of automatic writing, of the ouija or planchette, or of the table, but in the contents of the message. If the content represents normally acquired information, we explain the message by subconscious action of the writer's mind. If the content is unmistakably foreign to normal experience, we seek for the external stimulus or mind that may account for it. The method of delivery is of secondary importance.

Another method of communication is by raps. They are not always connected with the motor action of the psychic. No doubt some raps are simply ordinary automatisms like automatic writing and other unconscious actions. But they are often independent of any intervention by the human organism as revealed to sense-perception. They are used as signals of answers to questions; and, being foreign to either conscious or unconscious action of the organism, another explanation must be sought for them than for automatic writing. The latter assumes at least the intervention of the physical organism with its powers and habits. But raps may involve no such intermediary; and in this case they must be regarded as independent physical phenomena. They can be used only for answers to questions or for spelling out words in various ways. Their method of communication is crude, in the sense that it takes time and trouble to get intelligible messages; but they signify the possibility of communication with an outside world without the mediation of the subconscious or normal machinery of the human organism.

Clairvoyance and clairaudience are very different processes. Clairaudience is the hearing of apparently foreign messages, by means of voices. usually "internal voices." Possibly they are sometimes apparently external, but since those who experience the facts are not always adept in analyzing and describing the experiences, we are not sure that the experiences are other than subjective or hallucinatory, though the stimulus may be foreign. Both clairaudience and clairvoyance are sensory phenomena, unconnected with motor action, whereas automatic writing and other forms of communication, except independent raps, are connected with the motor functions.

Clairvoyance, however, is a term that does duty for three distinct types of phenomena. (1) It denotes generally the power of mediumship in so far as the messages are obtained by impressions or visual pictures. It is even very often used to denote any type of communication with the dead, and so is made synonymous with mediumship, excluding purely physical phenomena. (2) It is more technically used to denote the acquisition of foreign information through visual phantasms, as clairaudience is used to denote auditory hallucinations of the veridical type. (3) Lastly, still more technically, it denotes the perception of concealed physical objects whose whereabouts are not known by any living being. It represents the visual perception, transcendental in nature, of facts or things that cannot be known through telepathy. It presupposes supernormal perception at a distance, and excludes all mind-reading. This is the more technical conception of the process. Telæsthesia is probably a better term for this conception of clairvoyance.

There is another popular conception of communication with the dead, which gives rise to the errors regarding the physical means of communication. This popular notion is that the communication is quite like our own communication with each other. The circumstance that it comes in speech or writing or some use of the physical organism creates the impression that the process is a mere substitution of the discarnate spirit for our own in the use of the human organism. This is not true, despite the appearances to that effect. Superficial characteristics make it appear as if a spirit simply took hold of the physical organism and used it just as the living personality uses it. On the contrary, the subconscious does not cease to function; and, when the normal consciousness is made the vehicle of the communications, no part of living control is lost. The popular misconception leads to the interpretation of messages as if they were not colored by the mind which serves as the medium of transmission, an assumption which is provably false. There is nothing clearer to investigators than the fact that all messages are affected by the mind of the medium, normal or subliminal, according to the conditions under which communication takes place. If the messages come through normal consciousness, the form of the message will be deeply affected. Memories, interpretation, and language determine the form of the message. To some extent the subconscious will affect it in the same way in a trance, when normal consciousness is suspended. Control of the living organism is either indirect or totally wanting when the communications are going on, except possibly in exceptional cases of possession, such as the "Watseka Wonder." (See Myer's "Human Personality and its Survival of Bodily Death," Volume I, pp. 360–368.) In most cases at least the influence of the living mind on the results is such that it gives rise in the scientific mind to doubts about actual spirit communication, but only because it has borrowed from the popular mind a preconception of what communication would be if it took place at all — namely; that the communication would be direct and like normal intercourse with the living.

Normal communication among the living is a species of mimicry. This mimicry is not apparent in language; but when language cannot be employed, we quickly resort to some form of symbolism that is a modification of mimicry. In this way we instigate more or less the same thoughts in others as in ourselves; but we do not communicate or transmit thoughts. We transmit only mechanical effects from one organism to another, and the mind connected with that organism interprets the effect in accordance with its own experience in sense-perception.

The external and superficial characteristics of the phenomena purporting to be communications from the dead, especially automatic writing and automatic speech, very strongly suggest the same process; and, as the popular mind assumes that thoughts and ideas are actually transmitted from one person to another, it very naturally supposes that communication with the dead is direct transmission of ideas. But careful examination of the facts makes it quite clear that there is a radical difference, despite the resemblances between spiritistic and normal communication. The fact that no thoughts are directly transmitted between the living, unless we admit telepathy as an exception, gives us pause in our assumptions about the process, and further examination reveals complications that show the process to be wholly different from normal intercourse.

We can describe certain steps in the process of normal intercourse or conveyance of ideas. There is first the idea in the mind, which will usually take the form of a mental picture or a series of pictures. Next, there is the volition to express the idea in words.

The word is recalled and the vocal organs are moved to convert it into physical sound. There are no doubt intermediate stages between the thought and the vocal expression; but what goes on in the nerve filaments connecting the brain centers with the vocal organism is purely conjectural. When the sound is produced it is conveyed from the person talking to the recipient of the sound, who receives an auditory sensation, which he interprets. The sound is a symbol, which we interpret as meaning the same experience for the communicator as for the listener. In this way we learn his idea, but only by reproducing it from our experience, not by having it directly transmitted to us.

The process of communication with spirits includes all these and no one knows how many more complications. We need not go beyond telepathy between the living to see that the process is very different from normal communication. Telepathy does not involve any known stimulus upon the sense-organs. What its process is we do not know. We only know that it does not affect the sensory apparatus as does a physical stimulus.

The various methods recognized by laymen and set up as mysterious do not appear to the psychologist to be of any importance in determining the nature of the process of communicating with the dead; hence he seeks some further characteristic which will make the phenomena intelligible. He notices first that all the phenomena can be reduced to two types, *motor* and *sensory*. The motor type is manifested in automatic writing, planchette, ouija board, and table-tipping. The sensory type is exhibited in apparitions, clairvoyance, clairaudience, and other sensory phantasms, whether of touch, taste or smell. The relation between the sensory and the motor types will be the subject of later consideration. At present we need only note that the essential feature of the process is most likely to be found in a characteristic common to the two types of phenomena. We shall first consider the sensory type, and may there find a clue to what goes on in the motor type.

We cannot read ancient literature, Oriental, Hebrew, Greek, or Roman, without observing evidence of *visions*, though only in recent times have they become intelligible. The influence of science for several centuries, with its accusation of hallucination and delusion to account for every event inexplicable by material forces, has deprived the term vision of its original meaning. From the beginning of organized psychic research, the idea that a medium saw what she claimed to see was disparaged or ridiculed. The claim was regarded as evidence of fraud, or of hysterical hallucinations or delusions. But psychic researchers found what they called *veridical* hallucinations, experiences related to external events, often unknown to the subject, in a manner to give the hallucination a significance much more important than that attaching to *subjective* hallucinations. The psychologist and psychiatrist had always regarded hallucinations as caused by some intraorganic stimulus, and the resultant hallucination was supposed merely to simulate reality. But veridical hallucinations were referable to an external cause to which they bore a relation like that of normal sensation to its stimulus.

It was discovered very early in the investigation that telepathic subjects had apparently visual perceptions when receiving the impressions presumably created by the thoughts of the agent. The existence of these sensory phantasms is not questioned, though they are probably often subjective instead of veridical. If telepathy of any kind has been proved, the existence of veridical hallucinations has equally been proved. Apparitions illustrate the same phenomenon; and, indeed, from the outset of their investigation it was apparent that many, if not all, of them must be classed as sensory hallucinations, veridical or subjective. Mr. Myers and Mr. Edmund Gurney conceived them after this fashion. On this understanding, we may concede to the skeptic the phantasmal character of the experience, and yet insist on its definite relation to an external cause. The phantasm may not at all adequately represent that objective cause. On this assumption the paradoxes of the situation disappear; for instance, spirit clothes which have been so sore a perplexity to the average man, no longer present any difficulties. To conceive apparitions as veridical hallucinations or phantasms, is only to translate into mental terms what had before seemed to be physical or quasi-physical phenomena. The assurance that there is a foreign or external cause of the appearance, guarantees the existence, though not the characteristics, of spirits.

These considerations prepared the way for a more extensive application of the conception to the problem of communication with the dead. It is probable that Mr. Gurney and Mr. Myers fully appreciated the meaning of this new discovery, though they did not develop it into a completely expressed doctrine. However this may be, it is certain that, though I knew that their conception of apparitions and of telepathy involved the idea of veridical hallucinations, I did not see the full significance of the theory until I had communication with Professor James after his death. I then saw what the founders of the Society had meant by their doctrine of veridical hallucinations. I thought at first that the theory was my own, but I soon discovered my mistake; later it became apparent that Swedenborg had anticipated all of us, though he had not worked out his ideas scientifically.

So much for the development of the theory. What was necessary in ascertaining the process of communicating was to consider something more than the physical means of delivering the messages. It was evident that the process involved more than the physical instrument, and that something unusual was at the bottom of the process. The most obtrusive fact was that the two general forms of communication, sensory and motor, corresponded to the two channels by which the mind is connected with the physical world. In the sensory field the most conspicuous phenomenon is clairvoyance; but it is apparent to the student of psychology that auditory phenomena represent in reality the same type. The voices are as veridical as the visions. Consequently, all sensory contacts with the discarnate world are simply veridical phantasms, visual, auditory, tactual, olfactory, or gustatory, and, perhaps we may add, emotional. The main point is, that supernormal sensory experiences are all of the same type and reducible to a single law, expressed by the *pictographic process.* This process means, that the communicator manages to elicit in the living subject a sensory phantasm of his thoughts, representing, but not necessarily directly corresponding to, the reality. The motor process, giving rise to automatic writing, does not represent anything pictographic, though pictographic processes may precede it. What chiefly interests us here, however, is the development of the process which expressed itself in sensory imagery and which, interpreted after the analogies of sense-perception, gave the impression that the spiritual world was a quasi-material reality.

I must now let the records tell their own story; they will at the same time illustrate the difficulties of communicating. The main object is, to give those facts which are more or less evidential of the pictographic process and its importance, while they also represent actual communications on the question itself.

A friend of Dr. Hodgson, whom in his report he calls George Pelham, died in 1892, while Dr. Hodgson was carrying on his experiments with Mrs. Piper. She knew nothing about the man, though he had had one sitting with her. By communications begun about two weeks after his death, of which Mrs. Piper was probably uninformed, he finally was able to convince Dr. Hodgson of the scientific truth of the spiritistic theory. G. P., as he is called in the records, gave excellent proof of his personal identity, and showed himself desirous of telling all he could about the problem that Dr. Hodgson was trying to solve. In the course of his account he took up the process of communication and the mistakes and confusions in the messages. The following statement appealed to Dr. Hodgson as having unusual interest.

"Remember we share and always will have our friends in the dream-life, that is, your life so to speak, which will attract us forever and ever, and so long as we have any friends *sleeping* in the material world; — you to us are more like as we understand sleep, you look shut up in prison, and in order for us to get into communication with you, we have to enter into your sphere, as one like yourself asleep. This is just why we make mistakes, as you call them, or get confused and muddled, so to put it, H."

This statement, with its reference to sleep as the condition for communicating, as well as further incidental evidence, induced Dr. Hodgson to apply the hypothesis of a dream-state in the spirit as more or less necessary to communication with the living. He worked out the theory at some length in his report, which I followed with further evidence and defence. Before his death, Professor James knew the hypothesis well and admitted its cogency, but was not convinced of its truth. Very soon after his death and in an early communication through Mrs. Chenoweth, who knew nothing about his views on this specific question, he made the following statements, after referring to the probable interest of the newspapers in his "new revelation":

"It opens my eyes to some of the real difficulties in the way of actual communication to try the experiment myself."

(Yes, do you find Hodgson and I were right about the difficulties?)

"I think so, but it is too early for me to have positive conclusions."

(All right, take your own course.)

"I am of the opinion that some of the messages are produced without volition and they are caught by contact. Hence the broken and imperfect utterance on paper. Actual and complete contact would make the circuit and running capacity for trains of thought. Do you understand my expression?"

(Yes, satisfactorily.)

"I desire to have the work complete, less jerky and disjointed than Richard gave us."

This characteristic passage, reflecting the personal identity of Professor James, indicates one new fact, abundantly illustrated since that time, namely, that some messages are involuntary. The cause of this involuntary communication was indicated later in a definite way. Nearly a month later Professor James, through Mrs. Chenoweth, spontaneously took up the matter without a hint from such a question as I had put in the passage quoted above.

"I seem to be able to reason while I am at work and that pleases me. So much of the work recorded in the past lacked that function."

(That is correct.)

"It always stood between me and my theories of what ought to be and often I said: This seems more like snatches of broken recollections detached and left solitary or wandering brain —" [Pause.]

(Actions?)

"No, photographs. You may recall what I am trying to tell you."

(Phantasms?)

"Yes, fugitive phantasms, unreal."

(I understand.)

"Unattached, floating in ethereal waves, caught, retained, expressed, as if by subliminal states not able to distinguish between the attached and unattached. The embodied or fugitive phantasms. This I was forced to consider when I would gladly have thrown it away as inadequate."

The sudden reference to "photographs," accepted as phantasms after I had so interpreted the word, was an interesting allusion to the pictographic process, though I did not see its meaning at the time. The qualification of them as " fugitive " was another reference to " involuntary messages." The evident allusion to marginal mental pictures was not apparent to me at the time, nor the meaning of the expression " fugitive phantasms," which was an epitome of both the idea of involuntary messages and of the pictographic process. It remained for G. P. to make the matter clear later.

Nearly a month later Dr. Hodgson took up the subject and evidently tried to clarify it. He referred to the desire of Professor James in his communications to prevent the disjointed character of which he had to complain when living.

" His one desire is to be slow and let nothing come that is not his own. No fugitive ideas to float in unawares into the communications. This is not a new phase of thought to you and me. The fugitive expressions you understand."

(Yes, perfectly.)

" But we are seeking to eliminate all that, as far as we can at least, but it is almost impossible to completely inhibit one 's self and thought and let nothing but the pure present expression come. Try it yourself in the ordinary conversations of life and see how the fugitive drops in and is constantly bringing misunderstandings of the idea you are trying to express to your most intimate friend."

The " fugitive " in this instance is evidently what comes from other minds present, when another communicator is trying to send messages; but the second reference is to the phenomenon in the mind of the communicator. The allusion to the inability to control one 's own mind assumes the possibility of " fugitive phantasms " from both the mind of the communicator and of others present. While the passage does not explicitly recognize involuntary messages, it implies them. Evidently Dr. Hodgson was not able to make his message clear. Two days later Professor James recurred to the subject and made clearer what he wished to say.

" I have been making note of things to recall here and it is possible that some will be dropped in without special relevance, but with the statement that it is to be so. You understand."

(Yes I shall.)

" It may look like a French exercise book, but it is to be done with malice aforethought."

(All right, all the malice prepense you like.)

"So it will be absolved from the charge of dreams, dream talk, our old theme, a theory we more than once discussed and discarded and discussed again."

The allusion to "dream talk" was clearly to Dr. Hodgson's hypothesis, suggested by the communication of G. P. quoted above, as an explanation of the confusions and mistakes. The earlier reference to "fugitive phantasms" was an attempt to explain the same fact, but the communicator got no further with the problem at this time. Some days later he took it up again.

"Not all the evidence need be twaddle nor all the twaddle evidence."

(Good.)

"It is the spirit of a man which survives, all that makes up his day, his weeks and years, tone, the quality, and I desire to prove, and not to give you a sample of deteriorated or disintegrated capacity. Have I made it clear?"

(Yes, if I assume that you have to overcome a trance on your side.)

"I am not entranced."

(All right. Is there danger of going into a trance on your side and thus of preventing communications?)

"On that subject we have had our conversation before."

(Yes, how much is true?)

"I passed into this life and we were obliged to assume that such was the case for two reasons. First, we were informed so by Imperator; second, the evidence submitted implied as much in many instances. But I must confess that the trance is absent in my case."

Again we meet with the denial of the trance or dream state as necessary for communications, but the key to the problem is still to come, and it was given by G. P. some months later. I quote his statement in full. I asked a question and G. P. seized the opportunity to go into the subject of immediate response to such queries and the difficulties involved.

"Your question sets thought working, but after a while I will tell you if I can."

(All right. Go ahead.)

"One good thing about working with you is your understanding of the difficulties and patience with us and we are never afraid to tell you the exact situation. The mental action is just the same here as with you, becomes visible to you for it expresses in words. The body is a cloak for mental processes. Do you know what I mean?"

(I can get sufficient idea not to worry about that.)

"Every word from another sets a train of thought in motion and if your thoughts find visible or audible expression, you would be thought wandering in your mind the greater part of the time, but the whole process is almost instantaneous, and so you are saved the ignominy of the charge. But with us the thoughts are found on the paper sometimes and before we know it, and so it takes practice and will to keep the line steady and express only what we desire. Much of the past in various quarters can be explained in this statement."

I saw at a flash what this remarkable statement meant. If our thoughts, which are realized in mental images, whether central or marginal or both, were to become visible or audible to a friend in conversation with us, as they would if they were transmitted to him as veridical phantasms, they would make him think that we were "wandering in our minds." This idea, taken with the denial that the communicator was in a dream state and that the communicator could not inhibit the expression of his thoughts, together with the reference to "fugitive phantasms" or marginal thoughts whether of one's own mind or that of others present, explains the confusion in messages and shows that pictographic phenomena are the clue to the understanding of the problem. I saw the whole meaning of the theory of Mr. Gurney and Mr. Myers about veridical phantasms. If we add the idea that G. P. clearly perceives what is going on all the time in all minds, living or dead, to the idea that transmission takes the form of hallucinations or mental pictures, we have an explanation of clairvoyance and a clear idea of the process of communicating.

It required but an extension of this principle to the other senses, to render the whole field intelligible, in so far as sensory functions are concerned. It still remained to be ascertained whether the pictographic process lies back of communication by motor expression. The process is less clearly apparent in motor phenomena; but further communications have rendered it probable that mental pictures lie behind the motor expression, and that automatic writing may involve special difficulties in transmitting the thoughts of the communicator. If the medium have the habit of interpreting in speech her own visual imagery, she may be qualified to transmit in automatic writing the thought that comes to her mind in pictures.

This pictographic process is what G. P. probably meant in the passage quoted from his communications through Mrs. Piper; the message was possibly distorted in the transmission. He was apparently describing the similarity between the living and the deceased mind in the comparison with the "dream life." This is not evident on the surface of his statement; but, when we consider that the spirits have access to our minds through the subconscious, which is well described as the "dream-life," and that the subliminal of Mrs. Piper either did not catch the true meaning of his message or distorted it by abbreviation, we can realize that he may have been trying to show that the panoramic stream of images in the communicator's mind, both central and marginal, voluntary and involuntary, is transmitted to the mind of the medium and there has to undergo either abbreviation or interpretation and selection. In this way arises confusion which we do not experience in ordinary intercourse with each other in normal life, because we can inhibit what we do not wish conveyed to our friend in conversation.

It is impossible to go into the significance of this pictographic process with adequate detail. Though we can only name it without describing the intimate nature of the process, we can understand that it makes communication more intelligible than does the study of the mechanical devices or methods of communication. We are nearer the heart of the problem when we are able to recognize a psychological process in it. We do not know in detail all that goes on, but when we can conceive that a mental picture in the mind of a communicator is transmitted, perhaps telepathically, to the psychic or to the control; even though we do not know how this occurs, we can understand why the message takes the form that it does in the mind of the psychic and why the whole process assumes the form of a description of visual, or a report of auditory images. The whole mass of facts is thus systematized as a single process, whose specific form of transmission is determined by the sense through which it is expressed.

The pictographic process was not apparent in the work of Mrs. Piper, except in the transition from the subliminal to the normal state. Here she was a spectator of transcendental events or of the phantasms transmitted to her mind and taken for realities. But in her deep trance the visual functions apparently were not employed. A careful examination of the records shows that, in the deep trance for automatic writing, she was the recipient of auditory rather than visual impressions, and hence there was no distinct evidence of the pictographic process in the automatic writing. Now Mrs. Chenoweth is *par excellence* a visuel only and nothing of an audile. Mrs. Chenoweth showed no aptitude for auditory phantasms; it took two or three years of training to elicit any of them to help out the meaning of the visual images, which she received with comparative ease. The association of the two is a great help in the interpretation of messages, as it is in ordinary experience.

The popular mind fails to appreciate the real complexity of the problem. It assumes that, if the medium is honest or unconscious of the communications, the whole material comes from the spirit; it does not take into account the subconscious of the psychic, the various processes of the mind going on under the threshold of consciousness. But when we introduce into the problem the pictographic process, we are able to concentrate attention on a better conception of the problem.

It is apparent that the pictographic process introduces into the communications various sources of mistake and confusion, and thus explains much that the ordinary man with his view of the messages cannot understand. Mental pictures have to be interpreted, either by the control or by the subconscious of the psychic, probably by both. But whether interpreted or not, and whether the subconscious is as important a factor in the result as the mind of the control, interest is centered in the pictographic process itself, with its measure of identity between the thought of the communicator and of the percipient, with its aptitude for bringing confusion and mistake into the ultimate form of the messages.

I have referred to the control as another mind than that of the psychic. Laymen usually assume that the whole process is one between the spirit and the medium, or, if the medium is in a trance, between the spirit and the sitter. The process is in reality much more complex. The pictographic process is but one factor in a complex situation, which involves not only the mind of the medium, conscious and subconscious; but also the mind of the control. A study of the records will give overwhelming evidence of this modifying influence on all messages.

In the work of Mrs. Chenoweth, the guides distinguish between what they call the direct and the indirect method of communicating. The direct method seems superficially to be automatic writing, though it is more than that; the indirect method is always the use of the pictographic process, which requires the control to act as an intermediary between the communicator and the medium. The communicator simply allows his mind to run over his memories in a panoramic form; these are transmitted to the control as veridical phantasms, and are there interpreted, and either transferred directly by automatic writing through the psychic or again through her subconscious by mental pictures and reinterpreted there. When we add to this situation the fact that the communicator cannot determine just what shall be transmitted to the control or the subconscious of the psychic, and that marginal images in the mind of the communicator may be picked up instead of the central or intended ones, we can understand why the messages do not always give the impression of perfect rationality and why so much real or apparent confusion occurs. Every message has to run the gauntlet of selection in the mind that sends it and in the mind that receives the pictographic images, and then be subject to the liabilities of misinterpretation and distortion, by the minds both of the control and of the psychic.

But the complexities do not end here. As the process of transmission is not always under the complete regulation of either control or psychic, there are evident in many messages phenomena like "crossed wires" on the telephone. Sometimes A, communicating to B on the telephone, unconsciously transmits his message to some one else whose wire "crosses" with A's, and without intention on the part of either A or the unknown receiver that this latter should obtain the message; mechanical conditions accidentally arise in which the words of A are picked up and transmitted to some one else. Something analogous to this often occurs in spiritistic messages. Conditions accidentally arise in which the thoughts of some one other than the intended communicator are picked up and transmitted without the knowledge of either the control or the medium that it is the wrong message. This phenomenon occurred frequently under the Phinuit régime with Mrs. Piper. Those near at the time had their thoughts unwittingly picked up and transmitted, with a resulting impression of false or irrelevant messages. Sometimes, with Mrs. Piper, there would come to a sitter messages that were wholly false to him; but, on inquiry of a previous sitter, it was found that the statements were true of that person. Whether they were subliminal resurgences of previously received messages, or the accidental transmission of present thoughts by a previous communicator who happened to be present, is immaterial.

Here are two instances in my work with Mrs. Chenoweth: On one occasion, as she began to go into the trance, in the subliminal stage when she sees pictographic phantasms and describes them, she saw a lady whom she had never seen or known, and identified her by name; a moment later she remarked that Dr. Hodgson was standing beside her. She went slowly over what Dr. Hodgson was saying to her, then reached for the pencil, and wrote a message from Dr. Hodgson, who said that it had not been his intention to communicate. In the other instance, a lady was having a sitting. On previous days her father and mother had communicated. On this day, however, some one else began a series of very intimate messages. As soon as the sitting was over I asked the lady if the messages were relevant; she said that they were wholly meaningless. I knew the communicator by the signature of his pet name and wrote to his widow to ask whether the messages were correct. Her reply was that they were, and as none of us present knew about the incidents communicated, they had much evidential value, though they were wholly irrelevant to the sitter.

In both these instances, it was probably the diversion of the medium's subconscious attention from the persons wanted to the person in whom she was interested, that established rapport and gave rise to irrelevant messages. It is the business of the controls to prevent or inhibit such phenomena, but they may be unsuccessful, either because of the diverted attention of the psychic or of the greater intensity of some other personality.

But the process is yet more complex. Often a whole group of controls is involved in the effort to get a message through from a given person, and one long used to the phenomena can detect evidence of their coöperation in stray messages that slip through after the manner of indirect messages just described; cases are even on record in which there is marked evidence of the interfusion of the thoughts of two or more persons in a message that purports to come from one person. This interfusion explains the failure to discover the personal characteristics of the purported communicator. I have even remarked it in the hand-writing, which showed the characteristics of two controls, while the essential characteristics of the normal hand-writing of the medium were also clearly discernible.

To imagine the pictographic influences of a dozen minds hovering around a psychic, all exposed, like a delicate mechanical mechanism, to various undulations and influences, is to form some conception of the difficulties of communication between the discarnate and the incarnate. It is probable that there are hidden intermundane conditions and processes necessary to the transmission of mental pictures or to the transformation of the thoughts of the communicator into pictorial impressions. Future investigation must fill in the remaining gaps between the thought of the communicator and the picture received and described by the control.

The relation of the pictographic process to automatic writing has not been determined, but it is fair to imagine that it may bear some resemblance to the influence of our own mental imagery upon the motor system. At any rate, the direct method involves conditions in which, whatever place the control still preserves in the process, he is either not so near the psychic or can let the communicator's thought influence the medium more directly than when receiving the pictorial figures and interpreting them. The pictographic process may lie behind that of automatic writing, though its presence is not so easily detected as in the indirect method.

PART III

EVIDENCE OF SURVIVAL

CHAPTER XI

EXPERIENCES OF WELL-KNOWN PERSONS

IT has frequently been the accusation that experiences purporting to represent the supernatural are confined to the ignorant and superstitious. The work of the English Society has been a convincing refutation of this reproach; there can be no doubt of the respectability and intelligence of those who reported the facts of their experience. It is true enough that "old wives' fables," and dreams of sailors, porters, and coachmen will never affect the minds of scientific psychologists, for obvious reasons. It is just as true that experiences from these classes, if subjected to cross-questioning and to corroboration, have interest. But the mere word of an intelligent person secures attention, and in scientific matters may often go far to silence ridicule or to invite investigation.

The first instance of note is the apparition of his friend, appearing to Lord Brougham. It is taken from "Phantasms of the Living," where it was copied from his own biography. He and a friend at the University of Edinburgh had discussed the immortality of the soul, and had signed in their own blood an agreement that whichever died first should appear to the other. Soon after they left the University the friend went out to India in the government service, and was there some years; meanwhile he was almost forgotten by Lord Brougham. The latter was travelling in Sweden in cold weather, and at about 1 P. M. he was taking a hot bath. Suddenly he saw an apparition of his friend in the chair where he had left his own clothes. He got out of the bath; but, on recovering from what was evidently a trance, he found that his friend had disappeared. He wrote down the facts, with the date, in his journal. He returned to Edinburgh; and some weeks later received a letter from India, bearing the same date as that recording his experience in his journal, and telling of the death of his friend.

Mr. Andrew Lang records that he once saw an apparition which he took for Professor Conington; he ascertained afterwards that the time coincided very closely with that of Professor Conington's death. The latter was one hundred miles distant at the time.

James Cotter Morison, a literary man well-known in England, is sponsor for an incident of some interest. He writes to the authors of "Phantasms of the Living":

"My mother and grandmother were together in the dining room of their house in the Isle of Wight, occupied in some domestic matter which made the exclusion of chance visitors desirable. A sudden knock at the door caused my grandmother to hasten to it with a view to taking the stranger into the drawing room. The knock was heard by both mother and daughter. On opening the door with the least loss of time possible, my grandmother was surprised to find not only no one there, but no one even in the long corridor which led to the drawing room. My mother distinctly remembered the look of astonishment in her mother's face as she returned from the door. Nothing more was said on the subject, but in a short time afterwards a letter was received from London from my grandmother's sister, saying that she (the sister) had been most seriously ill, at death's door indeed, but was now a little better, and wished my grandmother to come and see her. The latter went up to town and found her sister still very ill, but slowly recovering. After the mutual endearments natural to such an occasion, my grandmother said:

"'Do you know, such a strange thing occurred, exactly at the time, it seems, when you were supposed to be dead or dying.'

"'I know what you are going to say,' said the other. 'When I was in the trance which was mistaken for death, I thought I went to your house in the Isle of Wight and knocked at your drawing room door. You opened it instantly and looked much affrighted at not seeing me or any one, though I saw you.'

"The singular point in the story is the anticipation by the one sister of what the other was going to say.

"No theory or inference was ever deduced by my relations from the circumstance and it was only mentioned as an odd coincidence by them and their friends, who, as well as my mother, have often told me the story"

Mr. Morison then adds that his grandmother was a woman of "strong understanding" and "had an aversion to what she called superstition, belief in ghosts, etc."

G. J. Romanes, the contemporary and scientific peer of Charles Darwin, narrates the following as his own personal experience. As an evolutionist, his name is known the world over.

"Towards the end of March, 1878, in the dead of night, while believing myself to be awake, I thought the door at the head of my bed was opened and a white figure passed along the side of the bed to the foot, where it faced about and showed me it was covered head and all in a shroud. Then with its hands it suddenly parted the shroud over the face, revealing between its two hands the face of my sister, who was ill in another room. I exclaimed her name, whereupon the figure vanished instantly. Next day (and certainly on account of the shock given me by the above experience), I called in Sir William Jenner, who said my sister had not many days to live. (She died, in fact, very soon afterward.)

"I was in good health, without any grief or anxiety. My sister was being attended by our family doctor, who did not suspect anything serious; therefore I had had no anxiety at all on her account, nor had she herself."

Robert Louis Stevenson reported to Mr. Myers four different experiences which represent dissociation or split consciousness. It is not necessary to detail them here.

Professor J. Estlin Carpenter reports a case of apparition within his own knowledge, though it is not evidential.

Ben Jonson had a vision of his son "with a bloodie cross upon his forehead," coincidental with the child's death at a distance.

Among experiences of Americans, the first case of interest is that of James G. Blaine as told by Gail Hamilton in a little brochure called *"X-Rays."* She collected there a large number of significant experiences; the present incident is connected with death visions and represents two different persons seeing the same deceased man or an apparition of him at different times. Mrs. Coppinger was the daughter and Walker was the son of James G. Blaine.

"Mrs. Coppinger died two weeks after the death of her brother Walker. In the later stages of her illness, she more than once spoke of his presence and tried to convince others of it. 'Do not you see Walker?' she asked. 'He is looking at you as if he loved you.' When, two years afterwards, her father was near the other world, as he lay quiet and silent in the evening dusk, a sorrowing watcher said, in a low voice, 'I am dreading all the time to hear him talk of Walker. Don't you remember Alice?' The next evening at the same hour we were sitting in the same place, when Mr. Blaine suddenly exclaimed 'Walker!' in the familiar tone of slight, pleasant surprise."

Such visions are not necessarily premonitory of death, though they are invariably indications that the person is near death. He or she may recover, but as the larger proportion of people so near death actually die, the popular belief has arisen that such visions are premonitions.

Carl Schurz, an officer in the Civil War and afterwards a member of the United States Senate from Missouri, tells the following experience in his "Memoirs," which were published in "McClure's Magazine" for April, 1908. He was a scholar of the best type as well as an able statesman.

"On the way to Washington, something strange happened to me which may be of interest to the speculative psychologist. In Philadelphia I had supper at the home of my intimate friend, Mr. Tiedemann, son of the eminent professor of medicine at the University of Heidelberg, and brother of Colonel Tiedemann, one of whose aides-de-camp I had been during the siege of the Fortress of Rastatt in 1849. Mrs. Tiedemann was a sister of Frederick Hecker, the famous revolutionary leader in Germany, who in this country had rendered distinguished service as a Union officer. The Tiedemanns had lost two sons in our army, one in Kansas, and the other, a darling boy, in the Shenandoah Valley. The mother, a lady of a bright mind and a lively imagination, happened to become acquainted with a circle of spiritualists, and received 'messages' from her two sons, which were of the ordinary sort, but which moved her so much that she became a believer. The Doctor, too, although belonging to a school of philosophy which looked down upon such things with a certain disdain, could not restrain a sentimental interest in the pretended communication from her lost boys, and permitted experiment to be made in his family. This was done with much zest. On the evening of which I speak it was resolved to have a séance. One of the daughters, an uncommonly beautiful, intelligent, and high-spirited girl of about fifteen, had shown remarkable qualities as a 'writing medium.' When the circle was formed around the table, hands touching, a shiver seemed to pass over her, her fingers began to twitch, she grasped a pencil held out to her, and, as if obeying an irresistible impulse, she wrote in a jerking way upon a piece of paper placed before her the 'messages' given her by the 'spirits' who were present. So it happened that evening. The names of various deceased persons known to the family were announced, but they had nothing to say except that they 'lived in a higher sphere,' and were 'happy,' were 'often with us,' and 'wished us all to be happy,' etc.

"Finally I was asked by one of the family if I could not take part in the proceeding by calling for some spirit in whom I took an interest. I consented and called for Schiller. For a minute or two the hand of the girl remained quiet; then she wrote that the spirit of Schiller had come and asked what I wished of him. I answered that I wished him by way of identification, to quote a verse or two from one of his works. Then the girl wrote in German the following:

> Von Lichtern hell. Wer sind die fröhlichen?
> Ich höre rauschende music, das Schloss ist

"We were all struck with astonishment; the sound of the language was much like Schiller's works but none of us remembered for a moment in which of Schiller's works the lines might be found. At last it occurred to me that they might be in the last act of 'Wallenstein's Tod.' The volume was brought out and true enough there they were. I asked myself, 'Can it be that the girl, who, although very intelligent, has never been given to much reading, should have read so serious a work as 'Wallenstein's Death'; and, if she has, that those verses, which have meaning only in connection with what precedes and follows them, should have stuck in her memory? I asked her, when the séance was over, what she knew about the Wallenstein tragedy, and she, an entirely truthful child, answered that she had never read a line of it.

"But something still stranger was in store for me. Schiller's spirit would say no more, and I called for the spirit of Abraham Lincoln. After several minutes had elapsed, the girl wrote that Abraham Lincoln's spirit was present. I asked whether he knew to what purpose President Johnson had summoned me to Washington. The answer came: 'He wants you to make an important journey for him.' I asked where that journey would take me. Answer: 'He will tell you to-morrow.' I asked further whether I should undertake that journey. Answer: 'Yes, do not fail.' (I may add, by the way, that at the time I had not the slightest anticipation as to what President Johnson's intention with regard to me was; the most plausible supposition I entertained was that he wished to discuss with me the points urged in my letter.)

"Having disposed of this matter I asked whether the spirit of Lincoln had anything more to say to me. The answer came: 'Yes, you will be senator of the United States.' This struck me as so fanciful that I could hardly suppress a laugh; but I asked further: 'From what state?' Answer: 'From Missouri.' This was more provokingly mysterious still; but there the conversation ceased. Hardly anything could have been more improbable at that time than that I should be a senator of the United States from Missouri. My domicile was in Wisconsin, and I was thinking of returning there. I had never thought of removing from Wisconsin to Missouri, and there was not the slightest prospect of my ever doing so. But — to forestall my narrative — two years later I was surprised by an entirely unsought and unexpected business proposition which took me to St. Louis, and in January, 1869, the legislature of Missouri elected me a senator of the United States. I then remembered the prophecy made to me at the spirit séance in the house of my friend Tiedemann in Philadelphia which, during the intervening years, I had never thought of. I should hardly have trusted my memory with regard to it, had it not been verified by friends who witnessed the occurrence."

Inquiring on my own part of a friend in Philadelphia, a physician, I ascertained that he knew this Dr. Tiedemann, and, from another who knew him well, I found out that he was a man of intelligence and that the phenomena were entirely private and had no connection with professional mediumship, a fact apparent in the account of Mr. Schurz.

The following incident, published in the "Journal" of the American Society for Psychical Research, Volume VII, p. 129, can be found in the life of Laura Bridgman, the blind, deaf and dumb girl of especial interest for her intelligence as manifested through the tactual sense alone.

"Miss Paddock and Miss Wight [two teachers in the 'Perkins Institute,' each of whom had Laura as a special pupil] were greatly attached to each other, and spent much of their leisure time together. They often noticed, as they sat talking of an afternoon, with Laura near by knitting at her purses or pretty lace edging, that she would suddenly lay down her work and begin talking [with her fingers] of the person or topic they had been discussing. The two young women were so much impressed by the frequency with which Laura took up the subject of their conversation when no possible clue of it had been given to her by word or act, that both believed the girl often knew what they were talking about, and the girls often said to each other, what they would have been abashed to say to older and wiser people, that Laura always knew what they were thinking of, *if* their thoughts were strongly concentrated upon an idea or a person."

There was an excellent opportunity here to investigate either hyperæsthesia of touch or telepathy, but no scientific spirit existed and a transcendent opportunity was lost.

Horace Bushnell in 1858 published a book called "Nature and the Supernatural," in which he mentions a number of incidents that show he anticipated psychic research. He was a reforming theologian, founder of the "moral theory" of the atonement, and perhaps the forerunner of all progressive theology in this country. Some of the incidents which he narrates would not stand the test of science, but one of them so accords with what has been proved by later investigation that it deserves quotation. He reports from an apparently reliable source the fact of an interesting coincidental dream, which was told by him by the dreamer, Captain Yonnt.

"About six or seven years previous, in a mid-winter's night, he had a dream in which he saw what appeared to be a company of emigrants, arrested by the snows of the mountains, and perishing rapidly by cold and hunger. He noted the very cast of the scenery, marked by a huge perpendicular front of white rock cliff; he saw the men cutting off what appeared to be tree tops, rising out of deep gulfs of snow: he distinguished the very features of the persons and the look of their particular distress. He woke, profoundly impressed with the distinctness and apparent reality of his dream. At length he fell asleep and dreamed exactly the same dream again. In the morning he could not expel it from his mind. Falling in shortly with an old hunter comrade he told him the story and was only the more deeply impressed by his recognizing, without hesitation, the scenery of the dream. This comrade came over the Sierra by the Carson Valley Pass, and declared that a spot in the pass answered exactly to his description. By this the unsophisticated patriarch was decided. He immediately collected a company of men, mules and blankets, and all necessary provisions. The neighbors were laughing in the meantime at his credulity. 'No matter,' said he, 'I am able to do this, and I will, for I verily believe that the fact is according to my dream.' The men were sent into the mountains, one hundred and fifty miles distant, directly to the Carson Valley Pass. And there they found the company in exactly the condition of the dream, and brought in the remnant alive.

"A gentleman present said, 'You need have no doubt of this; for we in California all know the facts, and the names of the families brought in, who now look upon our venerable friend as a kind of savior.' These names he gave and the place where they reside, and I found afterwards that the California people were ready everywhere to second his testimony."

Psychic researchers are familiar enough with coincidental dreams and would have no difficulty now in accepting this one.

Louisa M. Alcott tells a story, corroborated by the physician, of an experience relating to the death of her sister.

"A few moments after the last breath came, as mother and I sat watching the shadow fall on the dear little face, I saw a light mist rising from the body, and float up and vanish in the air. Mother's eyes followed mine, and when I said, 'What did you see?' she described the same light mist. Dr. G. said it was life departing visibly."

The character of the experience as shared, removes it from easy explanation as an ordinary hallucination; and the character of the informant makes it the more impressive.

Mark Twain had an experience which he called "mental telegraphy"; he offered it to the publisher of a well-known magazine, but it was rejected as one of his jokes. He kept it some years; and, after psychic research had become respectable and coincidences of the kind had become credible, the magazine published it. He also had a premonitory dream, which his biographer, Mr. Albert Bigelow Paine, records. Mark Twain (Samuel Clemens) was a steersman at the time on one of the Mississippi steamers.

"One night, when the *Pennsylvania* lay in St. Louis, he slept at his sister's house and had this vivid dream:

"'He saw Henry [his brother] a corpse, lying in a metallic burial case in the sitting room, supported on two chairs. On his breast lay a bouquet of flowers, white, with a single crimson bloom in the center.'

"When he awoke, it was morning, but the dream was so vivid that he believed it real. Perhaps something of the old hypnotic condition was upon him, but he rose and dressed, thinking he would go in and look at his dead brother. Instead he went out on the street in the early morning and had walked to the middle of the block before it suddenly flashed upon him that it was only a dream. He bounded back, rushed to the sitting room and felt a great trembling revulsion of joy when he found it really empty. He told Pamela [his sister] the dream, then put it out of his mind as quickly as he could. The *Pennsylvania* sailed from St. Louis as usual and made a safe trip to New Orleans. [Henry and Samuel both being employees on the steamer.]

"It is doubtful if he remembered his recent disturbing dream, though some foreboding would seem to have hung over him the night before the *Pennsylvania* sailed on the return trip. . . . On this particular night the elder, Samuel, spoke of disaster on the river. Finally he said:

"'In case of accident, whatever you do, don't lose your head — the passengers will do that. Rush for the hurricane deck and to the life boat, and obey the mate's orders. When the boat is launched, help the women and children into it. Don't get in yourself. The river is only a mile wide. You can swim ashore easily enough.'

"It was good manly advice, but it yielded a long harvest of sorrow. Henry was burned on the return trip by the escaping steam from the steamer's engines, four of which blew up, causing an immense loss of life by drowning and scalding. Henry, clear of danger and able to swim ashore, returned to help others and was scalded by breathing steam and died after several days.

"He, Samuel, saw the body down to the dead room, then the long strain of grief, the days and nights without sleep, the ghastly realization of the end, overcame him. . . . It was many hours before he awoke; when he did . . . he dressed and went to where Henry lay. The coffins provided for the dead were of unpainted wood, but the youth and striking face of Henry Clemens had aroused a special interest. The ladies of Memphis had made up a fund of sixty dollars and bought him a metallic case. Samuel, entering, saw his brother lying exactly as he had seen him in his dream, lacking only the bouquet of white flowers with its crimson center — a detail made complete while he stood there, for at the moment an elderly lady came in with a large white bouquet, and in the center of it was a single red rose."

This is a graphic incident; but the details of the premonition must excite skepticism, which would be supported by the risk of paramnesia, an illusion of memory, especially since his biographer speaks of Mark Twain's liability to strange mistakes of memory, probably connected with the intensity of his imagination. But such as it is, he told his biographer the story as a fact.

Professor James obtained through Frank R. Stockton a narrative of some experiences in his sister's house which, though not his own, he could vouch for. His sister was the subject of them. They consisted of apparent footsteps in the house, which, though not assuredly extraordinary, were inexplicable, and were made the subject of critical examination.

James Otis, the celebrated lawyer, had often expressed the wish that he should meet his death by lightning. While staying in the country, he was standing in the door when he was killed by a sudden stroke of lightning. The coincidence is hardly evidence of a supernormal premonition, but it is reported as a fact.

An experience of Mr. Chauncey Depew, former United States senator from the State of New York, has at least the suggestion of premonition. The following is the newspaper account of the experience, which Mr. Depew confirmed by a personal letter to Professor Newbold, of the University of Pennsylvania, in which he states that " the story is substantially true as written." It occurred on the eve of the political convention which nominated Theodore Roosevelt for the governorship of New York State. This was in October, 1898.

" On Saturday afternoon, before the Republican Convention was to meet, Mr. Depew went to the Country Club, at Ardsley-on-the-Hudson, which was his temporary home, and after luncheon he went out upon the piazza, from which a beautiful vista across the Hudson can be obtained.

" He sat there, lazily intent upon the scenery, which was especially agreeable to a man who had been for a week in the thick of the most exciting business undertakings. By and by the vista seemed to pass away. He saw as vividly as though the scene were real the convention hall in Saratoga. He saw the delegates stroll in. He looked at the presiding officer, whose name he did not know, as he called the convention to order.

" He heard the temporary chairman's speech, he saw the various details of preliminary organization, and all the work in the convention was as vivid as though he were a part of it at the moment. Then at last he saw Mr. Quigg make a motion for the nomination of candidates and heard the brief comment with which Mr. Quigg accompanied that motion.

"He did not, it is true, know that as a matter of fact Mr. Quigg was to make that motion; nevertheless he saw him do it. He said to himself, 'Your time is come for your speech placing Roosevelt in nomination.' He saw himself rise, address the chair, and heard himself deliver the speech and felt the glow of satisfaction at its reception, which is the highest reward of eloquence.

"After that, the convention hall, the voices of the orators, the faces of the delegates faded away as in a dream, and Mr. Depew again saw the vista of the Hudson and the distant mountains across the stream. He got up, went to his room and wrote out with his own hand the speech, exactly as he afterward in fact delivered it.

"The address which the delegates heard was the address which by that singular preoccupancy of the mind, Mr. Depew composed on that dreamy Saturday afternoon. Afterward, at the convention, he was amazed to discover that the picture which he saw with his mind's eye was perfectly reproduced to his physical eye and ear in the convention, even to the words of the chairman and the manner and motion of Mr. Quigg."

We should like to have had the details of the "vision" before it was fulfilled at Saratoga. Though we cannot obtain these, the experience has the character of Mr. Depew to give it interest.

Ernest Thompson-Seton, the traveler, tells some experiences in connection with prediction and clairvoyance among the Indians. There was an especially reliable old guide whom he asked to accompany him on an important trip. The old Indian went, taking with him "a new shirt and a pair of pants"— this was the outfit of a corpse; and the Indian explained that he was to die, "when the sun rose at that island" (a week ahead), before the officer in charge came back. A week after they had started he put on the new clothes and said, "To-day I die when the sun is over that island." The author adds: "He went out looking at the sun from time to time, placidly smoking. When the sun got to the right place he came in, lay down by the fire and in a few minutes was dead."

Auto-suggestion is probable in this case; but we do not know what auto-suggestion is! It may be as supernormal as any materialization would be. The main point is, that the incident is vouched for by a reliable and disinterested reporter.

Dwight L. Moody, the evangelist, had an experience which apparently forecast some danger to him, a few days before the arrest of a lunatic, who felt himself commissioned to assassinate Mr. Moody and had tried for days to get an opportunity to stab him. The incident is not striking, and would have no standing alone in a scientific court; but it is one of a large number with good credentials.

Sir Henry Stanley, the African explorer, narrates a personal experience of the coincidental type. While a private in the Confederate Army, he was captured at Shiloh and sent to Camp Douglas near Chicago. His biographer writes the account as he told it:

"On the next day (April 16, 1862), after the morning duties had been performed, the rations divided, the cooks had departed contented, and the quarters had been swept, I proceeded to my nest and reclined alongside of my friend Wilkes in a posture that gave me command of one half of the building. I made some remarks to him upon the card-playing groups opposite, when suddenly I felt a gentle stroke on the back of my neck, and in an instant I was unconscious. The next moment I had a vivid view of the village of Tremeirchion and the glassy slopes of the hills of Hirradog, and I seemed to be hovering over the rook woods of Brynbella. I glided to the bed chamber of my Aunt Mary. My aunt was in bed and seemed sick unto death. I took a position by the side of the bed, and saw myself, with head bent down, listening to her parting words, which sounded regretful, as though conscience smote her for not having been so kind as she might have been, or had wished to be. I heard the boy say, 'I believe you, Aunt. It is neither your fault nor mine. You were good and kind to me, and I knew you wished to be kinder; but things were so ordered that you had to be what you were. I also dearly wished to love you, but I was afraid to speak of it, lest you would check me or say something that would offend me. I feel our parting was in this spirit. There is no need of regrets. You have done your duty to me, and you had children of your own, who required all your care. What has happened to me since, was decreed should happen. Farewell.'

"I put forth my hand and felt the clasp of the long thin hands of the sore-sick woman. I heard a murmur of farewell, and immediately I woke.

"It appeared to me that I had but closed my eyes. I was still in the same reclining attitude, the groups opposite me were still engaged in their card games, Wilkes was in the same position. Nothing had changed. I asked, 'What has happened?'

"'What could happen?' said he. 'What makes you ask? It is but a moment ago you were speaking to me.'

"'Oh, I thought I had been asleep a long time.'

"On the next day, the 17th of April, 1862, my Aunt Mary died at Fynnon Beuno [in Wales]!"

General John C. Fremont, who was the first candidate for the Presidency of the newly formed Republican party, and who was also a United States senator, and an explorer of some ability, once came near starving on the western plains. In his biography by his daughter, the following incident is told. It is abbreviated here.

After the escape from danger, he wrote in his diary an account of the facts and felt relief at the thought that his wife would be glad to know of his safety. In Washington, D. C., his wife had suddenly been seized with foreboding and despondency about him and could not sleep, eat, nor go into company on account of her fears. She had the feeling that he was starving. This weight of fear, however, was lifted as suddenly as it had come. Her sister Susie and others had returned from a wedding and they sat down by the fire. Mrs. Fremont went out to get some wood; and, as she knelt to pick up a stick, she felt an invisible hand on her shoulder and heard the laughing voice of her husband whisper her name, "Jessie." There was no sound. When she came back to the others her sister Susie uttered a scream and fell on the rug. Her cousin asked Mrs. Fremont what she had seen, and she explained that she had seen nothing but had heard her husband tell her to keep still until he could scare Susie. Peace of mind came to the wife instantly. When General Fremont returned home it was found that the wife's fears coincided with the time he was starving in the desert and his diary showed that at the very time he was writing the journal note of his escape and happiness his wife had her experience and lost her anxiety.

Henry Wikoff, a lawyer, who traveled much and who at one time was employed by Lord Palmerston as a secret agent, tells a detailed story of the apparition of his deceased cousin, which lingered for two hours in spite of repeated efforts during that time to dispel the "hallucination," as he regarded it. He does not remark any coincidence in it, naturally enough, since he thought it an unaccountable delusion.

Dean Hole, of Rochester, England, tells in his memoirs some personal experiences and some incidents which came to him from others. He wanted information which only one man could give him, and that man was dead. Dean Hole, however, saw him in a vision, and his answer to Dean Hole's question told the latter all he wanted to know. He told the incident to his solicitor and the latter mentioned a similar experience of his own: a dream in which his father appeared to him and conveyed desired information.

These incidents, taken alone, have no evidential values, but similar experiences are well authenticated and can be shown to have evidential importance. We have quoted the foregoing instances not for their scientific value, but simply for the unimpeachable character of the witnesses. We require only better credentials in the way of record at the time and more striking incidents of detail to arouse scientific interest.

CHAPTER XII

SPONTANEOUS INCIDENTS

THE only spontaneous incidents which can serve as evidence of survival are apparitions. And among these the penchant for telepathy as an explanation of so many types of coincidences requires us to select only phantasms of the dead. As we have already seen, phantasms of the living and the dying cannot be quoted as evidence, at least as evidence free from the suspicion of telepathy. We are therefore obliged to select apparitions which cannot so easily be referred to that process. Some of them at least, if not all of them, may be exposed to simpler objections than is telepathy; but I am sure that, if telepathy has supplanted chance coincidence and subjective casual hallucination as an explanation for phantasms of the living and of the dying, these latter explanations will not any more easily apply to certain phantasms of the dead. We shall suppose here that chance coincidences and subjective hallucinations have been excluded from the collection with sufficient care; the remaining experiences are impressive collectively, and, so far as they go, are suggestively evidential. We resort to experiment for more conclusive testimony.

In taking up apparitions, however, as preliminary evidence for survival, I shall first select from a special type that are perhaps more impressive than the others and that have more or less corroborative support. I refer to *visions of the dying.* They are peculiarly free from the ordinary objections to apparitions, though they may have to contend with other difficulties in the way of proof. They have the advantage of being identified by the dying person at the outset, and are not exposed to the suspicion of being ordinary illusions caused by some casual stimulus. Chance coincidence may account for some of them, but hallucination and illusion due to sensory stimuli are less applicable to them than to many other types of apparition. Besides, they are numerous enough to deserve special consideration.

The first examples of visions of the dying are taken from the first number of the "Journal" of the American Society.

The first of this group was dictated to me by the two persons who knew the facts and was taken down verbatim. Both are intelligent and trustworthy witnesses, no more liable to errors in such matters than all of us. It involved circumstances which give peculiar value to the incident, as the story itself will show. I quote the narrative as I took it down.

"Four or five weeks before my son's death Mrs. S—— was with me — she was my friend and a psychic — and a message was given me that little Bright Eyes (control) would be with my son who was then ill with cancer. The night before his death he complained that there was a little girl about his bed and asked who it was. This was at Muskoka, 160 miles north of Toronto. He had not known what Mrs. S—— had told me. Just before his death, about five minutes, he roused, called his nurse for a drink of water, and said clearly: 'I think they are taking me.' Afterward seeing the possible significance of this I wrote to Miss A—— and asked her to see Mrs. S—— and try to find why the word 'they' was used, underscoring it in the letter, as I always supposed the boy's father would be with him at death. Miss A—— went to see Mrs. S——, and did not mention the letter. When I saw Mrs. S—— more than a week later we were having a sitting and Guthrie, my son, came and told me how he died. He said he was lying on the bed and felt he was being lifted out of his body and at that point all pain left. His first impulse was to get back into his body, but he was being drawn away. He was taken up into a cloud and he seemed to be a part of it. His feeling was that he was being taken by invisible hands into rarified air that was so delightful. He spoke of his freedom from pain and said that he saw his father beyond."

The intimate friendship of Mrs. S—— with Mrs. G——, the mother of the boy, makes it possible to suppose that hints or suggestions may have been unconsciously conveyed to the boy before his death or that something was said at the experiment which might deprive the incidents of that importance which they superficially seem to have. The boy's experience of a strange girl at his bedside, and the allusion to the plural of the pronoun are quite possibly correct accounts of the facts. A record of the later sitting would be necessary to be assured that the allusion to the father was not in response to a suggestion.

I quote next a well authenticated instance on the authority of Dr. Minot J. Savage. He records it in his "Psychic Facts and Theories." He also told me personally of the facts and gave me the names and addresses of the persons on whose authority he tells the incidents. I am not permitted to mention them; but the story is as follows:

> "In a neighboring city were two little girls, Jennie and Edith, one about eight years of age, and the other but a little older. They were schoolmates and intimate friends. In June, 1889, both were taken ill of diphtheria. At noon on Wednesday, Jennie died. Then the parents of Edith, and her physician as well, took particular pains to keep from her the fact that her little playmate was gone. They feared the effect of the knowledge on her own condition. To prove that they succeeded and that she did not know, it may be mentioned that on Saturday, June 8, at noon, just before she became unconscious of all that was passing about her, she selected two of her photographs to be sent to Jennie, and also told her attendants to bid her good-by.
>
> "She died at half-past six o'clock on the evening of Saturday, June 8. She had roused and bidden her friends good-by, and was talking of dying, and seemed to have no fear. She appeared to see one and another of the friends she knew were dead. So far it was like the common cases. But now suddenly, and with every appearance of surprise, she turned to her father, and exclaimed, 'Why, papa, I am going to take Jennie with me!' Then she added, 'Why, papa! Why, papa! You did not tell me that Jennie was here!' And immediately she reached out her arms as if in welcome, and said, 'O, Jennie, I'm so glad you are here.'"

As Dr. Savage remarks in connection with the story, it is not so easy to account for this incident by the ordinary theory of hallucination. We have to suppose a casual coincidence at the same time, and while we should have to suppose this for any isolated case like the present, the multiplication of cases, with proper credentials, would suggest some other explanation.

I shall turn next to two instances which are associated with the experiments and records of Mrs. Piper. Both present the allegation of death-bed apparitions, and give statements through Mrs. Piper purporting to be communications from the deceased, showing a coincidence with what was otherwise known or alleged to have taken place at the crisis of death. The records in these cases are unusually good, having been made by Dr. Richard Hodgson. I quote his reports. The first instance is the experience of a man who gives only initials for his name, but was well known to Dr. Hodgson. It occurred at a sitting with Mrs. Piper.

"About the end of March of last year (1888) I made her (Mrs. Piper) a visit — having been in the habit of doing so, since early in February, about once a fortnight. She told me that the death of a near relative of mine would occur in about six weeks, from which I should realize some pecuniary advantages. I naturally thought of my father, who was in advanced years, and whose description Mrs. Piper had given me very accurately some week or two previously. She had not spoken of him as my father, but merely as a person nearly connected with me. I asked her at this sitting whether this person was the one who would die, but she declined to state anything more clearly to me. My wife, to whom I was then engaged, went to see Mrs. Piper a few days afterward, and she told her (my wife) that my father would die in a few weeks.

About the middle of May my father died very suddenly in London from heart failure, when he was recovering from a very slight attack of bronchitis, and the very day that his doctor had pronounced him out of danger. Previous to this Mrs. Piper (as Dr. Phinuit) had told me that she would endeavor to influence my father about certain matters connected with his will before he died. Two days after I received the cable announcing his death my wife and I went to see Mrs. Piper, and she (Phinuit) spoke of his presence, and his sudden arrival in the spirit world, and said that he (Dr. Phinuit) had endeavored to persuade him in these matters while my father was sick. Dr. Phinuit told me the state of the will, and described the principal executor, and said that he (the executor) would make a certain disposition in my favor, subject to the consent of the other two executors when I got to London, England. Three weeks afterward I arrived in London; found the principal executor to be the man Dr. Phinuit had described. The will went materially as he (Dr. Phinuit) had stated. The disposition was made in my favor, and my sister, who was chiefly at my father's bedside the last three days of his life, told me he had repeatedly complained of the presence of an old man at the foot of his bed, who annoyed him by discussing his private affairs."

The reader will remark that the incident is associated with a prediction, but that is not the subject under observation at present. The chief point of interest is, that the prediction refers to a will affecting private business matters, that the sister reported a number of visions or apparitions at the man's death-bed, and that after his death, apparently not known to Mrs. Piper, the statement was made by Phinuit that he had influenced or tried to persuade the man in reference to these matters. The coincidence is unmistakable and the cause is suggested by the very nature of the phenomena and the conditions under which they occurred. But we need a large mass of such incidents to give the hypothesis something like scientific proof.

The next case is a most important one. It is connected with an experiment by Dr. Hodgson with Mrs. Piper, and came as an accidental feature of the sitting. The account is associated in his report with incidents quoted by him in explanation of the difficulty and confusion accompanying real or alleged communications from the dead. It will be useful to quote the report on that point before narrating the incident itself, as the circumstances associated with the facts are important to the understanding of the case, while they also suggest a view of the phenomena which may explain the rarity of them.

"That persons 'just deceased,'" says Dr. Hodgson, "should be extremely confused and unable to communicate directly, or even at all, seems perfectly natural after the shock and wrench of death. Thus in the case of Hart, he was unable to write the second day after death. In another case a friend of mine, whom I may call D., wrote, with what appeared to be much difficulty, his name and the words, 'I am all right now. Adieu,' within two or three days of his death. In another case, F., a near relative of Madame Elisa, was unable to write on the morning after his death. On the second day after, when a stranger was present with me for a sitting, he wrote two or three sentences, saying, 'I am too weak to articulate clearly,' and not many days later he wrote fairly well and clearly, and dictated to Madame Elisa (deceased), as amanuensis, an account of his feelings at finding himself in his new surroundings."

In a footnote Dr. Hodgson adds an account of what this Madame Elisa communicated regarding the man. I quote this in full. Referring to this F. and Madame Elisa, he says:

"The notice of his death was in a Boston paper, and I happened to see it on my way to the sitting. The first writing of the sitting came from Madame Elisa, without my expecting it. She wrote clearly and strongly, explaining that F. was there with her, but unable to speak directly, that she wished to give me an account of how she had helped F. to reach her. She said that she had been present at his death-bed, and had spoken to him, and she repeated what she had said, an unusual form of expression, and indicated that he had heard and recognized her. This was confirmed in detail in the only way possible at the time, by a very intimate friend of Madame Elisa and myself, and also of the nearest surviving relative of F. I showed my friend the account of the sitting, and to this friend a day or two later, the relative, who was present at the death-bed, stated spontaneously that F., when dying, said that he saw Madame

Elisa, who was speaking to him, and he repeated what she was saying. The expression so repeated, which the relative quoted to my friend, was that which I had received from Madame Elisa through Mrs. Piper's trance, when the death-bed incident was of course entirely unknown to me."

The apparent significance of such a coincidence is evident, and its value is much enhanced by the cross reference involved in the work of Dr. Hodgson. The following incidents are perhaps less evidential, but may be trusted as actual events.

The next case is a very important one, because the percipient did not know that his teacher was dead. Unfortunately the mother took an unreasonable position in regard to narrating the facts. The state of mind of religious people on such a matter is incomprehensible, except on the ground that they take a selfish view of the question of survival after death. This determination not to help others in such matters only tends to confirm the skeptic's judgment both that there is no evidence for the belief and that the believers in it have only a selfish interest in a future life. Unfortunately this is too often true. In the present instance we have the statement of another witness and though it is not as complete as we might wish, because she had not appreciated the value of the incident, the refusal of the mother to testify is a negative confirmation of the facts.

February 4, 1907.

" Dr. James H. Hyslop,
" Dear Doctor: —

" I am on the track of a very strange circumstance that happened in the family of a cousin of mine living in Greeley, Colorado.

" It seems their child was dying and a very short time before death told his mother that the teacher (public school teacher) was in the room. The child's mind, so far as they could tell, was clear. The strange part is that a very short time before, perhaps an hour or so, the teacher had suddenly died. Her death was unlooked for and the child knew nothing of it, and so far as I can learn none of those with the child knew of teacher's death. Would such a circumstance properly vouched for be of any value? I find it very hard to persuade people to relate or tell about such things. This family above mentioned are worthy people, the mother being for years a teacher in the Greeley, Colorado, schools.

" Yours truly,
" Dr. H. L. Coleman."

I wrote to Dr. Coleman asking him to make an effort to secure the lady's statement of the facts, for obvious reasons, and the following is his reply after making the attempt:

"March 15, 1907.

"Dr. James H. Hyslop.

"My Dear Sir: —

"I am sorry to inform you that I have resorted to every means to obtain from the mother of the child a full account of the vision, but she absolutely refuses to give me any information. She belongs to the class of people who regard such things as Psychical Research as unholy and wrong, though in other matters she is a woman of education and standing in society. She is strictly orthodox (a Methodist) and no influence myself or any of my friends can have on her will in any way change her views. I feel sure the case was one of great value. A cousin who talked to her about the matter told me as follows: The day before the little boy died he and his mother and the nurse were alone together in the room. The child said his Sunday school teacher was in the room with them, told how she was dressed, etc. At the time this took place the teacher, who had suddenly died, was lying in her casket. *The child had not been informed of her death.* The child talked to her much as one would talk to himself. The boy was regarded as very bright and was highly regarded by his Sunday school teacher. The child was about eight or ten years old. I will take the liberty to send you part of the letter from one of the cousins who has been trying to help me find out about the case. Part of the letter is personal, which you will please pardon, as I can send you nothing of value for the S. P. R., as it all came in too much round about way; I will return the stamp you sent me. If later I can find out anything more or introduce you into the case will do so, but can't now.

"Yours truly,

"DR. H. L. COLEMAN."

"I will try to answer the question you asked as near as I can; had I been talking to her myself I could have remembered it and wrote it down, but Annie did n't pay much attention to it.

"The child saw his teacher the day before he died; he did not know she was dead; he saw her soon after her death; he described the way she was dressed as she lay in her coffin. No one said anything to him about it. He talked as if talking to himself. No one saw child except the mother and nurse. This child was about eight years old and very bright; and a pet of his teacher. Now, Harry, I have written about all Annie can tell me and you will have to content yourself with this. If I get to see Clara this coming June I will talk to her myself.

"Your cousin,

"ELSIE."

The following incident was not dated in the informant's reply, and, as it was not a new incident, its interest has to rest on the authority of the informant. He was one of the ablest physicians in his city and himself attached some value to the facts, though not believing in a spiritistic hypothesis. The case must stand for what it is worth.

" BUFFALO, N. Y., [June, 1908].

" My Dear Mr. Hyslop: —

I have not been entirely inattentive to your letter of May, though your recent note gave my purpose a needed jog.

" Mrs. H—— has asked me to lay the following facts and circumstances before you: —

" Her brother died in 1876, at the age of twenty-one, after an illness whose entire course extended intermittently over several years. His grandfather had died when he was a small boy of about five.

" The grandfather's memory was dear to his mother and her family, but during this brother's illness, and especially toward the last when he knew he was dying, it is said that the grandfather's memory was not especially recalled.

" About seven in the evening, after he had been sinking and was supposed to be dying, the family being gathered about him, he opened his eyes and said " Grandfather," and looked as though he saw some one whom he addressed thus. He lingered through the night and died the next morning early.

" So long a time has elapsed that more detailed incidents are not available, and would scarcely be reliable, I fancy.

" An aunt of Mrs. H—— died a few years after the death of her sister, Mrs. H——'s mother. As she was dying she in the same manner as though recognizing some one dear to her, said ' Sis '— a title she was accustomed to giving her sister. The bystanders remarked the similarity to the manner and speech of the long-time dead brother of Mrs. H——.

" So far as these incidents are of service you are welcome to make use of them without name, unless necessary for verification of their truthfulness.

" With kind regards I am,

" Cordially yours,

" FRANK WHITEHILL H——."

The following incident came from one of my former students, now a lawyer. His special interest in the matter was not awakened until he lost his wife. At my request he reported the present incident, after narrating it to me personally. The gentleman who might have corroborated it in writing was reluctant to do so, though he confirmed it *viva voce*.

"March 3, 1908.

"Dear Professor:—

"I wish to give you the written account which you asked for of my observation when my wife died: she was a very spiritual girl and I always imagined in consequence that she did not have a very strong grip on life and was ready—psychologically and not voluntarily—to relinquish her hold. She was the youngest of a large family and was the particular pet of her father when a girl. Both her parents had been dead about ten years. She was not in the habit of mentioning her parents particularly, and all her interests were centered in her home. The last thing she said to me before she died was that she complained of being sleepy and from then on to the end, some two hours, she was not very conscious, as far as we could see, of her surroundings. When she was in the last struggle she called out 'Mama' once or twice, and later 'Papa! Papa! take me up, *they are killing me*.' (I remember this distinctly.) Shortly afterwards, some ten minutes, she passed away.

"Considering that she did not frequently speak of her parents, that at and shortly prior to her death she was too weak to speak to me, but nevertheless called out in a loud voice just as she was passing away, the incident is interesting as bearing upon the mental states at such transitional periods.

"Yours faithfully,

"HARRISON CLARK, JR."

The following incidents explain themselves; one of them is especially interesting because it is associated with a death vision by the lady herself of the same personality that had appeared as a warning of the death of others. That is, we have an ordinary apparition premonitory of the death of others and also of the subject herself when she died, giving a double interest to the facts and showing that the two types must have the same explanation.

"MILWAUKEE, WISCONSIN, March 18, 1907.

"Dr. James H. Hyslop.

"Dear Sir:—

"My mother used to say that whenever there was about to occur the death of a friend or relative, she saw her own mother standing beside her and looking at her. The first time that I knew of this vision of hers was when I was a girl of about twelve. My mother's most intimate friend, outside her own family, was dangerously ill. In the evening mother came from the friend's house and coming into my room got into bed with me. When I awoke in the morning mother was sitting on the edge of the bed in a brown study. I spoke to her and she roused herself and said: 'I fear Mrs. F—— is no more.' I asked her why she said that and she replied: 'Mother appeared to me just now.' Then she explained her belief that grandmother always appeared to her before the death of anyone she loved, and added: 'As I opened my eyes this morning, lying there beside you, I saw mother standing looking over the foot-board of the bed at me, very intently.'

"In less than an hour my aunt came up from Mrs. F.'s to say that she had passed away early in the morning.

"I do not distinctly recall any other instance of this hallucination of hers until the morning before her own death, about fifteen years later. She had had an attack of pneumonia, but the doctor had said that she was better and I was feeling much easier about her. I was taking care of her alone that night. About four in the morning, when I went up to the bed to give her medicine or stimulant — I have forgotten which — she aroused from a light slumber, looked up at me very keenly and said: 'Mother has just been with me.' The significance of it flashed over me at once and I could hardly control myself enough to give her the medicine I had in my hand. I went into the other room at once to call father to go for the doctor. Before he could arrive she had sunk into a stupor, and passed away in a few hours. Those were the last conscious words, or rather I should say intelligible words that she ever spoke to me. They were spoken in as clear and distinct a voice as she ever used.

"She died of heart failure, a reaction from pneumonia. My grandmother died a month before I was born.

"Another incident that I have only by hearsay was this: My mother told me that her father, on his death-bed, and when they thought he was just about gone, suddenly raised a little from his pillow, opened his eyes wide and called out in a glad, clear tone: 'Why, Dada!' This was the name of his wife's brother with whom, as a young man, he had been very intimate, and who had been dead for many years."

Instances of the same kind are much more numerous than those we have quoted, though they are not recorded as they should have been. One good instance, which happened in the family of Mr. James G. Blaine, mentioned in the preceding chapter, should have been recorded in detail. But the witnesses of it seem not to have appreciated its scientific interest. Probably the majority of similar incidents escape all but the immediate witnesses and generally they are regarded as too personal for scientific notice. They are not quoted here as of themselves satisfactory scientific proof of survival, though in sufficient numbers and properly observed they might be adequate even to that purpose. They at least suggest what other methods might establish or corroborate, and are so free from objections obtrusive in other phenomena that they deserve a first place among spontaneous incidents in favor of survival.

I next take up another type of apparition which requires specially good credentials to escape the suspicion of casual hallucination. But, as chance has been excluded from the explanation even of phantasms of the living, we may illustrate a type from whose interpretation telepathy is also excluded, though, apparently at least, they are not so common as phantasms of the living, including those of dying persons.

Phantasms of the dead are not easily classified as examples of telepathy. We cannot specify the agent without either unwarrantably extending the telepathy or making the deceased person the agent. The latter assumes that the facts are evidence of survival; and we may take such instances as spontaneous evidence for survival, though we may not regard this evidence as conclusive unless the facts become numerous enough and well enough established to be on the same level as experimental phenomena.

The first report of the English Committee on Haunted Houses mentions a number of good instances. One of them involves experiences by two persons.[1]

"In the early spring of 1852, Mr. X. Z. went to reside in a large old house near C——. Mr. X. Z. only occupied part of the house, the remainder being inhabited by a friend of his own, Mr. G——, and some pupils. Mr. G—— had occupied the house about a year before Mr. X. Z.'s arrival; and two servants had, in that interval, given him warning, on account of strange noises which they had heard. The house, which is a large one, was let at an extremely low rent.

"On the night of the 22nd of September, 1852, at about 1 A. M. Mr. X. Z. went up to his bedroom. The house was in complete darkness, and he took no candle with him; but on opening a door which led into the passage where his room was situated, he found the whole passage filled with light. The light was white like daylight, or electric light, and brighter than moonlight. At first Mr. X. Z. was dazzled by the light, but when his eyes became used to it he saw, standing at the end of the passage, about thirty-five feet from him, an old man in a figured dressing-gown. The face of this old man, which Mr. X. Z. saw quite clearly, was most hideous; so evil was it that both expression and features were firmly imprinted on his memory. As Mr. X. Z. was still looking, figure and light both vanished, and left him in pitch darkness. Mr. X. Z. did not, at that time, believe in ghosts, and his first thought was (he had lately read Brewster's 'Natural Magic,' and had been much impressed with the striking cases of spectral illusion recorded in that work) that he was the subject of a

[1] "Proceedings," English S. P. R., Vol. I, p. 106.

hallucination. He did not feel at all frightened, but resolved to take a dose of physic in the morning. The next day, however, remembering the tales told by the two servants who had left, he made inquiries in the village as to the past history of the house. At first he could find out nothing, but finally an old lawyer told him that he had heard that the grandfather of the present owner of the house had strangled his wife and then cut his own throat, on the very spot where Mr. X. Z. had seen the figure. The lawyer was unable to give the exact date of this occurrence, but Mr. X. Z. consulted the parish register, and found the two deaths recorded as having taken place on the 22nd September, 179— (the precise year he could not now (1882) remember). The lawyer added he had heard that the old man was in the habit of walking about the house in a figured dressing-gown, and had the reputation of being half an imbecile.

"On the 22nd September, 1853, a friend of Mr. G——'s arrived to make a short stay. He came down to breakfast the following morning, looking very pale, and announced his intention of terminating his visit immediately. Mr. G—— rather angrily insisted on knowing the reason of his sudden departure; and the young man, when pressed, reluctantly explained that he had been kept awake all night by the sound of cryings and groanings, blasphemous oaths, and cries of despair. The door of his bedroom opened on to the spot where the murderer had committed suicide; and it was in the bedroom which he had occupied that the murder had been committed. In 1856, Mr. X. Z. and his friend had occasion to call on their landlord, who lived in London. On being shown into the room, Mr. X. Z. at once recognized a picture above the mantel-piece as being that of the figure which he had seen. The portrait, however, had been taken when the man was younger, and the expression was not so hideous. He called Mr. G——'s attention to the painting, saying: 'That is the man whom I saw.'

"The landlord, on being asked whom the portrait represented, replied that it was the portrait of his grandfather, adding that he had been no credit to the family."

The incident lacks nothing in dramatic interest, but is old, though well authenticated. It would take many such to enforce a conclusion; and only the certification of a large number of more recent cases, such as those which "Phantasms of the Living" presents, could justify the use of such an incident for illustration. But there are similar instances.

In a paper by Mrs. Sidgwick on "Phantasms of the Dead" [1] an incident is recorded, which will have to be abbreviated. Its interest lies in the unconscious testimony of a child to an experience whose meaning he did not know.

[1] "Proceedings," English S. P. R., Vol. III, p. 87.

A man died in 1875, leaving a widow and six children. The three eldest children were admitted to an orphanage. Three years afterwards the widow died, and then the three remaining children were admitted to the orphanage. Some visitors came one day; and, as the place was full, the warden took a bed in the little ones' dormitory. In the night he suddenly awoke and saw a soft light in the room. He saw that it was not the gas light from the hall, and, turning round, he saw a wonderful vision. Over the second bed from his, and on the same side of the room, there was floating a small cloud of light, forming a halo of the brightness of the moon on an ordinary moonlight night. In this bed slept the youngest of the six children. The warden took the trouble to note that he was not dreaming, but went to sleep again. In the morning, while dressing, this youngest child looked at the warden with an extraordinary expression, and said: "Oh, Mr. Jupp, my mother came to me last night. Did you see her?" The warden did not answer the child, though astonished at the statement, and nothing more was said about it.

This is practically a case of shared experience, as two persons had an experience at approximately the same time. The following is from the same list by Mrs. Sidgwick. It was received from Mrs. Windridge, whose address was given in the account.

"November 9, 1882.

"About the year 1869, I was much interested in a poor woman who was dying in my neighborhood. I used to visit her frequently, until my friends prevented me from going any more, as the excitement rendered me ill. Eventually, when she died, they concealed the fact from me for some days.

"I was taking my little boy, three years old, up to bed one evening. It was dusk; and, when half-way up the first flight of stairs, I distinctly felt a pressure and a rustling of a dress at my side, as if a woman had brushed past me. There was no one there. On the second flight the pressure was repeated, but more unmistakably. The occurrence made me so nervous that, having put the boy to bed, I decided to remain with him until my husband came in. I accordingly lay down on the bed, facing him.

"Suddenly the boy started up. 'Oh, mother, there is a lady standing behind you!' At the same moment I felt a pressure which I knew to be that of my friend. I dared not look round.

"When my husband returned, I heard for the first time that my friend had died three days before."

Again the experience was shared, and bears the marks of purpose. The next has a human interest and is from the same collection. It was recorded by the Rev. C. C. Wambey.

"During my residence in B. C., as curate in charge, it was my custom in the summer evenings to walk over the neighboring downs.

"On the evening of Sunday, August 20, 1874, I was strolling on the downs skirting Marlcombe Hill, composing a congratulatory letter, which I proposed to write and post to my very dear friend W., so that he might have it on his birthday, the twenty-second, when I heard a voice saying, 'What, write to a dead man; write to a dead man!' I turned sharply round, fully expecting to see some one close behind me. There was no one. Treating the matter as an illusion, I went on with my composition. A second time I heard the same voice, saying, more loudly than before, 'What, write to a dead man; write to a *dead* man!' Again I turned round. I was alone, at least bodily. I now fully understood the meaning of that voice; it was no illusion.

"Notwithstanding this, I sent the proposed letter, and in reply received from Mrs. W. the sad, but to me not unexpected, intelligence that her husband was dead."

Here is another brief instance from the same collection; it was the only experience of Mrs. Haly, who reported it.

"On waking in broad daylight, I saw, like a shadowed reflection, a very long coffin stretching quite across the ceiling of my room, and as I lay gazing at it, and wondering at its length and whose death it could foreshadow, my eyes fell on a shadowy figure of an absent nephew, with his back towards me, searching, as it were, in my book-shelf. That morning's post brought the news of his death in Australia. He *was six foot two or three inches in height,* and a book, taken from that very bookcase, had been my last present to him on his leaving England.

The next instance from the same list, a long one, is also reported by a clergyman. The writer was the Rev. Gerrard Lewis, of St. Paul's Vicarage, Margate. The account was given in a letter to Mr. Podmore. The story had been published in "Temple Bar."

"I have nothing to add to my 'true ghost story' in 'Temple Bar.' As to dates, he died on Thursday, September 19, 1866. I saw his appearance on Sunday, September 22, and officiated at his funeral on Wednesday, September 25.

"My wife's mother had in her service a coachman named P., with one son, James Henry P., who had been brought up by friends at a distance, and was apprenticed to a trade in London. His father had only twice casually mentioned him to me, and he had almost entirely slipped out of my mind, for, with a large seaside parish on my hands, of which I was curate, my time and attention were fully taken up with matters nearer home. I mention this, lest in the course of the following story my readers should chance to think that a deep impression, previously made on my own mind, had predisposed me to see what I saw, and afterwards to regard it in a supernatural light. I cannot, therefore, too emphatically repeat that

I knew next to nothing about James Henry P., my friend's son; that I had never seen him; and seldom, if ever, thought of him at all.

"It was a hot and bright afternoon in summer, and, as if it were only yesterday, I remember perfectly well walking down the broad bright street in the broad bright afternoon. I had to pass the house of P. I remarked indeed that all his window blinds were drawn carefully down, as if to screen his furniture, of which his wife was inordinately proud, from the despoiling blaze of the afternoon sun. I smiled inwardly at the thought. I then left the road, stepped up on the side pavement, and looked over the area rails into the front court below. A young man, dressed in dark clothes, and without a hat, and apparently about twenty years of age, was standing at the door beneath the front steps. On the instant, from his likeness to my friend P., I seemed to recognize his son. We both stood and looked very hard at each other. Suddenly, however, he advanced to that part of the area which was immediately below where I was standing, fixed on me a wide, dilated, winkless sort of stare, and halted. The desire to speak was evidently legible on his face, though nothing audible escaped from his lips. But his eyes spoke; every feature in his countenance spoke, spoke, as it were, a silent language, in which reproach and pain seemed equally intermingled. At first I was startled; then I began to feel angry. 'Why,' I said to myself, 'does he look at me in that manner?' At last, annoyance prevailing over surprise, I turned away with the half-muttered thought: 'He certainly knows me by sight as a friend of his father, and yet has not the civility to salute me. I will call on the first opportunity and ask his reason for such behavior.' I then pursued my way and thought no more of what had just occurred.

"On Wednesday it was my turn to officiate at the local cemetery. On my asking who was to be buried, I was told that it was a young man from my quarter of the town, who had died of consumption. I cannot give the reason, but immediately I felt startled and ill at ease. It was not that I had the least suspicion that anything extraordinary was about to happen. I had quite forgotten young P. The feeling which I think was uppermost in my mind was annoyance at the fact that anyone should have died of such a slow disease in my parish, but without my knowledge. I asked without delay for the registrar's certificate. My eyes fell on the words, 'James Henry P., aged twenty-one years.' I could scarcely believe my own senses.

"I lost but little time before calling on P. and his wife. I found the latter at home, and what she had to say only made me more uncomfortable still. James Henry P. bore such a close resemblance to his father that all who saw him remarked on the striking likeness. In addition to this, during the last three months of his life, which he spent under his father's roof, he had often wondered that I did not come to see him. His longing for an interview with me had been most intense; and every time he saw me pass the house without going in he had both felt and expressed a keen disappointment. In fact, he died terribly in earnest, wishing in vain to the last that I would come. That thought pierced me through and through. I had not gone to him, but he had come to me. And yet I would have gone, if I had but known. I blame the doctor for not telling me; I blame the parents for not sending for me; and with that awful look he gave me in my remembrance, I blame myself, though I cannot tell why.

"James Henry P. had died on the Thursday before the Sunday on which I had seen him. He had died, too, in the front room, on a level with the area, into which its window opened. He had also lain there till the Wednesday following, awaiting burial. His corpse then was lying in that very room on that very Sunday, and at the very moment, too, when I had seen his living likeness, as it were, in the area outside. Nobody, I found, had passed through the area that day; the door there had been locked and unused all the Sunday. The very milkman, the only person who called, had come by the front steps to the house; and P. and his wife were the only inmates at the time."

Another long case follows this, and tells of the appearance of a young man, to say that he did not do what he was accused of. Inquiry showed that he had been accused of committing suicide. Later it was found that the accusation was not true. Another represents two persons seeing a phantasm of the same person whose relation to the place was wholly unknown to them, though afterwards verified.

Mr. Myers quotes from the "Census of Hallucinations," Volume X of the English "Proceedings," a case of which that report says: "Unless we accept the hypothesis of chance coincidence, the evidence for the agency of the dead is certainly strong, because any other explanation compatible with the veracity of the narrators requires a very complicated and improbable hypothesis." The following is the narrative [p. 383]:

"RIO DE JANEIRO, March 12, 1892.

[After relating his first meeting, in June, 1886, with "Deolinda," a child whom he had found in great poverty and had taken charge of, and her death from consumption shortly afterwards, Señor Cabral continues: —]

"Some months passed, and my family (which now included my wife's other sister, Amelia) went to stay at a plantation belonging to friends. I escorted them thither, and returned to attend to my obligations in the city. In order not to be alone, I accepted the invitation of my friend, Barboza de Andrade, and went to live with him in S. Christovam. One month afterwards, a sister of Barboza's, who was ill, came into his house. She grew daily worse, and after the lapse of a few months had sunk so low that we had to sit up with her at night.

"One night when I had taken my turn at nursing, I felt sleepy, and went to lie down. Two sisters, Donnas Anna Ignez Dias Fortes and Feliciana Dias (now deceased), took my place. I had made their acquaintance but a few days before. After stretching myself on the bed, I was filled with a feeling of unbounded joy. I was happy, and could not imagine what was the cause of my happiness. I had a sensation as if some one were holding my head and placing something round it.

"Astonished at my experience, I called to the ladies who were watching in the next room, and Donna Feliciana, though from the place where she was seated she could not see me, answered me back, 'I see at your bedside a spirit child clothed in white. She places on your head a crown of roses. She says her name is Deolinda, and she comes to thank you for the kindness and charity with which you behaved to her.' I was amazed at such a declaration, for that very day was the anniversary of Deolinda's death, and neither I nor any other person in the house had recollected this. Besides, I had never spoken on the subject.

"ULYSSES CABRAL."

The two ladies write that they knew nothing of the story of Deolinda and confirm the narrative as told. The incident is especially interesting as involving a tactual phantasm by Señor Cabral himself, veridical in nature, and probably affected by the condition of the dying woman, as it is possible that phantasms of the kind require some energy supplied by the living who are in a state to generate it, a state on the border-land of death.

The next case is remarkably interesting, as it is not only a phantasm of the dead, but is accompanied by the account of a phantasm of another person definitely related to the decedent and appearing to other persons as a premonition of her death, and is also a vision of the dying person, so that it combines three characteristics of great interest. It also is quoted by Mr. Myers from the "Census of Hallucinations." Mrs. B. is the writer of the narrative.

"April, 1892.

"At Fiesole, on March 11, 1869, I was giving my little children their dinner at half-past one o'clock. It was a fine hot day. As I was in the act of serving macaroni and milk from a high tureen, so that I had to stand to reach it, and give my attention to what I was doing,—on raising my head (as much from fatigue as for any purpose), the wall opposite me seemed to open, and I saw my mother lying dead on her bed in her little house at ——. Some flowers were at her side and on her breast: she looked calm, but unmistakably dead, and the coffin was there.

"It was so real that I could scarcely believe that the wall was really brick and mortar, and not a transparent window—in fact, it was a wall dividing the hotel in which we were living from the Carabinieri.

"I was in very weak health — suffering intensely with neuralgia — having gone through a bad confinement, brought on by traveling, the baby was almost still born, on January 31.

"Owing to a family quarrel, I had left England without telling my people where I was going; but I was so fond of my mother that, when in Paris, I made an excuse to write to an old servant, who lived with my mother, to ask her for a toy which we had left with her,— the object being to get news of my mother. Reply came that for years she had not been so well and strong; thus I had no reason for imagining her to be dead.

"I was so distressed at the vision, that I wrote to her (my mother) to give her my address, and entreat her to let me know how she was. By return of post came the statement that she had died on March 5, and was buried on the eleventh. At the hour I saw her, she was removed from her home to Kensal Green Cemetery. She had wished to see me so much that letters had been sent to a great many continental cities, hoping I might be found; but I never got a letter from my sister till long after I had received the news of my mother's death.

"When I was married, my mother made me promise, as I was leaving home, to be sure to let her know in any way God permitted if I died, and she would try to find some way of communicating to me the fact of her death — supposing that circumstances prevented the usual methods of writing or telegraphing. I considered the vision a fulfilment of this promise, for my mind was engrossed with my own grief and pain — the loss of baby, and my neuralgia, and the anxieties of starting a new life.

"My youngest sister, since dead, was called to my mother and left Devonshire, where she was staying with friends, to come home. When she arrived at home, she entered the drawing-room, but rushed out terrified, exclaiming that she had seen godmamma, who was seated by the fire in my mother's chair. Godmamma had been dead since 1852. She had been my mother's governess — almost foster-mother; had lived with her during her married life, been godmother to her eldest girl, and when my father died had accepted the duty of taking his place as far as possible in the family, to shield her from trouble and protect her — a duty which she fulfilled nobly.

"My other sister went into the drawing-room to see what had scared K——, and saw the figure of godmamma just as K—— had. Later in the day, the same figure stood by, then sat on the edge of my mother's bed, and was seen by both my sisters and the old servant, looking just as she had when alive, except that she wore a gray dress, and, as far as we could remember, she had always worn black. My mother saw her, for she turned towards her and said 'Mary'— her name."

This is also an instance of what the English investigators call a "compact case," which means an instance in which the parties concerned had made a promise between them to return. George Pelham was a case of the kind and Mr. Myers enumerates twelve such cases. But I turn now to some American instances of the kind; I shall only summarize the first case.

A man died on April 12, 1905. On the twentieth of May following, the sister-in-law was washing the dishes in the kitchen, and her sister was playing the piano, when the sister in the kitchen saw an apparition of her brother-in-law lying in bed straight in front of her just where she had seen him for the last month of his life. The music played on the piano was the same that the sister had played for him during his last illness.

The next case I must also abbreviate, as it is very long. It is reported by Dr. Heysinger, who took it from the autobiography of Captain Little, of the merchant service out of Baltimore. The book was entitled, "Life on the Ocean; or, Twenty Years at Sea."

It was a clear night. All had turned in. About midnight the captain was called by the sailor on the watch, who said that there was on deck a woman dressed in black, who was calling for him. Believing the sailor to be half drunk, as was generally the case at that period, the captain drove him away; but the sailor persisted in his statement and pointed out the place where he had seen and talked with the woman. Diligent search revealed nothing and they all turned in again. About two hours later another sailor, who was a perfectly sober man, called the captain again with the same story of a woman calling for the captain. The crew corroborated his testimony. Search was made again but without effect. The sailors, being somewhat superstitious, wanted to be discharged, but the captain would not listen to it. They felt that the apparition was a premonition that the ship was going down. On the captain's stubborn refusal they went to work, and the ship stood out to sea. On the second day they encountered a terrific storm and all were fearful of the consequences. At midnight, precisely, the ghostly vistor appeared again, but neither Captain C—— nor the narrator of the story saw it. The vessel reached Martinique safely and went thence to Guadaloupe, where yellow fever seized some of the crew; during the raging of this malady the same visitor was seen again by the crew. On reaching home after the return voyage, Captain C—— received a letter saying that his wife was dead.

On comparing the time of her demise with that of the first appearance of the lady in black, while the ship lay in Annapolis Roads, he found that the time exactly corresponded.

But for the subsequent apparitions this case would be classified with phantasms of the living or of those just dying. The next instance is a "compact case" and was reported to me by the Rev. A. B. Weymouth, a missionary in the Hawaiian Islands.

"LAHAINA, HAWAIIAN ISLANDS, October 24, 1910.

"Dear Dr. Hyslop:

"When I was living in Los Angeles, California, I became acquainted with Mrs. Jennie D—— who seemed to be a congenial soul. In the autumn of 1888, Mrs. D—— and I made a verbal agreement that the one who should first enter the spiritual world should return (d.v.) and appear to the other. In the spring of 1898, the lady became seriously ill and after a few months of suffering passed away. As no tidings came from the deceased, I supposed that some unexpected obstacle prevented her return. But at last the long silence was broken. On Saturday evening, October 22, 1910, I retired to rest soon after nine o'clock. After refreshing sleep I awoke, with the impression that something unusual was about to happen. Then I distinctly heard a voice saying: 'Jennie D. is coming.' A few moments later, something like a bright cloud appeared in my bedroom. In the midst of the cloud I recognized the form of my long lost friend. While hovering in the air she sang two verses sweetly. Then other spirit forms appeared (the faces not recognized) and joined in the refrain. I had never heard the words or the music before; and I regret that I cannot recall the words. They were very beautiful and so was the melody. When the music ceased, the bright cloud and the celestial visitors disappeared and my room was dark again. I arose immediately, lighted a lamp, looked at my watch and made a record of the incident. The time of the vision was 12.30 on Sunday morning.

"Sincerely yours,

"A. B. WEYMOUTH."

Mr. Albert J. Edmunds, librarian of the Pennsylvania Historical Society, reports a case in fuller detail than that given in the report published by the English Society, and again by Mr. Myers in his great work, "Human Personality and its Survival of Bodily Death." We shall have to abbreviate it, though it is published in detail in the "Journal," of the American Society for Psychic Research (Volume VI, pp. 439–448). The man who saw the apparition was well known to Mr. Myers, who took down the statement from this man himself.

"In 1880 I succeeded a Mr. Q. as librarian of the X Library. I had never seen Mr. Q. nor any photograph nor likeness of him, when the following incidents occurred. I may, of course, have heard the library assistants describe his appearance, though I have no recollection of this. I was sitting alone in the library one evening late in March, 1884, finishing some work after hours, when it suddenly occurred to me that I should miss the last train to H., where I was then living, if I did not make haste. It was then 10:55, and the last train left X. at 11:05. I gathered up some books in one hand, took the lamp in the other, and prepared to leave the librarian's room, which communicated by a passage with the main room of the library. As my lamp illuminated this passage, I saw apparently at the further end of it a man's face. I instantly thought a thief had got into the library. This was by no means impossible, and the probability of it had occurred to me before. I turned back into my room, put down the books and took a revolver from the safe, and, holding the lamp cautiously behind me, I made my way along the passage — which had a corner behind which I thought my thief might be lying in wait — into the main room. Here I saw no one, but the room was large and encumbered with bookcases. I called out loudly several times to the intruder to show himself, more with the hope of attracting a passing policeman than of drawing the intruder. Then I saw a face looking round one of the bookcases. I say looking *round,* but it had an odd appearance as if the *body* were *in* the bookcase, as the face came so closely to the edge and I could see no body. The face was pallid and hairless, and the orbits of the eyes were very deep. I advanced towards it, and as I did so I saw an old man with high shoulders seem to *rotate,* and with a shuffling gait walk rather quickly from the bookcase to a small lavatory, which opened from the library and had no other access. I heard no noise. I followed the man at once into the lavatory; and to my extreme surprise found no one there. I examined the window (about twelve by fourteen inches), and found it closed and fastened. I opened it and looked out. It opened into a well, the bottom of which, ten feet below, was a sky-light, and the top open to the sky some twenty feet above. It was in the middle of the building and no one could have dropped into it without smashing the glass nor climbed out of it without a ladder, but no one was there. Nor had there been anything like time for a man to get out of the window, as I followed the intruder instantly. Completely mystified, I even looked into the little cupboard under the fixed basin. There was nowhere hiding for a child, and I confess I began to experience for the first time what novelists describe as an 'eerie' feeling.

"I left the library, and found I had missed my train. Next morning I mentioned what I had seen to a local clergyman who, on hearing my description, said, 'Why, that's old Q!' Soon after I saw a photograph (from a drawing) of Q., and the resemblance was certainly striking. Q. had lost all his hair, eyebrows and all, from (I believe) a gunpowder accident. His walk was a peculiar, rapid, high-shouldered shuffle.

"Later inquiry proved he had died at about the time of year at which I saw the figure."

Two assistants in the library some time later saw a spectral light in the room in which Mr. Q. *used to sit late at night writing articles.* This was in 1884. About 4 P. M., April 1, 1885, Mr. J., one of the persons who had seen the spectral light, was sitting at the head of a long table, and asked Mr. Edmunds, the sponsor for this story, to stay a minute, as something was the matter with the table. The upshot of the matter was, that Mr. Edmunds, after proving that other conjectures were not correct, shouted out the suspicion that it had something to do with "old Q." What they had heard was a "half-bell-like vibration, which sounded something like a tuning fork when struck and held to the ear." Just as Mr. Edmunds suggested that it had something to do with "old Q.," Mr. R., who had seen the illuminated room, came in. "He was the only member of the staff that had worked under Q." The three men put their fingers lightly on the table, and, as soon as Mr. R. touched the table, the sound came ringing out of his sleeve. Two of the party rushed to R. and looked into his sleeve, but found nothing there. Recalling that such phenomena sometimes occurred on the anniversaries of deaths they decided to find out when Mr. Q. had died. A messenger was dispatched to some one who knew and he returned with the information that Mr. Q. had died on the first of April, 1880, between four and five o'clock in the afternoon.

Mr. Edmunds then asked R. whether, when Q. was alive, he was accustomed to hear in this library any sound that at all resembled the ringing; he replied that he was. Upon that spot on the table whence the sound appeared to proceed there used to stand an old cracked gong, which when Q. wanted one of his boys, he used to strike; it sounded like the vibration which the three men had heard. Thus, on the fifth anniversary, to the very hour, of the old man's death, a phantasmal bell reminded them of his presence.

A number of experiments were then held, and the alleged Q. was interrogated with some success. But the important fact is, that a series of shared experiences and of real or alleged messages came, strengthening the significance of the first apparition; it is only the phantasmal phenomena that are important in this connection.

The following incident has a romantic and perhaps pathetic interest. It was in the collection of Dr. Hodgson, which came to me after his death; and, as I knew the person who had reported it, I took the pains to have it fully confirmed. It was written out by the lady herself and reported to Dr. Hodgson in 1904. Mrs. Howell did not date her account.

"In the year 1865 I had a lover by the name of John A. Broadhead. Owing to several circumstances I was obliged to give him up, although I was deeply attached to him. When he found that he could not marry me, he left the town of Mount Morris, where I lived, but before he left he said to me: 'Mary, I think this separation will kill me, but if I die and a spirit can come back to earth, I will come to you.'

"I replied, 'Oh, no, don't; for that would frighten me dreadfully.' 'No, it would not,' he answered, 'for I should come so calmly that you would not be at all afraid.'

"In 1868 I married George R. Howell, a Presbyterian minister who knew all about my affection for John Broadhead. In April, 1871, I was visiting my old home with my husband and baby boy. About one o'clock one Sunday afternoon (I think it was April 12) I sat in the parlor of my father's house, my baby in my arms, on the long old fashioned sofa on which I had so often sat with my old lover. My husband sat across the room with his back to me, reading. The sofa was unusually long and I sat at the end of it near a door opening into the hall.

"Suddenly I felt a pressure against my knee and limb as though some one had come very close to me, and I looked up expecting to see one of my brothers, but to my great surprise saw my old lover, John Broadhead, standing there beside me. I felt greatly distressed, for he lived in a distant city. I had not seen him since 1865, and I thought it an unwarrantable intrusion that he should enter my father's house thus unannounced. It never occurred to me that he was not alive. I noticed every detail of his dress and can even now distinctly remember the black and white necktie which he wore. Before I had a chance to speak he raised his right hand and said, speaking very slowly and gently: 'Be very calm, Mary. I am what they call dead. I died in the West three weeks ago to-day.' Then, lifting his left hand, he pointed to a newspaper which lay at the other end of the sofa about three feet away from me and said: 'You will find my death in that paper.' Then without moving a muscle he vanished while I gazed at him.

"I was not at all afraid, but felt completely overcome by the shock of suddenly learning that he was dead, for, much as I loved my husband, I had never gotten over my old feeling for John Broadhead; and if it had not been for the baby in my arms I think I would have fainted away. As it was, I could not speak or call my husband, but I managed to hitch along the sofa till I could reach the paper to which he had pointed. This turned out to be a copy of the New York 'Times' that had never been taken out of the wrapper in which it had come through the mails. I tore it open and there, among the death notices, I found this paragraph:

"'Died in Burlington, Iowa, March 22, 1871, John A. Broadhead of this city in the thirty-fourth year of his age.'

"MARY SEYMOUR HOWELL."

It is certain that these phantasms of the dead cannot be explained by telepathy between living persons, except by proving an extension of thought-transference that has never been justified by any facts whatever. It is an interesting fact that out of the twelve cases of compact before death, three fulfilled their pledge before they died! They were very ill, near death, when they appeared to the other party to the promise, but recovered health, some of them still living when the facts were reported. This circumstance strongly supports the application of telepathy; and the scientific men who had to consider them were entirely right to pause before accepting a spiritistic interpretation of phantasms of the dying. The facts made it necessary, if phantasms of any kind were to be regarded as testimony of survival, that they should be of the type to which no proved telepathy could apply. The present instances seem to be illustrations of the desired kind. If telepathy applies to them at all, it will be that form of it which is not an alternative theory to belief in spirits, but the name of a process of communication which will apply alike to the agency of the dead and of the living. It is probable that the same process lies at the basis of all phantasms and that the differences lie only in the agents. But the main point here is that the phantasms of the dead show no traces of being initiated or instigated by the living. I have chosen for the most part those which have a teleological aspect; and teleology is not suggested by any known telepathy.

Such phenomena, however, can never constitute the scientific proof for survival that the experimental investigator will require. It is conceivable that they might be accumulated until they did establish the probabilities so overwhelmingly that experiment would not seem imperative. But always experimental proof is more satisfactory than spontaneous phenomena. The spontaneous phenomena suggest the problem and go far toward making the conclusion reasonable, though we may feel some hesitation in each case about accepting their evidential character. They often contain features that associate them psychologically with the phenomena obtained through mediumistic sources. We cannot dwell on this circumstance. We only remark it as an additional characteristic that tends to support the genuineness and significance of the facts.

CHAPTER XIII

EXPERIMENTAL INCIDENTS

EXPERIMENT is always the most important resource of science when it wants to obtain assurance on any point. Spontaneous phenomena are exposed to unexpected objections, often when we feel most sure about them, while the fear that malobservation may have vitiated some conclusions keeps the judgment in suspense, until experiment, in which we can determine conditions, has supplied us with the evidential desideratum. The phenomena of psychic research, which are sporadic even under the most favorable circumstances and more so under test conditions, offer special difficulties in the way of either their reproduction or discovery under evidential conditions. Whatever the difficulties, however, science insists on experimental production of the phenomena for better observation and security as to their genuineness and significance.

For some years experimental results have been obtained by investigators all over the world. There is to-day such a mass of well-authenticated facts affording a selection of incidents having the desired evidential value, as to make any other than the spiritistic hypothesis exceedingly improbable. Facts intelligently selected with reference to proving the personal identity of the deceased are not of the kind exhibited in telepathy. They are usually such as would most naturally express the mind of the alleged communicator, and, with various other characteristics of the phenomena themselves, they so commend themselves to a spiritistic theory, that no other view of them can be rational.

In such a summary of the facts as I give I cannot be expected to tell all the circumstances which exclude normal knowledge as the source of the messages. The detailed records do this quite fully. The reader will have to be content with the general statement that no incident which has not stood that test has been selected and that I have endeavored to eliminate all bias in recording and selecting the facts here used. I am primarily interested in their importance for establishing supernormal knowledge and the personal identity of the communicator. In some cases the very description of the facts will be a half-guarantee of genuineness, and often very little will have to be said to protect them against skepticism.

The first incident that I select is strong and complicated. It involves what is called a "cross-correspondence." There is a technical distinction between "cross-correspondence" and "cross-reference." The former implies the latter. but "cross-correspondence" involves the completion through a second psychic of a message obtained through another, or an increment that is relevant and not given at the first station. "Cross-reference" need be no more than the delivery of the same message from two independent sources. For our purposes there need be little difference between them, though the "cross-correspondence" appears to many people to be the more cogent.

The incident is not fully reported in the paper by Mrs. Verrall in the "Proceedings" of the English Society, and hence for the part which pertains to what Dr. Hodgson did I shall have to depend on my memory. He told me that, at a sitting with Mrs. Piper, in which Mr. Myers purported to communicate, Mr. Myers referred to Miss Helen Verrall as the daughter of Mrs. Verrall and remarked that she was "a better light than the mother," adding that he had got her to see a vision of a hand and a book. Dr. Hodgson, seeing an opportunity to get a cross-reference, and knowing nothing about the daughter, asked the communicator to make her see a hand and a spear, varying the picture as little as possible. Rector, the control, to whom the request was given, did not understand the word "spear" and interpreted it as "sphere." Dr. Hodgson corrected it and spelled the word "spear" and then Rector caught it, repeating the word "spear," and asking Dr. Hodgson if he meant some flying weapon. Dr. Hodgson said that he did, and there the matter stood, so far as events in Boston were concerned. This was on January 28, 1901. When he made inquiries later as to what had happened in England, he ascertained that the daughter, Miss Helen Verrall, had received no vision of either a hand and book or a hand and spear. But Mrs. Verrall's record of automatic writing on January 31, 1902, three days after Dr. Hodgson had sent the message, contained the following script in Latin and Greek, the first word being a mongrel of neither language.

"Panopticon *σφαιρᾶς ἀτιτάλλει συνδέγμα μυστικον. τί οὐκ ἐδίδως; volatile ferrum — pro telo impinget.*"

On February 4, the communicator through Mrs. Piper said that he had succeeded in getting "Sphear" through to the daughter Helen. This statement is not correct; but it is apparent that Mrs. Verrall got the exact idea, except for the hand, in the words "*volatile ferrum — pro telo,*" with the word *σφαιρᾶς*, which is the Greek for "sphere," representing the misunderstanding in Boston of the word "spear," which Dr. Hodgson had given and which had been mistaken for "sphere."

The significant point here is, that what was started in English was translated into Greek and Latin when delivered in England, with the same mistake there that had been made in Boston. *Volatile ferrum* is the Latin for "flying iron," or arrow, and *telum* (ablative *telo*) is the Latin for javelin or *spear*. The remainder of the message shows the filling that comes through the transmitter or the subconscious of Mrs. Verrall. The chief points lie in the coincidences between the words "spear" and "sphere" at one end of the line and *volatile ferrum — pro telo* and *σφαιρᾶς* at the other end. No serious difficulty is met in the mistake about "sphear" in the sitting with Mrs. Piper on February 4th. That is a natural error on the part of the subconscious, which had started with the impression that Miss Verrall was the subject of the experiment. In fact, this mistake and that of transforming the word "spear" into "sphere" and putting it in Greek in England is in favor of a spiritistic interpretation of the coincidences, as it would be natural in the complicated circumstances under which such a message has to be transmitted. But the reader can judge of all this for himself.

A similar mistake in regard to the personality through whom a message was intended to be delivered was made in the St. Paul cross-correspondence. Dr. Hodgson purported to be communicating through Mrs. Piper in England when Sir Oliver J. Lodge was present as sitter. It was the communicator, Dr. Hodgson, that proposed the name of *St. Paul* as an experiment, saying that he would go to Mrs. Holland and deliver this message at once.

This was on November 15, 1906. But no reference to St. Paul appeared in the work of Mrs. Holland. By this time, however, Miss Helen Verrall, like her mother, was doing automatic writing in foreign languages. On January 12, Miss Verrall received the following in her automatic writing. It began in Latin and ended with the statement wholly unconnected with it: "The name is not right, robbing Peter to pay Paul? sanctus nomine quod efficit nil continens petatur subveniet."

There is the mention of the name St. Paul here to suggest the possibilities, but it does not prove the int ention. But, on February 26, the following came, making rather evident the intention of the reference. Readers should notice how it is buried in a mass of apparently irrelevant matter. The first passage shows that a peculiar device had to be adopted to get the name through, if it refers to the cross-reference at all, and I have several times observed in the work of Mrs. Chenoweth a similar circuitous method. Here is the second passage.

"A tangle of flowers with green grass between wall flowers, pansies, which such hurry. Did you know that the second way was shorter. You have not understood about Paul. Ask Lodge. Quibus eruditis advocatis rem explicabis non nisi ad unam norman refers hoc satis alia vana. A tower of ancient masonry with battlements."

The intention here is unmistakable, especially since the reference has no logical connection with its environment, save as this environment is explanatory. In connection with the reference to St. Paul on January 12, Mr. Piddington, who writes the article, translates the Latin to mean: "Holy in name (i. e. with the title of saint) what she (or he) is doing is of no use (i. e. by itself). Let the point (*continens*) be looked for; it will help." The Latin words of February 26 he translates to mean as follows: "By calling to your aid what learned men will you explain the matter? (You will not explain it) unless you refer to one standard. This is enough; more is useless."

Mr. Piddington adds that the names Peter and Paul do not occur elsewhere in the automatic writing of Miss Verrall, so that it seems reasonable to suppose that the cross-reference is intentional.

As stated above, the writing of Mrs. Holland did not contain the name St. Paul, but Sir Oliver Lodge notes that, on December 31, there is an approach to the subject, which is thought to suggest an explanation of the words in Miss Verrall's script. The statement in the writing of Mrs. Holland was: "II Peter I: 15. This witness is true. It is now time that the shadow should be lifted from your spirit — 'Let patience have her perfect work.' 'This is a faithful saying.'"

The verse II Peter I: 15 is: "Moreover I will endeavor that ye may be able after my decease to have these things always in remembrance." It is quite apparent that this verse is not relevant to the name of St. Paul, though the references and quotations following it are more or less relevant. This fact was noted by Mr. Piddington and the relevance of the remainder of the statements. But Rev. Dr. Walter F. Prince, in a review of the whole cross-correspondence in connection with the name of St. Paul, calls attention to a possible mistake in the reference to the Epistle of Peter by showing that, if it had been "II Peter III : 15" the reference would have been extraordinarily apt. He assumes that the mistake was "one" for "three," or "first" for "third," assuming an auditory transmission. The verse reads: "And account that the longsuffering of our Lord is salvation; even as our beloved brother Paul, according to the wisdom given unto him, has written unto you." Dr. Prince notes that this reference to St. Paul is not only direct, but also that it is "the one verse in the midst of 166 Petrine verses, and that it is likewise the only verse mentioning him out of 734 which make up the body of the non-Pauline epistles." The possible significance of this fact is apparent when we note that the other several passages referred to have special relevance to St. Paul. The expression, "This witness is true," Dr. Prince notes, is in St. Paul's Epistle to Titus, I : 13, though similar expressions are found in St. John. "This is a faithful saying" occurs at least three times in St.

Paul's Epistles, according to Dr. Prince, and he adds a fourth instance. He also explains how the other two statements are reminiscent of St. Paul, but we need not emphasize the fact beyond recording Dr. Prince's opinion. As the main coincidence is clear, we need not stress the more enigmatical coincidences. It is only our knowledge that such circuitous methods are often employed that allows or requires us to tolerate or admit the cogency of the connection. The instance is the least cogent of the cross-correspondences.

Another instance may be briefly cited. At a sitting on January 16, 1907, with Mrs. Piper, Mr. Piddington asked the communicator, who happened to be Mr. Myers, to attach a sign to any message he got through as a cross-correspondence, and suggested that this sign be something like a circle and a triangle. "A circle and a triangle inside it appeared in the script of Mrs. Verrall at the foot of a remarkable communication embodying a successful cross-correspondence" on January 28, 1907, just twelve days later than the date of Mr. Piddington's suggestion. As he had mentioned Mrs. Verrall and Mrs. Holland as subjects for the experiment, this coincidence has much value, especially as showing that the circle and the triangle were signs of a cross-correspondence message. The automatic writing of Mrs. Holland did not show any circle and triangle in it; but on May 8, 1907, it did show geometrical figures, among which were a circle and a triangle, though the triangle was not in the circle. Mrs. Piper was in London, Mrs. Verrall in Cambridge, and Mrs. Holland in India.

This instance, however, as we have noted, is connected with the next, which is so complex that its meaning is unmistakable to all careful readers. It is called the "Hope, Star and Browning" incident. It will be apparent also that more than one personality is probably concerned in it. On February 11, 1907, came the following at a sitting with Mrs. Piper, Mr. Piddington being the sitter and Mr. Myers the supposed communicator.

Did she [Mrs. Verrall] receive the word "evangelical"?
("Evangelical"?)
Yes.
(I don't know, but I will inquire.)

I referred also to Browning again.
(Do you remember what your exact reference to Browning was?)
I referred to Hope and Browning. I also said "star." [Interruption.]
(Now, Myers, I must say good-by, as the friend is here.)
Meanwhile look out for "Hope," "Star," and "Browning."

On returning from the sitting, Mr. Piddington examined the record of Mrs. Verrall and found there on an earlier date, January 28, 1907, evidence of allusion to this cross-correspondence. On the next day, February 12, he asked Mr. Myers, the communicator, about the word "evangelical," as it had no meaning to him. Mr. Myers explained, without any suggestion from Mr. Piddington, that it was an attempt to give the name, Evelyn Hope.

He then quotes from the two records of January 23 and 28, 1907, to show the reference to "Hope, Star and Browning," though in an indirect and enigmatical form, showing evidence of the presence and influence of Dr. Hodgson. I quote first the record of January 23, 1907.

"Justice holds the scales. That gives the words, but an anagram would be better. Tell him that — rats, star, tars and so on. Try this. It has been tried before. RTATS, rearrange these five letters, or again t e a r s. s t a r e: s e a m, s a m e, and so on. Skeat, takes, Kate's, Keats, stake, steak. But the letters you would give to-night are not so many — only three — a s t."

The explanation of these anagrams will follow the next quotation, as a similar process is involved in that record. It is the sitting of January 28, 1907.

"A s t e r [star], τέρας [wonder or sign]. The world's wonder, and all a wonder and a wild desire — A WINGED DESIRE ὑπόπτερος ἔρως [winged love].

"Then there is Blake and mocked my loss of liberty. But it is all the same thing — the winged desire, ἔρως ποθεινός [passion] the hope that leaves the earth for the sky — Abt Vogler for earth, too hard, that found itself or lost itself — in the sky. On the earth the broken sounds, threads, in the sky the perfect arc. The C major of this life. But your recollection is at fault."

[Then follows an arc with the triangle in it, and then a full circle with the triangle in it.]

Both these passages are in the records of Mrs. Verrall. The indication that Browning is meant lies in the allusion to Abt Vogler. Mrs. Verrall recognized this allusion, but did not know what it meant, not knowing that any cross-correspondence had been attempted. Note that this occurred on January 23, nineteen days before the matter was alluded to through Mrs. Piper on February 11. The passage from Browning is not correctly quoted in the message. The word "hope" is in it, but instead the word "passion" is in Browning. This idea is recognized in the Greek word for "love" or the god of love. The line in Browning is: "The passion that left the ground to lose itself in the sky." Mrs. Verrall queried if ὑπόπτερος was an attempt at "bird," as it means "winged," and did not remark what Mr. Piddington notes, namely, that 'bird' is suggested by the line in Browning, which runs, "O lyric Love, half angel and half bird." This line in Browning precedes the words in Mrs. Verrall's record, namely, "And all a wonder and a wild desire." Thus the passage is packed with Browning, and the word "hope" is found in one of the statements.

The anagrams contain a remarkable intimation that Dr. Hodgson was behind a part of the cross-correspondence. They had no meaning to Mr. Piddington, but finally he remembered having seen something of the kind among the papers of Dr. Hodgson when he was in America settling the affairs of the American Branch. He found on investigation that he had kept a paper on which several of these very anagrams were made by Dr. Hodgson himself while living. Several papers containing them had been destroyed, but he had happened to keep one of them. On it is the list of words: "Star, tars, rats, arts, tras." Besides it contains "tears" and "stare," and the word "aster," which is the English for a species of flower, and the Greek word for "star," which comes out through Mrs. Verrall, is an anagram play in the Greek on the word for wonder or sign, serving at the same time for a transition to Browning. It throws much light on the process and the subliminal action of the medium's mind.

But the cross-correspondence did not stop here. Miss Verrall had not been told what was happening. One day she got in her automatic writing the drawing of a star with the following:

"That was the sign she will understand when she sees it. diapason, δια πασων ρυθμος [rhythm through it all]. No arts avail. The heavenly harmony ως εφη οπλατων [as Plato says]. The mystic three and a star above it all. *rats* everywhere in Hamelin town. Now do you understand. Henry."

It was Browning who wrote the "Pied Piper of Hamelin," and in the passage quoted there is not only a definite allusion to "star," but there is also the allusion to "rats" and "arts," two words in the anagrams mentioned through Mrs. Verrall. For brevity's sake I omitted one statement in the quotation which, in Greek as it was given, means "a foreign physician"; the "Pied Piper" cured Hamelin of its plague of rats. The same circuitous reference to Browning, apparent in the automatic writing of Mrs. Verrall, appears here. We have then three psychics alluding to the same complex group of ideas; the circumstances not only prove the cross-correspondence, but also show very clearly the difficulties in communicating.

The evidence for cross-correspondence is not the best. If it were as direct and meaningful as desired, there could be no skepticism based on the ground that the connections are fantastic and circuitous, or dependent on the interpretation of the reader. But, while some concession must be made to critical readers, the difficulty is not very apparent in the next instance, which is called that of "Crossing the Bar." It requires some preliminary explanation.

Mrs. Verrall had been struck with some indication of the personality communicating in the messages of Mrs. Piper; and, knowing that her personal acquaintance with Mr. Myers before his death precluded trusting her own messages reflecting his personal characteristics, she resolved on a test which would eliminate the subconscious knowledge of Mrs. Piper and perhaps strengthen the evidence for the presence of Mr. Myers. She looked about for something to use at a sitting with Mrs. Piper, that might provoke a significant reaction from the alleged Myers as communicator. She required a sentence or words which Mr. Myers would naturally recognize and which Mrs. Piper would not understand. Finally she hit upon a few words from a passage in Plotinus, used as a motto to a poem by Mr. Myers himself. The words were *καὶ* αὐτὸς οὐρανὸς ἀκύμων, or, spelled in English, *kai autos ouranos akumon*, meaning "the very heavens calm." Mrs. Piper did not know Greek, and so she would not be able even subconsciously to know the meaning of the terms when uttered to her control in the trance. Armed with these Greek words, Mrs. Verrall went to Mrs. Piper on January 29, 1907, and gave three of the words to the supposed Myers, omitting the first of the four, *kai*. She expected some reference to the following:

1. A translation into English of the three words.
2. A reference to Myers's poem on Tennyson.
3. A reference to Plotinus and the latter part of "Human Personality," the title of Myers's great work.

On January 30, at the sitting with Mrs. Piper, Mrs. Verrall received an allusion to a "haven of rest," purporting to come from Mr. Myers; and it was thought that it contained a remote reference to what was wanted. But this is only conjectural, as it may be a plainer English version of the expression "celestial halcyon days," another cross-reference having some associations with the present subject. Not until March 6, were distinct traces of the translation noticeable. In the meantime, Mrs. Verrall's automatic writing had taken up the subject and discoursed about it in a remarkable manner with results that seem evidential in some instances, though much of the matter is exposed to the suspicion of being subconscious production. The details would make too long a story here. But the messages purporting to come from Mr. Myers through her script refer to Tennyson's "In Memoriam" and his poem on Lucretius, both of which in some passages have affinities to thoughts in Plotinus. Though Mrs. Verrall had read Tennyson's "In Memoriam" in her college days, she had no suspicion that there were passages in it referring to Plotinus, until she re-read the poem in order to discover them. Passages from Tennyson's "Lucretius" were introduced very directly into the automatic script; they were almost a literal translation of the ideas in the three Greek words she had given Mr. Myers at the sitting with Mrs. Piper. This circumstance, of course, is not evidential; but these very ideas came back through Mrs. Piper, who knew nothing about either the Greek words or the relation of "In Memoriam" and "Lucretius" to their meaning. These records extend from February 12 to March 11, while the communicator was silent on the matter all this time, in so far as Mrs. Piper's communications were concerned, except that on March 6 Mrs. Piper's trance personalities began the translation and the system of pertinent cross-correspondences. I quote Mr. Piddington. He alone was at the sitting.

"On March 6, Myers, in the course of announcing various cross-correspondences which he claimed to have transmitted to Mrs. Verrall, gave without explanation three words, 'Cloudless, Sky, Horizon,' followed by the phrase: 'a cloudless sky beyond the horizon.' In the waking stage Mrs. Piper uttered the words: 'moaning at the bar when I put out to sea.' A little later she pronounced the name 'Arthur Hallam'; then almost directly said it agani: 'Arthur Hallam. Good-by. Margaret,' Margaret being Mrs. Verrall's Christian name."

The mention of Arthur Hallam, the subject of "In Memoriam," was very pertinent here. Mr. Piddington adds in his remarks:

"Though no claim was made to have given a translation of the words of the test question in the phrase 'cloudless sky beyond the horizon' it would be difficult to suppose that chance had furnished so satisfactory a paraphrase as this of αὔτος οὐρανὸς ἀκύμων (kai autos akumon); but preceded as the phrase was by references to Mrs. Verrall and followed by the quotation from 'Crossing the Bar' and the name 'Arthur Hallam,' it is practically impossible to attribute its appropriateness to chance. Moreover, this paraphrase seems to indicate knowledge not only of the meaning of the three words of the test question but also of their original context."

Mr. Piddington then quotes the whole of the original passage from which the three words were taken and shows that the Greek word for "air" preceded that for "heaven" and that the latter meant what was beyond the air; as we in English often use "sky" for the region occupied by the air, the phrase "beyond the sky" points to a knowledge of the whole passage.

At this time Mrs. Verrall had not consciously grasped the meaning of her own automatic writing in connection with the references to "Arthur Hallam" and "Crossing the Bar." It was March 12 before she saw the connection. On March 13, at a sitting with Mrs. Piper by Mr. Piddington, Myers communicating drew lines which were said to represent a bar, evidently referring to Tennyson's poem or indicating an attempt to make a sign at the end of a cross-correspondence. But nothing more of importance seems to have come until April 29, when Mrs. Verrall herself was present. At this sitting the only item of interest in this connection was a reference to "azure" and "blue sea," perhaps not as cogent as may be desired, but apparent to careful students of the record. No allusion was made to Plotinus or to "Human Personality." On April 30, however, when Miss Johnson was present at a sitting with Mrs. Piper, Rector, the control, said:

> "I have seen Mr. Myers and he gave me his reply to your Greek words and I gave them to the other lady before you appeared. Tell her to speak them. All right. Homer's 'Iliad.'"

Later in the sitting Mrs. Verrall came in; she was given the name Socrates and was told that it reminded the communicator of Homer. At first Mrs. Verrall thought the allusion to Socrates and Homer's "Iliad" was nonsense. "But later in the day," says Mr. Piddington, "a dim impression came to Mrs. Verrall, after thinking it over, that in the second volume of "Human personality," close to the passage about the vision of Plotinus in which occurs the translation of the words *kai autos ouranos akumon* (Greek letters given in original) was an allusion to the famous vision of Socrates, in which the woman of Phthia addressed him in a line from the 'Iliad.'" An unmistakable allusion in Mrs. Verrall's own script of the next day, May 1, to the "eagle soaring above the tomb of Plato"—a phrase descriptive of Plotinus, quoted in the ninth chapter of "Human Personality"—led her to investigate further with the following results.

> "In the last two chapters of 'Human Personality,' twice and twice only, is the word 'vision' used; the first time, of the vision which came to Socrates in the prison house, when the 'fair and white-robed woman' had 'given to Achilles's words'—'On the third day hence thou comest to Phthia's fertile shore'—'a more sacred meaning'; and the second time of the vision of Plotinus."

It should be added that the passage is translated in "Human Personality," but the words of it were not mentioned in the book, so that any supposed reading of the book by Mrs. Piper is not a valid criticism. But one more message was required to complete the reference desired by Mrs. Verrall, and that was the name of Plotinus. She told Mrs. Sidgwick and Miss Johnson of this defect; and, just when Mrs. Sidgwick intended to tell the trance personality at her sitting of May 6 that the name of the author was wanted, Mr. Myers, purporting to communicate, said.

"Will you say to Mrs. Verrall — Plotinus." The last word was not deciphered by Mrs. Sidgwick, and was thereupon repeated in large letters, PLOTINUS. Mrs. Sidgwick then asked: "What is that?" and Myers replied: "*My answer to autos ouranos akumen.*" [*akumon*].

This completes the data necessary to clinch the cross-correspondence, and, whatever readers may think of its evidentiality, it bears unmistakable indications in its complications and indirections of being what it claims to be, though I can quite understand that the incident may seem inconclusive to those who assume that communication with the dead should be more direct and obvious, if it is to be convincing.

The next instance of cross-correspondence is especially interesting because it involves the giving of the contents of a posthumous letter before the person who wrote it had died. By a posthumous letter we mean one written by a living person and sealed, so that no living person normally knows the contents; the intention is, if possible, to reveal the contents after death. The contents in this case purported to be given by Mr. Myers while he made an experiment in cross-correspondence with the contents. To understand the significance of the case, we should know some preliminary facts.

Mr. Myers, when he read the work of Stainton Moses, was impressed by one incident, very important if genuine. Mr. Moses, when doing some automatic writing, asked Rector, the control, if he could read the contents of a book; on his answering in the affirmative, Mr. Moses put him to the test, and, if we accept the account of Mr. Moses, he succeeded in a remarkable manner. Mr. Moses named the book, the shelf on which it stood, the number of the book and the page from which he wanted some passage read. Mr. Moses did not himself know what was on the page. When Mr. Myers heard of this phenomenon, he at once thought that, if such a thing were possible, it would be very difficult to prove the identity of any discarnate spirit who gave the contents of any document as evidence. He at once saw the relation of the possibility to posthumous letters, and came to the conclusion that the proof of survival would depend upon the concordant results of a large number of insignificant facts from different sources. He, therefore, based his method of deciding the question upon a system of cross-correspondences which should rightly articulate in illustrating the personal identity of a given person. After this discovery he did not attach so much value to posthumous letters as he had done before.

After his death, evidently with some sense of humor, he proceeded to prove his theory by giving messages which illustrate cross-correspondence and the obtaining of the contents of a posthumous letter. I summarize the facts in tabular form. On July 13, 1904, Mr. Piddington sat down in the office of the Society and wrote out his posthumous letter, which contained references to the number seven, and expressions including it. He said that he would try, after death, to communicate a written number seven, adding: "I should try to communicate such things as: 'The seven lamps of architecture,' 'The seven sleepers of Ephesus,' 'unto seventy times seven,' 'We are seven,' and so forth." He went on to say that he seemed to have an organic interest in the number seven, and that it might have made such an impression on his mind that he would be able to recall it as a spirit, if he survived. With this explanation and the date of the letter, the following table will explain itself. It represents the dates and contents of automatic writing through the several psychics named.

The force of the coincidences referring to Mr. Piddington's letter will be more apparent if we quote the whole of the passage that came through Mrs. Verrall on July 13th, 1904. The whole passage runs: "It is something contemporary that you are to record — note the hour — in London; in London half the message has come." Then after referring to the posthumous letters of Mr. Myers and Professor Sidgwick, the passage ends with a reference to Mr. Piddington as follows: "Surely Piddington will see that this is enough and should be acted upon."

There are certain marked weaknesses in this instance of cross-

(1) THE POSTHUMOUS LETTER.

DATE.	WRITER.	INCIDENTS.	POSSIBLE ALLUSIONS TO LETTER.
July 13, 1904.	Mr. Piddington	Mr. Piddington writes Letter.	In London half the message has come.
July 13, 1904.	Mrs. Verrall.		Contrast between potency of dead and living.
July 15, 1904.	Miss Verrall.		

(2) REFERENCES OF AUTOMATISTS.

DATE.	WRITER.	INCIDENTS.	POSSIBLE ALLUSIONS TO LETTER.
May 8, 1908.	Mrs. Piper.	We are seven. Seven of us in the distance.	
May 12, 1908.	Mrs. Piper.		
July 23, 1908.	Mrs. Holland.	There should be seven in accord.	

(3) DANTEAN ALLUSIONS.

DATE.	WRITER.	INCIDENTS.	POSSIBLE ALLUSIONS TO LETTER.
Aug. 6, 1907.	Miss Verrall.	A rainbow: the sevenfold radiance.	He himself will seem to have transferred this.
May 11, 1908.	Miss Verrall.	We are seven. Many mystic sevens. Jacob's ladder. Seven candles and seven colors in the rainbow.	
June 11, 1908.	Mrs. Frith.	The mystic seven and the golden candlestick.	
July 23, 1908.	Mrs. Holland.	Green beyond belief—Green Ray.	
July 24, 1908.	Mrs. Home.	Seven times seven and seventy seven.	

(4) ASSOCIATION AND OTHER EXPERIMENTS.

DATE.	WRITER.	INCIDENTS.	POSSIBLE ALLUSIONS TO LETTER.
Aug. 28, 1907.	Mrs. Verrall.	Let Piddington choose a sentence and send a part to each.	
Jan. 27, 1909.	Mrs. Verrall.	Has Piddington found the bits of his sentence scattered among you all?	

correspondence. The dates of the incidents create a doubt about the intention; and the Dantean allusions, though they contain frequent mention of "sevens," do not assure us by anything said about their reference that they were meant to indicate Mr. Piddington. We have only the contents of the messages to suggest him, and the skeptic probably would not be satisfied that they have this import. But the allusion to Mr. Piddington in London and to the hour, with other references to sevens make it fairly probable that his posthumous letter, written at the time of the first reference, was meant. The allusion, if accepted, shows that Mr. Myers was trying to prove that deceased persons might read the contents of posthumous letters before their writers had died, and so might impersonate the writer. In this way, while the securing of the contents of posthumous letters of the living or the dead might disprove telepathy between the living, it would not prove personal identity and might be explained by telæsthesia or clairvoyance by either the living or the dead. Apparently to emphasize this theory, Mr. Myers, on January 27, 1909, remarked in his message: "But even if the source is human, who carries the thoughts to the receivers? Ask him that." He had mentioned Mr. Piddington in the message, which shows exactly the same conception of telepathy as that mentioned in a message through Mrs. Chenoweth on November 28, 1911, when he actually used the word "carry" for the process and said that it was the "guide" or "familiar" that "carried" or transmitted telepathic messages. This aside, however, the main point is that in this real or apparent cross-correspondence he is demonstrating that not the posthumous letter, but the articulation of bits of evidence through a large number of psychics, is the crucial evidence for survival. The whole episode is remarkable on any theory; and, quite apart from the question of cross-correspondences, it gives good evidence of the personal identity of Mr. Myers.

I think I can give some instances of cross-reference in which the bare statement of the facts will carry the weight of evidence. Those already quoted require so many explanations that many people will not fully appreciate their value. The main point is the accuracy with which they point to the literary and classical tastes of Mr. Myers as he was known to his colleagues.

A lady whom I have called Mrs. Quentin, who was a person of good social standing in New York, was able to use the ouija board. At a sitting with her on October 4, 1906, four other persons being present and only three of us at the table, the following was spelled out. George Pelham purported to be present and controlling the messages.

(Well, George, have you seen any of my friends recently?)
" No, only Richard H." [Richard Hodgson, then deceased.]
(How is H.?)
" Progressive as ever."
(Is he clear?)
" Not very."
(Do you mean when he communicates or in his normal state?)
" Oh, all right normally. Only when he comes into that wretched atmosphere he goes to pieces. Wonder how long it will take him to overcome this."
(Do you see Hodgson often?)
" Yes, our lives run in parallels."

Mrs. Quentin knew about both George Pelham and Dr. Hodgson, so that this message is not evidential. The allusion to his going to pieces in our wretched atmosphere is pertinent, as it was quite true of him up to that time, in all the messages I had heard from him. But the passage has interest in the light of what follows.

On the tenth of October, six days later, without revealing a word of my experience with Mrs. Quentin, I had a sitting with Mrs. Piper. Dr. Hodgson purported to communicate soon after the preliminaries.

" I am Hodgson."
(Good, Hodgson, how are you?)
" Capital. How are you, Hyslop, old chap?"
(Fine.)
" *Good,* glad to hear it. Did you receive my last message?"
(When and where?)
" I told George to give it to you."
(Was that recently?)
" Yes, very."
[After some further statements irrelevant to the present issue I put another question.]
(What light was it that George spoke about?)

[I thought of the Smead case, expecting something would be said about it.]

"He spoke about this [Mrs. Piper] and the woman you experimented with."

[G. P. did speak spontaneously of the Piper case at the sitting with Mrs. Quentin and also made some pertinent and true statements about the Smead case, agreeing with what he had said about it through Mrs. Piper some years before; the facts had not been published and hence were not known to Mrs. Quentin. After a further interruption the communication continued.]

"Did you hear me say George?"

(When?)

"At the lady's."

(No.)

"I said it when I heard you say Van."

(Was that the last time I had an experiment?)

"Yes, we do not want to make any mistake or confusion in this Hyslop."

(Did G. P. communicate with me there?)

"*He certainly did.* Wasn't that Funk?"

(No, Funk was not there.)

"Was it his son?"

(No, it was not his son.)

"It resembled him, I thought. I may be mistaken, as I have seen him with a light recently."

(Do you know anything that George said to me?)

"I cannot speak his exact words, but the idea was that we were trying to reach you and communicate there."

(Do you know the method by which the messages came to us?)

"We saw ——"

[Mrs. Piper's hand ceased writing and began to move about the sheet of paper exactly as did the hand of Mrs. Quentin when she spelled out the words by the ouija board. The most striking feature of this resemblance was the tendency of Mrs. Piper's hand to move back to the center of the sheet, as Mrs. Quentin's always did after indicating a letter.]

(That 's right.)

"You asked the board questions and they came out in letters."

(That 's right.)

"I saw the *modus operandi* well. I was pleased that George spelled his name. It gave me great delight. I heard you ask who was with him and he answered R. H."

(I asked him how you were.)

"He said first rate or very well. I am not sure of the exact words. Do you mind telling me just how the words were understood. Was it very well or all right?"

(The words were 'progressive as ever.')

"*Oh yes!* I do not exactly recall those words, but I heard your question distinctly, Hyslop. I leave no stone unturned to reach you and prove my identity. Was it not near water?"

(Yes.)
"And in a light room?"
(Yes; that 's correct.)
"I saw you sitting at a table or near it."
(Yes, right.)
"Another man present and the light was near you."
(Yes.)
"I saw the surroundings very clearly when George was speaking. I was taking it all in, so to speak."

The reader can see for himself without any explanation the connection between the two sittings. I have only to say that I do not know any one by the name of Van and nothing was said about such a person at the sitting with Mrs. Quentin. Nor was Dr. Funk present. He might have been experimenting about that time, as he was doing much work on the subject. Dr. Hodgson knew something of the man, Mrs. Piper little or nothing. The record indicates the correct incidents and all that we need to know is that Mrs. Piper could not have known the facts.

At the end of the message I saw my chance to have another cross-reference; and, as I had previously made arrangements to have a sitting with Mrs. Chenoweth, my first and made for me by another person, who did not give my name, I at once took up the matter as follows:—

(Now, Hodgson, I expect to try another case this afternoon.)
"Chenoweth." [Real name written.]
(Yes, that's right.)
"I shall be there, and I will refer to *books* and give my initials R. H. only as a test."
(Good.)
"And I will say 'books.'"

I was alone at the Piper sitting. Mrs. Piper was in a trance, from which she recovered without any memory of what had happened or has been said during it. Three hours afterward I went to Mrs. Chenoweth, who did not know that I had been experimenting that day with Mrs. Piper and who did not know who I was. The communication through Mrs. Chenoweth was by speech in a light trance, not by automatic writing. It must be remembered in reading the record that the process was pictographic and that the control or the subconscious must interpret the mental pictures which come to his or her mind. After a few preliminaries in which I said nothing about my work, the following came, just after the mention of an unrecognizable name.

"Beside him is Dr. Hodgson. It is part of a promise to come to you to-day, as he had just been to say to you he was trying not to be intense, but he is intense. I said I would come here. I am. I thought I might be able to tell different things I already told. Perhaps I can call up some past interviews and make things more clear. Several things were scattered around at different places. [Correct.] He says he is glad you came and to make the trial soon after the other."

[I put a pair of Dr. Hodgson's gloves which I had with me in Mrs. Chenoweth's hands.]

"You know I don't think he wanted them to help him so much as he wanted to know that you had them. You have got something of his. It looks like a book, like a note book, with a little writing in it. That is only to let you know it."

[At this point the subject was spontaneously changed and I permitted things to take their own course, and a little later the previous subject was resumed.]

"There is something he said he would do. He said: 'I would say like a word.' I said I would say — I know it is a word. Your name is n't it? [Apparently said by psychic to the communicator.] I said I would say — each time the word slips. [Pause.] I am afraid I can't get it. It sounds — looks as if it had about seven or eight letters. It is all shaky and wriggly, so that I can't see it yet.

"Can't you write it down for him so I can see? [Apparently said to the communicator.] C [Psychic then shakes her head. Pause. Psychic's fingers then write on the table.] Would it mean anything like 'Comrade'?"

(No.)

"He goes away again."

(All right. Don't worry.)

"Let me take your hand."

[Said to me: I placed my left hand in the psychic's.]

"No good. I'm trying to do it. I know that he has just come from the other place, and kept his promise to say a word."

This passage also explains itself as an apparent, but unsuccessful, attempt to get his name. He was able to indicate that he had promised "at the other place" to come here. The talk about a book requires no explanation. But in the course of the communications I got also a reference to "a pen which he carried in his pocket." He had referred at the sitting with Mrs. Piper to a "stylographic pen" which he had always carried in his pocket, while his pencils were carried in his bag. The "stylographic pen" was specially kept for the Imperator personality to use in the automatic writing through Mrs. Piper. It was, therefore, pertinent to mention it in both cases.

I went again that evening to see a young girl who was just developing psychic power. She did not know that I had had any sittings on that day. I had carefully concealed the fact from her and from her mother, purposely conducting the experiment in a manner to make them think I had just arrived in Boston. I put Dr. Hodgson's gloves into the girl's hands and she began immediately to talk about books. The coincidence with the other two sittings is apparent, but I did not secure further evidence of the connection.

I should perhaps add one more cross-reference, to which I have referred before, but which is so good that it should perhaps be repeated in detail and with its complications:

On February 7, 1900, at a sitting with Mrs. Piper, soon after I had had a sitting with a psychic whom I thought to be a fraud, my father, evidently alluding to the experiment, gave me a pass sentence in a language which Mrs. Piper did not know, and suggested that, unless I received it at first in any such experiments, I need not try for it. On March 7, 1901, I conducted an experiment with Mrs. Smead. She was the wife of an orthodox clergyman, exempt from all suspicion of trickery, and in no respect a professional psychic. In her trance, when my father purported to communicate, I asked for the pass sentence. After some struggle I got the first word of it very clearly, probably the second word, and a letter or two of the third, but certainly not the whole word. Mrs. Smead also did not know the language in which it was to be written. On May 31, 1902, I had a sitting with a lady whom I shall call Miss W——, an assistant to a physician. In the course of the sitting the communicator came to the sentence spontaneously and without a hint from me. The following is the passage.

"I doubt if I can give you the one thing you most desire this moment.

(What do I desire this moment?) [I was not conscious of any particular desire.]

"The sign, well not exactly password, but the test. If you will keep motionless, I can be able to give even that. I shall not be able to give that and much else without the full coöperation of the messenger. Let us not ask too much, James."

It was called both a "password" and a "test" in the records of Mrs. Piper, which had not been published at that time. It is clearly referred to here, though not given, and the allusion is evident in the expression, "coöperation of the messenger." Imperator always called himself a "Messenger" in the work of Stainton Moses and Mrs. Piper, and Miss W—— had seen none of the work of either of them. Besides, Imperator always claims to help the communicator when he is present and his aid is needed. Miss W—— knew nothing of these circumstances.

Later still, the date is not important, I had an experiment with another person who knew nothing about the facts, as they had not yet been published; and, on my asking for the pass sentence, she also not knowing the language in which it was to be written, I got the English of it.

In quoting incidents which establish personal identity, I shall give first an illustration of the difficulties attending the application of the telepathic hypothesis to the facts. It involves events which happened in various parts of the world and yet purport to come from the only person who ever had the knowledge of them all in his mind.

A lady of whom I had never heard in my life wrote me from Germany asking if I could recommend to her a psychic, saying she had lost her husband and in her distress of mind wished to be convinced of a future life, hoping that communications from her deceased husband would convince her of it, if he actually survived and could communicate. I replied to her inquiry that I did not know of any psychic in Germany, but that I could give her sittings when she returned to America. She replied that she could not come to America, but that she had a sister living in Boston who might take the sittings in her place. I then wrote her for name and address of this sister and asked her to send me an article wrapped in a special covering and said I would arrange for the sister's presence in due time. I had never heard of her husband, who had been a teacher of philosophy in a small western university of which also I had never heard. This institution was on the Pacific coast. He fell ill there and went to Germany, his native place, where he died.

As soon as I could fix dates for sittings I did so and arranged for the lady's sister to see me at my hotel at a certain hour on the date of the first sitting. I did not tell her whom we were to see or where we were going. I never give sitters any information of the name or address of the psychic. I also put her into a trance before admitting the sitter. These conditions were observed on the occasions of the present sittings. The following facts summarize the results.

As soon as the automatic writing began, the letter O was written, or the circle which had been used for the sign Omega by Professor James in his communications three years before. After the circle had occurred several times the sign of the cross was made inside or over it. I recognized its import but said nothing in recognition, though I saw no reason for its appearance on this occasion. I had never known nor heard of the communicator I was seeking and knew not whether he had any connections with Professor James. The sequel showed that they had been personal friends, and the significance of the circle and the cross was indicated in response to my query a little later, when I wanted the record to explain its significance. When the desired communicator broke down, Jennie P. came in to write; in the course of her automatic writing I asked her what the circle and cross meant, though knowing well enough. Her reply was, " W. J.", and I was satisfied that these were the initials of Professor James, as they have nearly always been used to denote him.

The giving of the circle and the cross was followed by a short communication from Imperator intimating that he soon expected to fulfill a desire of mine with reference to another case which I had brought to Mrs. Chenoweth, wanting the judgment of Imperator on it. Immediately following Imperator came another communicator. It took some time to make clear that I was on the right track. I simply let the communicator take his own course. The very first sentence took the right direction.

"I will try to write for her, for it is good to have the chance to do so. We are four over here in a loving group this morning. One woman, three men, all so anxious to tell her about the life we remember and the life we live now. There are others who wish to come, but they will wait.

"I am not entirely new to this belief and neither is she and her own experiences ought to help at this time."

(Yes.)

"I know the questionings of her intellect and also her belief in the power, and I would not scoff nor laugh now, but rejoice that the time is given me to try my own power."

(Good.)

"I did not want too much of this talk before, but I cannot get enough of it now. I did not want to die. I don't know as any one does, but any way I wanted to live and accomplish things and finish my work, but it was no use, I could not weather the gale."

The first sentence implies that it was a lady who wished to hear from the communicator. Of course a lady was present, and the critic will say that the psychic knew this and that the reference on that account has no significance. But we must remember that the psychic had not seen the sitter, neither in her normal state nor in her trance, and had no means of knowing whether it was a man or a woman who was present, unless she guessed from hyperæsthetic perception of her walking upstairs and into the room, or the slight noise from the movement of her dress when coming into the room. But Mrs. Chenoweth never shows this power in other instances. In fact she is very often normally mistaken about the situation, sometimes thinking a person is present when he is not, or thinking none there when a sitter is present, and sometimes, I might say always, ignorant of the sex, unless told. Besides, a little later, after a few sentences, the communicator referred to the lady who wished to hear from him as "belonging to me," an expression constantly used in this work to denote husband or wife, and hence not applying to the sitter, though a guessing medium might try the phrase for leverage. But he soon remarked that his "father was over here," which was true of the communicator. Soon after this statement and some general and non-evidential messages the communicator gave up and was followed by Jennie P.

As soon as I could ask Jennie P. what the circle and cross meant, she replied by the initials "W. J.," which were correct. She then made some flings, in her humorous way, at cross-references, and then proceeded with the following statements:

"Did you know that the lady is psychic?"

(No, I did not.)

"She has had some experiences of her own. I do not mean with other lights, but alone, and she really has clairvoyant power, if it were only unfolded; but she is one of those cautious kind and does not want to let her imagination run away with her. Do you know anything about a mother in the spirit?"

(Yes, his mother is dead.) [Sitter nodded head.]

"And there is such a desire on her part to come here to-day. She has been gone some time and she has not much acquaintance with this sort of business. Is that true?"

(That is correct.) [Sitter nodded head.]

The communicator's wife, not present but in Europe, is quite psychic, a fact that I did not know at the time. I learned it from inquiries after the sitting. She had had a number of experiences of her own and it was probably these that induced her to apply to me. She distrusted her own experiences, fearing that they were imagination or subconscious action. Her mother was dead, a fact not known to me, but known to the sitter. Her mother was of a very religious nature and had known nothing of these phenomena.

The communications went on with some correct, though not striking, statements about this mother, among them that the communicator had "a deep reverence for his mother." This was followed by a reference to the sitter implying, though not asserting, that she was his wife. Jennie P., acting as an intermediary, made the statement with this implication and I did not correct it. I then asked what the nature of his work was and the answer by Jennie P. was that it was "philosophical" and that "he philosophized about everything." This was true. He was a teacher of the subject. General messages of a non-evidential character followed, until I was asked whether I knew any one named William with whom the communicator was associated. I replied by the query whether it was "W. J." and Jennie P. at once answered that she did not know it was he and proceeded to say that she would leave, but finished with the statement:

"Just as I said I go, he put his hand to his mouth and I saw a cavity as if one or two teeth had been extracted and the funny part of it was that I saw him take them out himself. It looks as if he had something happen to his teeth. Did he have a tooth which he lost and had replaced by a new one?"

(I don't know.)

"It seems to be a space about big enough for one, perhaps two, but not more than that and here is something about some dentistry which involved that space."

This incident came suddenly and apparently irrelevantly. Of it the widow writes: "He lacked just one tooth, but the cavity was not visible. He had, however, a tooth filled in Portland, Oregon, about a year ago, and was very much dissatisfied with the dentist and refused to pay the exorbitant price he asked."

Nothing more came in the automatic writing, but the first thing that appeared in the subliminal stage of the recovery was the capital letter T., which was the initial of his name. The subliminal, however, suspected the name Theodore, which was the name of the communicator of the week before. I denied that this was correct when asked by the subliminal if it was, but I said no more.

The automatic writing of the next day began with general observations on the communicator's new life and experiences, as if he were merely practising until he could get control; he then made an allusion to my desire for evidence and at once began the effort to give it.

"There was a great deal of pain in my head. I could not seem to think clearly, so much confusion, you know what I mean."

(Yes perfectly.)

"And the confusion of ideas made everything seem unreal and some of the things I said were meaningless, like one talking in his sleep. Still I was not asleep nor yet irresponsible entirely. It seemed as if there were more people about than there really were, but just at the last moment there was peace and hush and no more hurrying to and fro. I longed for home."

Mrs. Tausch writes in regard to this statement that he did suffer a great deal of pain in the head and that a short time before his death he was delirious and talked incoherently at the last. When she arrived at his side she was not sure that he recognized her. There were only two at his side when he died, Mrs. Tausch and her sister-in-law.

The messages continued immediately with reminiscences of the last illness, one or two of much interest. The allusion to his longing for home implied that he died away from it, a fact which I did not know. But to help make the allusion clear I began with a question.

(Did you not pass away at home?)

"No, I did not mean that I was away from home, so much as that it was not like home at all and the noise of the feet on the floor troubled me. You know what I mean, the footsteps, first on the carpet, then on something bare.

"I wish to recall something gray which was thrown about me as I was lifted up to take something from a cup. It was only a partial lifting but this gray garment was over my shoulders. So weak I could not do it myself."

He then evidently attempted to refer to his mother, who was dead, and then referred to his children as living.

He left two children when he died. He died, not at his home in America, but at his old home in Germany. Mrs. Tausch thinks that walking on the floor disturbed him, but she was not a personal witness of the fact. He was constantly getting up and sitting wrapped in his mother's gray dressing-gown. It is probable that he drank medicine or nutriment from a cup. Outside of his sick room was a pretty scene. It was a picturesque village with an old convent in view. Of the children he said they needed him more as an advisor than as provider. The reverse was true. They needed his provision more than his advice at their young age. But he went on with his message.

"I wish to prove to them all that I was not a fool to be interested in this belief of spirit. You know what I mean."

(Yes.)

"It is not so easy to prove as it is to believe."

(Yes, that is right.)

"I also had some records I had been much interested in."

(Yes, do you mean they were your own?)

"No."

(Whose?)

"Others. My personal experience was limited."

(Yes, do you know whose records they were?)

"Yes, J. had some."

(Let me be sure what the J. is for?)

"My friend James."

Now Professor James was a friend of the communicator, and Mrs. Tausch wrote in response to my inquiries that Professor James had given them records to read and that they had done so. Of course I knew nothing of this fact, and indeed nothing of the man and his life.

This message was followed by a reference to a long country road with birch trees on its sides, a stone wall, and the road winding round a hill.

He intimated also that he had suffered from shortness of breath, apparently caused by climbing the hill referred to. Mrs. Tausch says he did walk over such a road the last year of his life, but there were no birches on it. He suffered from shortness of breath, caused by asthma, not by climbing the hill, though the latter would probably produce the same effect. He then referred to his wife with an initial B., which is a letter in her name, but not significant here. He referred to himself as a philosopher, which was correct, and then to "some things near an old furnace," which could not be verified. He referred to Harvard and Columbia Universities, claiming to be a graduate of Harvard, which he was not. But he had visited both universities and knew the head of the philosophy department at Columbia. He referred to the name Fiske and connected it with a place which he said his wife would know, saying that the man was dead. He had patronized the Fiske Teachers' Agency. I have not been able to verify the death of the man. But he went on with other incidents.

"Does she remember how I used to fuss about clocks? I wanted them to be right. Does she not know what I mean?"

(She does not know.) [Sitter, sister-in-law, shook her head, knowing nothing about his private and domestic life.]

"I was always fixing things. [Hand then seized the article on the table which was a purse enclosed in oiled silk.] My purse."

(Yes.) [Might have detected it by touch.]

"Well, well, that ought to bring a man to his senses. I am getting hold a little now, but is it not hard work?"

(Yes.)

"My books, does she not know about my books and library, so many of them which have been annotated for use. T h T." [Pencil fell and control lost.]

Mrs. Tausch says that he did fuss about the clocks a great deal, especially a cuckoo clock which he always wound up. As to annotating his books Mrs. Tausch says: "Well, he was the greatest man for that. He always read with *pencil in hand*."

The letter is the initial of his name and "h" the last letter in it. As he came to the end of his message he evidently tried to sign his name, but broke down, and the automatic writing came to a close.

In the subliminal recovery, reference was made to "Rome in New York." The sitter knew no reason for referring to it, but Mrs. Tausch, though she could give no special meaning to it, said that he had travelled about New York State lecturing in various places, and Rome may have been one of them. A further reference was made to Niagara Falls and Mt. Tom with a house on it. Also a yellow building was described, with the intimation that it was on Mt. Tom. This house is not recognized by Mrs. Tausch, as having any meaning, nor has the reference to Niagara Falls. But Professor Tausch visited Little Falls, in New York, and, in a mental picture, which was the method of communication employed here, this mistake might easily occur and influence the subliminal. Mt. Tom Mrs. Chenoweth knew nothing about save that such a place existed. It seems that the reference to Mt. Tom has no relevance to Professor Tausch, but he had visited Mt. Chocorua, on which there is a conspicuous house. Mrs. Chenoweth knew the latter very well, having taught in that locality.

At the beginning of the next sitting, after a few general remarks while getting control, the communicator gave the following incident:

"Do you know about a man younger than I, still alive in your world, most near to me and my work, C—— yes C—— and I want to write about something which was done by a group of men in connection with my death, resolutions and something in the way of a tribute which was sent by my associates to the family. You know about that."

[I asked the sitter whether she knew about this, but she shook her head.]

(I don't know. I shall inquire elsewhere.)

"Yes, I knew about it and it was a pretty thing to do and I wonder if she knows who M is, alive. Ask her M."

(Yes.) [Sitter nodded head and said: "My name is" . . . I waved my hand before she uttered it and stopped her.]

"Dear to me and alive, that is what I mean."

(What relation to you is this M?)

"When you ask a question, every spirit in the room begins to answer mentally and that knocks the pins out from under me. You know I told you it seemed to be a mental process and every man here has his head on his shoulders and hears your question. I will do the best I can."

Later the relationship was stated, and the message went on with a new incident to be given presently. The initial of the lady present was M. I did not know it myself. But it is the incident given just prior to this initial that is most interesting. The sitter knew nothing about it and Mrs. Tausch writes me regarding it,

" His death was published in Ohio papers and I was asked by a former fellow-professor — not a close friend — whose first name was Clement, to send biographical notes of his life. Besides there came a great many letters of condolence with handsome tributes to him." The communicator's position as a teacher was, as indicated, in Oregon, not Ohio, so that the incidents here mentioned refer to friends who knew him in another State.

Without a break then the new incident was taken up:

"I want to speak about a glass and a small bag in which I carried papers, manuscripts, and the glass was a magnifying, reading glass. Ask her if she recalls either of those, the bag I used to put other things in, but the papers went to the bottom always."

(I shall ask about it.)

"And I recall trying to do some work just before I came here. That you probably know already."

(I myself do not know it, and perhaps you had best tell just what it was.)

"I had planned and arranged to do some particular work and tried to complete it, but it was beyond my strength."

Mrs. Tausch writes regarding these incidents: "He carried a bag in which he put his manuscripts. He did not use a magnifying glass, but carried eye glasses in his bag and always lost them. He had planned an essay on 'The Relation Between Science and Religion.' But he died before he could do anything with it. An American college offered a prize for such."

It is probable that the eye glasses magnified somewhat, so that Mrs. Tausch, not understanding the pictographic process of communicating, may not have noticed the approximate truth of the communication.

There followed a long passage which had many characteristic hits in it, though mainly expressed in isolated words. For instance, he referred to ethics and his interest in the subject, which his wife says was one of his passions. He also intimated his reason for staying in the church though his own creed was too liberal for strict adherence, and he gave as his reason for remaining in the church against his liberal creed that it was better to be associated with the good than with those who disregarded it. This was true of his career in life. The name Lizzie came in the same connection; it was the name (Elizabeth) of his living wife; he said that she was alive. The sitter, however, thought he was giving the name "Leslie," which she recognized, and so spoiled the completion of the reference. He described a brick church, but the wife does not recall it.

Then came the effort to give his name. I got, without any help on my part, variously Taussh, Tauch, and Taush, once "Tucah" and once "Tach." The reader will see that I got all the letters and two or three times the name phonetically. I then began speaking German to him and I got a few disjointed replies in German, among them the relationship of the sitter to him: "Geschwister," and a few other words. Mrs. Chenoweth does not know German, save four words: "Federmesser," and "Wie viel Uhr," the latter of which she speaks incorrectly.

Then a reference was made in the subliminal to the railway and a long trip, and the statement was made that after his death his body was taken on a railway. This was not correct. Perhaps the whole passage should be quoted.

"Do you know where there is a long stretch of railroad track?"

(No.)

"A long long track."

(Where?)

"Oh, I don't know. Wait a minute. Has there been a spirit here whose body was taken on a railroad track after his death?"

(No.) [Sitter shook her head to my inquiry.]

(That spirit who has been here did not have his body on the train, but perhaps some friend of his did.)

"No, it seems connected with him, connected with him just near his death. I can't get it very clearly. I seem to want to go to his grave. There are two or three trees there that look like evergreens and are in some sort of a conical shape right near his grave. They don't grow that way, but are cut in conical shape."

Professor Tausch took a long railway trip from Oregon via Quebec to Germany just before he died and was physically exhausted by it. He returned to Germany because of bad health in connection with asthma. Probably this incident got confused with the reference to his grave, as he was trying, pictographically, to give an account of these last events. Mrs. Tausch knew nothing about the evergreens and so I asked her to have photographs taken of his grave. This was in Silesia. She directed that my request be fulfilled and when I received the photographs conical shaped evergreens were visible not far from the man's grave.

There were minor points of interest, but it would require the whole record and much comment to bring out their significance. What I want to emphasize is the fact that the incidents required confirmation by correspondence with Mrs. Tausch, who was in Germany and who was the only person who knew the facts, and even she did not know some of them, inquiry having to be made in Silesia to verify them. The believer in telepathy will have to stretch that theory inordinately to meet the situation, and that is the value of the facts; namely, that they put that process to its wits' end to vindicate its rationality.

Another case is interesting because it involves something like a cross-correspondence or cross-reference, and also contains a complication of some interest because of the connection between remote personalities.

A man in the practice of international law had a lady, Miss De Camp, as his secretary. She developed automatic writing and was soon writing stories purporting to come from the late Frank R. Stockton, who had died in 1902. Miss De Camp's work began in 1909. The stories were sufficiently like those of Mr. Stockton, despite subconscious influences, to enable Mr. Henry Alden, the editor of "Harper's Monthly," to say that they were "very real." Mr. John R. Meader, who had specially studied Stockton, said that the stories were "very characteristic." There were occasional indications of personal identity in the expression as well as the plot of the stories. But, as Miss De Camp had read "The Lady or the Tiger" when she was a small child, though nothing else of Stockton's, we had to allow for the possible influence of latent subconscious knowledge. When I learned that the New York "World" was going to publish some of the stories, I resolved to make some cross-reference experiments before the stories were made public. I therefore took Miss De Camp to Boston and had her registered in a hotel under an assumed name. I then took her to Mrs. Chenoweth under the conditions so often described. Miss De Camp entered the room after Mrs. Chenoweth was in the trance, and left it before Mrs. Chenoweth recovered normal consciousness.

At the first sitting the name "Frank" came. This was referred to several times before he communicated directly; then I got the name "Frank Richard Stockton," with some confusion about Richard at first. This was the middle name, not consciously known to either myself or Miss De Camp. He also gave Francis, which was his real name, not given in the "Century Dictionary." He then told when and where he died; namely, in Washington, D. C., in April. He discussed at some length the work he was doing with Miss De Camp, showing that he was the source of her stories, whatever allowances be made for the influence of her subconscious, which, it must be said, is not apparent to any large extent.

There were many touches of personal character and wit, though these were probably colored by the influence of the control and the subconscious of Mrs. Chenoweth; but one passage in this vein will be interesting and serve as an example of many more. I had brought up the question of skeptical critics in order to make him see, as a communicator, the necessity of evidence for personal identity more specific than a general avowal of what he was doing through Miss De Camp.

"I really have a desire to do a certain kind of work, but deliver me from the class who cut up their relatives to see how their corpuscles match up.

"I think I won't do for your business at all, but personally I have no fight with you. You can go on and save all the critics you can, but don't send them to me when they die."

(All right.)

"For I would make no heavenly kingdom for them. I had my share of them while I lived, and I wash my hands of the whole lot."

(I understand.)

"I do remember some pleasant times I had with my little friend when I was alive. That sounds like an Irishman's toast, does n't it; for I would hardly be talking unless I were alive. Do you know the Irishman's toast?"

(I don't think I do.)

"May you live to see the green grass growing over your grave. Do you see the comparison?"

There is much that is more evidential than this passage, but it would require too much explanation to quote it here. The next point of interest is the appearance of the man who had introduced me to Miss De Camp. He was Mr. George F. Duysters. When living, he had taken his secretary, Miss De Camp, with the family on a strolling trip in the mountains, and Miss De Camp had asked for a drawing of the scene where they had camped near a stream of water. Mr. Duysters was a good draftsman, and drew a rough sketch of the place, intending some day to finish it. It consisted of a hollow stump with a charred hole in its side, some lines for the stream of water, an outline of a small fir tree, the covered wagon with three circles for the wheels. It was put away for keeping. But before he had finished the drawing, Mr. Duysters died. Soon afterward he purported to communicate through Miss De Camp, and one day she heard a voice say, "Fetch the picture and I will finish it." Miss De Camp got it and taking her pencil automatically finished the picture. She drew a double tree on the stump, drew the pot and hook used for cooking their meals, drew the dishes on the rectangular outline which represented the table cloth, the meaning of which she had not noticed in the drawing, finished the fir tree, put in the stones, bank and lines for the water in the stream, inserted the spokes in the circles for the wheels, drew the fourth wheel, and behind the wagon made a tree to which they had hitched the horse. I had all this, picture and all, in my files before I took Miss De Camp to the sitting.

But Mr. Duysters and the drawing and the scene itself were so well known to Miss De Camp that I could attach no evidential value to the communication from him and the finishing of the picture through Miss De Camp. However, he appeared through Mrs. Chenoweth and gave his full name, George F. Duysters; and, as soon as this was done and because it was the last sitting, I at once put to him a query to see if I could get a reaction bearing more completely on his personal identity, with the following result.

(Do you remember drawing a picture for the lady?)

"Yes, I do, and I will try and do more some time. I have to have more exact conditions, more than some, but I can work at some places and some times."

(Yes, what was that picture?)

"Trees and water, you know, and that is the sort I like. It was an illustration of a time and place of other days. I will come again to her and here also, but I cannot stay now. I finished it. Yes I finished it, the picture, I mean."

(I understand perfectly.)

"I thought you meant the name, George F. Duysters."

It is especially significant that both personalities should appear to communicate. They are not in any way connected with each other in life, and neither of them were relatives of Miss De Camp.

There is another complicated incident which is practically an instance of cross-reference, but is quoted here because of its relation to the associated physical phenomena, and the difficulties of explaining it by the telepathic hypothesis.

I had given a lady some sittings with Mrs. Chenoweth. The first four of them were quite unsatisfactory. This was in December, 1912. The fourth sitting was on Monday. On Tuesday morning I was awakened in my hotel by hearing *raps* on the headboard of the bed in which I was sleeping. I suspected that the noise was made by my breathing or heart action on the springs of the bed, though I had never heard them before in spite of the fact that I had slept for years in that bed. I determined to test the matter and lay perfectly still, trying not to move a muscle, and at intervals stopping and starting my breathing. When I discovered that the raps often continued when I had stopped breathing and stopped at times though the breathing went on, I saw that the breathing was not the cause of them. I then asked a *mental* question: "Is any one rapping?" There immediately followed three loud *raps,* the second and third having a very short interval. I then again asked a *mental* question: "Will you spell out a message?" The answer was a whole volley of raps on the bureau ten feet distant. They could not have been produced by my breathing or heart action. I then began slowly to go over the alphabet *mentally;* that is, without saying the letters aloud. When I reached certain letters there was a single distinct rap; this occurred at the letters which spelled *cat*. When this was done the raps ceased.

In the morning I wrote out an account of what had happened, and then experimented on the bed, first by lying down on it and shaking my body in various ways to see if I could produce similar noises on the springs; but I totally failed to produce any such sounds. I then kneaded the bed with my hands in every direction, and failed again. I then tapped on the headboard of the bed with my knuckles, and obtained exactly the same quality of sound that had occurred in the raps. I wrote out these facts in the record.

On the way to the sitting I told the lady what had happened; she showed decided interest, but did not tell me why. Arriving at the place for the sitting, the sitter, as usual, waited down stairs until Mrs. Chenoweth had gone into the trance, and was then admitted. In the subliminal stage of the trance, Mrs. Chenoweth saw an apparition of Dr. Hodgson. He lingered, and as I had not heard from him for a long time, I bethought myself that he had some reason for appearing. I therefore asked him, through the psychic, of course, if he wanted to say anything; the answer was, that he and G. P. were trying to " give undeniable proof of identity to his mother and some *post mortem* facts which would clear up the mystery." The pronoun " his " was the first intimation of personality at this series of sittings, and referred, as later allusions show, to the deceased son, from whom the sitter wanted to hear. I then asked Dr. Hodgson if " he knew whether any one was in my room last night "; the answer was, that he himself had been there, but " was merely a spectator of a manifestation made by Jennie P., one of the controls." The subconscious then got the impression that some moving object was involved, and, though this impression was wrong, I did not correct it. Automatic writing then followed. After preliminaries, the communicator said " the boy was there," meaning in the room, and said he wanted to do so much. But Dr. Hodgson did not succeed in telling me exactly what had happened. In a few moments the control evidently changed and I got the words: " Was ich eine mutter," [What I a mother] and my deceased wife followed with the statement: " I thought I could write something myself." She knew German well; Mrs. Chenoweth did not know it at all. Then there was again a change of control and the boy began communicating in the automatic writing. He soon wrote: "I knew if I could knock or rap then that you would take notice and it would be a good evidential . . . ," and then went on making allusion to the noises and their purpose. In a few moments came the following words: "Was ich die Katzie," imperfect German for "what I the cats." The boy also had known German, I learned later, but the mother, not knowing it, did not appreciate this allusion until it was converted immediately into English by the communicator, who added: "I thought you would see [that] the meaning of any unusual sound was always the cat." The sitter at once broke down sobbing, as she saw the point, but did not explain a feature in the incident which I did not know at the time. After we left the house she told me that for the previous two months and for the first time in her life, she had been so deeply interested in cats that her petting them and giving them catnip on the street had brought them into trouble with the police who, thinking they had hydrophobia, had taken them to the pound. She had never before had any interest in cats.

I then told her that, years before, when I had stayed all night at her home in a Western city, I had been awakened in the morning by hearing raps on my pillow, and that I turned over and over again to stop them, without success. I added that I had written out an account of the facts and filed it without telling her about the incident. She admitted that I had not told her, and added that the boy had died in that room — a fact, of course, which I did not know.

The complex interest of these facts is apparent without explanation on my part, except that we can hardly account for the raps in my room at the hotel by telepathy, and we cannot accuse the medium of fraud without implicating myself as in collusion with her. The sitter will testify that I did not know of her interest in cats, so that it appears as if the interest itself had been instigated on the other side and the rest of the phenomena planned to get results which would prove to the sitter's suspicious mind — for she was very suspicious — that the facts would have no easy explanation. The chief interest of the incident is just that fact. It does not prove the personal identity of the boy. It proves only the association of mental and physical phenomena, unless you wish to regard the raps as hallucinatory. I should not object to that. They systematically spelled out the word cat, and were veridical, as the experiment at cross-reference showed; as hallucinations they would have the same evidential import as genuine physical phenomena, in so far as spiritistic explanations are concerned. The main point is their complexity and the difficulty of normal explanation.

CHAPTER XIV

ROBERT SWAIN GIFFORD

THE present chapter will summarize a set of phenomena which I have usually described as the "Thompson Gifford Case." It is not necessary to regard it as giving a final solution of the problems which it suggests; it is presented here for the sake of its psychological interest and any other conclusion which it may help to establish. The case came to my attention in the manner described below; in giving the account of it I shall follow the chronological order of events.

Some time in the summer and fall of 1905, Mr. Frederic L. Thompson, who was a goldsmith, not an artist, was suddenly and inexplicably seized with an impulse to sketch and paint pictures. Accompanying this impulse were numerous hallucinations or visions of trees and landscapes which served as models for his work.

Mr. Thompson had had no training in art. He had obtained only the slight education which the public schools give a boy until he was thirteen years of age. He had had a few lessons in drawing, such as the public school give. He then had to go to work, and was employed as an apprentice at engraving. He served at this work for some years. His employers discovered that he had some taste at sketching, and the foreman of the department encouraged this as a means of helping Mr. Thompson at his engraving. While employed at this task, Mr. Thompson formed what may be called a partnership with an artist to turn photographs into oils. Mr. Thompson did none of the finishing; his partner, Mr. Macy, executed the artistic work of the paintings. Only a few photographs were finished in this manner, as the work did not prove remunerative. This was the last of Mr. Thompson's experiences with anything like painting until, in the summer of 1905, the impulse seized him to sketch and paint. The meantime was spent in his work as a goldsmith, which he took up in New York City after he left New Bedford, Massachusetts. His experience with turning photographs into oils had taken place a number of years before.

It is apparent that he had had no education nor important experience in painting, so that whatever merits his painting may have do not represent the usual result of education and practice. When he was seized with the impulse to sketch and paint he seemed to lose his interest in the work of a goldsmith and began to show some unusual powers as an artist in oils. While he did this work he often felt that he was Mr. Gifford, Robert Swain Gifford, and remarked to his wife at times, "Gifford wants to sketch." He did not know at this time that Mr. Gifford was dead. He had some years before been slightly acquainted with Mr. Gifford, having met him once or twice on the marshes about New Bedford while Mr. Gifford was sketching there, Mr. Thompson himself being out hunting. He talked with him a few minutes only on one of these occasions, and on the others merely saw him sketching. Once he called on Mr. Gifford in New York to show him some jewelry, but saw nothing more of him.

Between the period indicated, the summer and autumn of 1905, and the latter part of January, 1906, Mr. Thompson kept on at his sketching and painting. In the latter part of January he saw notice of an exhibition of the late R. Swain Gifford's paintings at the American Art Galleries and went in to see them. He learned at this time and not before, that Mr. Gifford was dead. Mr. Gifford had died on January 15, 1905, some six months before the impulse seized Mr. Thompson to sketch and paint. While looking at Mr. Gifford's paintings on exhibition he seemed to hear a voice, apparently issuing from the invisible, say, "You see what I have done. Can you not take up and finish my work?" This incident may be treated as an hallucination or as a fabrication, unless evidence can be produced to make it credible. Whether genuine or not it had sufficient influence on the mind of Mr. Thompson to induce him to go on with his sketching and painting. From this time on the impulse to paint was stronger, and between this date and the next year he produced a number of paintings of artistic merit sufficient to demand a fair price on their artistic qualities alone, his story being concealed from all but his wife.

In January, 1907, Mr. Thompson came to me with the fear that his visions and hallucinations were threatening his sanity. He had been constantly the subject of them ever since he saw the exhibition of Gifford pictures, and a scene of gnarled oak trees haunted him perpetually, with the strong impulse to paint them. He drew several sketches of them, but the insistence of these visions made him begin to doubt the normal condition of his mind. I interrogated him for two hours on all aspects of his experiences, which included the story just told. As I saw no evidence of anything supernormal in the account, I diagnosed it as disintegrating personality, that is, some type of hallucination and a symptom of mental disturbance. I advised him not to continue the work of painting, but to go on with his vocation as goldsmith, as I could not see any reason to believe that he could well earn his living in painting, especially if he had to explain how he did his work. Besides, I feared that the tendency, if not due to morbid mental conditions, would not last. But, since it would require time to prove whether the case was one of morbid hallucinations, and since we might never know, until an autopsy would show, what the real trouble was, it occurred to me that I might take a shorter path for finding out what was the trouble. The incident of hearing a voice in the American Art Galleries suggested that view of the case which many instances on record in the publications of the English Society for Psychical Research indicate, namely, the hypothesis that the dead may occasionally intrude their influence upon the living. There was no evidence of this in the story of the voice as Mr. Thompson narrated it. But I saw that an interesting set of alternatives was placed before me. I had no way of proving that his visions and the voice were purely subjective hallucinations without waiting, possibly for years, to watch their development. On the other hand, it suddenly came into my mind that I might test the matter in a very simple manner. I thought that, if the hallucinations were really inspired by the source apparently claimed for them, I ought to get traces of Mr. Gifford through a medium. If I did not get any trace of him the presumption would be all the stronger that the phenomena were ordinary and not supernormal. As a consequence I asked Mr. Thompson if he had ever seen or consulted a medium. He replied that he had not and that he always despised the subject of spiritualism, laughing at it with others. I further asked if he would go with me to a medium, and he replied in the affirmative.

This was on January 16, 1907. I immediately arranged for a sitting to take place on the second evening after this, the 18th. I did not tell Mr. Thompson whom he was to see nor where we were going. I had him meet me at my house at a suitable hour and took him to a medium whom I here call Mrs. Rathbun. I introduced him as Mr. Smith and took the notes myself, also requiring Mr. Thompson not to say anything and not to ask any questions until I signified permission. In a few minutes after we sat down the medium apparently described some one whom Mr. Thompson recognized as his grandmother, the evidence not being of the kind to assure any one of its genuineness, and then allusion was made to a man behind him who was said to be fond of painting. No hint whatever had been given of either Mr. Thompson's character or the nature of his experiences. Mr. Gifford was described in terms recognizable by Mr. Thompson, and in a few minutes the locality of Mr. Gifford's birth was described, and a group of oak trees, even to the fallen branches and the color of the leaves that had appeared in his apparitions. The communicator said that it was a place near the ocean, that it was not England, but that you had to take a boat to the locality. It was this group of trees that had haunted Mr. Thompson's vision for eighteen months, and that he had described in our conversation two evenings before. The real group was afterward found in the locality described. It was on one of the Elizabeth Islands on the New England coast. (See Fig. III.)

The outcome of this experiment pacified Mr. Thompson's mind and relieved my own, as to the cause of his hallucinations, and he resolved to go on with his painting. Before this time he had painted only six or eight pictures, but had a large number of sketches, rather crude, all of them, sketches and paintings, being based on his visions. Without telling the story of his experiences, he showed some of his paintings to a few persons interested in art and sold two or three of them. One he sold to Mr. James B. Townsend on its merits and without telling his story. In the course of his examination of the picture, Mr. Townsend remarked that the painting resembled those of R. Swain Gifford; Mr. Thompson then told him something of his story. Soon afterwards he sold another painting, under similar circumstances, to Dr. Alfred Müller, who was pleased with the excellence of the work. This experience, with the encouragement offered by my experiment with the psychic, led him to continue serving the impulse which haunted him.

While Mr. Thompson went on with his work I resolved to make a second mediumistic experiment. I was experimenting at the time with Mrs. Chenoweth, and brought Mr. Thompson to a sitting. He was not admitted to the room until after Mrs. Chenoweth had gone into the trance, and left it before she came out of the trance, so that at no time in her normal state did she see or hear him. At this first sitting some twenty incidents of a coincidental character were told, many of them bearing on the personal identity of Mr. Gifford. Among them was a reference to his fondness for rugs and rich and flesh colors, a reference to a tarpaulin which it was his habit to wear when boating and painting, and more or less definite accounts of his relation to Mr. Thompson, the sitter. The latter could not be given any important evidential value, as some things were said, or implied by Mr. Thompson's questions, which might have suggested this influence to the subconsciousness of the medium. The facts mentioned about Mr. Gifford's private habits are more suggestive; but there were incidents even more pertinent than these. Reference was made to his sudden death, his unfinished work, to the condition of his studio, to apparently the same woman who had appeared in the experiment with Mrs. Rathbun, to misty scenes, which were a favorite with Mr. Gifford, and finally to the same group of trees and their locality mentioned above. This passage should be quoted.

Mr. Thompson said to the psychic: "There is a picture of an old group of trees near the ocean. I would like to get it. Can you see it?" He had reference to his vision as before described, and said too much about it for any details to have evidential value.

Mr. Thompson thought that possibly Mr. Gifford had painted such a picture, but he wanted to find where the trees could be found that he might paint them himself. He assumed rightly enough that, if Mr. Gifford were actually present, he might tell where the trees could be found and something about them. The following was the result of the inquiry, taken down by a stenographer at the time, the matter in parentheses representing what Mr. Thompson said:

"Do you think that it is one that he is giving you?"

(I think it is, yes. I feel that I must go out into nature and paint those trees.)

"I want to tell you, little boy, I think he has seen the trees and I think he is giving you the picture of it. I think you will see them too. I don't know the place, but it looks like that to me. When you go up here on this hill, as I told you about, and ocean in front of you it will be to your left, and you will go down a little incline, almost a gulley, and then up a little bit and a jut out. This is just the way it seems. Now you have this so that you can follow, can't you? They look like gnarled old trees. There is one that stands up quite straight, and some roots that you can see, not dead, but part dead. Some are roots and gnarled and then the rest. They are nice."

(Beautiful coloring.)

"O, beautiful! But that is what you will get if you are right on the spot. You will get those soft colors, just like this old rug, that he likes very much that has some soft colors."

When the group of trees was finally found it was proved that this description was perfectly accurate, though it probably would not have led any one to either the locality or the special scene. The account supplements that given by Mrs. Rathbun. When facing the sound or ocean one had the group of trees on the left, and had to go down a little gulley to reach them. They were gnarled oak trees and standing as described. There were no dead roots nor partly dead roots visible. But there was near the ground one dead limb which resembled a very crooked root of a tree. It is represented in Figure VIII. The trees were situated on a little promontory and so a "jut out." When painted in the autumn the trees had colored leaves of the red and brown tones which were favorites of Mr. Gifford. The rug alluded to, Mr. Thompson found at the foot of Mr. Gifford's easel; it contained the same colors as the leaves in the autumn scene which he painted of these trees.

THOMPSON - GIFFORD CASE

Figure I

Figure II

Figure III

Figure IV

Figure V

Figure VI

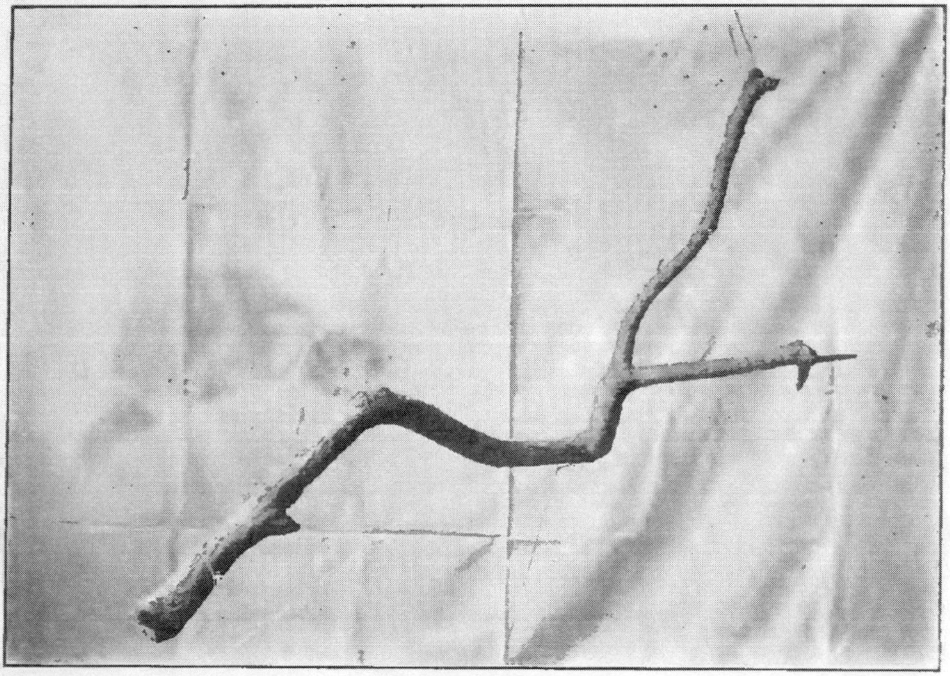

Figure VII

Figure VIII

Sketch from hallucination

Photograph from actual scene

A few things were said that were pertinent to Mr. Thompson and that did not bear upon the identity of the dead. They assumed an influence over Mr. Thompson. For instance, Mr. Thompson was told that he would go out to the place where the trees were and paint them and that he would return when the weather was "crisp and cool." He did find the trees and after painting them returned to New York in December, in the "cool and crisp" weather indicated. This fulfilment of the prediction, however, may be regarded as the result of suggestion.

But I have somewhat anticipated the story. I desired, however, to explain the incident of the trees, and to call attention to the facts which, in this first sitting, gave encouragement to pursue both the investigation and the painting. It is noticeable that these first sittings give evidence of supernormal information; and, as they took place under test conditions, we do not have to raise the issue of the mediums' character. No hint of the communicator's name was given by either psychic. One or two pertinent names were given, but no special importance could be attached to them.

These results sustained the hypothesis which the first experiment with Mrs. Rathbun suggested, and Mr. Thompson resolved to hunt up the scenes of his visions or hallucinations and to paint them. On the second of July, 1907, he, therefore, put into my hands a number of sketches which he had made in the summer and autumn of 1905. I wrote a note to that effect and locked them up in my files. Mr. Thompson first went to Nonquitt, Massachusetts, where he expected to find the scenes which had haunted his visions. He states that he had known nothing about this place, except that it was the summer home of Mr. Gifford. It is situated near his own old home in New Bedford, but is inaccessible except by boat. Mr. Thompson found a few of the scenes of his visions and took photographs of them, but ascertained that Mr. Gifford's favorite haunt was one of the Elizabeth Islands. He then resolved to go out to the islands and to make an attempt to verify his apparitions. But, as fortune would have it, Mrs. Gifford took him into the studio of Mr. Gifford, which had not been greatly altered since his death two and a half years before. To his surprise, he saw on the easel an unfinished sketch, which was identical with one of the sketches left in my hands more than a month before. He said in his diary at the time that it almost took his breath away to see the identity of this painting with his visions and sketches. The reader may observe this resemblance himself by comparing Figures I and II. There were on easels two other pictures identical with sketches which he had made, but which had not been left with me.

The case does not wholly depend on the veracity of Mr. Thompson. He had left the sketch in my hands before he saw the painting by Mr. Gifford. Mrs. Gifford testifies that the picture was rolled up and put away until after Mr. Gifford's death, when it was taken out and put on the easel. Mr. Thompson had had no opportunity to see it, and his impulse to paint did not arise until six months after Mr. Gifford's death.

Mr. Thompson then went out to the islands and accidentally on the island of Nashawena came upon the exact scene of this picture by Mr. Gifford, and painted it. He had never been on this island before and hence had never seen this particular view.

In his rambles over another of the islands, whose name I am not permitted by the owner to give, Mr. Thompson found a large number of scenes that had appeared in his visions. He states, and the evidence is fairly conclusive, that he had never before been on this island. It is extremely difficult for visitors to get to the island without a permit, and Mr. Thompson had to obtain one to visit it. He painted several pictures of actual scenes which he had seen in his visions, and some of which he had sketched from his visions before he visited the islands. Among these is a peculiar group of trees. He stumbled upon them in his wanderings about this island and had started to sketch them, when he heard a voice similar to the one he had heard at the art gallery say: "Go and look on the other side of the tree." Though some sixty feet away he went forward and on the opposite side of the tree found the initials of Mr. Gifford carved in the bark of a beach tree in 1902.

I photographed the initials about two months later and they had long grown up and could not have been cut by Mr. Thompson.

Finally in October he accidentally found the group of gnarled oak trees described by both psychics, and painted it. He had put into my hands a sketch of the trees seen in his visions, as remarked, on the previous second of July (Figure III).

The next problem was for me to find these trees and photograph them myself. The story of their finding should be told in some detail, as the facts tend to make the whole incident more evidential than it would otherwise be.

After some directions as to where I should find the group of trees, said to be near or in the edge of what is called the Black Woods, I went out to the island. I found the place, but no tree like those desired. There were plenty of gnarled oaks and storm blown trees of all kinds, and one group of trees which Mr. Thompson had painted, but no group representing any specific resemblance to Figures III and IV, save in isolated details. I photographed a few trees, thinking that perhaps Mr. Thompson had put trees from various localities together and had made an idealized picture. The specific points of his sketch and painting, however, were not found in what I had photographed. As soon as Mr. Thompson saw the photographs he said that they did not represent the scene he had painted and that the trees he had found were all together just as painted. I therefore took him with me on a second trip to the island, and we went to the same spot. We found the group of trees which he said would serve as a guide to the place where the desired group was to be found. But there was no trace of the trees we were searching for. There was nothing but a sand-waste. We had to give up the search and return home.

The third trip was more successful and contained some interesting episodes. On the second trip, when he failed to find the trees, I remarked to Mr. Thompson that he must have painted the picture from an hallucination; but his reply was, that this was impossible, because he had carved his initials on one of the trees. He conjectured that he might have painted it on the north shore of the island, as the day in question was stormy and foggy. We made the third trip on order to investigate this north shore. We investigated this shore for two or three miles and examined every tree and group of trees, but there was not a trace of any single tree or group of trees that had any specific resemblances to the desired scene. Nor was the shore itself sufficiently like that needed for a technical resemblance. There were gnarled oaks in plenty, but nothing that suggested the picture. We then resolved to sail around the island into Vineyard Sound and examine a small group of trees not investigated on the second trip.

Before leaving New York, Mr. Thompson said to me that he had come to the conclusion that he could never find the trees by himself, and went to consult a psychic, a lady whom I personally know well and who is not a professional in the usual sense of that term. She told him the following, which Mr. Thompson wrote out from memory for me before the steamer left the dock in New York; I had the record in my possession from that time on.

"I see the trees. They are on a rounding bank. The land slopes down. One limb is not there. It has blown away or been struck by lightning. It changes the appearance of the tree."

(Do you see any landmarks by which I can locate them?)

"The water bends around quickly and beyond is where men have been at work. I see something like a round building. I can't see what it is: it may be used for cattle or a bridge, like a rustic bridge. In front is a cleared place, then trees beyond."

(On what part of the island is it?)

"You face the rising sun. I see houses near it. It is not exactly east, when you face the rising sun: it is on your left hand."

(Are there trees near it?)

"When you stand on the bridge and face south they are on the left hand."

The reader may remark some resemblance to the statement by Mrs. Chenoweth, which I have quoted above. I shall not take the time or space to discuss details. But after we had examined the north shore of the island we sailed into Hadley Bay and anchored there, taking a row boat with the purpose of going into Vineyard Sound, and in trying to row under a bridge found the tide coming in so strong that we could not get through. Mr. Thompson threw his coat upon the bridge and helped us to carry the boat around and into the water. He went back for his coat, but instead of getting it took his stand on the bridge, facing east, and, ignoring three separate calls to get his coat and come on, he seemed to go into a sort of trance. Soon he ran down the bridge, leaving his coat there for some one else to get, and ran with all his might around the shore to a small promontory, shouting back that he had found the trees.

He threw into the air the old grocery box which he had said before leaving New York that we would or ought to find on the spot where the trees were. Mr. Thompson's initials were on one of the trees.

We then photographed the trees and the shore. They are represented in Figures V and VI. One of the important limbs presenting a specific characteristic for identification had been blown down by the wind, but was found and tied in its place for the photograph. Another, the S-shaped limb in the tree at the right, had also been broken off by sheep. It too was found. The two limbs are represented in Figures VII and VIII. The limb on the tree at the left, which turns on itself, was not a part of the real scene; but, as Mr. Thompson had always said that he had himself inserted this from another tree, no importance attaches to this discrepancy. But the branched limb on the ground was there, and the cut will show the two large rocks lying in position. The decayed spot in one tree, the one at the left, was there. There was no storm at the time of our visit and hence no such appearance as the picture represents. But the group of trees were a little to the left when one faces the east, and when facing the south there was a wood on the left. The bridge was not exactly a rustic bridge, but had some resemblances to such. On the left of the bridge was a "slope down," which had to be crossed in reaching the promontory where the trees were. The houses were west of this spot and not visible.

The reader will observe from the cuts that there is more distinct resemblance between the sketch which had been placed in my hands in July, 1907, and the painting represented by Figure IV than between either the sketch or the painting and the photographs of the real scene. But the specific characteristics which determine identity are all there, and unmistakably indicate the right trees, though the painting, as is usual, idealizes the scene.

The two most important pictures thus seemed to bear the investigation, and the fundamental question of Mr. Thompson's veracity, which was the first thing to be determined, was settled. Of course there are other important evidences of the supernormal, not connected with his veracity, namely, the mediumistic phenomena in my own experiments. As many of the circumstances described protect the genuineness of the phenomena affecting the two pictures, we may feel less difficulty in accepting other instances where similar identity exists between sketches made from his visions and the actual scenes afterwards found. There were several of these. There was one of a forest, rather dense, which Mr. Thompson sketched from an hallucination and then found on another easel, though he did not recognize it at the time, having forgotten his sketch. There were also two sketches of a seashore and a man with an ox team, and on still another easel in Mr. Gifford's studio was a painting by Mr. Gifford representing the same scene.

Mr. Thompson had many other interesting experiences which he recorded in his diary at the time. When he was on the island searching for the scenes which had haunted his visions, he often heard music like that of a guitar or violin and hunted about to see if it was produced by any one. He found no evidence of any human cause. In fact, there seems to be but one house on the island, except the three or four at the eastern end of it. The island has no population except the two or three families of care-takers. Besides, this music was heard at different times and places on the island, and once Mr. Thompson ran up a hill to see if he could find some one whom he fancied he heard singing, but found no one. Usually the music he heard was instrumental. A friend of Mr. Gifford states that Mr. Gifford was passionately fond of music, especially of the violin. Whether there is anything more than a coincidence in this circumstance must be determined by each one for himself.

These incidents made it necessary to try further experiments with psychics to see if I could obtain more specific evidence of the influence of Mr. Gifford. I therefore held a number of sittings with Mrs. Rathbun and with Mrs. Chenoweth, some of them before the public knew anything about my work on the case. I shall briefly summarize the results, indicating those obtained before the psychics had any means of suspecting that I was experimenting with Mr. Thompson and before they knew anything of the case.

The first sitting was on April 3 with Mrs. Rathbun, and was held before I had made the search for the trees mentioned above. She did not recognize Mr. Thompson, whose first sitting had occurred more than a year before. At this sitting Mrs. Rathbun soon made the following very relevant statement:

"You have been questioned regarding your honesty, so far as intuitions, impressions or — some might call them hallucinations, for you have a very peculiar power."

Then came an allusion to a lady who was said to be influencing him from the other side of life, practically implying what was indicated at the first sitting more than a year before. Then a reference was made to the confused state of Mr. Thompson's "material" conditions — a statement that was exact, if it can be said to describe the effect of these impulses on his financial situation. Then a reference was made to "uniform," which might possibly be interpreted as pointing to the tarpaulin, and then he was told that he had twice nearly passed out of the body. This was exactly true, if his own feelings are to be taken as the guide. When he had finished the painting of the group of trees above described, and called the "Battle of the Elements," he had felt so ecstatic that he could describe his sensations only as dying. This impression was recorded in his diary. At another time he was nearly dashed to pieces while painting the sea in a tarpaulin, and had to lash himself to a rock to keep his position. These facts were known only to Mr. Thompson. The medium mentioned the "hurt or blow" connected with the exposure.

A striking allusion was made to an operation upon a man who was said to be communicating; Mr. Thompson while on the island, had witnessed the funeral of a man who had died from an operation, and the scene had produced a profound emotional effect on Mr. Thompson. There was some confusion by the medium of this incident with the personality of the artist supposed to be influencing his work. Some striking statements were made about a ring which Mr. Thompson was wearing, namely, that he had made it himself and that the stones in it had been changed, and a number of other even more important incidents, which I need not mention except to indicate their irrelevance and yet evidential character for the supernormal.

One little incident of great relevance was mentioned. It was, that there was a little woman who worried a great deal for fear that he would not be practical, and that she wanted to get him into his every-day line of work. Every word of this was true with reference to his wife, and when under this obsession Mr. Thompson was not very practical as the world goes. Then the medium went on to describe exactly the attitude of mind which his relatives had toward his experiences, saying that they thought him going insane and that they "would rather you were more practical than interested in the spiritual," adding that "they cannot stop you, because it is not hallucination or insanity." She added that his work was influenced by spirits about him, though she did not at this time know anything about the case.

A direct allusion was made "to peculiar scenes and visions" and "lots of them" that he had around him, with the remark that some "extraordinary happenings had happened to him within the last ten months." Then came a spontaneous reference to the ocean and a shipwreck and again to his "uniform" and a reference to what must be taken as some one guiding him in his work from the "other side." The pertinence of this reference is apparent, whether it is evidential or not. One remark describes an exact scene in his life, when he was painting on the shore of the sound. The detailed record will be clearer and more interesting than these excerpts, and also will contain a number of incidents which, though not bearing on the issue, do show indications of supernormal information about incidents in Mr. Thompson's life.

At the second sitting there was much relevant matter concerning Mr. Thompson's life, and a reference to a box, said not to be a satchel, but describing Mr. Thompson's means of carrying about his materials. In the first of the two sittings it was clearly indicated that he was an artist, and this idea is made still clearer in this second experiment. The most important allusion, however, was to a Latin word which the medium said had come to him. Mrs. Chenoweth at a later sitting alluded to the same word. Mr. Thompson had had a communication from an alleged spirit, giving the Latin words "*alter ego*," as the influence affecting him, and purporting to come from a lady. There was then an allusion to a woman and a child, representing something that he had seen in his visions and that he would paint. The fact was that, as he finished the painting of the group of trees in the "Battle of the Elements," he saw the vision of a woman and a child interfused with the scene, and had been haunted ever since by the desire to paint this representation of a madonna and child. The statement that he drew much under trees was true and pertinent. There was, however, no definite identification of Mr. Gifford. The two sittings discovered only incidents associated with the life of Mr. Thompson, with a few vague indications of the source from which his apparent inspiration came.

The next two sittings were with Mrs. Chenoweth on the dates of April 10 and 11. Mrs. Chenoweth goes into a light trance for her oral work. Mrs. Rathbun was normal in her sittings. There was a great deal of subliminal "chaff," if I may so describe the non-evidential matter, but interfused with it were incidents that clearly represent supernormal information. Mr. Gifford was fairly well described in several characteristics physical and mental, with some errors, and the intimation was made that he was influencing Mr. Thompson. Mr. Thompson's business was indicated in fairly clear terms. The reference to a woman in the "spirit world" and the entire account of her relation to Mr. Thompson fitted what had been told through Mrs. Rathbun in her first and later sittings and also what was said the year before through Mrs. Chenoweth, though she did not know that I had brought the same sitter. We may assume that her subconscious recognized the man. Mr. Thompson's middle name was given and an allusion, like that of Mrs. Rathbun, was made to his unsettled condition of mind and body, a very pertinent statement because of the embarrassed state of his finances at the time. This was followed by a description of Mr. Gifford's work at painting, evidently to identify him, but the medium wholly misinterpreted it to refer to writing. The incident as understood by her was wholly false. But immediately thereafter she described a pocket-book, brown, old and shiny, long as a bill-book, with papers in it. Later in the deeper trance and by automatic writing the same psychic referred to it again with more details. Mr. Gifford had no such pocket-book, but he did have a sketch-book and in fact many of them, which might be so described. In the later sitting it was said that this pocket-book had a strap about it and contained a burial permit. Mr. Gifford used rubber bands about his sketch-book, but had no burial permit in it. He did carry in his sketch-book a permit to visit the island of Nashawena.

Then came the following statement: "Did you ever have a feeling as if you were away from the body, above everything, sometimes?" Mr. Thompson replied in the affirmative, and further statements refer to the outside influences producing this effect on Mr. Thompson.

Then came the statement: "Another thing. You have got a sort of hearing. It is not definitely unfolded yet, but there are times when you can get strains of music, just as though it floats about you. People don't seem to understand you, do they, around you?" There then followed a long and accurate description of Mr. Thompson's habits at the time, none of it specifically evidential, except the allusion to "dreams that he has sometimes" and to his "throwing himself down at night and looking and trying to see the spirits and as though he felt such dreams." The reader will recognize the relevance of the allusion to music and the "dreams," which apparently refer to his visions; he did at times exactly what is here said, throw himself down and give way to his visions.

The next sitting contains a large amount of pertinent matter, too vague to summarize, and open to the interpretation of inference from admissions by Mr. Thompson. But there were a few incidents specific enough to attract attention. The first was a statement that he, the sitter, had a lot of unfinished canvases, and a reference to a yellow cliff and the blue sea, this being a very definite reference to a picture which Mr. Thompson had painted at Cuttyhunk and which he had long before sketched from a vision. Mr. Thompson had never seen this bluff. Following this was an apparent allusion to Mr. Thompson's occupation as a goldsmith, then to influences from older and deceased artists for which there was no specific evidence.

The next specific incident was a reference to a vision of a woman; no mention of a child is made in connection with it, but he is told that he is to paint this. The reader will recognize the allusion to the vision Mr. Thompson had when he had finished painting the trees, and the similar reference of Mrs. Rathbun. Mr. Thompson was told that in connection with this inspiration he would slip away by himself and cry, and that now, when off alone tears would often come, tears of joy at his work. This statement was true.

But the evidence of personal identity in these sittings with both Mrs. Rathbun and Mrs. Chenoweth is entirely unsatisfactory. There is evidence of supernormal information; and a critical analysis of the whole mass of statements, in spite of its "chaffy" character, will reveal interesting pertinence throughout. But my dissatisfaction was so great that I resolved on a different type of experiments. Those just summarized represented work previous to any possible knowledge on the part of the psychics of what I was doing and of Mr. Thompson's experience. The public, by this time, as a result of my inquiries on the Elizabeth Islands, had learned something of the case; very little that was relevant, however, got into the papers, and nothing that is attributable to that source of information came out in the records. However this may be, it was necessary to experiment further to satisfy the requirement for better evidence of personal identity in the alleged communicator, and the deeper trance afforded me a better opportunity for testing the case. The experiments were conducted without admitting Mr. Thompson to the room until after Mrs. Chenoweth had gone into her trance. The results were much better than before. I summarize them briefly.

It took some time to obtain an adjustment at the first sitting. The communicator who first appeared through the automatic writing purported to be Professor Sidgwick. Not a hint was given of any one related to Mr. Thompson until he moved in his chair; then, as if awakened by this, the medium at once referred to some one near him and began at once to tell incidents related to Mr. Gifford. Allusion was made to a man with a whip in his hand and familiar with horses. This was not especially significant, but immediately following it was a reference to a gang-plank, a steamer, and a trip, not on the ocean, and then to the "wallet" smooth and shiny with the burial permit in it, apparently an allusion to his sketch-book, as explained above. The account of his room and desk with their papers was accurate enough, considering that he taught as well as painted, but it had no value as evidence, while the immediate statement that he had taken a little journey just before he passed away was true and quite pertinent, as he had taken a little trip with Mrs. Gifford just before his fatal illness. When the automatic writing came, the first allusion was to a woman who might have been regarded as Mr. Thompson's grandmother, though she was not evidentially indicated. Then the control took up the personality whom we were seeking and referred again to the journey before he passed out, and added that there were two services in connection with the funeral, which was true of Mr. Gifford. There arose a clear idea that I was seeking incidents to identify this personality. There followed an earnest effort to supply these, though the success for some time was not marked. An allusion was made to certain "black figures, like stellar geography" scattered through a book that was mentioned, which would fit some of Mr. Gifford's illustrating, though the incident cannot be regarded as evidential. Finally the communication became so confused and equivocal that I indicated that the whole thing was perfectly blind; in order to identify the man more clearly an allusion was made by the control to "color, more color, and more again." I hinted that they were now on the right line, and there came an allusion to the "paper hand-book again," with a statement, very true of Mr. Gifford, that the "blue and the sky were always fascinating to him."

At this point there was an apparent attempt on the part of the communicator directly to control the writing himself, but he was unable to effect his object, though he made the remarkably interesting statement that "it was so much of an effort to keep his memory and all the work at the same time." The sitting then came to an end.

As Mrs. Chenoweth came out of the trance she said some things relevant to the identity of Mr. Thompson. She described a large horse and said it was one that he used to ride "back to," with some reference to peculiarities in Mr. Thompson that took him out of the athletic class, though he has an athletic body. All this was true about his riding a horse when a boy, and it was just such a horse as was described. She then stated that he was an artist and made a reference to the influence of colors on him, specifying his love of yellow, which was true.

On the next day there elapsed considerable time before any relevant facts appeared. Apparently the controls tried subliminal methods instead of automatic writing, hoping that identity might be better established by that means than by writing. A great many things were said that were true, but not evidential. The first incident that promised to be valuable was the following:

"I think he smokes. It is something that he holds in his mouth. He does n't seem to be always smoking, but it seems that he holds something in his mouth quite a lot; really, like a — like — I think it is like a cigarette. I think he gets nervous and rolls them up and then holds them there and then sits down and does a little and does that again, just that little nervous anxious way."

Now, as fortune would have it, inquiry showed that Mr. Gifford did not smoke, and, even if he had smoked, the incident would have been without evidential importance. But I learned that Mr. Gifford was in the habit of holding a stick in his mouth when he was at work, rolling it about and chewing it as some people use cigarettes or cigars. The description of the medium does not clearly indicate assurance as to what it is, and the expressions "holds in his mouth" and "does n't seem to be always smoking" suggest the interpretation of the passage in conformity with the facts as I ascertained them.

Then came a reference to a "soft cap, not a skull cap" which might have meant a Scotch cap which he used to wear. The mention of his desire to paint a pearl was not verifiable. But, on being asked to describe the picture that was on his easel, the communicator, or the subliminal of the medium, made the following statement:

"Yes, indeed, I see it. It is quite a good-sized one. Yes, indeed, there is a picture there and it is a picture of a scene. It is not a person. It is a scene and I can see away off in it. It is n't all done, you know. It is partly done, but mostly done so that you can see pretty nearly what it is. Oh, but it is beautiful, you know. But there are some trees in it and there is some foreground that is lighter and then the background seems dark, but some trees and I think I catch some glimpses of light in through. It does n't seem like a scene around here. It seems as though there is some sky in it and that everything is very brilliant. Everything he did is brilliant, brilliant colorings. He likes those things, you know."

The reader may determine for himself the measure of accuracy in this account by comparing it with the cut represented in Figure II. This represents the picture that was on the easel and that corresponds to the sketch which Mr. Thompson made from a vision without ever having seen the original. This original was an unfinished sketch of Mr. Gifford's. The inaccuracy in the account is the reference to the background as dark. But this is apparently corrected by the allusion to light being visible through it. It is possible that the very dark field occupied by the trees might be taken by obscure perception for the background. In any case the other characteristics mentioned do apply to this picture.

The next incident, perhaps as suggestive as that just marked, was the statement: "There is another little thing that stands up, or else it is pinned up, but it is something like a small thing. It is thinner and smaller than the picture. It is not a study of the picture. It is something different and seems to be up on one of the posts."

Now Mr. Gifford had a smaller sketch of this same scene, from which he had painted the larger one represented in Figure II, and it too was on the easel, placed very much as indicated.

After a number of pertinent, though non-evidential, allusions, I was told that he had illustrated poetry and had done work in "black and white," both of which I was able to verify. The allusion to "atmosphere" as characteristic of him was true and suggestive. The reference to his having many unfinished canvases was true and more or less evidential.

After some confused allusions to travel, came an evident attempt to describe his old home and its surroundings. That it was a "goodcolored" house and a landmark was true, and also that there was a "piece at the end"; there was an "L" on the house. That it was inland was true. That he could look over water from it was true and that there was "a lake near where he was" was almost correct, as Hadley Bay, shut up by the surrounding land, looks like a lake. Still more pertinent was the statement that it "had beautiful views around it, and then hills rising soft like billows."

Another incident is very interesting. I quote it in full.

"I want to know if you know anything about a little loft. It seems as though — I have got two places that this spirit worked in; one is off, you know."

(Yes.)

"In the country. One is in the city."

(Yes.)

"You know. Well, do you know anything about what I would call a little loft? It seems almost like going up in a barn or a shed, and there is a smell of hay and a smell of things around, but some things are kept up there — and working there sometimes."

(All right. I think I shall find out about that.)

"It is a place. It is not a house, you know. It is like a place that you go and can open doors wide and look out, upstairs, you know, and it smells of hay."

Mr. Gifford had two places for work, one in the country and one in the city. Early in his artistic career he had a studio in a barn and he and Mrs. Gifford used to work there, as indicated. All the incidents were true as stated, even to the wide doors.

Then the means of communication changed to automatic writing. The communicator was asked, after he had intimated that he was influencing the sitter, whether he knew what particular things he had impressed upon the man. The reply was:

"Of course he knows or rather he knew there was a scene which he was trying to project which he has never yet given. It is a misty day on the old road or a misty day on the marshes. I do not know which. It has come over our friend a number of times that a misty day, a soft gray day would be a good subject."

Every word of this is true. Mr. Gifford had had a great liking for misty days and atmosphere, as perhaps many artists have; but Mr. Thompson states that he has often been haunted by apparitions of misty scenes and days to be painted. This remark was followed by the statement of the communicator or the medium that Mr. Thompson had trouble in selecting his paints, and that he had especial difficulty with his grays, while the yellows turned up more easily. All this was perfectly true.

The next sitting was with Mrs. Rathbun. The first allusion was to a picture, which was said to be at my house; I had only a short time before taken one of Mr. Thompson's pictures to hold it against a cheap sale. It was the "Battle of the Elements." The last incident, indicating the supernormal though not evidence of communication with the dead, was Mrs. Rathbun's allusion to something in Mr. Thompson's pocket, which she said had been cut in Paris. Mr. Thompson had in his pocket some crystals from Paris; it is not possible that Mrs. Rathbun knew anything about them.

Mrs. Chenoweth was the subject of the next sittings. The first evidential circumstance was an account of what was in his house. The medium indicated that he had a lot of old-fashioned furniture in it; that he had some straight-backed rush-bottom chairs, and that there was an old-fashioned bureau "with legs that curve out." Mr. Gifford was fond of old-fashioned furniture, and had in his house such a bureau, with bird-claw legs, and some rush-bottomed chairs.

The next incident is as interesting for its mistake as for its aptness. The medium said that the artist had something "almost like a basket near a shelf with a lot of brushes in it," and that he "kept an awful lot of old brushes," and that when he came to paint "rocks and things that were rough" he resorted to these old brushes, and that he seldom threw a brush away. Mr. Gifford did keep his old brushes and use them in this way. They were not kept in a basket, but in a ginger jar.

When asked whether he had communicated elsewhere he admitted that he had, and indicated the number of times with fair correctness. Then a reference was made to an intended picture for Mr. Thompson, a symbolic painting about the past and the future, which Mr. Thompson took to represent his vision, interpreted to mean immortality. After some apparent effort to recall, the communicator mentioned a man by the name of Cox, saying that he was an illustrator. Mr. Gifford had a friend by this name, but he was an architect, not an illustrator. Mention was made of his having painted a fish, an incident that Mrs. Gifford says was true; in response to the question whether he liked sublime scenery, the reply was, that he liked wild things better, which was true. In a few minutes he or the medium spontaneously indicated that he had painted Dutch scenes, windmills and the like. This was true. The paintings that had made his reputation were of the Dartmouth salt works, with windmills in them, and resembling many of the Dutch paintings. He was said by the psychic to have admired Dutch painting, a statement which seems to have been true.

Then came a remarkable passage which is too long to quote but which is full of evidential matter. Reference was made to "scraggly and gnarled oaks" and "an overhanging bank" with a boat near and "the ocean in front." Mr. Gifford had actually painted such a scene near his cottage. I have a cut of it. It was not the ocean in front, but Buzzard's Bay. Immediately after this came a reference to the "river in back," and suddenly an allusion to the lighthouse there, saying that its light was not one "of the revolving kind," but steady, and that the lighthouse was "straight and white," and was called the "Farmer's Light." It was Dumpling light that was near his cottage. It was white and the light was not a revolving one, but was steady as affirmed.

The account of his painting in storms would have been correct if it had been asserted of an occasional trial, but it applies more fittingly to much that Mr. Thompson had done. After an unsuccessful attempt to describe his house in the city, the communicator described a favorite picture. Mrs. Gifford did not recognize the special picture described, but said that several favorites were, in character, much like the one described.

The communicator said that he had lost a child and that he had once or twice tried to paint the boy's face in some picture. I ascertained that this was true. The name of the child was incorrectly given.

At this point the subliminal communications ceased, and the communicator attempted to control directly, with rather remarkable results. Besides referring correctly to the "blue and disheartened" days through which Mr. Thompson had passed, and to the effort which he, the communicator, had made to influence him, he asked the sitter, Mr. Thompson, the following very remarkable question:

"I have been to him as in dreams at times."

(Yes, I understand.)

"And will do so again."

(Thank you.)

"Ask him if he remembers an incident when, standing on a bridge and looking down, he saw pictures in the water like reflections and a great desire came over him to paint?"

(Yes, he says he remembers that well.)

"I was there and followed him for some time. Sometimes in the old days he was so disheartened and blue, as if had not found the right path, but now he is far happier and life seems more complete."

The reader will appreciate this passage when he knows that, early in his visit to the Elizabeth Islands, as Mr. Thompson stood on the very bridge from which we discovered the group of oak trees painted in the "Battle of the Elements," he was looking at the reflections of the rocks, covered with moss and sea-weed, when they appeared as landscapes to his vision, and there came over him an ecstatic desire to paint. He was a very much disheartened man before and after this experience, but, with the resolution formed on that occasion, he went about the island discovering and painting the various scenes that had haunted his visions.

At the next sitting Mr. Gifford, if I may assume that he was really communicating, tried direct communications again; and, among a number of true and pertinent incidents not especially important, he asked me, in Mr. Thompson's absence, how I liked the comparison of the picture and the real scene. The interest here lies in the fact that I had a few days previously been on the second trip to search for the trees that we finally found in July. Mrs. Chenoweth knew nothing about this trip, though she had known after the middle of May that I had been investigating the case on the coast of New England. When I asked the communicator what scene and what picture, as we had not yet found the object of our quest, he replied, the small one, and described it as "the marsh and tree and you know it was the misty one," and asked me, "How do you explain the bit of red in a sunset sky? It was good, but the red was put in as an afterthought." We had not noticed any such scene and did not know of any such picture. But Mrs. Gifford told me that he had once painted such a picture and that he had afterwards put in the red of the sunset. The communicator then went on to remark that he had in mind a picture of death represented by a beckoning angel with one hand pointing to a path leading up a mountain, and that Mr. Thompson had seen it as in a dream. The main features of this are true.

As I had never obtained Mr. Gifford's name in the communications, and as I desired to strengthen the evidence by experiments through Mrs. Smead, whose motives could not possibly be suspected, I brought her from the Southern state where she lived, some thirteen miles from a railway and almost inaccessible to information about the case.

The first few experiments did not show any evidence of the communicator's identity. At the first sitting it was distinctly intimated that Mr. Thompson had to do with art, as a gilt-framed painting in oil, representing a landscape, was referred to as standing near his door. This was correct. At the next sitting the communicator was identified as an artist and I was told that "he likes that picture which you have," apparently referring to one of two that I had. I had taken the "Battle of the Elements," and had been given another picture of merit, in fact one of the best that Mr. Thompson had painted. Mrs. Smead knew nothing about them, as one of them had been put away out of sight, and the other was hanging unexplained in my parlor. Some very good advice was given Mr. Thompson about his pictures, and a reference was made to teaching, relevant to the personality of Mr. Gifford. The next experiment was similar; in the last one the most interesting incidents were given to establish the identity of the communicator. I was usually sent out of the room by the control, in order to leave Mr. Thompson alone with the communicator, but before leaving on this day, I asked Dr. Hodgson, who was acting as amanuensis, that is as control, to try to give the communicator's name. At once he write out "R. G. yes." I conjecture that "yes" was a mistake for "S," the probable intention being to give "R. G. S." — Robert Swain Gifford was his name. Soon after, "R. G. S." was given and the "S" repeated.

After I had left the room, the communicator referred to a picture "on the canvas with the rock on the coast" and added "yes, the ocean" and then drew a picture representing a pile of rocks mounted by a cross, and wrote out "and my name is on it." Later in the sitting an allusion was made to it again and the cross was drawn again and this time apparently not on a pile of rocks but on a ground of sand washed by the waves.

While on the shore last summer, Mr. Thompson saw some

wreckage ahead of him, and on approaching it saw on it a cross, caused by a rib of a boat crossed by a piece of timber. As he went nearer he saw the initials of Mr. Gifford on it, but as he went still nearer, the initials disappeared. He wrote out an account of this experience at the time and sent it in a letter to Mrs. Thompson. She gave the letter to me on November 10, and I had it in my files at the time of this sitting, December 9.

The communicator then indicated that the scene was in "our West Indies," a fair indication of the locality. Soon a statement was made by the communicator that he had sketched at a place which he had tried to indicate, apparently getting the word "Island." He soon said that "swimming was a sport of which I was very fond there on the island shore." I have not been able to verify the statement about the swimming, but a correct reference to a cottage and his mother, as his early home was there, makes it probable that the statement about swimming, though not evidential, is correct. His allusion to the house as their "spot" was also true, and the term apparently a characteristic one.

In connection with the reference to the house, he mentioned that he used to climb and sketch the trees there. After stating that he had sketched them, he made an excellent evidential remark. He said "the wind used to blow them dreadfully, yes, away over. Can you remember the storms we used to have there?" That coast is a very stormy one, and the trees in that locality are remarkably storm-blown. I have seen some whose tops had been made, by the winds, to grow at right angles to the trunk. Immediately he was asked to give the name of the island where he had done his work. Apparently he got the capital letter "E" and more probably the word Island, the letter "I" being found clearly written several times. The suggestion of Elizabeth Islands is thus clear. This was followed by his initials "R. S. G." in their correct order. After repeating the reference to the storms and waves circular lines were drawn to represent the rolling of the waves on the shore, and a reference, probably correct, was made to skipping rocks on the water when a boy; then in reply to the second request to give the name of the island he got the word

"Marchan," which will suggest to any reader what island was meant. This ended the sittings.

It is impossible within the compass of this chapter to discuss these incidents and their import. Suffice it to say that they have the same general character as those which come from Mrs. Piper, Mrs. Verrall and others, and, assuming that they are free from suspicion, must have the same interpretation. The circumstances make some of the facts less evidential than others. But it will not be necessary to defend or apologize for the weaker incidents. We may discard the sittings with Mrs. Rathbun and Mrs. Chenoweth after the middle of May, when we may suppose them to have had the opportunity to make inquiries. The reader may feel assured that they did not do so, but the opportunity may be conceded, on account of their knowledge that I was investigating the case. Discounting all sittings after the middle of May, we nevertheless have a number that give evidence of supernormal information under test conditions. Besides, whatever we may assume as possible regarding the others, the careful student will examine the facts and may come to the conclusion that they afford internal evidence of good faith; many of them could not easily have been obtained by any sort of inquiry without betraying the purpose.

Whatever suspicion may be entertained regarding a part of the record connected with Mrs. Rathbun and Mrs. Chenoweth, cannot be applied to that of Mrs. Smead, where the evidence, though often confused, is unmistakable, and shows that ordinary explanations cannot be applied to her sittings.

On any theory we ought to recognize that the identity of Mr. Gifford is clear. There are perhaps no single incidents that would force one to accept this view, but their collective force is overwhelming and constitutes a mass of relevant hints inapplicable to any one else. One of the most interesting and significant circumstances, which could not be indicated in a summary of the facts, is the constant assumption and frequent assertion that the communicator has been and still is influencing Mr. Thompson, and influencing him to paint. Besides this, the mediumistic phenomena corroborate the spontaneous experiences of Mr. Thompson and point in the same direction. Superficially, at least, all the facts point to the spiritistic hypothesis, whatever perplexities exist in regard to the *modus operandi* of the agencies effecting the results.

A striking character of the phenomena is, that the hallucinations cannot be rationally accounted for by telepathy between the living. We might suppose telepathy and telepathic phantasms from the dead, but to do this is to concede that the facts either tend to prove the spiritistic hypothesis or are explicable by it, while the mediumistic incidents support it independently and confirm the character and significance of the visions.

The critical inquirer should go to the detailed report for a correct understanding of the facts and of their evidential nature. They occur in the midst of much chaff and confusion, and a summary like this necessarily makes the case appear stronger than it might appear to one who had to wade through the entire records. On the other hand, he who takes this trouble will discover, by careful investigation, that there is a connected relevance in much of the non-evidential matter, which may appear to strengthen the case instead of weakening it.

I have not mentioned the cross-references in the records. There are several, representing the same or similar messages through different psychics. The most notable are the references apparently to the painting and scene representing the "Battle of the Elements" and the picture on the easel. But I shall not dwell upon these. The reader may discover them for himself in the detailed records. They very much strengthen the evidence, and the manner of their delivery more or less protects them from the ordinary suspicions. The instances mentioned occurred under test conditions and there is no reason to minimize their importance.

One thing it is important to remark: Not all the facts in the record bear upon the personal identity of the communicator. The important thing was to ascertain, if possible by mediumistic experiments, whether the superficial interpretation of Mr. Thompson's experience would be borne out in mediumistic results; this interpretation seems to have been confirmed in the evidence both of the identity of the communicator and of a connection between the visions of Mr. Thompson and that communicating personality.

CHAPTER XV

PROFESSOR JAMES

PROFESSOR JAMES died on August 26, 1910. On the next day, August 27, Mrs. Smead, living in the mountains in one of the Southern states, thirteen miles from a railway, before any newspaper or other news of James's death could reach the place, had an apparition of a man in a long black gown. She did not recognize him, as she had never seen a picture of Professor James. On the following Tuesday, August 30, she accidentally learned that Professor James was dead. A Baltimore paper giving an account of the fact had reached the mountain village, and Mrs. Smead's son casually remarked to his mother that Professor James was dead. Mr. Smead burned the paper before Mrs. Smead had had an opportunity to read it. Some time later she was shown a picture of Professor James and recognized it as identical with the apparition.

On August 31 Mr. Smead held a sitting, but nothing whatever occurred to suggest that Professor James was present. Another sitting was held on September 1, and almost immediately an attempt was made to give the Greek letter Omega, which succeeded at the second attempt. The meaning of this was not apparent either then or later until I got the same letter through Mrs. Chenoweth as the sign of Professor James. It might have signified, as this letter does in literature, the last person to have come to that side, but no indication of this meaning was given.

There was some further stumbling about with Greek letters, and reference to a college sign, but nothing evidential. On September 2 an allusion was made to an elm said to be near Professor James's "earth home." Inquiry proved that this was true of his Cambridge home, a fact which the Smeads did not know and could not have known. In the meantime I had promptly made arrangements to have some sittings. The first was on September 12.

There was no attempt at first to present Professor James. My wife purported to communicate and referred apparently to a deceased brother. She was followed by my father for a few moments and then came a change of control and Dr. Hodgson came to the helm, reporting the presence of Professor James and Mr. Myers. A statement was made that they had tried to appear "at the lady over there," apparently referring to Mrs. Verrall, a wavy line being drawn to signify the ocean, as is usual with Mrs. Smead. Many months later I learned from England that on this very date, some hours before my sitting, Mrs. Verrall had had a dream in which she thought Professor James was trying to communicate, and that she had made a record of the dream.

The next day there were several pertinent allusions which did not reach the rank of good evidence, but were interesting, when we consider that Mrs. Smead knew absolutely nothing of Professor James and his habits of thought. One allusion was to his wanting to believe, and to his believing "only partially." Reference to the religious aspect is also significant. A pertinent reference was made to the difference between himself and Mr. Myers, in the statement that the latter had written poetry and that he himself had not. This was true, and the Smeads knew nothing of the facts. This was followed by a very natural remark about letting the Piper records go out of "our possession," pointing probably to the policy of allowing sitters to have records which the office did not keep. The Smeads knew nothing that could make this subconscious knowledge. Other matter is such as new experience might suggest, but is not evidential, though an allusion or two to the cause of confusion shows that his mind was turning to one of the perplexities which had troubled him during life.

On the next day the first references that would suggest an attempt at evidence were to psychometry, in which it is not known that Professor James had ever been interested. Some observations on his own obstinate doubts and the influence of the Imperator régime in the Piper case were very characteristic and represented knowledge that Mrs. Smead did not have. The reference in this connection to the "amusement of earth-bound souls" was evidently a description of the work of Phinuit and described his character perfectly in a manner not at all familiar to Mrs. Smead, but with just such knowledge of Phinuit's work as Professor James had in life. A little later reference was made to the process as a "reservoir of information," a very characteristic expression of Professor James, not at all known to Mrs. Smead.

On September 19 Mr. Smead had a sitting in which some reference was made to the "Huldah episode," which Professor James had discussed in his report and about which he had had some correspondence with the Smeads. On September 21, another sitting was held and some pertinent, but not evidential, remarks were made about public mediums, suggested by a question of Mr. Smead.

Just a month after the death of Professor James I had my first sitting with Mrs. Chenoweth, who knew a little more about him than did Mrs. Smead, but not enough to affect most of the material that purported to come from him.

At the first sitting, on September 26, 1910, Professor James did not try to communicate. He apparently wrote his name William at the end of the automatic writing, after G. P. and Dr. Hodgson had alluded to him in various ways. G. P. alluded to the promise that James would give me a sign, a circumstance of some significance, since Mrs. Smead had made a similar allusion, accompanied by the sign Omega, as we have seen above, wholly unknown to Mrs. Chenoweth. He also made a very pertinent reference to Mr. Dorr, who had been a warm friend of Professor James, a fact which, it happened, Mrs. Chenoweth did not know. In the communications of Dr. Hodgson, with reference to him, there were allusions to his own failure in a somewhat chaffing vein that would be natural when the two old friends met. Dr. Hodgson said for him, however, that some papers marked for the two Societies would be found; but nothing of the kind has turned up among his papers. An allusion to his fear of a "phantom existence" was relevant, as he had made remarks of this kind in his life.

The description of Dr. Hodgson's communications as "jerky and disjointed" was very characteristic, and closely connected with it a reference to his not being a "deteriorated personality" was very striking, as it represented an opinion he had had of such communications before his death. He had always been discouraged by the disjointed and trivial character of the communications, and had never been induced to speak tolerantly of them until Dr. Hodgson offered his dream theory to account for the confusion and fragmentary character of the messages. There was also a very pertinent reference to the use of the word "death" and the reluctance of the Imperator group to use it through Mrs. Piper. Mrs. Chenoweth knew nothing of this peculiarity, which was very characteristically discussed here, the communicator explaining that he had emphasized it because Imperator had disliked it. It was also characteristic to ask me to get Mrs. Chenoweth to write down all she knew of him, this being the policy of the Society with Mrs. Piper when there was no other way to prove the exclusion of normally acquired knowledge regarding specific incidents. He then gave the sign Omega and stopped writing.

I had no more sittings till October 20. On that date he wrote again. No distinct incident came out that would show by its environment that it could not have any other source, but most of the communications had characteristic touches. The description of the attitude and manner of scientific men was very like the author, who adopted an apologetic tone and a sympathy of their situation which were far from the natural feelings of Mrs. Chenoweth. Reference was made to his own disappointment at not having been able to finish a certain work that he had undertaken, which I found by inquiry to be true and not known by the psychic.

On October 29, Professor James came first. In alluding to the clearness of his memory he approached the problem of the confusions and mistakes, a characteristic question with him in life. Here he, like other communicators, ignores the "dream theory" and refers all mistakes to limitations of the psychic. He correctly indicated that his son was always called Harry in the family, a fact not known by Mrs. Chenoweth, but possibly guessable. He referred to a work which he said was nearly finished. This I found to be true and not known by Mrs. Chenoweth, whatever we may think about its exposure to the objection of guessing. The statement that his set of English "Proceedings" was not complete seems to have been untrue. The immediate reference to Sir Oliver

Lodge, though not evidential, is characteristic enough to be genuine. In the subliminal stage reference was made to "a little trunk, light yellow, for his affairs up stairs in an upper room, with a lot of little things in it, papers, articles and various little things placed away." At first no knowledge of such a trunk existed in the family, but later several trunks were found in the attic packed with such material.

In the sitting of November 2, little was communicated that even requires mention from the evidential point of view. The allusion to the fact that the public thought him always occupied with psychic matters when it was not a fact was true and probably not at all known by Mrs. Chenoweth. The additional statement that he passed judgment on the work of others was also true and probably not known by the psychic. The reference to the demands of a university on him as an excuse for not occupying himself with the subject and his reliance on Dr. Hodgson for information were very pertinent, whatever value we give them.

On November 3, he returned to the effort, and soon correctly characterized the work of Dr. Hodgson and his influence, and his own disappointment with the results when he came to them at first hand. All this represents matter which would not naturally come to Mrs. Chenoweth, with her slight knowledge of the man. Some interesting wit was shown in the passage which was more characteristic of the two men than of Mrs. Chenoweth. There was an interesting denial of having written a definite letter for the purpose of communicating it, because the communications often seemed to imply that there was such a letter and the public had been saturated with the belief that he had written one. There is no evidence in responsible quarters that he wrote it, though he did write an important letter after Dr. Hodgson's death. There was also an allusion to the illegibility of the writing in the Piper case, which had been a subject of discussion in life; the psychic most probably, I could say certainly, did not know the fact. The statement that he had much trouble with his eyes during the last year of his life was not correct.

Then came the following important statements:

"Do you recall coming to me once in the winter when snow was on the ground and we talked over these things and I gave you something to take away."

(I recall the event very well.)

"At that time we talked of the cleryman s wife who had the power of talking automatically."

(Yes.)

"Since then I have seen her or rather since I came into this life."

(Yes, good.)

"And I have made an effort to write with some success but not for long at a time. She does better when you are present."

(Good.)

"Altho I find enough power to make some good expression when you are not there."

(Good.)

"It is more spasmodic than here but that is largely a question of environment and companionship and desire. At that visit at my home you had to hurry away at last and some things were left for another time. I had been planning for a long time to see you. Indeed I was always planning for a time to talk more with you."

In the winter of 1906, while a heavy snow was on the ground, I had called on Professor James, and we had had a long talk on these matters, and he had given me a package of French publications to take away with me. We talked of Mrs. Smead especially on that visit. She is the wife of a clergyman, this fact being known to Mrs. Chenoweth, but not that Professor James and I had talked about her on this or any other occasion, though it might be guessed that we would do so, at least on some occasion. But this was the only time we ever talked about her. That he had seen Mrs. Smead since he came into the new life has its evidence in the sign of Omega and perhaps other incidents in the detailed record.

The accompanying statement that Mrs. Smead does better when I am present is true and also not known to Mrs. Chenoweth. The description of the case as "more spasmodic" than the present case was correct also and not known. Then allusion to my last call on him as a hurried one was correct also and not known. Whether he had planned, as said, to see and talk with me, is not verifiable. Then came the following:

"I have a recollection of meeting you first with Richard. Do you recall that?"

(I do not at this moment, but may later.)

"It was at some small gathering or small company and after it was over we met and talked. That was about your own work with Mrs. Piper. I do not recall whether that was my first introduction to you. But it was about that time."

(Yes, I think I recall something about it.)

"It was not important enough then to make lasting impressions."

(Yes, I think it was about the time of my talk at a certain house in Cambridge.)

"I think so and I was impressed with your fervor and laughed with Richard about it afterwards."

(I expect you did.)

"I said to him that you would have that high hope shattered after a while."

(Yes, I was converted long before Hodgson and you knew it.)

"We had been through the stages of Imperator wonder and worship and still had the problem of Moses' identity unsolved. You remember how we were harassed by the conflicting statements and contradictory evidence."

(Yes, perfectly.)

"It was enough to make us swear but we stuck to the task and hid our chagrin as best we could."

This is, in fact, a remarkable passage. I do not remember just when I first met Professor James. But it is very probable that we became acquainted with each other about 1899, when I addressed an audience at some conferences of Dr. James in Cambridge and at a symposium at the Hollis Street Theater on the subject of psychic research. A little later I addressed the meeting of the Society in Boston, which Professor James probably attended. I do not remember. If I met him before that period I do not recall it. I remember, however, that once, when in Boston for some purpose, I went with him to a meeting of a little post-graduate club of philosophy students, to talk to them on my Piper work.

The statements about the Imperator "wonder and worship" and the difficulties into which the failure of Stainton Moses to prove his identity and that of Imperator and the group of alleged spirits with him, are all quite true and represent knowledge which Mrs. Chenoweth could not have without direct inquiry or casual information of an unusual kind. She might possibly learn the general state of mind regarding the phenomena as a whole, but would not get the reasons here assigned.

On November 10, in the subliminal stage of the recovery of

normal consciousness, the psychic remarked that Professor James had a little boat that looked like a motor boat and that it was at his summer place. He did have a row boat, but not a motor boat, at Chocorua. Then immediately came the following:

"I see a roll like a diploma. It would all be in French except his name, and it is something very recently come into his life. It has never been hung up, but is still in the roll as if sent to him. He takes it out of a paste-board case and holds it up. It is an honorable thing. It pleased him very much. He saw it only a little before he went away."

Mr. Henry James, Jr., the son, writes regarding this incident: "He received an honorary degree from the University of Geneva in 1909 after July. It was in French and is still in the roll."

On November 11 came the following:

"Bread and milk and berries often made the meal at night in the summer and the vegetable kingdom furnished a large part of my food always. I was fond of apples and some kind of fish. These may seem remarkable things to return from heaven to talk of, but you will appreciate their value."

(Yes, perfectly.)

"I can see the headlines in the newspapers now if this were given out, but if I had said I had broken bread with the Saviour or Saint Paul there would have been many who would have believed it a part of the life of a man of my reputation in my new sphere."

In reply to inquiries, Mr. Henry James, Jr. writes: "For some years before his death my father was a small eater and ate little meat. He was fond of apples and of course had his preferences in fish. He often ate berries with milk and cream, and I think sometimes mixed bread with them, but he practically never drank milk." The remarks about the newspapers are perfectly relevant for the communicator, but not at all beyond the intelligence of Mrs. Chenoweth.

On November 12 I asked a question about a person, not mentioning his name, who had furnished him certain incidents in his book "Varieties of Religious Experience," not named there, but known to me. I did not get the reply I wanted, but he named the man in the following manner, after indicating that he had not caught the drift of my question at first. "I know what R. H. told me of his own religious convictions after long investigations with the Imperator group." Dr. Hodgson was the name I wanted, and, though his relation to the book mentioned is not given, the reference to the effect of the investigations of the Imperator group on his religious convictions is correct and was most probably, one might say certainly, talked over with Professor James.

In the communication he also said that I had told him some things. This was true and wholly unknown to Mrs. Chenoweth.

He also made a spontaneous allusion to the endowment fund that I was seeking, and I remarked that he had made a slight gift to it. His reply was: "That is a small sum. You refer to the first $100 subscription." He had agreed to double his fee of $10 a year for two years, and had paid the first installment. It was not $100, as it appears to be here. But the word "first" is the interesting one in the message.

On November 18, he referred to the appearances of "deteriorated and disintegrated capacity" in the messages, which had been a subject of much perplexity in his life, and when I started a discussion of it by alluding to the "dream or trance" theory of the communicator's condition he replied, correctly enough, that we had been told this by Imperator and that "the evidence submitted implied as much in many instances." Mrs. Chenoweth knew nothing of these facts, and whether they were inferable from what she might have seen in allusions to the theory in his report must be determined by each reader for himself. He denied the existence of a trance in himself, but admitted that there may be cases of it. A little later G. P. remarked that Professor James had "knocked down some of the nine pins" and then on the next day he remarked that Professor James had "given a black eye to one of Dick's theories," referring to Dr. Hodgson, who had first advanced it.

On November 19, the following came:

"Do you remember the experience you had with Shaler and my thought about it?"

(I do not know the thought.)

"I laughed when I read it and I knew the meaning of passing between the light and the connecting current, for we had been taught at the Piper light. It was not so realistic a lesson but we got it."

This is an interesting incident and nothing of it can be ascribed to previous knowledge on the part of Mrs. Chenoweth, except that the Shaler incident could have been known by her subconscious, but not by her normal consciousness. At a sitting some years before in New York, Professor Shaler purported to communicate. An accident occurred in which he got locked up for nearly an hour in the organism of the medium, and quite a dramatic incident happened in releasing him. I sent the record to Professor James and I have no doubt he laughed about it, and it is true that the same causes were assigned for similar phenomena through Mrs. Piper. The facts were not known to Mrs. Chenoweth.

In the subliminal stage of the recovery he communicated indirectly the following:

"I can see the front of Professor James's house and I see a lady going there with flowers for Mrs. James. She opens the door and the lady stays only a few minutes."

(Did you say "a man and a lady"?)

"No, just a lady. Perhaps I said *and*. She has a big bunch of flowers. I think she is taking them for Thanksgiving. They are big flowers and look like chrysanthemums, not all yellow but some violet ones."

Inquiry brought the following information from Mr. Henry James, Jr.: "A friend of my mother's, a lady, made a short call just before Thanksgiving, leaving chrysanthemums. She was let in by the housemaid." This, of course, was not known by Mrs. Chenoweth.

On November 27, while controlling directly, he said that the last thing he remembered eating was a bit of bread of which he ate but a taste or two, and then referred to uncooked eggs. My information in reply to inquiry was: "Not true as to the eggs, but he ate a part of a piece of bread the morning before his death."

On December 8 Professor James remarked that he treated letters on the subject of psychic research with the same care and respect as if he had been engaged by the Society to answer them, which he was not, and that the whole community seemed to look on him as an adviser in these matters. He added also that Mrs. James tried to relieve him when they became too much for him. Inquiry showed that this was true, save that Mrs. James was not the only member of the family that aided him in such situations. It might have been guessed that he received many letters, but his manner of treating them, which was correctly stated, would not be so readily guessed. After a failure correctly to answer a question by me he lost control, and Dr. Hodgson, acting as amanuensis for him, mentioned a ring which was said to have been put away. Inquiry showed that he never had a ring. But the next incident was more successful. He referred to his father's watch and stated that he had used it for some time. Inquiry showed that he had worn his father's watch many years.

Following this was a reference to an English cap which he was said to have worn; it was compared with Dr. Hodgson's, said to have been Scotch. Dr. Hodgson had had a Scotch cap and I learn from inquiry that Professor James had had several English hats and caps.

I arrived at the Smeads on May 28, and learned that on February 6 Mrs. Smead had had a vision of the Greek letter Omega and a monogram of the letters F and P, the initials of Mr. Podmore. The meaning of these they did not understand until May 4, when Mr. Smead learned for the first time that Mr. Podmore was dead and Mrs. Smead was told the facts because the "Outlook," in which his death was mentioned, was likely to be read by her. But the Omega had no meaning to them. When told of it I recognized it, but said nothing, hoping to have it come in the writing. The letter, however, as readers will recall, was given through Mrs. Chenoweth as Professor James's sign and was also alluded to earlier through Mrs. Smead.

In the first sitting the communicator purported to be Mr. Podmore and in the course of the writing the Greek letter Omega was drawn with a cross after it. Seeing that there might be confusion I asked who had made that sign and a little surprise was expressed at my not recognizing the sign. In a few moments I was told that it was Mr. Podmore's. I saw that this statement was wrong, but quietly accepted it as if it were correct and said nothing. On June 6, Professor James appeared for the first time in the series, and after mentioning his son William, evidently intending his son Henry, however, as I judge from the contents of the reference, he twice wrote the Greek Omega with the cross in it and explained that it was he that came with Mr. Podmore. This explained and corrected the erroneous statement that the Omega had been given by Mr. Podmore.

Allusion was made to his heart trouble, which Mrs. Smead did not know about, and to his having said little about it to his family. A fairly clear reference was made to his difficulty in breathing, about which Mrs. Smead knew nothing. He had suffered from oedema of the lungs. Apparently in the message, however, reference is to earlier periods of difficulty in breathing, which gave rise to his retirement from college; the circumstances were explained in the communications with fair definiteness, Mrs. Smead knowing nothing about the facts.

Then followed a reference to the Piper case, which I quote for its pertinence, omitting the confusion.

"I have so many times thought of our mistaken views of the whole problem when we began in the early days before you joined in our experiments. It was more with some a case of amusement. Do you know that little Frenchman has not yet put in his appearance to me."

(No, that 's good.)

"No, I think we will have some interesting talks."

(I hope so and you can report them.)

"I certainly will if it is possible. I will try to find out why he was so stubborn, yes, persistent, in having it as he wished. He may try to go back to the light now that we are not using it."

It was correct that the earlier experiments with Mrs. Piper were attended by many people more out of amusement than for any serious scientific purpose, in the early days before I had even heard of the case, much less joined in the movement. All this Mrs. Smead knew absolutely nothing about. She may have known that the control claimed to be a Frenchman, but of the other incidents she was wholly ignorant. She was equally ignorant of the obstinacy of Phinuit and of all that is implied in the true and characteristic way in which the period and conduct of Phinuit are here described. He then terminated his communications with the sign Omega and the cross.

On June 7 he communicated again, and referred to "a mountain that looks like snow all over," and remarked that "it is only a short distance from our house." He added that he "could do no mental work while there" and that "we were nearer that mountain than you" and that he "was glad to have you talk with me during my sojourn there."

I recognized Chocorua in the reference to the mountain and his house near it. His summer home is at the base of that mountain, which is quite bare and white in appearance. I spent the summer in which he died nine miles from his place, and called to see him, though he was too ill to see me. Mrs. Smead knew that he had died at Chocorua and had herself lived not far from it many years before; she would therefore remember its appearance. She also knew that I had spent the summer not far away. But she did not know that he could do no work there nor that I had called.

He then recurred to his son, apparently for the purpose of making a reference to his city home, which he mentioned as the place where his son was living. His son is living in the old home in the city, a fact not known to Mrs. Smead.

I asked him whose picture was in the library, having in my mind the picture of Hodgson that he had mentioned through Mrs. Chenoweth. In reply he asked if I meant the picture in a frame on the wall, and I replied that I knew nothing about the frames. He then said he had several in the books, and in a moment he said, the telephone having rung in the hall and possibly producing some confusion in Mrs. Smead's mind, "I cannot remember just now, but I said I had one of each of us, Hodgson's and myself too."

I had previously learned from Mr. Henry James, Jr., that he had a picture of Dr. Hodgson on the wall; and after this sitting I learned that he also had a painting of himself. Mrs. Smead knew nothing of either picture.

On June 14 he indicated that he had been trying to make his presence felt to Mrs. James, and requested me to ask her whether she had not felt him. Inquiry proved that she had not had any impressions of his presence. A few minutes later he indicated that his son Will, whose name the Smeads did not know, had cared for his correspondence and helped him in his work at the college. It was apparent to me that he had his son Henry in mind; and it is curious to note that Mrs. Smead knew his name but not the name William.

Inquiry showed that all the members of the family had at one time or another helped him in his correspondence, but none had helped him in the college.

Professor James then referred to his daughter, of whose existence Mrs. Smead knew nothing, and implied that she was psychic and might write. No trace of psychic power in her is known.

In the course of his allusions to the surprise which some people felt on their arrival in the other world, I made the remark that it is easy to believe in atoms, but not easy to believe in a soul. The reply was a confused but very characteristic discussion of the atomic and ether hypotheses, in which he said that they are mere hypotheses and aids to our thinking and memory, thus expressing scientific conceptions which are entirely foreign to the experience of Mrs. Smead. During the discussion he expressed the desire to discuss the ethereal body at length, I remarked that it would not be proof of identity, and then asked him if he remembered Pragmatism. The reply, very pertinent, was: "Yes, but not identity either. Only interesting to the philosophers." This was a correct appreciation of the case. Mrs. Smead does not know the word "pragmatism," nor that Professor James represented that school of thought.

Thus terminated the experiments for Professor James. At the last sitting another communicator came. The messages from Professor James through Mrs. Smead were not any better than those through Mrs. Chenoweth. They are wholly different in style, owing to the different types of mediumship and despite the fact that the method of automatic writing is identical so far as we can see. There is less chaff in the work of Mrs. Smead than in the work of Mrs. Chenoweth, probably due to the method of development and the controls, together with the different habits and temperaments of the two ladies. However this may be, it is noticeable that through Mrs. Smead Professor James can get at the gist of a subject more clearly than through Mrs. Chenoweth, though his messages are so fragmentary that the evidence does not seem to be any better.

There is one incident of peculiar interest and importance, which adds much to the value of Professor James's messages. It is a most interesting piece of cross-reference. On the twelfth of September,

1910, Professor James, purporting to communicate through Mrs. Smead, said that he had tried to communicate through Mrs. Verrall living in England, naming her and her locality, the latter simply as "across the water." Two months later through Mrs. Chenoweth he again mentioned having tried through Mrs. Verrall. Later inquiry in England of Miss Alice Johnson, secretary of the English Society, resulted in the following report. Mrs. Verrall had a dream on September 12, 1910, in which she felt that Professor James was trying to communicate. My sitting with Mrs. Smead was held at 10 A. M. of that date, several hours earlier than London time, so that her dream must have been that morning. A record of the dream had been made by Mrs. Verrall. The reference through Mrs. Chenoweth was made, as indicated, two months later, but coincides with the fact that Mrs. Verrall had been impressed with the effort of Professor James. That is to say, Mrs. Verrall had had the impression of the presence of Professor James and two mediums in America, or Professor James through them, soon afterwards stated in their trances that Professor James had tried to communicate through Mrs. Verrall. No other psychics were mentioned. Both psychics knew that Mrs. Verrall did similar work, but they had the same opportunities to know of others also doing the same work. The most natural person to mention was Mrs. Piper, as her reputation and supposed work at the time would most naturally provoke subconscious guessing. But not a hint of her appeared and during the whole series of experiments both psychics were either remarkably silent about Mrs. Piper where they had years before referred to her freely or they acted as if Mrs. Piper was not active in the work, which was the fact, unknown to myself as well as to the psychics. Hence the coincidence with respect to Mrs. Verrall is all the more striking.

But there is one set of incidents which are perhaps as important as any that I know in connection with Professor James. I must go back a little to make them clear.

Some years ago after the death of Dr. Hodgson and before that of Professor James, while the latter was lecturing in England, a reference was made to him through Mrs. Chenoweth in a somewhat pertinent way. At about the same time Dr. Hodgson, purporting to communicate through Miss Gaule, said that he had seen Professor James in *pink pajamas* and that he looked cute in them. I wrote to Professor James, and received the reply that he was wearing "pink pajamas" at the time. It is not possible for the psychic to have known the facts, whatever we may think about guessing. To test the reaction, when he was claiming to communicate through Mrs. Chenoweth, I once asked him if he remembered anything about "pink pajamas," and the reply was in no respect evidential, though apparently appreciative of the significance of the mention of them. Later I thought to try a cross-reference with Mrs. Smead and asked him to say "pink pajamas" there. In the series of sittings held with her there was an entire failure to allude to them.

But recently a young boy in the family of a clergyman developed mediumistic powers; and, both in automatic writing and by crystal gazing, in messages appearing as visual writing, *when I was not present at all,* Professor James purported to communicate, and, mentioning me, referred to *pink pajamas* and to a *black necktie.* He said: "I want you to give Hyslop two pairs of pink pajamas and a black necktie for Christmas." The parents referred to the facts as amusing, without any knowledge of their significance. I had kept the incidents absolutely to myself. They were quite astonished to find how pertinent they were. The black necktie I used at sittings, and it had belonged to Professor James. The reference to "pink pajamas" explains itself as the cross-reference which should have come through Mrs. Smead. The association of his name and mine with them strengthens the reference.

When we estimate the messages that thus purport to come from Professor James, we have to admit that they will disappoint the general public. While errors and false statements are not evidence against the claim that the effort originates from Professor James, the public is so ignorant of what the problem is that it will, as usual, commit worse errors in its judgment than spirits commonly do in facts. Of course, we cannot claim that errors are evidence, unless they are of a certain type, but they are not objections; they are problems. The actual errors, however, are not the primary weakness of the data purporting to come from Professor James. It is rather the paucity of the messages that lessens their value. The weakness, moreover, is much increased by the nature of the circumstances. Professor James was so well-known to the public generally that it is extremely difficult to obtain facts whose value might not be nullified by previous knowledge. A more obscure person would have far better chance of transmitting evidence of identity. But there are instances that cannot be discredited in any way. The Greek letter Omega and the cross cannot be impeached except by accusing me of collusion. The records were known to no living person but me, as I had made them myself and locked them up out of sight. The same assurance may be given of the "pink pajama" incident, my visit to Professor James and the package, the talk before his "seminar," his diet, his last meal from a crust of bread.

There are many facts as evidential as these, which cannot be made clear to general readers. They can be appreciated only by those who knew the mind of Professor James intimately either from personal acquaintance or from his books. But any one who examines these obscure incidents illustrating characteristic ideas will find that, while one or two of them might be obtainable from reading his published writings, the large number could not easily be obtained except by a minute acquaintance with his writings, which neither psychic possesses.

On the whole his evidence is not what was desired, at least for the satisfaction of the hungry public. Fortunately Professor James himself remained true to his ideas of the subject while he was living, namely, the need of small and trivial facts to prove personal identity. In the investigation of psychic phenomena no one ever insisted more rigidly than he that personal identity is the fundamental problem and that only the remotest trivial facts would prove that identity. The "pink pajama" incident cannot be surpassed for evidential value, especially in its cross-reference, to anyone who intelligently understands this problem. The only disappointing thing for those interested is the paucity of the evidence, not its omission of characteristic phrases.

The present writer is not at all surprised at the outcome. His experience has been that intellectual minds have special difficulty in establishing personal identity. Their preoccupation is with themes, which do not lend themselves to sensory imagery. The pictorial or clairvoyant way of representing thoughts is adapted to sensory imagery, more particularly of the visual type. The abstractions of philosophic thought do not lend themselves to accurate representation by this method.

One incident should not remain unnoticed. The newspapers published widely at the time of his death the report that Professor James had left a posthumous letter whose contents he was to divulge, if he found himself surviving death and it was possible to transmit them. Allusion was made through one of the psychics to something of the kind, but a thorough investigation showed that there was no evidence whatever anywhere known to the family or anyone else that such a letter had ever been written.

CHAPTER XVI

MARK TWAIN

SOON after I had published a review of the work of Patience Worth, I learned from one of the persons connected with that work, Mrs. Emily Grant Hutchings, that she was getting Patience Worth through another psychic. Just as the interest in this fact was beginning to grow, and when I had formed my plan for a cross-reference experiment to see whether I could get Patience Worth myself, the whole work of this new psychic changed. She began to get communications purporting to come from Mark Twain.

The psychic in the case was a Mrs. Hays, of St. Louis. The circumstances, however, were such that Mrs. Hutchings was as necessary to the phenomena as was Mrs. Hays. Both ladies had to hold a hand on the index or planchette part of the ouija, otherwise it would not move. The interest in this fact lies in the attempt to measure the probabilities that the subconscious of both ladies could act harmoniously enough to spell any word whatever, to say nothing of writing books characteristic of a man whose works only one of them had read. Under these conditions two volumes were spelled out.

Both ladies are in private life, Mrs. Hutchings being a writer on art for the St. Louis "Globe-Democrat," and Mrs. Hays a writer for various papers. No pecuniary reward was involved in the work, except such as might come from the risks of publication. No taint of professional mediumship is contained in either case and all ordinary objections may be discounted at the outset. The mediums are open to any investigation of character that skepticism may adjudge desirable. The first question to occur to the curious inquirer would be whether the work was not done as a literary adventure merely pretending to come from Mark Twain, a sort of *jeu d'esprit* to help in the advertisement of the work by the claim that it came from the celebrated humorist. The one fact which might arouse this suspicion is, that both ladies are writers and are not in a trance when the work is done. But students know that automatism is not limited to trance conditions. It is quite common in normal consciousness. Any question on this point must be answered by the critic's own study of the two ladies.

Mrs. Hutchings had not read anything of Mark Twain's until after much of the work had been done. Mrs. Hays was more familiar with his work. There are four sources for a theory of subconscious memory to account for the phenomena. (1) Mrs. Hays had read something of Mark Twain's work. (2) She had expressed the desire that he would communicate, thus providing the condition for a Freudian explanation for his appearance. (3) She has a very keen sense of humor herself, with a tinge of Mark Twain's drollery, though with less compass and depth. (4) She also, like Mark Twain, possesses a vein of melancholy, though without his irony. Perhaps it would favor the same interpretation to add that Mrs. Hays has psychic powers in other directions, which favor the dissociation necessary to produce work of the kind.

The suspicion that subconscious fabrication might be the explanation made it necessary to experiment in a decisive manner. The conditions just mentioned were ideal for the theory of subconscious production, and without experiment for cross-reference it was idle to maintain that the work was supernormal. There was absolutely no internal evidence of the supernormal, except little incidents and references in the work, and perhaps its general character involving a better digest of his writings than was normally probable. These suggested independent origin, despite the general presumption that prior knowledge inspired the main subject. But these points would not be conclusive to the hard headed skeptic; hence it was necessary that I should try experiments for cross-reference for evidence that Mark Twain was at the bottom of the affair.

After about half the sittings were over, Mrs. Chenoweth one day remarked to me that she had recently felt impressed that she should read Mark Twain, adding that she had never read him, but thought she ought to know something of the great American humorist. It thus appears that she was quite ignorant of his work.

Nothing that had reached the knowledge of Mrs. Chenoweth had been published about the case. A western paper or two had mentioned it, but the one that had said most about it is not a daily and has a very small circulation in the East. But it would not have helped her any to have known the facts. My purpose and the identity of the persons concerned were effectually concealed from her. She had never seen nor known the ladies and did not know that I intended to experiment with them. Moreover they were taken separately to the sittings. In her normal state she did not even see either of them, and she could not see them in her trance, because they sat behind her, being admitted to the room after she had gone into the trance. Every precaution was taken to conceal their identity from her. Under these circumstances ten sittings were held; I then continued the experiments after the ladies had left Boston. I took Mrs. Hays first because she was the less prominent of the two ladies and was evidently the main psychic. Mrs. Hutchings then followed with her five sittings. At intervals between the sittings with Mrs. Chenoweth I had sittings with the two ladies themselves, using the ouija board, with a view to giving suggestions at these sittings as to what I wanted with Mrs. Chenoweth, so that I could remain silent in the main experiments, and also with some hope that these sittings might help in the effort to get cross-reference.

Evidence of the supernormal appeared at once, but there was very little hint of Mark Twain until several sittings had been held. The kind of work he had done was obscurely indicated, but not until the fifth sitting did specific evidence of his identity appear.

At the first sitting for Mrs. Hays the first sentence was: "The Girl is a light." This was not only a correct hit, but the use of the word "Girl" was especially significant, as it was the name by which Mark Twain called her with Mrs. Hutchings in the ouija board experiments. Immediately the control remarked that "her sensitiveness was of interest" to me, which was especially true, and the first time that so prompt a recognition of such an interest had taken place. In a moment an allusion was made to her father, who is dead, and his desire to communicate indicated, and then some diagnosis of her powers followed. Immediately reference was made to "hands and visions," with the remark that she "sees things sometimes." Mrs. Hays is quite clairvoyant and has pictographic visions in one type of her work. Evidently the allusion to "hands" was a fragmentary intimation of the ouija board work, but it was not further developed at the time. It was said that some of these experiences were "written to make clear to some one else that they occurred." If this referred to the work of Mark Twain it was correct. It was specifically stated that these experiments were "not coincidences," which is particularly true of Mark Twain's work, which consists of posthumously written stories. It was stated that this work has "a real purpose."

Allusion was then made to the mother and to an Aunt Elizabeth; the former was dead and it was not known whether the latter was dead or not, though such a person and relationship were correct. Then came an intimation that a little boy was present, a child of the sitter. She had lost a stillborn boy some ten years previously. The sitter was said to be quite nervous. This was true.

When I asked who it was that was doing the work at home, understanding of my desire was indicated, with the intimation that identification would have to be established by messages "given through another source," implying the need of cross-reference. As the reason for this need, there was made what was tantamount to the admission that the subconscious might color a personality in the transmission: for the communicator said that "there is often a play of imagination to contend with, not always in the mind of the girl, but within the minds of the others," suggesting that more influences than the subliminal of the medium are likely to affect the results.

Reference to her father followed, and to his lack of interest in the subject, which was true in his lifetime. An allusion to the trance of the sitter was not correct, though there were signs of an incipient trance in some tendencies to anæsthesia and numbness. There followed a reference to an aunt and to some prophetic power of the sitter. The latter point is correct, but the identity of the aunt was not indicated. In a moment came a statement about "Jess," which suggested vaguely what I wanted to ascertain;

namely, the influence of Mark Twain; but it was not developed into anything definite.

At the next sitting the first communicator gave no evidence of his identity or of the supernormal, but on a change of control an allusion to "voices and sounds" was made, which was not especially important, though relevant, as raps had once been heard just before the death of the sitter's daughter. "Voices" do not form part of the psychic experience of the lady, but Mark Twain's daughter is a vocalist. A reference to "dexterous movements of the hand" was made, probably representing an attempt to speak of the work on the ouija board. Then came an allusion to music which was very pertinent, whether it meant something in the mind of Mark Twain or of the lady, as the latter is passionately fond of music and often hears it, as it were, in the form of auditory hallucinations, and the former stated later that music was referred to in the interest of establishing his own identity, as the living member of his family is a musician. But I am not sure that this later statement by him referred to this special incident. I denied, in the course of the communications, the pertinence of what was said, not knowing the meaning of the allusion to music.

It is possible that the allusion to music was a confused attempt to mention his daughter and her husband, the former of whom is a singer and the latter a pianist.

We had not yet any distinct hint of what I wanted. The supernormal had been vaguely indicated, but nothing that would lead me to believe that Mark Twain was present.

At the next sitting the first thing that occurred was an indication that Mark Twain was present and that the course of affairs had changed. His initial "M" and possibly the second letter "a" came at once, and then a message about his purpose, which was amply confirmed in the work at both places; namely, to help the world on a vital matter. He had signified this purpose in the work with the two ladies. He referred to the difference between his work at the present light and with the ladies; and to a "manuscript," in a statement which represented its nature well enough and coincided with what had just been done by the ladies, who had submitted it to a publisher in Boston. He described the work as "philosophical," which is not strictly correct, though "allegorical" would have described it. I had not seen the work and could not tell its nature, nor had I at that time been told its character.

For some time the communications continued to be pertinent though fragmentary, containing an evident attempt to give his name. "M two" or "M 2," which was very significant, came at once. Then the attempt resulted only in a possible reference to Stainton Moses, which I interpret "Moms" to be, and then Myers, both of whom often help in such crises. But "Ma" came clearly enough and then the subliminal made a prolonged effort to get the full name. "Ma" came first and then "S. T.," which were initials of his name, the first of his real name and the second of his assumed name. Then followed "Mark," whose meaning is apparent, and the initial of his second name. But the subconscious evidently supposed that Saint Mark was meant and alluded to "Saint." Then the name Mark was spelled out, though the subconscious evidently thought that Mark Hanna was intended, as Mrs. Chenoweth asked me if I knew any woman by the name of Hannah. The next day Mark Twain alluded to this mistake in a humorous way. But the most significant indication of his identity was the "M two," as it came before the subconscious had any hint of his identity. This expression was a correct indication of his name, which he had adopted after his experience as a pilot on the Mississippi River. It came in full later, but from this time on the case was clear. It is important that he thus established his identity with Mrs. Hays before Mrs. Hutchings took her place at the next sitting.

At the next sitting the most interesting phenomenon is the deviation from the usual course, which is for only relatives of the sitter to appear. Instead, Mark Twain came at once. First he tried to give his real name rather than his *nom de plume,* which, whether intentionally or not, is especially significant, as it did not exactly continue the effort with which the sitting of the day before closed. I got first the capital letter "S" and then "Sam," followed by "Cl," his name, as everyone knows, being Samuel Clemens. From the confusion with Mark Hanna on the day before, it is evident that the subconscious had not yet any inkling of his identity. With the failure of the effort to get the full name came the following statement: "Funny man cannot write his own name without so much fuss, but when one assumes so many titles one must inevitably make a mark in the world of literature, even if that literature assumes the ponderousness of Psychic Research or Christian Science."

This last sentence is packed full of marks of his identity. Evidently the use of the word "mark," especially in association with the reference to "titles," was intended as a play on his pseudonym; the allusion to Christian Science is to the title to one of his works. We must remember that the subconscious had not yet caught on to the real name. Immediately after the sentence quoted he referred to "Hartford" and the statement added: "Place, not person. To think that any one could take a Connecticut Yankee for an Ohio Statesman. Joke lost on you. To think a man of my superior hirsute growth should ever be mistaken for the bald and baby face of him who ruled a President."

Here again is a statement packed full of evidence of personal identity. It refers to Mark Hanna, who had the reputation of ruling President McKinley. Mark Twain had a very bushy head of hair and Mark Hanna was bald and clean shaven. Mrs. Chenoweth, of course, knew of Mark Hanna and possibly of Mark Twain's old home at Hartford, Connecticut. But she did not know normally that he was communicating nor that his presence had any connection with the sitter.[1] Immediately came the following spontaneously, connecting the present with the previous sitting:

"The 2 Marks, my name, exactly fits the case, the 2 Marks. Never mind. You know who I am now and it is all right for me."

(I knew it all along, but we stubborn scientific men have to get it on paper.)

"I forgive every Scientist except the Christian, and that is a matter of principle with me."

[1] Reference to his "A Connecticut Yankee at the Court of King Arthur" is also probably intended, and was "lost on" J. H. H., being noted by Miss Tubby, his secretary, when reading proof of this record.

The reader can see the point of this from the remark above that "2 Marks" came from his experience as a pilot, and from his relation to Christian Science, which he treated contemptuously.

He then referred to his living in New York, whither he had gone after leaving Hartford. He then explained, after indicating why music had been referred to before, that his return had the importance of being intended to show that he "was not a dead one." He then stated that this was not his first appearance, and that he had "practiced some through the hand of the girl," this term "girl" being the name by which he had called the two ladies in his work with them. He then compared his work with that of Frank Stockton, remarking that the latter had better look after his laurels. The whole passage was full of humor.

After this humorous account of his purpose he turned to the serious aspect of it and remarked: "I have a way of making light of it only that I may better keep hold, but it is the vital matter of creation." This reflected the serious aspect of his nature, which was not so well known as the humorous, the serious trait being known only to a few, or to those who could read between the lines. Mrs. Chenoweth had not read any of his works.

He took up the humorous vein again in a passage too long to quote and not otherwise evidential. But he returned to say that he had been somewhat familiar with the general subject of psychic research before his death. I knew this to be a fact and asked him to give an instance or two. He referred to a "vision like a mist rising and forming a picture before me," and then to conversation with some friends. I had in mind his experiences in "mental telegraphy," as he called them. But he did not mention these. The sitting terminated with a reference to "Samuel," his first Christian name, too well-known to be evidential.

At the next sitting Mark Twain began with the effort to get the name of his living daughter, which I did not know at the time, and succeeded in all but the letter "a" in Clara, which he completed later. He gave the name Mark in connection with it, and then made an effort to give the password which he had agreed on in St. Louis, but in which he did not succeed at the time, though he got the first letter of it, which I did not acknowledge. I did not understand it until he explained what he was trying to do. He went at it in a roundabout way. The following long passage shows what he was doing:

"It is not a safe thing for a man to go to a foreign land without his passports and I begin to think this is worse than any customs a traveler passes through, for passports are not enough. He must give his ancestry and his innermost purposes to a hard headed wretch who sits in command of the light. By the way why do you call the automatist a light?"

(It was originated by the Imperator group beginning with Stainton Moses and the Piper case, and I followed suit.)

"It may be to keep light craft away, as the rocks and shoals make havoc with all except strong swimmers."

(I understand. Do you remember the password?)

"You are referring to work done at another place which was to be repeated here s . . . or anywhere, if I found myself able to come."

(Yes, exactly.)

"And I have known from the first that I must get that through in order to prove that I was the same spirit who has been doing some things at home."

(Yes, exactly.)

"Now I referred to passports with that in mind and I intend to make good my plan to help them. You know whom I mean, the girls."

(Yes.)

Much of this explains itself. It has been true in recent years, though not before his death, that a traveler has to give his ancestry and purposes to custom officers or government officials, as well as a passport. Mrs. Chenoweth knew absolutely nothing about this. The query about the use of the word "light" turned out to be especially relevant. Mrs. Hutchings told me that Mark had used the word "automatist" in his work with her and Mrs. Hays. He is only the second person who has ever used the term through Mrs. Chenoweth, the other being Mrs. Verrall, who used it regularly in life. The word "light" or "medium," usually the former, is the one used in the work of Mrs. Chenoweth.

It was a fair hit, not necessarily implied by my query about the password, to refer to work elsewhere and then ask me if I knew what he meant by "the girls." The word "Girls," as already explained, was the one used by him to denote the ladies. The letter "s" is the first one in the password. This came later, but the consciousness of its importance is clear in the passage here.

There followed at once a reference to the sitter's mother as one who helped with the work. Mrs. Hutchings's mother was dead, and in a moment she apparently took control, but the sequel showed that Mark was the intermediary. The only evidential incident in her message was a reference to her head being dizzy. She had died from diabetes and during the last months of her life she had been very dizzy much of the time. The reference to a child was not clear until a little later. Mark Twain assumed control for a time and then the mother came and tried again but got only the initial " S " of Mark Twain's real Christian name. Then the subliminal came on for a time, during which the allusion to the " child," now said to be " a little brother " of the sitter, made it evident who was meant in the first reference. The sitter's mother had lost a little boy, who was, of course, a little brother to the sitter. She then made a reference to " Two Sams," which was very important, though wholly unknown to me. Sam Jones and Samuel Clemens, Mark Twain, had both come to the ladies in St. Louis.

The automatic writing then returned with an attempt to give the initials of Mark Twain's real name; they were given as " S. C. C.," which were incorrect, though I did not know it at the time. Later he spontaneously corrected the error. He then alluded to some experiences as he was dying, stating that he had seen his wife while he was in a semi-conscious state. After some non-evidential remarks he tried to correct the mistake in " S. C. C.," but failed. He then compared me to P. T. Barnum, saying under oral control that I " had an elephant on my hands in the work."

At the beginning of the next sitting it was evidently the mother of Mrs. Hutchings who occupied the time at first, though her communications were invaded by an effort to get the name Clara, which was that of Mark Twain's living daughter. It was evident throughout that the communications were an interfusion of the mother and Mark Twain, as they combined the mental attitude of the sitter's mother with some of the affairs of Mark Twain connected with the dictation of the two volumes through the ladies and the ouija board. The mother was probably the intermediary. There was an allusion to a picture, said to be a photograph of himself, in the room where the work was done.

This reference to a photograph has considerable interest. The record shows that it was associated with his daughter Clara. Now Mrs. Hutchings had a picture of Mark Twain in the room where she and Mrs. Hays did their work. It was a photograph taken at the time when he made his lecture tour around the world, his wife and daughter Clara with him. In the communications he had always used the word "home" to mean the place where the communications were made to the ladies. He was evidently referring to his daughter in this connection in order specially to identify the picture, as there were many photographs of himself besides this one.

Then came a reference to the "writing board," which definitely implied the ouija board, and then an effort to tell the nature of the work done, which was said not to be "personal messages, but more like editorial," with emphasis on the word "editorial." So far as this went it was correct enough, and also the further statement that the work was now almost complete. The following is the message on the point just mentioned:

"You have both been so careful to eliminate all that would mar the beauty of the pure expressions he wished to use."

(I understand, and do you know the name of . . . ?) [Writing went on.] "Book." (Yes.) "Of course I do, for was it not a part of the plan over here to have the complete work, name, title, size, description given to you about the make up &c."

(Yes.) [Sitter nodded assent.]

"It is not a joke at all, but a very earnest endeavor to make an addition to literature, a sort of posthumous work, see?"

(Yes, perfectly.)

"And the fact that the style and the form may be well-known to you does not make it less valuable spirit autobiography."

(I understand.)

"I feel that it is right to have this go on, because it will wake up some of the sleeping friends who had no idea of the possibility of such contact.

"I want the love we feel to be the incentive to further effort. Harpers people may help. You will know best what to do about that."

This is a very accurate description of what went on in the ouija board work. The dictation delivered through the board was often in incomplete and abbreviated sentences and these had to be filled out by the ladies. There was no doubt of what was meant, because the abbreviated sentences were clear, though unessential words were often omitted. The name, title, etc., were taken up and decided. The book, though abundant in humor, I understand, has also a serious purpose, and though its evidential value is marred by Mrs. Hays's knowledge of Mark Twain's work, it is said to be very autobiographic in respect to characteristic features in it. I had not seen it. The allusion to "Harpers" is very significant because the Harpers were the publishers of Mark Twain's works. Mrs. Chenoweth knew nothing of this.

The communications continued in the same vein, with characteristic and pertinent statements which do not require to be quoted at length. But a definite allusion was made to the "cracked sentences that had to be pieced together," which I mentioned just above. When asked what share he would have in the royalties, the reply was that it would be a "share of heavenly percentages," which was exactly the answer he had given to the same question through Mrs. Hays. He then gave the initial letter of the title to the first of the two books, though it is not stated that the initial was so intended.

At the next sitting he began the automatic writing with general communications that were interspersed here and there with evidential touches. He spoke of the work as having been undertaken with a purpose to help the whole world, which was an avowed object in the work with the ladies, and he spoke of it in an interesting manner as "keeping up the connection in a natural and supernatural way," meaning the contact with the material world. He showed that he was well aware of the pitfalls of fraud in any effort to do his work through the professional type and stated that he had given them a "sign password which would give the clear idea of my presence." It was not exactly a password, but was a sign to prevent successful impersonation by others who had tried to palm themselves off as Mark Twain, either in their work or elsewhere.

He then indicated, what was true enough, that one message was not sufficient to prove his case, and that the work which had been done at the other center was the kind he wished to put in the foreground, and remarked that he "sometimes found the flow of words very easy to start for her and then sometimes I have to wait a little, even when she gives me opportunity." Mrs. Hutchings recognized that this was correct. He then spontaneously corrected the error made previously about the initials of his real name, giving them now as "S. L. C." instead of "S. C. C." as before. I did not know or recall that he had a middle initial. I knew him only as Samuel Clemens. I had not read any of his works but two, and these some thirty-five years before.

He then turned to some personal matters and gave correctly the name of his living daughter Clara. Among his personal statements were references to his love of the old home in Hartford and his choice of New York for its opportunities, speaking of Hartford as the place where he "had so much happiness and pain," alluding probably to the loss of members in his family, as well as financial losses. He then mentioned a ring with some detail, but the daughter could not verify it. Some further statements were made about his desire to continue work through the ladies, and he then closed the communications with references to his interest in this subject when living. But while it was true that he knew something about it, the special incident stated could not be verified by the daughter. He spoke of feeling the presence of her mother, his wife, after her death and his endeavor sometimes alone to have her come to him. It is not known whether this is true or not. The sitting ended with the name Margaret coming in the subliminal recovery. It was the name of Mrs. Hutchings's deceased mother.

At the next sitting Mark Twain began by expressing approval of all such efforts and made a humorous allusion to substituting communication with the dead for "Catholic masses for the repose of souls," and then went on to give a very characteristic message:

"I am quite serious about this, although I have always had to labor about being taken seriously. If I preached my own funeral sermon with tears rolling down my back, no one would think I was at all serious about it, and some one would begin to cheer for the funny things I was saying, but I really have the revolutionary spirit in my bones, and it is with me now, and I think that the work that I have done at home and shall continue to do will help to revolutionize some ideas of my friends, if it does no more."

This passage, I understand, represents many actual experiences in his life. He was often cheered for humor when he was serious and he had to tell his audiences so. I never knew this and Mrs. Chenoweth knew less than I did about him.

The communicator then turned to a personal matter and reiterated that his wife's face was the first one he saw when he died. This, of course, cannot be verified, but it is a phenomenon that has been verified in a few other instances.

There then followed a long set of communications intermingled with evidential hints, and characteristic throughout. The ouija board or "planchette" was indicated as the method of his work through the ladies. Then an allusion to an "old spirit who now and then shows such a look of age on her face drawn and worn," with further reference to the mother of Mrs. Hays, coincides with the change in Mrs. Hays's face when her mother may be present. What was said about the personality exactly fitted her mother and described her characteristic facial expression in life.

In the subliminal Mrs. Chenoweth saw a man in white clothes. This exactly described the habit of Mark Twain. He used to wear a white suit a great deal. Mrs. Chenoweth told me that she knew nothing about his manner of dress.

The ladies left Boston after the sittings which I have just summarized and further experiments were conducted in their absence. At the first of these sittings Mark at once recognized that the ladies were not present, a fact not normally known by Mrs. Chenoweth, and after getting adjusted remarked how "good a receiver the little lady was," evidently referring to Mrs. Hays. This was correct, as the books will show, though it may be doubted if she could do systematic work of the evidential type as well. At an earlier sitting, as well as at a sitting with Mrs. Hays, I had asked Mark to give me the name of the personality who had preceded him in his work with the ladies. I had Patience Worth in mind, but I gave no hint at these sittings with Mrs. Chenoweth of what I specifically wanted. I did not know that Mark had been preceded by others as well as Patience Worth. He immediately referred in the present sitting to this request of mine and after some confusion he said: "Just a little patience," and paused, and then wrote "W."

This was almost the name Patience Worth in an indirect and oracular manner. The interest in it is the fact that this is the first time in the history of my work with Mrs. Chenoweth that the word "patience" has been used in the sentence asking me to wait. It has always been "Just a moment," "Just a minute," "Wait a moment" or "Wait a minute," so that it looks as if "patience" had been used as he had used the word "mark" to identify himself without making it a name. But immediately following this effort he said the "W" was wrong and evidently tried to give the name of "Rector," getting the first three letters of it, and then in the confusion got "J," which was the initial of the name of the book I wanted mentioned. The effort, however, ended in confusion. After a subliminal interval the automatic writing tried it again and got nothing more than the "J."

At the opening of the next sitting came the letters "Br," the first two letters in the title of the second volume received by the ladies, but it was not stated that they were so intended.

At the next sitting Mark Twain came with oral control at the outset. He spelled the first three words by letters and then spoke the words as wholes. He closed by giving his full name and address with great ease: "Samuel Langhorne Clemens, Hartford, Connecticut." Neither Mrs. Chenoweth nor I had ever heard his middle name. I knew the rest. But the chief significance lies in the ease with which proper names came in this instance of oral control. It suggests that, if we could eliminate the pictographic process usual with Mrs. Chenoweth, we might use clairaudience more effectively in getting proper names. It remains to prove this possibility in practice.

At the next sitting another communicator came and it was several sittings before I was able to get his name and identity established. It was Washington Irving. He claimed to have helped Mark Twain in his work with the two ladies. But there is no evidence of it in the record of the material for the two books. But on several occasions a friend was present who called for Washington Irving and he purported to communicate. As a cross reference this is not strong. But apart from this there was some evidence, not at all striking, that Washington Irving was helping in the work with Mrs. Chenoweth. Whoever it was certainly knew about the facts more or less.

He referred to something begun and discarded, which I learned to be true, and then to the trance, which was incorrect. He then referred to Robert Ingersoll and indicated that he had been present at a sitting, but did not say that he had communicated. Inquiry showed that a few days before the ladies started for Boston, they had a sitting in Columbia, Mo., and on a question being asked about him were told through the ouija board that he was present and had come out better than Henry Ward Beecher. As Mr. Beecher was a communicator here a few sittings earlier, this association of the names has some coincidental value, all the more when we know that Beecher and Ingersoll were personal friends, a fact not known to Mrs. Chenoweth. A pertinent allusion was made to religion in connection with him and a correct description of his facial appearance, but Mrs. Chenoweth knew enough of Ingersoll's connections and appearance from pictures to deprive the facts of evidential importance. In the passage about religion a comparison of the different sects to the rainbow induced me to inquire of his biographer whether he had ever used this simile in his lectures or writings. The reply brought out the fact that his biographer knew of three separate instances in which he had used the simile, but not in connection with religion. Mrs. Chenoweth has never read any work or lecture by him and does not like his views, thinking they were too negative.

Mark Twain followed with some communications, but they were not evidential enough to find a place in this summary.

Washington Irving apparently came again the next day and possibly tried to get his name through, for George Pelham was referred to as apparently helping him. The interesting thing is that George Pelham's real name was given by the communicator whom I suppose to be Washington Irving, as has been done by other strangers who would not naturally know that the pseudonym of Pelham was the regular one employed. An effort was then apparently made to tell me where I had gotten the password before. But it is not clear enough for me to be sure of it. Two or three coincidences suggest it, but an allusion to a phantom rather tends to nullify the hypothesis.

The next day Washington Irving evidently came again, but he did not get anything through that can be clearly described as evidence either of identity or of any special incidents in the work of Mark Twain. The capital letter " C " and then " Ch " which came were not intelligible at the time, but probably refer to Charles Dickens, who reported later.

The next day Mark Twain got the name of Washington Irving through and cleared up the perplexity of previous sittings in that respect. " Travels Abroad " were mentioned evidently in an attempt to mention " A Tramp Abroad " or " Innocents Abroad." When Washington Irving came himself he finally got the name of Rip Van Winkle through. Mrs. Chenoweth did not know or recall who created Rip, and associated him only with Joseph Jefferson, who played him. She might have heard about it and forgotten it. She had, however, never read it or any other work of Washington Irving, though she knew that he had written " Bracebridge Hall."

At the next sitting Charles Dickens was mentioned in the subliminal entrance into the trance and then followed automatic writing by Washington Irving. Nothing was given to prove his own identity except a casual allusion to John Jacob Astor, saying that he, Washington Irving, was present when Mr. Astor communicated with his wife, and then an allusion to the older John Jacob Astor. There was no hint of his presence when the John Jacob Astor, who went down on the *Titanic,* communicated with his wife, which was several years ago. But I turned to the " Life of Washington Irving " and found that he had been intimately acquainted with the elder John Jacob Astor, a fact about which Mrs. Chenoweth knew nothing. But Washington Irving was not present to prove his identity. He was explaining the object of Mark Twain's work, and he well summarized it in the statement that a group of literary spirits had felt that it was time to abandon rappings and knocking furniture about and to give some mental phenomena which might more effectually prove to the world what could be done by spirit communication.

He characterized Mark Twain's object and work in an excellent manner and it is impossible to give a complete conception of it without reading the detailed record. He continued this subject in the next sitting and discussed Charles Dickens and Shakespeare, indicating that their work had been influenced by transcendental agencies, but denying that his own work and that of Mark Twain when living were so affected.

At the next sitting Mark Twain came, announcing his presence by his real name, Samuel L. Clemens, and then remarked what is probably true, that, with the ladies he was Mark Twain and with Mrs. Chenoweth he was Mr. Clemens. He had difficulty saying what he wished, but assumed oral control again after it had broken down once and mentioned in a peculiar way the title of the most of the books he had written. He gave them in the form of a story in which the heroes of them played a part.

The next day Charles Dickens came and indicated that he had taken part in the work with the ladies, but if this be true it was as a silent partner. There is no trace of his presence there. He admitted that he had tried to finish " The Mystery of Edwin Drood " after his death and told where he had done so. After some difficulty I found that this was true in detail. Though Mrs. Chenoweth was very fond of his works and had read many of them, and knew that he had left an unfinished novel, she refused to read it and had never heard of any attempt to finish it after his death. But there was no evidence of his personal identity that I could treat as probably supernormal, except that Mrs. Chenoweth, just before she came out of the trance and for some time afterward, yawned a great deal. This was only the second time that such a phenomenon had ever occurred in my work with her and I suspected that Dickens was tired when he died. I went to Forster's biography of him and found that the symptoms of his approaching death were great weariness.

At the next sitting Mark Twain made the attempt to give his password. He failed by the direct method and Jennie P. came in with George Pelham to try the indirect method. She first mentioned the word " Tramp," which was not correct, but was the first word in the title to one of his books. Then the name " Susy " was given, which was the name of one of Mark Twain's deceased daughters. I did not know the fact and had to ascertain it from the living daughter. Then Jennie P. said: "Do you know about two words; that is a compound word, which is apparently one which he wishes to give as the password. It is something like O p e n S e s a m e."

Sesame was the password which he had given me in St. Louis and which a few days later he had given me in Toledo through Miss Burton, (on whom I had reported in Volume V of the "Proceedings.") In her case I got it written in letters of fire, so to speak, in the air. She was in a trance and I was the only person who could read it, which I did not do aloud. It was in pitch darkness. I mention it only because of its relation to the present cross-reference. It came spontaneously in Toledo and without my asking for it and without any possible knowledge of Miss Burton that I had been in communication with Mark Twain. Mrs. Chenoweth was equally ignorant normally of the facts.

Before the trance came on at the next sitting I happened to be talking to Mrs. Chenoweth about the unethical action of falling in love with married people or taking liberty with the moral law generally in such matters, and mentioned Petrarch and Laura, and Abelard and Heloïse, thinking of Mark Twain and his comments on the latter two in "Innocents Abroad," but being very careful not to mention Mark Twain in my remarks. Immediately on his beginning the automatic writing, Mark Twain referred to the subject and spoke of me as a good defender of his belief and referred to the case of Abelard and Heloïse by name, saying that he did not mean Petrarch and Laura. I asked where he had mentioned it and after some difficulty and mentioning first "Travels Abroad," he got the correct title of "Innocents Abroad." On inquiry I learned that Mrs. Chenoweth had never read any of Mark Twain's works and had not seen "Innocents Abroad," and did not know that Mark Twain had ever referred to Abelard and Heloïse. She, as a child, had heard her parents reading "Roughing It," but was too young to understand the humor of it.

At the next sitting Mr. Myers opened the communications with some general remarks, saying that the oral work would be stopped for a time and then be the next step in the development of Mrs. Chenoweth's work. He then made some evidential statements about Sir Oliver Lodge's family and his own. They are not relevant to the present matter. Then he was followed by Mark Twain, who referred to Mr. Beecher and Dr. Funk relevantly, and made some statements about smoking which repeated more or less what he had mentioned long before in a message. But he got through nothing else, though I suspected that he was trying to give the name of the book, which I wanted.

At the next sitting another communicator, who did not reveal his identity, referred to the Harpers as publishers of his books, and made a very pertinent observation about their character as publishers. He then mentioned Mr. Howells, who was an intimate friend of Mark Twain, saying that he might have chosen him to deliver the message, but that trained minds would so influence the work as to make it lose all personal distinctiveness, and that he had chosen the ladies because they would affect it less. This was a correct conception of the problem and an admission that the subconscious or normal consciousness can deprive a message of its individuality. After indicating, perhaps in jest, a possible title for another book by Mark Twain, the communicator began the effort to give the name of the book I wanted. I got "Jo," which was incorrect, and then "Jul," which was also incorrect. It was the Fourth of July and fire-crackers were being shot off outside, so that noise disturbed the sitting. Finally "Jim" and "Jerry" were given, both wrong, but found later to have a relevance which at the time I did not recognize. Then the oral control came and I got "Jack," "Jas," and then "Ja," when Mrs. Chenoweth recovered normal consciousness and said she kept hearing "Jappy." As "Jap" was the name I wanted I thought this wrong, but I later learned it was especially relevant and in fact correct.

At the next sitting, after some general communications which were quite characteristic, the attempt to give the name of the book was resumed. I got "Jack" again, and "Jasper," both of which I thought were wrong, and then "Jap" followed by "n," which is the last letter in the second part of the name.

I afterward learned from Mrs. Hutchings that incidents were

much more evidential than I had supposed. "James Jasper Herron" was the name of the character who gave the name "Jap Herron" to the book. "Jacky" was the name of the father, and Jasper had been called "Jappy" or "Jappie" by one of the characters in the book. I had known nothing save that "Jap Herron" was the title of the book to be published.

An interval of two weeks followed, during which Professor Muensterberg occupied the time, appearing suddenly and without suggestion on my part. It was apparently a part of a scheme of the controls to have him communicate at a certain crisis of present events and his own conversion to reason in regard to the war. At the end of this time Mark Twain took his place. As soon as he got control he took up the matter of cross-reference and compared his position in it to the Colossus of Rhodes requiring that he should have a foot at each place of communication while his head was in the clouds watching events beneath. The comparison was not natural for Mrs. Chenoweth, though I cannot make it specially evidential. I gave him a statement to report in St. Louis through the ladies, asking him to say that I was a cabbage head. I employed this phrase for a double reason. First I wanted to see the reaction and secondly I wanted to see what it might be possible to say about it at the other end of the line. I knew it would be a rude message to deliver, but it was one that was calculated to appeal to his sense of humor, and it did. His reply at once was: "How do you expect me to be so blunt. That message shows no consideration for cabbages." This answer could not be surpassed for humor and is Mark Twain to the core. Mrs. Chenoweth is not capable of it. She never indulges in humor, though she enjoys it when presented.[1]

[1] Circumstances which cannot be explained here, the matter being too personal, have prevented my getting the cross reference in this instance. The experiment could not be made as I desired.

On the evening of January 26th, 1918, I had a sitting with Miss Burton, 800 miles from New York. Without any hint of what I wanted, not mentioning a name or asking a question, I received three cross-references. Among them was the word *cabbage* given several times and accompanied by the word *mark*. These were written in the air in letters of fire. The séance was held in pitch darkness. The words were purposely not recognized until written several times, as I wanted to avoid mistake in reading them. When I read them aloud, three raps signifying that I was correct were given.

At the next sitting the attempt was renewed to get the name "Jap Herron" after some general communications by a friend who came to help in this very work. I got "Jap" and "Jappy" and then "He," but no more at this sitting. In the midst of this I got "C" and "CL," which were a part of his name, but spontaneously denied as incorrect. "B" came, which was the initial of the name of the second book, "Brent Roberts," but was spontaneously said to be incorrect, which it was for the book he was trying to name, but correct for what I also wanted. Two other letters came which are not clearly conjecturable.

Only occasionally had Mark Twain tried to identify himself to the remaining member of the family, already mentioned. He had mentioned a ring which the daughter could not recognize and as the situation made the incident rather equivocal, I resolved to broach the subject when I could and see if my conjecture about it was correct. The response was immediate and my supposition was supported.

In the original statement the name of the daughter Clara was given and in a few minutes allusion made to "Mamma's ring," which was said to have been given to the daughter, worn a while, put aside and then to have been in the possession of the communicator himself. The context shows unmistakably that the most natural interpretation was as I have stated it. But on the denial of the daughter that it had any meaning for her I put the matter before the communicator to have it cleared up, but without hinting at what I suspected and without telling anything more than that it had no significance to the daughter. The communicator then said that his wife was helping him in that message and that he was referring to *her* mother and his wife, her daughter. As Mark Twain's living daughter would not reply to inquiries I appealed to Mr. Bigelow Paine and he ascertained from the living sister of Mrs. Clemens, Mark Twain's wife, that Mrs. Clemens's mother had a beautiful emerald and diamond ring which she specially bequeathed on her death-bed to Mrs. Clemens, who constantly wore it and for some reason not known it disappeared, the sitter thinking that it was lost. The incident thus turned out to be true substantially.

However, I took occasion to ask what the attitude of his daughter was toward the subject, just to see the reaction. At first she had shown cordial willingness to answer questions, but finding the incidents trivial she had revolted against the matter and requested me not to communicate with her about it again. I had said nothing of this to the psychic either in or out of the trance, and hence I wanted to see what reaction I would get by asking what her attitude toward the subject was. In general the reply was correct, as I could easily see from her two attitudes as revealed to me. But as she did not reply to further inquiries I cannot be sure of details. Mark Twain, however, evidently saw the situation and resolved to press upon her some evidence of his identity. He mentioned her by name in one sitting and inquiry of Mrs. Chenoweth showed that she not only did not know that there was such a person but that she did not know that Mark Twain had any children at all. In a desperate effort to impress her in the last sitting he gave the following message:

> "It is to speak now of some foot trouble — that is, some little difficulty, which was his in the last years of his life when he could not walk as much or as well as he used to, and it was a source of annoyance to him. It was not simply growing old, but something had happened to his foot which made it necessary to be more careful in walking and in the choice of shoes, and as he had always been a great walker, very active and interested in all things out of doors, it was more or less of a cross to him.
>
> "That is one thing he wishes to speak of, and another is a small article, a watch charm, and it had some special reference to some group or body of people. It seems like a charm which may have been a symbol of some order, but he did not use it all the time, and as he shows it here to-day, it seems like a gift which he now and again looked at and felt some pleasure in the possession of."

The first incident about the foot difficulty seems quite clear. The daughter failed to reply to my inquiries to say whether it was either true or false, but inquiry of his biographer, Mr. Albert Bigelow Paine, brought the information that it had at least a modicum of truth. It is not exactly stated. Mark Twain always had tender feet that made it important to be careful in the choice of footwear. It was not due to old age, but, so far as Mr. Paine knows, it gave no special trouble near the end of his life, though he did not walk much during the last year, so that the record is not quite accurate at this point, and yet near enough to be significant.

Mr. Paine, however, writes that Mark Twain did have a watch charm as described, which was presented to him by the Yale Greek Society. Whether he took the emotional interest in it mentioned is not verifiable.

He then took up the effort of completing the name of the book I wanted and succeeded in getting *Jap Herron* through the subliminal, after failing by the direct method. The experiments stopped at this point and there was no opportunity to try that of *Brent Roberts* and I had to remain content with the previous hints of it that came involuntarily as I thought at the time. But as Brent Roberts was one of the minor characters in *Jap Herron* its association with the effort to get the name of Jap was very natural.

This cross-reference was tried and was more or less successful with another psychic, Mrs. Salter, who has not been mentioned since the study of the Thompson-Gifford case. While I was carrying on my experiments in Boston with Mrs. Hays and Mrs. Hutchings, I wrote my secretary, Miss Tubby, in New York, whom I did not inform of my work in Boston, to arrange for sittings with Mrs. Salter. I mentioned no names even to my secretary and she was as ignorant as the psychic of the persons whom I wished to see Mrs. Salter. Again they were taken separately without introduction, Miss Tubby not knowing Mrs. Hays at any time until after the sittings, and not knowing that Mrs. Hutchings was to have any sitting until that of Mrs. Hays was finished. As there was but a short sitting for each, the results were not so striking for our purposes as those of Mrs. Chenoweth. The best evidence for the supernormal in these sittings was irrelevant to the Mark Twain incidents, but in the course of them the initials of several persons connected with the case were given and the word "Jap" came. Correct names of places were given connected with both the story and the home of the ladies. While the initials given were often intelligible, they were not as evidential as is desirable. But the name "Jap" was an unmistakable hit of some interest. Considering that this immediately followed what occurred in Boston, though it was fragmentary and did more to prove the difficulty of communicating than anything else, the coincidences must be accorded some weight, though taken alone their meagerness would deprive them of scientific value.

It will be interesting to find some incidents from Mark Twain long before the experiments were made to test his relation to Jap Herron. He came spontaneously to Mrs. Chenoweth in February, 1913, and when the subconscious of Mrs. Chenoweth asked me if I knew any one by the name of Mark, I replied that I did, not thinking of Mark Twain, but Mark Hanna whom I might expect to be mentioned by a recently deceased friend of my own. When the automatic writing began the following came.

I ought to tell you first who I am for fear you might be under the impression that you are talking to Saint Mark, or some other great ones. I am S. C. and think it about time I dropped the *nom de plume* which gave me a following; namely, Mark Twain.

(Thank you. I know.)

I see so little to make me better comprehend what the meaning of it all is that I am not in the least tempted to mount a pulpit and preach to the lost. I only know that I am saved and that I have a few choice friends along with me and we are not worrying about the state of the rest of the world. It is most wonderful to be able to see so much at once. That is the one thing that stands out more clearly to me. It seems as if we had gained a double capacity to see. Do you understand what I mean by seeing?

(No, not exactly. Explain a little.)

Two worlds instead of one. We see double, in other words, and no one seems intoxicated either.

(Does the old physical world look as it did before passing?)

Sometimes it looks pretty much the same. It depends on where you float. Wall street looks very much like — shall I say what I think — (Yes) Inferno. It seems to have no saving grace as an atmosphere about it, but it always does look like that to a man who is not on the inside. I find a smoky atmosphere plenty good enough for me.

I think I ought to file a protest against some of the malevolent criticisms that have been made in my absence. Do you know how I have been hashed up since I died?

(No, I do not. I suppose I shall be done up when I get over there.)

So we are in the same boat. Let's take a pipe and smoke away our trouble.

(What made you choose the simile of a pipe?)

Nothing particular, only because I knew you would not smoke and I would do it all myself. You may learn when you get over here. You never can tell how soon a thing like a great truth may dawn upon a poor benighted man.

(Well, I hope it will not be one kind of smoking.)

I have not yet seen the sulphur pit, but I presume that there is one. Most of us would be glad of a chance to toss an enemy in on the sly, but so far I have restrained my desire and made a great effort to keep the peace and not to mar the joy of heaven.

The communicator then, after some further statements, went on to mention Mr. Howells, who had been his friend, and spoke of their relation to each other in rather affectionate tones and then tried to mention some incidents in proof of personal identity, but was not successful. The passage quoted above, however, is characteristic of Mark Twain in its humoresque features and it is given for that reason rather than for the forcefulness of its evidence, though it has this characteristic: for readers must remember that at this time Mrs. Chenoweth had not read a line of Mark Twain's writings. She merely knew that he was an American humorist. His allusion to smoking will be understood by readers who knew his habits in that respect, and not known to Mrs. Chenoweth. He was an inveterate smoker and, knowing that, I put my question as I did to see the reaction. It was characteristic and humorous enough. He used to say when living as reported of him, that he never smoked except when he was not asleep.

The discussion of this topic need not be detailed. The problem is not the general one of spiritistic explanation, but the connection between the experiments with Mrs. Chenoweth and the work of Mrs. Hutchings and Mrs. Hays. The introduction showed that the evidence for the presence of Mark Twain in the work of the two ladies would not be accepted by the scientific students of psychology. They might be wrong in saying that Mark Twain was or is not the author of the volumes claimed, but their skepticism would have the defence that Mrs. Hays's subconscious memory might be adequate to the production of the result assuming that her moderate reading of Mark Twain might endow it with the material for the work. The believer would certainly have to contend and to prove that this reading and desire on her part for Mark Twain to communicate had not impressed the subliminal with the subject matter for both reproduction and fabrication of the results. The skeptic would undoubtedly have the advantage in the argument from this point of view, and it was this fact which made my experiments so necessary for the purpose of limiting the claims of destructive criticism.

It is true that there may be incidents and general characteristics in the books that transcend any knowledge conveyed by Mrs. Hays's reading. Only a patient comparison of her work with that of the works of Mark Twain while he was living would discover any such evidence of his independent influence, and even then this view would represent largely, perhaps, the opining of the student skilled in the detection of fine points of internal criticism. But we should always be without a criterion of the limitations of Mrs. Hays's subconscious mind. That of Mrs. Hutchings can be excluded because she had not read Mark Twain until after he had done much of his work through the ouija board. But the mind of Mrs. Hays cannot thus be exempt from suspicion. Her reading and desires offer the skeptic all the leverage he wishes for an excuse against foreign intelligence and in favor of any amount of credulity about the subliminal. But he has to be refuted.

I have called attention to one consideration which this argument of subconscious reproduction and fabrication ignores. It is the fact that neither lady alone could move the ouija board and that it would move only when each had a hand on it at the same time. This increases the improbabilities that the two subliminals would act harmoniously toward a given result in any other sense than as passive media for the influence of outside intelligence. But the advocate of subconscious origin must face and solve this problem evidentially prior to his assertion of his own hypothesis. Nor will it suffice to say that this harmonious action is conceivable. That may be true. What we must have is evidence that it is a fact and it will not be easy to produce any evidence for it, perhaps not any easier than for spirits. I shall not dwell on this, however. It is a vantage ground to which we may return when we require.

I said that the primary problem was not regarding the existence of spirits in the work of Mrs. Chenoweth. I have said many times that I regard this as proved. Here we are concerned with the question whether the books by Mrs. Hutchings and Mrs. Hays have the same explanation as the work done through Mrs. Chenoweth. Whether spirits are the first thing to consider is a distinct question, and we have first to decide whether the same explanation applies to both results. If you insist that secondary personality or subconscious memories explain the work of the two ladies you cannot apply that hypothesis to the work of Mrs. Chenoweth. If you account for Mrs. Chenoweth's work by telepathy you cannot apply that to the work of the two ladies, Mrs. Hutchings and Mrs. Hays. Neither one of these hypotheses covers the ground. Besides, you would find that telepathy does not explain all of the facts in the Chenoweth records, so that you have an independent difficulty in those alone. In any case you have to reject both secondary personality and telepathy from the explanation of the whole. You cannot combine them for the whole, for telepathy will not explain all of the records in the work of Mrs. Chenoweth. You might speciously say secondary personality in the work of the two ladies and telepathy in that of Mrs. Chenoweth, but you would be confronted by the fact that telepathy will not explain the latter and that secondary personality may have its limitations in certain characteristics and details of the books. Consequently, if you are seeking a single hypothesis to cover the ground you must find it in normal sources; namely, in conscious fraud on the part of the ladies and a similar hypothesis in regard to my own work with Mrs. Chenoweth. I do not object to this theory. I shall only demand scientific evidence for it. The slightest investigation into the character and work of the ladies will dispel illusions about their relation to it, and though I may not be able to vindicate myself from suspicion, I am open to investigation.

The fact is that there is only one hypothesis that covers the ground without complications, and that is the spiritistic. The influence of Mark Twain would explain the work of the ladies, whether you have the proof of it or not. The communication of Mark Twain is the only explanation of the work of Mrs. Chenoweth. You cannot import telepathy, inference, and suggestion into it to account for the whole of it, and whatever explains it will explain the work of Mrs. Hutchings and Mrs. Hays. There is one hypothesis that explains both, and so far as I can see only one hypothesis explains both sets of phenomena consistently. That is the spiritistic and the one that has all the superficial claims to application. There should be no doubt in any intelligent mind that the spiritistic explanation is the more natural one, and that all sorts of devices would have to be accepted to evade the application of it. I shall not further summarize the evidence for this conclusion. It has been vindicated in so many other cases that it requires little further evidence to sustain it and I take it for granted in the nature of the phenomena.

The important thing is the light which it throws on cases which would otherwise be referred to secondary personality. The value of cross-reference for establishing the nature of such cases is unmistakably reinforced by the present one. It adds one more instance to the class which might have been doubtful before. It confirms again what was supported in the case of Doris Fischer, though not as an instance of multiple personality, but as one which the psychiatrist and psychologist would refer to dissociation. Without the experiments in cross-reference, the work of Mrs. Hays and Mrs. Hutchings would be referred to secondary personality and to this explanation only. But we cannot suppose that the work of Mrs. Chenoweth has that explanation, because of the conditions under which the results were obtained. The facts sustain the hypothesis for the work of the ladies which applies to that of Mrs. Chenoweth and the confident *a priori* speculations of the psychologist must be challenged. The main lesson is that we begin a generalization which may alter the judgment in regard to all such phenomena. Secondary personality can no longer be dismissed as requiring no further investigation and we cannot be allowed entire freedom in theories of brain cells as sufficient to account for the facts, though they are always complicated with any other causes. Psychology will have to revise either its theories or its facts. At any rate a doubt is established about the dogmatism of the psychiatrist and the student of normal psychology. The ramifications of the conclusion will prove as great as in the Doris Fischer case, to say nothing of the possibly extended influence of discarnate agencies on the living where they care to exercise it.

One warning, however, I must issue against all critics of the spiritistic theory. In this instance, as in all others where I defend it, I am not unconscious of the objections which these critics will bring in regard to the characteristic nature of the messages. There is a prevailing belief that a man's personality or personal characteristics should be clearly reflected in the communications. This assumption is held alike by lay believers and scientific critics, more frequently by the latter. I usually find laymen more sensible about this matter than the scientific man. But at least for a chance to criticize, the skeptic seizes on uncharacteristic incidents or expressions for disqualifying the evidence. But if he supposes that I do not concede such features in the record when advocating the spiritistic hypothesis, he very much mistakes my position. I can excuse the illusion in laymen, but not in scientific minds. No doubt we have, and perhaps must have, something characteristic of the communicator, if only in the veridical character of the incidents told in proof of personal identity, but tricks of language and style need not be present at all. The skeptic who assumes that the lack of characteristic phrase and style is against the spiritistic interpretation does not know his business. The fundamental assumption of the theory is that the discarnate personality is subject to the limitations and modifying influence of the medium through whom he gets expression. And there is more than this. He also is subject to the influence of other minds than that of the psychic. Not only must all messages pass through the mind of the medium and be subjected to the coloring effect of her organic habits of thought and language, but they must also often pass through or be affected by the mind of the control, and in some instances by two or three other minds acting as helpers or intermediaries. The result on which we base our conclusion is a compound, an interfusion of two or three, or even half a dozen minds. No critic should approach the subject without recognizing that it is this that he has to refute and that he cannot do it by remarking that messages are "uncharacteristic." They are always this to a certain extent and rarely reflect the personality of the communicator in its purity. It should not be expected. Only an ignorant person would assume its purity, after investigating the facts.

It will be found that the subconscious of Mrs. Hays affected the contents of the book and that the subconscious of Mrs. Chenoweth affected the contents of Mark Twain's messages. This is unavoidable. Several minds are probably involved in both products and an expert student of the phenomena would easily discover this interfusion of personality in the result. It is the prominent evidence in the case that escapes explanation by the subconscious alone, even though it may be colored by that influence. The same law is discoverable in the language and thought of any normal writer who is appropriating style and thought of his past reading. Hence I shall make the critic a present of any objections based upon the impurity of the communications. The spiritistic hypothesis is based upon the incidents which transcend explanation by the mind of the medium alone, even though the result is highly colored by it.

I must warn readers, however, against assuming that the story itself has anything to do with the conclusion here adopted. I do not care whether it is a good or a poor story, whether it has literary merits or not, whether readers of it can detect Mark Twain in it or not. It is probable that some who are very familiar with the man, his style and habits of thought, and perhaps scenes of his boyhood, may find traces of the man, but the circumstances prevent us from attaching any special weight to these. My own knowledge of Mark Twain as a writer is too small to pronounce judgment on these points and I should regard them merely as corroborative and secondary evidence if I found them. But the telling facts for any hypothesis must be the cross-references which unmistakably associate him with the books. It is in Mrs. Hutchings's introduction to the story that we find psychological traces of work which only trained psychic researchers would recognize, and then the cross-references add the rest. The one thing that must dawn on us is the repeated evidence that cases which superficially show no traces of supernormal influences yet yield to experiment proving that superficial indications cannot be trusted and we may have to allow for supplementary influences from another world where we least suspect them.

Authorities differ in regard to the *vraisemblance* of the story to Mark Twain. His biographer, while conceding that the Introduction contains incidents like Mark Twain and some unlike him, sees absolutely nothing in the story of Jap Herron that would remind him of Mark Twain. The reviewer in the " New York Times " finds some things like Mark Twain, but regards the story itself as inferior to his work. It is probable that people would differ widely on these points, sometimes according to bias one way or the other about the alleged origin of the story, but more frequently because of the unavoidable differences of conception which people have of any man whatever. But, as remarked above, this makes no difference to the hypothesis defended here. We are neither asserting that the story is like Mark Twain nor assuming these conditions in the communications that would make it probable that his characteristics would be reflected in the story. In the contrary, we assume that the story would be greatly influenced in the transmission by the subconscious of the medium and also by the mind of the control and of any other helpers in the process of transmission. It might actually lose all the specific features by which we should recognize him. Through Mrs. Chenoweth he said he simply had to think and that his thoughts had to be *interpreted* by the medium. This process of interpretation would greatly alter any message transmitted, and the man who does not allow for this aspect of the hypothesis is not discussing the problem we have before us, but some *a priori* product of the imagination with which we are not concerned. We may be wrong, but the hypothesis here advanced is the one we ask to be met, and that is that the subconscious of the medium is an important factor in the results, and that the evidence from cross-reference fits in with this, even to the extent of supposing that the stimulus may be wholly spiritistic while the contents may be wholly subliminal. We have no proof that this is strictly true in this special case, but the fact that no trace of Mark Twain may be visible to most readers, or even all of them, does not affect the hypothesis here advanced. It would affect it if the process of communication were as simple and direct as the expectant reader assumes, though in normal life a story, unless reported verbatim, will undergo modification when transmitted through another mind. With a symbolic or a new method of transmission or communication, and a number of minds to reckon with in the process, we may little expect to find clear characteristics of the person alleged to be the chief communicator, while evidence that cross-reference supplies may force us to admit the origin of the facts, though we have to discount their purity because of the complex conditions affecting their communication. This is fully illustrated in the Doris Fischer case. Personal characteristics of the communicator, while they added to the proof, did not determine it, because cross-reference makes us independent of that aspect of the problem. Hence the important thing here is the repetition of cases which tend to show that phenomena otherwise assignable to secondary personality may be proved to have a supernormal origin by the method of cross-reference.

CHAPTER XVII

DR. ISAAC K. FUNK

DR. FUNK was well enough known to make it possible for the public and scientific men to propose certain objections to alleged communications from him. As we have to discount anything which the medium certainly may have known about an alleged communicator, the person who is well-known pays the penalty of skepticism regarding his efforts to prove his identity. Dr. Funk was well-known to the American public as a publisher and this exposes any alleged efforts on his part to communicate to objections based either upon fraud or casual knowledge on the part of the psychic. But it was not his reputation as a publisher that constitutes the greatest difficulty about alleged communicators. Mediums can hardly keep themselves informed about every well-known publisher or professional man. It would be a waste of time and money to do so. Their custom, so far as it has been practised at all and that is not one-hundredth as much as Philistines suppose and assert, has been to get information about persons interested in the subject and likely to appear as investigators with some degree of constancy. And they have been so limited in their power to get information, even in such cases, that the practice of it had to be given up as not paying for itself. Gossip was a more fruitful source of information than organized efforts.

Now Dr. Funk happened to be known all over the country as interested in the subject and as experimenting whenever he could. So he was exposed more than the average person to any predatory instances alleged of mediumistic detectives, and we have to allow for the objections of the Philistine in this respect. He was the author of two books on the subject, " The Widow's Mite " and " The Psychic Riddle," both rather widely read, and probably familiar to many mediums interested in learning what he had to say.

Mrs. Chenoweth, whose work we shall quote here, had not read or seen either one of them, though knowing he wrote the first one. She knew of Dr. Funk's interest in the subject, and the consequence is that, if she had been so minded, she could have ascertained much about the man to use in her work. But in her trance nothing came that can be accounted for by reference to "The Widow's Mite," except the name of Mr. Beecher connected with it and that not certainly, and neither work, as remarked, had been seen by her. The facts which I shall quote here will not be explicable by referring them to any such source. Whatever objections are made must be based on the liabilities of casual knowledge or deliberate effort to acquire the desired information, as I had no means of giving the facts pertinence to any friend of his present as a sitter except myself, and I was too well known to the psychic to plead cogency on the score of relevancy to myself. But there is always the reply to skeptics at this point, that Mrs. Chenoweth has so constantly succeeded under test conditions that the skeptic has no vantage ground on which to rest and it would be useless expense on her part to seek information consciously. Beyond that her honesty cannot be impeached, and though that has nothing to do with estimating evidence, it throws the burden of proof on the skeptic who would suggest or assert fraud. The facts which we shall quote will doubly obligate such minds to produce evidence for their doubts.

Dr. Funk died April 4th, 1912, and his first appearance through Mrs. Chenoweth was on October 2nd, 1912. He did not give his name at first, but mentioned New York and Brooklyn, and spoke of Brooklyn as his home, a fact not known by the psychic, though she did know his relation to New York. Soon afterward he gave his initials. This assured me who it was and his full name came later.

Soon after giving his initials, he remarked that he had not been the fool or dupe that some of his associates thought and on being asked by me who it was that thought him so, having conjurers in mind, the reply was his "business associates" and I asked who else. To the latter question I received a remarkable answer. He mentioned the "Editor of 'The Sun,'" referring to the owner and editor, who died before himself, and said that he had found out that his editorial ridicule of Dr. Funk had been mistaken. The special pertinence of this was not known to the psychic. I pursued my question and got a reference to the "Clergy," which was correct enough, but not in my mind and then, after alluding to scientific scoffing at him, possibly known to the psychic, he said he had done things I would not do. This was quite correct and was in all probability not known by Mrs. Chenoweth. Asked to say what kind of phenomena he investigated, he replied "dark and strange and physical," meaning dark seances and physical phenomena. This was true. He had investigated much of this type and I none of it. Mrs. Chenoweth did not know that I had not done this, though she might have known that Dr. Funk did some of it. He then alluded spontaneously to his having got better material than some of his friends and indicated his difference correctly with Dr. Hodgson, and remarked that they could both now afford to laugh about it. All this was correct and not known to the psychic. He had obtained much better material than his immediate friends and had a sharp controversy with Dr. Hodgson.

The next week, October 7th, he reported again and began with some very characteristic things which one could not appreciate without reading the detailed record, and that is too long to quote, referring to his interest in certain aspects of the subject, but not in abnormal psychology. Then he referred to Prospect Park and the cemetery where he was buried. He was familiar with Prospect Park in Brooklyn and I learned afterward that he was buried in Greenwood Cemetery, Brooklyn, not far from Prospect Park. Neither Mrs. Chenoweth nor myself knew this fact. He then referred to having left a posthumous letter whose contents he was to reveal after death. This was true and absolutely unknown to any one but myself and his son. After a few more characteristic things he referred to the fact that he had been regarded as a "hot headed enthusiast," which was true, and added as truly that this was "far from the truth." Then came the interesting statement.

"I accepted much tentatively, to disarm the psychic and produce results, but I reasoned out the evidence calmly enough alone later." He then referred to the crudeness of the conjurer's "ignorance of the laws of psychology." This message represented the exact facts about the man, and the point is that they were quite contrary to all that was believed of Dr. Funk. He was supposed to be the dupe of mediums and totally unacquainted with the methods of investigation, and to be swallowing everything that came along. This was an illusion, and he was quite willing for the public to think that he was deceived, if only he could get at the bottom of a case. He was worth a dozen conjurers in investigating most cases. The contrary opinion would have been all that casual information could have brought to Mrs. Chenoweth.

He then referred by name to his brother and to his brother's son, though the manner of doing it is not strongly evidential. On the next day he referred in the subliminal stage of the trance at once to the Bible and other literature of the same type among different nations, specifying the Veda as one of them. He was interested in comparative religions. Immediately he mentioned Luther R. Marsh and Miss Dis Debar, using V by mistake for R in the first name, and correctly described Mr. Marsh and his relation to this subject, stating at least one thing not known to the public about him. Miss Dis Debar had been connected with Mr. Marsh's debacle in Spiritualism and this was well known to the public and might have been known to Mrs. Chenoweth, as even confessed by the subliminal, but she did not know how pertinent it was for Dr. Funk to mention the incident.

When the automatic writing began he confessed that communication was not so easy as he expected to find it and he then gave an excellent statement of what the process is. "Thought produces images and unless the thought is concentrated on some particular thing, the image quickly melts into other images, a kaleidoscope movement," and having difficulty in spelling the word "kaleidoscope" he asked if he had spelled it phonetically. This last remark, or rather question, was very pertinent because of his great interest in phonetic spelling, a fact not known to the psychic, but known to me. The process of communication described is another version of the pictographic method and well put, having perfect accordance with what we know of the remote processes in ordinary streams of mental imagery, especially in deliria. Comparison with the kaleidoscope is excellent and Mrs. Chenoweth's knowledge of psychology is too defective to be so accurate. What he said of his interest in phonetic spelling was better than the mere reference to it, as it represented his reasons for his interest in it and these reasons were not common public property, but were correctly stated.

He spoke of a few converts to it and I asked who one of them was, thinking of Mr. Carnegie. But his answer was to "Big Stick," using this expression as a reference to Theodore Roosevelt whom he had converted to the need of reformed spelling. But this was publicly known. When I pressed him for the name I had in mind, he failed to give it, but made some pertinent personal statements about the value of getting names on which he differed from other investigators. His attitude on this matter was unknown. The passage also describes the usual method of the sitter about this and other explicit incidents, indicating the preference for spontaneously given messages, which he correctly enough said was the method I employed.

He then gave me a sign which he would use elsewhere in proof of his identity, just after having said that proper names were always difficult if it was important to get them, but easier when there was nothing to gain or lose by giving them, a fact of considerable truth in this work. This sign I shall not mention here. But suffice to say that I got it soon afterward by means of the ouija board through two private people who did not know it and who did not know that he was giving it as his sign. I carefully refrained from explaining it to them. Then I got it through Miss Burton who, though not a private psychic, did not know anything about either the man or his sign, and was not told that I got it in my work with her. It was given along with his name and both written in the air in letters of fire.

The next day, in alluding to this sign he made use of the term "riddle" in referring to the problem, and asked me if it meant anything to me. I recognized at once the pertinence of it, and as fortune would have it Mrs. Chenoweth knew nothing about its relevance in connection with the identity of Dr. Funk, as he had used it in the title to one of his books.

He then proceeded, as he said, to give "some memories of phonetic conquests" alluding to converts in reformed spelling, having previously alluded by the expression "the Big Stick" to Mr. Roosevelt. He began with the capital letter C and after some confusion got the name Charles. I knew what he desired, but kept still and did not help. After some struggle and confusion, he got the name Carnegie. This was correct and though it was not known by the psychic that Mr. Carnegie had any relation to Dr. Funk, it might have been known that he was interested in phonetic spelling. As soon as he got out the name I asked the communicator if Mr. Carnegie had not been asked to do something else and the answer came promptly that he had been asked to endow psychic research. Dr. Funk had done this three times, but was rebuffed in it, the last time very emphatically. After explaining what he had done and how his request had been received he added significantly:

"It is so stupid to wait till a thing is assured before you give it sustenance. I think the uses to which rich men apply their wealth are subject to inquiry as to whether they are not suffering from hallucinations."

While not evidential this is too true to leave unquoted. In a moment he again took up his own method of experiment and gave a characteristic message.

Gullible was not exactly what I should have been called, but I saw nothing to be gained by spoiling the case at the start by suggestion or manner of disbelief. Let the spirits, if there are any, have their own way and take what comes and do the sifting of evidence in your own conditions. (Exactly.)

I knew that I got many things passed me that I could discount, but I would never have gotten it if I had done as the world thought I ought to have done.

(That 's right.)

God confounds us with combinations of good and ill, weak and strong, in every expression of His, and psychic matters are not exceptions to the rule. I thank God I leaned out far enough to catch the light of the dawn before I came into the full glory of the eternal day.

This was exactly his method and belief about the subject, and he was regarded by people who neither knew him nor his methods as "gullible" and deceived. He simply laughed at public opinion and went on with his work.

He had raised the questions, in our conversations, of "demons" or evil spirits, as mentioned in the New Testament, as possibly explaining the facts we had, and so I asked him at this point about the matter to see the reaction. The answer was not clear, though he gave an answer clear enough to what he supposed I meant by the query; namely, that "mistakes were not demoniacal," and referred to them as like crossed wires in the telephone, a conception which exactly represents what involuntarily occurs at times.

He did not communicate any more until January 14th, 1913. He began on that occasion with general observations, not evidential at first, except as they were generally characteristic, and then turned to this subject and its effect on the future. He said:

> There will be no mighty revolution which disintegrates and destroys the civilization of the Christian Era, but noiselessly as the morning dawns the work will awake and the sun of demonstrated truth will be high in the heavens, and the night of sorrow will have passed away and the wondrous beauty of the law of God will be revealed and understood. No revolution but revelation. That is my watchword now. In giving you this statement, I realize that I am using time which might well be given to the work of establishing my personal identity, but this also is part of my identity, I hope, as much as the memory of a particular collar button and its present location. Our friends, the critics, are amused that we busy ourselves in recalling Welsh Rarebits, when there are Bibles to be translated, but we dare not descend into literary efforts or they stone us because we cannot remember the wart on grandfather's finger.
>
> (Good.)
>
> What a contradictory jury we try our case before, and what an inconsistent judge passes sentence on us, because we dare show our faces at a place, in fact, the only place where we can get some inkling of the truth. No respectable people believe in spirits, they tell you, and when an eminently respectable and respected man dares to show an interest, they at once do their best to make him the reverse of respectable. [Pause after word "him."] I could not think of the word although I once fathered a dictionary.

In the last sentence he was referring to the word "reverse." The passage is a good summary of many a remark he made in conversation with me. He took exactly that attitude toward the public as a jury in the phenomena, and knew exactly what kind of evidence was necessary and what absurd things the public wants for its satisfaction and delectation. His relation to a dictionary is too well known to make a point of it, although the knowledge of the man by Mrs. Chenoweth is so small that we may well believe that she does not know the fact well enough to apply it so aptly. But casual knowledge may have been forgotten.

After further general observations he undertook to give some specific things in personal identity which could not easily be questioned in their evidential nature. He first mentioned the Orange Mountains, and then described in some detail a wooden building with Corinthian columns in a small town in view of the mountains and with maple trees on the street. It was said to be a church without a steeple, but with a square bell tower.

He lived the last few years of his life in a town near the Orange Mountains in New Jersey, but the church he attended there had no resemblance to the one mentioned, and no one seems to know of the building so minutely described. Mrs. Chenoweth knew nothing about his home near the mountains named. Nearly all his business life was spent in Brooklyn, New York.

On the next day, January 15th, after general communications of no evidential value, he referred to "pictures" and "physical experiments" he had made. But the confusion was considerable for some time, as I would not help in the message, tho surmising what he was trying to do. He got away from the subject, and as the incident had never been made public, I resolved to have him stick to the subject and I began the matter by recalling him to it.

(Now, were you referring to a picture that you got in one of your experiments?) Yes. (Now, who took that picture or made it for you?)

I have been trying to write that, for I knew it would be good evidence.

(Yes, stick to it.)

It was quite a curio. My mother was supposed to come and I could not see how it was done.

(I understand. That was the picture I had in mind. Now where and who was it that made it for you?)

I want to tell that also; for, while I was not sure of the method, I had doubts and suspicions, but there was the result before my eyes.

(Yes I remember.)

You know all about that and I have more to say about it now.

(Yes, go ahead.)

Two who had the work in their home and the way it was produced seemed most open and above reproach. And yet, if it were done as supposed, the world ought to stand still at the stupendous marvel. I left the answer to time, for I could not answer it myself. I was not a juggler nor sleight of hand artist. One thing I always said was that it was light bright.

(Yes, you mean that it was bright when the picture was taken?) Yes. (And two persons had to do with the making?)

Yes and they had their own conditions and time and home. I went to them, but it was after I was known to be interested in these matters.

(Yes, and can you tell where it was you went to them?)

B . . . On the train. I first went away from home.

(In what direction?) W e s t. (Yes, and I was seeking to have it on paper for evidence.)

Yes, of course, and I saw some slight changes in the picture to anything I had seen before as a picture of my mother. Such changes, however, could have easily been made by an artist. It was more than a photograph. (Yes.) I intended to say that before. (I understand.)

But it was not a bad piece of art nor superior, but still not execrable.

(I understand. What was the reputation of the artists in the matter?)

As varied as the clientele. Some cried, Impostors, some cried, Most gifted of the world's psychics. C . . . C h . . . Chicago.

(Good, that is the place.)

Yes, that is where I went. L . . . L . . . M . . . Bangs.

(That is good.)

Sisters. They talk as devotedly to the subject as you or I, but I have an idea it is trade talk, but do not yet know the methods used. It would be easy if collusion were discovered.

Dr. Funk visited the Bangs sisters to try their work at what was called spirit paintings. The conjurer can duplicate such phenomena with considerable ease. But Dr. Funk had an old photograph of his mother and did not show it or take it out of his pocket. He got a picture of her which he regarded as a good likeness and his son told me that he saw the likeness of his grandmother in it. I myself saw the painting, but not the original. Dr. Funk had not made up his mind about its character. That he told me in my conversation with him when I saw it at his home in Brooklyn. He was puzzled to account for it under the conditions, as that picture was so rare. The L and M are the initials of the Bangs sisters' Christian names.

Mrs. Chenoweth knew of the existence of the Bangs sisters and the nature of their work. But that was all, in so far as the present incident is concerned. The subliminal might have guessed the place after the allusion was made to the fact that "two" were concerned in the picture and after my admission that it was "West," Chicago and the Bangs sisters would be a natural guess after that, for any one who knew them and their work. But she did not know the other facts. The intimate personal traits and opinions of Dr. Funk on this incident were not known to her and were known to very few even of his acquaintances. His attitude toward the incident is described with perfect correctness and accuracy. The description of the two sisters as having a reputation as varied as their clientele is literally correct and well known to Dr. Funk, and could be known to Mrs. Chenoweth, but the terms of the description are not like Mrs. Chenoweth and are like Dr. Funk.

Dr. Funk did not appear again until June 14th, 1916. I was busy with other work in the meantime. When he did appear he first gave his name and began with a reference to the picture which I have mentioned in detail, and spoke of the cost of such work in rather humorous terms. Then he immediately took up his posthumous letter and warned me that it would take a little time to deliver its contents. He again referred to simplified spelling, but got no further at that sitting.

At the next sitting, June 15th, he began by explaining the difficulties in communicating and, though at first it contained no element of personal identity, it soon revealed a very subtle characteristic imbedded in ideas beyond the knowledge of the psychic. He began with his Christian name and then came the following.

I am here again and it does not seem at all strange. In fact it is so natural that it is with some difficulty I realize that I am making a bridge of myself.

You know how easily one drops into conversation with interested friends and when a specific matter is questioned the mind becomes unruly and questions its own knowledge, even when perfectly sure ten minutes before that the knowledge was exact and correct. I think that is exactly what happens here or anywhere when we try to express a particular idea. It seems more like that to me than like trying to master or conquer another outside element which you people have named the subliminal of the medium. I think we need not go outside our own experiences to find ample reason for the disturbances mentally when trying to recall. It is very like trying to recall what certain things would be in French or German or a language we did not commonly use, a sort of translating process because we are not as dependent on language as you are.

(I see.)

Sounds were not always the means of communication in earlier tribes of men, but developed powers given new expressions, and signs and symbols were left behind, and with some difficulty new methods of speech were adopted and the mongrel method of signs and sounds, still used by the race, is a left over condition. So much that comes to us is a mongrel expression of a past form of intercourse, and much that we commonly use drops into the effort and leaves hiatuses which seem like sorry efforts at communication.

I have wanted to pass this theory of mine down to you for some time, but have had no chance. It is not in the least like telepathy, this method of communication between us here, but has as much to do with vision as sound.

The subtle point of personal identity in this is the reflection of Dr. Funk's study of the principles of language, when living, in order to work out a scientific basis for simplifying our spelling evidence of which I often remarked in his office. On this question the message is not perfectly clear, except in reference to certain points. But it is evident that he is trying to compare our own normal methods of intercourse and those which prevail on the other side and affect the process and the contents of the communications received by us. The statement that with them vision has as much to do with the process as sound is only a recognition of the pictographic process and includes the similar characteristic in sound. That is, clairvoyance is as much a factor in communication as clairaudience, and the connection between their methods of transmitting to us and our own intercommunication by the symbolism of language which is sound only and involves physical phenomena, is that the symbols are quite different. We should say that it was like telepathy in that respect. Dr. Funk denies this, and it is at this point that he indicates a point of personal identity, as he knew nothing about the pictographic process and thought telepathy a transmission without the use of symbols or hallucinatory pictures.

There is no trace to me of Mrs. Chenoweth's knowledge in the passage, though the terminology is at least partly hers. The expression "left over" is hers for certain mental phenomena, noticeable in her own conscious experience, but the ideas are more subtle than anything she knows about language and the processes of human intercommunication. The whole subject reflects the deeper aspects of Dr. Funk's mind on the question of language. But he went on a little later and stated that there was a telepathic communication between them and us and that it was the result of "some other contact." I saw that he had opened a question as to the nature of telepathy and asked him if he meant to say that telepathy between spirits and the living required the aid of another party, and his reply was the query to know if I was "referring to the message bearer theory now." On my assent, his reply was a most interesting one, though we cannot verify it. Of the transmission he says:

"That is often purposely done, but conversations, spirit contact and consequent knowledge of situations and emotions, often fall into the consciousness of a sensitive quite irrespective of definite purpose, but such knowledge is being expressed somewhere at the time, else it could not overflow."

Here we have an intermediary involved in the telepathic transmission of thoughts of the dead to us and with the fact also the involuntary transmission of thoughts going on elsewhere at the time, a phenomena which I have often remarked in the work of the psychic. While it does not directly assert that the same process is connected with telepathy between the living, it is more or less implied by the conception outlined and that intermediary would most likely be a discarnate spirit, and both the sporadic character of the phenomena in the apparent purposelessness of much of it would favor the view.

The next day, the 16th, he recurred again to his method of investigating and referred to dark seances which he had often had, though not constantly, the facts being wholly unknown to Mrs. Chenoweth. He remarked: "I have heard it said that I was easily fooled, an old idiot who could be fooled with his eyes shut, but I don't need to refute that statement here: for you know the best detective work is done when one is supposed to be unwary."

This was quite characteristic of the man and was a secret with himself and a few friends. Finding that he was getting confused in what he was saying, he changed the subject to the Bible and said he was a believer in it, which was true, and he thought, as he says here in the message, that "some light might be given to certain passages and statements by the study of the occult." I saw my chance and took up the subject.

(What passages, for instance?)

I thought the matter of some of the old Testament stories might well be explained by the understanding of the laws governing the modern manifestations.

(What in the Old Testament, for instance?)

Just a minute. I wanted to reconcile old and new mythological Biblical statements. Some of this you may know about, for it was a matter of interest to me, often expressed to my psychic research friends. The woman of Endor and Moses and the Commandments. Red Sea episode and Samuel. The misinterpretation of these with several others brought darkness rather than light, and I believe now as I did before I came here, that the light on the ancient Scripture will come through modern interpretation, through the knowledge obtained through psychic research work.

While we never discussed this subject specifically, he threw out remarks about the relation of psychic research to religion that prove this message to be very characteristic, as characteristic as it is correct about the problem. But Mrs. Chenoweth, whatever she believes, did not know Dr. Funk's views on the matter.

He then went on to state the change of view which he made in the doctrine of the resurrection and added that, "when we lift ourselves to the divine state, our communicators will be of that type, but while we are less than that, we receive visitors of our own ilk." I expressed my assent and we continued: "We have had some straight talks before I came here, and we were of the same mind on these things, and the conception of making our messages other than from people like ourselves never came to us, plain people returning in plain fashion."

This passage is a clear reference to what I knew to be characteristic of Dr. Funk when he once remarked to me in conversation that the dead were "not angels but just folks." He had no patience with the ordinary conceptions of the dead, and knew nothing about the processes necessary to get the more spiritual type of message. I tried at this point, without hinting what I wanted to see, if I could get him to refer to a view which he once mentioned to me as an alternative to spirits; namely, the "demons" of the New Testament, but he did not catch my point. He referred, however, to a perplexity which had troubled him at times; namely the "cosmic reservoir theory" and also "dual consciousness," which might be convertible with his "demon theory," and remarked that "we knocked down so many straw men before we built up our final form" of theory.

This too was the substance of many a conversation and represents his attitude and conception of the problem clearly enough. He did not appear again until June 19th and then began with the remark that he had known Whirlwind before he died. Whirlwind is one of the controls of Mrs. Chenoweth, otherwise spoken of as Jennie P. His statement was true as he had seen records of her work and was interested in her personality, a fact Mrs. Chenoweth did not know. He then went on to his own work again.

I knew the tricksters quite as well as you, or better, for I had the temerity to risk being duped, and one by one I found them out and piled up my evidence for and against. I thought it best to know for myself and not to take the word of some one else.

(I understand.)

I think it time that some of these people whom we both knew should take some responsibility toward shaping the destiny of the work.

(Could you not from your side influence one of them to help? You know whom I mean.)

Yes I think so, for there is more done from this side than is supposed. You refer to our friend in New York who has been approached before, through some friends of his, but who seems slow to see the importance of the endowment. I think endowment ought to be understood as meaning equipment to unearth the truth about this subject either for or against. Some very canny people would be glad to have a devil unmasked, but never care about putting aside the veil from the face of God's angels.

(Who tried to approach that man?)

Let me think. It was done, I think, before I came here.

(Yes it was.)

I mean before I died, and I thought at one time we might get something as well as the various towns and groups that did, and when I came here he was one of my first attacking points. Andrew Carnegie.

(Yes, that is correct.)

Peace seems to have needed ammunition, but he does not need to withdraw from that in order to give us a due interest. Angle worms get quite as much attention as angels.

Dr. Funk had investigated "tricksters" more than I had done. Mrs. Chenoweth did not know this fact, and he had studied the results as stated. The allusion to endowment, it will be seen, was quite spontaneous and I at once directed my tactics to see what he would say on that point. The result justified my expectations. Dr. Funk himself is exactly represented in views taken here, as shown in many a conversation with me, and he himself had tried three times to get Mr. Carnegie to help us, but without success. He was close enough to Mr. Carnegie in the matter of simplified spelling to venture on this, but was at last denied the matter in a rather plain way. The remark about angle worms is an interesting reminiscence of the work of Darwin as compared with the investigation of the human soul. It was exactly Dr. Funk's idea of the matter, though he never used that particular analogy to me.

Following this message immediately, he took up a subject of his own experience whose pertinence in this connection it would require much time to explain, but its evidential import is easy. He asked:

> Do you recall Brooklyn and work done there and some queer things that happened which were in the nature of evidence?
>
> (Yes, tell all about it.)
>
> Circles where some manifestations of a physical nature purported to be given and where ghosts, apparitions, sounds, lights came.

This is a clear reference to some dark seances in Brooklyn where just such occurrences took place and he always reserved his opinion about them, as intimated in the use of the term "purported," and owing to the incident of the "Widow's Mite" which occurred there, he took me once to the performance, at which nothing of interest occurred, except that I was convinced that the medium, a private person, was honest, though doing things which the conjurer would call fraud, but which were evidently somnambulic phenomena on the borderland of the genuine. Mrs. Chenoweth could know none of these things. The sequel is interesting as proving that I have rightly interpreted the incident.

Dr. Funk did not appear till June 28th, but on June 27th Henry Ward Beecher purported to communicate. The importance of this lies in the fact that he was for a long time the pastor of Dr. Funk in Brooklyn and was connected, as a communicator, with the very experiments mentioned in the last quotation from Dr. Funk. Mr.

Beecher began and communicated about the difference between his work and ours, but recognizing the far reaching import of the scientific side of it, and half jocosely treating of emphasizing the difference. I did not know who was communicating and I interrupted the generality of the message to ascertain his identity. It resulted in the following passage, with an item of unusual interest in the personal identity of both men.

(May I ask who is communicating?)

Your friend, I. F., Isaac Funk, is my friend and he laughed at some things I asked about your efforts and his, and he was to write today. He [was] always a clergyman with leanings toward the unusual. Did you know that he could preach?

(Yes.)

A sort of emergency fund. When he could do nothing else, he could preach, he told me, but he did too many other things to make his preaching the one great power in his life. I knew him and love him.

I am H. W. B. Brooklyn, Plymouth.

(Yes, that 's right.)

I could no more rest on a cloud of glory than Mark Twain. We have to find some way to get back, if it is only as a supply, when the regular pastor goes away.

(I understand.)

I have quite as much interest in my fellow travellers as Funk or you, even if I wrote no posthumous letters to startle an unsuspecting world.

(I understand. Did you ever communicate with Dr. Funk?)

Yes, yes, and tried to wake him up to the importance of the cause and he knew I came to him, too.

(What incident?)

There you go. What did I tell you?

(Yes.) [I laughed heartily as he was joking me on my evidential bent.]

It is not how you can make your power felt, but what kind of chips did you use to make the tea kettle boil. Well, if you must pin me down like a school master here it is.

I came to him several times, and on one occasion a message proved of value to him, and I always felt I would like to tell him that I did it myself. He used to wonder if I did it or got some one to do it for me. Money, there was money in that message.

(Yes, go ahead.)

And money that made him take notice. The old lady, the old lady, good old widow.

The control was lost at this point, but to those familiar with the facts the passage is clear. This is the story told in Dr. Funk's book "The Widow's Mite." In working up the Standard Dictionary, Dr. Funk got one of the ancient coins, called the "Widow's Mite," once owned by Mr. Beecher, to use in an illustration. At one of the sittings in Brooklyn referred to, in the passage quoted previous to the message immediately above, Mr. Beecher purported to communicate and referred to this coin and said it had not been returned. Dr. Funk said that it had, but Mr. Beecher said that it had not, and told just where it was. Dr. Funk went to his office and to the safe where he knew it had been kept at one time, but could not find it in the place to which he had been directed by Mr. Beecher. He then went to another sitting and Mr. Beecher again communicated. Mr. Beecher was told that the coin was not where he, Mr. Beecher, had said it was. Mr. Beecher described the situation more minutely. Dr. Funk went away and made a second and more careful search and found an envelop with two of the coins in it. But he did not know which one was Mr. Beecher's or which one was genuine. He knew that one of them was counterfeit. He thought the red one genuine. He returned to the sittings and told Mr. Beecher what he found and asked which one was genuine, and was told that it was the black one. Dr. Funk did not think so. He went home and sent both coins to the Philadelphia Mint and asked which was the genuine "Widow's Mite." The reply was the same as Mr. Beecher's; namely, the *black* one.

The pointedness of the incident explains itself, and considering that Mrs. Chenoweth had not seen or read the book in which the incident was made public, the reference to it here by the original sender in company with the receiver makes a cross reference of the incident as well as an incident in proof of the identity of both men. The only weakness in it is its liability to casual information from gossip about Dr. Funk and the "Widow's Mite," and its connection with Mr. Beecher. The connection, however, and the withholding of the communicator's name are so much in favor of the genuineness of the phenomenon here and also the manner of making the reference to the idea rather than to the specific incident when the subliminal should have reproduced the exact language of the recorded incident. The relation to the previous allusion to the Brooklyn sittings, about which Mrs. Chenoweth did not know the facts, also is some protection to the case and in all it has an unusual and complicated interest.

The next day Dr. Funk took up the matter and stated things that had not been recorded in his account of the facts. He said that "the British Museum held nothing better." This was true enough and no part of the incident as published. He then took up his experiments and mine in an instructive statement reflecting his personal identity in a way not known to Mrs. Chenoweth. He started with a reference to the contents of his posthumous letter.

I tried to make simple assertions, because we, you and I, had talked about the difficulties of getting complex statements through.

(Yes we did.)

And I knew that the vultures would be after my bones. I had been falsely identified with so many associations when I had only shown the interest of the passer by.

(I understand.)

You knew that and you kept away. We had to make a special arrangement for you, either at your house or another, for the public demonstration did not appeal to you.

(Correct.)

That will not help you much, though, when you die. They will lie just as glibly then as they do now.

I do not know about the first statement of this message, as it pertains to his posthumous letter which has not yet been opened. But the rest of the passage is exactly correct and not known to Mrs. Chenoweth, though she might have inferred by lack of interest in public demonstrations. But she did not know that Dr. Funk was aware of the fact, and especially did not know that he was exactly correct in stating that the only way he could get me interested was to make an appointment at my own house or some private house other than my own. The mental tone of it also is his, especially his consciousness of how he was regarded and his indifference to it. Mrs. Chenoweth did not know the man well enough to reproduce him in this manner.

Immediately he followed this message by one in reference to a psychic whom he had often met and with whom he had experimented, identifying her by reference to Judge Dailey by name with whom he was well acquainted and concerning which fact Mrs.

Chenoweth knew nothing, though she knew well enough about Judge Dailey and this medium. He referred to this medium in unmistakably clear terms, and then referred to another one in correct terms, comparing the two persons correctly and recognizing that the latter had genuine powers. This was recognized by Dr. Hodgson when living. While Mrs. Chenoweth knew about both psychics, she did not know that Dr. Funk knew them so intimately.

At the next sitting, June 29th, he alluded to Mr. Carnegie briefly again, and then passed to communications about things on that side. There was nothing in them that is verifiable, except some statements about religion which were characteristic of him and not in any way known to Mrs. Chenoweth. Though the passages are interesting they are too long to quote and have no value in proving anything when taken alone. In the course of them, however, he turned aside to mention a matter which required him to speak of his son which he did, the fact that he had a living son not being known to the psychic. But he first gave the name Benjamin which was the name of his brother who had died a short time before this and was not known in any way to the public. The circumstance had evidential character of considerable importance and later he corrected the mistake here made of confusing him for a moment with his son.

On June 30th he recurred again to Whirlwind in a correct way and evidentially, but for the previous reference to her, and then made the remark, while explaining the confusion about his brother and son, that spirits communicated automatically while they might be thinking on another matter. Though we cannot prove this individual statement, there is evidence that the statement is probably correct. At least the facts make it a legitimate hypothesis to be tested and proved in the future. It certainly explained why he mentioned his deceased brother Benjamin when he should have mentioned his living son, who was the only person concerned with the matter of his message at the time, and who was definitely indicated in the correction. He continued his communications on the process of transmitting messages and then turned to a matter still to be considered. At the sitting of July 1st which followed he referred first to an attack in the "Brooklyn Eagle" upon him for his adventures in this subject. This paper had attacked him along with others, and the fact was not known to Mrs. Chenoweth, as it occurred before the new American Society was organized, and was not known specially outside the city in which he lived. Toward the end of the sitting he referred to some old letters he had and specifying one as from Abraham Lincoln. Inquiry showed that he had corresponded with many public men about that time, but no letter from Mr. Lincoln was found.

On July 5th, after an interval occupied with another person, he returned to the work and referred to his library, and when I remarked that I knew nothing of it, he went on as follows:

You know nothing of my home?
(No, nothing save that I was in it once.)
I thought you had been there, but it was when something was going on.
(Yes, and you showed me that picture . . .) [Writing began before I had finished my statement.]
Yes mother's and there were some other things that went with it, slates, messages you know.
(Yes I do.)
And some were very apparent tricks and some were not so apparent, but possible tricks.
(Yes I understand.)
And I flatter myself that the perpetrators never knew my real opinions, for I wanted the result whatever it might be.

It was his mother's picture that he showed me on this occasion. I do not recall that he showed me any slates at that time, but he did show me slates and tricks he had witnessed on another occasion. His attitude on the phenomena is correctly indicated. The tricksters never found out what he thought about them. He was too sly to give himself away. The remainder of the sitting was taken up with another matter.

At the next sitting little came that I can easily make clear until the end. Then the following was given.

I wonder if you recall anything about a hotel interview in New York.
(With whom?) You. (Yes, go ahead.)
You and a medium, meeting with spirits.
(Yes, tell me all about that.)
I have been more eager to recall it, for there were several things involved that only you and I knew.

(Yes, stick to it.)

Sometime ago it was, and it proved of greater value than we knew at the time.

(Do you remember who the important communicator was?)

Yes, that I will tell.

The psychic suddenly came out of the trance before the message was completed. We had a sitting at a hotel in New York at which a mutual friend was present with Dr. Funk and myself. The psychic was a private person of good standing. The communicator was Thompson Jay Hudson and he answered a question of Dr. Funk's involving a private matter that passed between the two men and that none of us but Dr. Funk knew. To have gotten the name of Hudson at this juncture would have been a most excellent piece of evidence. But he failed at this time and later alluding to the matter again referred to a "man across the water." The other person present on the occasion was a man from England. Later he got the name Thompson through and thus cleared up his original intention and made the evidence excellent.

But in the same sitting he alluded to another incident of some interest which had been a very funny one. Professor Shaler had tried to communicate with me and got into serious trouble in the effort. His getting free was a very funny incident. Mrs. Chenoweth knew nothing about it. Dr. Funk was told it by me, because it was an incident he would enjoy and because it threw light on the difficulties of communicating. He here referred to him and the incident. It was better evidence of supernormal knowledge than it was of personal identity, though it had some features, as remarked, of this.

He did not appear again until July 11th and even then only an incident or two has special pertinence. He was referred to by the control as interested in "the Enigma of Existence" and I was asked at once if I saw "the semblance of the title" and when I assented, the statement came: "I thought you did. The Sphinx has spoken." He was then said to have known the Bible "from beginning to end." This last was perfectly true and not known by the psychic. The reference to the Sphinx and to the "Enigma of Existence" and the semblance of the title was evidently a reminder of the title to his book called "The Psychic Riddle," which Mrs. Chenoweth did not know.

Dr. Funk did not appear again until February 9th, 1917, when he appeared with Henry Ward Beecher again. I had been occupied in the meantime with another matter. Mr. Beecher did not reveal his identity, and my question brought Dr. Funk to the forc. He indicated who was with him, but only after he had made the following communication.

I want to speak of a bronze piece.

(Describe it.)

[A circle was drawn.] Medallion. Did I try to tell you something of a medal when I was here before? It is a medallion made of bronze with repousse figures. Much interest to me. I thought I wrote about it before.

(I do not recall it. Did it have a special name?)

What did you do to my old friend Henry Ward? [I had received the previous communication from Mr. Beecher with much indifference, as he did not identify himself and I was anxious to have something else.]

(Do you know?)

Gave him a chilling greeting. He is smiling here and says he thinks you would have no use for the Angel Gabriel, if you had an engagement with Jack Jones to give evidence.

To return to H. W. B. [Beecher.] This was an occasion earlier than this one to-day and he also tried to make connections at another place. You know Lee, not here, but another place, another light.

(I don't know anything about it.)

Do not be too hasty for this is sometime ago, and I was there too.

I did not recognize what was meant by the allusion to the "bronze medal," and inquiry showed that he had no such thing so far as the son knew. But the sequel showed that he meant the "Widow's Mite" which was of bronze, and the mental picture by which the message was transmitted involved a mistake by the control in the interpretation of the picture, taking the picture of this small coin as that of a "bronze medal."

The reference to Mrs. Lee was very striking, as the sequel proved it to be. Mrs. Chenoweth knew nothing about her. I had never mentioned the lady or her work to Mrs. Chenoweth, and I did not know what the reference here meant. I wrote to her at once to know if she had any photograph of either Mr. Beecher or Dr. Funk among those she had taken. She replied that she had one of Mr. Beecher taken sometime previously, but none of Dr. Funk, so far as she knew. She sent me the picture and no one whatever would question the identity of the man in it. It is an excellent photograph of him. It claims to be a spirit photograph and Mrs. Chenoweth could not know about the fact. I was familiar with Mrs. Lee's work, and published some of it in the "Proceedings," of which Mrs. Chenoweth knew nothing, but did not myself know about this photograph of Mr. Beecher.

Dr. Funk did not appear again until February 12th, 1917. He began characteristically with a quotation from 1st Thessalonians, but without definite meaning that can now be determined. He then went on to say that he thought the sacred books of the East might be studied with advantage to psychic research. But he accompanied the statement with the remark that "precepts" had accompanied the giving of "performances" and noted that Christ accompanied his precepts by "miracles." The importance of this statement is not its truth, which any one may know, but its special relevance to Dr. Funk whose saturation with biblical ideas was not known to Mrs. Chenoweth.

He followed this by a long statement of the process of communicating, which, though it is not evidential taken by itself, so conforms to what I have observed in the facts generally, that it deserves quoting. He had been preceded by Imperator or some such personality and wanted to take up the work of giving a special message prepared before death.

It is not to disconnect myself from that task, but to relate myself to it by saturating the subliminal mind, which merely means the more active mind of the light, of saturating that with my own personal feelings until I recall the past as a past, as a part of myself, and not as a detached piece of information, which seems so foreign as to challenge question in my own mind, and thus create active mind currents which tend to produce several sorts of evidence and make for incorrect statements.

One thing that friends who have tried to understand the working of this power have overlooked is that the sleeping light may be sleeping physically and have awakened more active brain currents than when in actual physical conscious contact with the present friend, and so it is not enough to be sure of the sleeping state. There must be a flowing in of other currents of knowledge in sufficient power, force if you will, to push out the remaining elements of the remaining inhabitant.

It is plain to me that it takes time and experience to do this, and that even when it is done for one, as it is sometimes by a guide like Imperator

&c., that guide will also leave somewhat of himself, which in turn must be pushed out, so when a man like Professor James or Frank Podmore or like myself begins to reason and argue and preach, you may know he is taking possession for future work of some more minute and definite import.

(I understand.)

It is for this reason, I believe, that the familiar guide has been employed in the usual work, and I can understand it as never before, and the less that familiar guide has of preconceived ideas of the methods of life and general activities, the more free it is to express without bias or prejudice the truthful picturing or imagery given by the outside and disconnected spirit.

(Is a guide always connected with a message?)

No, unless you call any one who is able to transmit a message.

(I meant to ask if a spirit always had the help of another when giving a message.)

Do you mean here at this light?

(Yes.) [I really meant anywhere, but would not divert the thought.]

Yes, because this is a very carefully ordered and organized work. But, for instance, in my own case now, I am alone in this effort to write and retain my will to recall, but as I took control I was helped by those who watch the process, and if I had imparted to my wife or mother, or some other, the exact words I wished to write. they would prompt me, but I might then be subject to imperfect hearing or seeing while in the act of controlling, and I preferred to play the part which the familiar guide plays, and that is what Imperator tries to do in all the cases where he is interested. That is why we always get into writing conversationally.

The interesting psychological point of this message, in its reference to saturating the medium with his own personality, in order to transmit a specific message, is that, as Mrs. Chenoweth came out of the trance, in the subliminal stage, *she thought she was a man,* and repudiated the idea with some vigor.

The whole picture is clear for those familiar psychologically with the work of Mrs. Chenoweth, though the passage is fragmentary and tinged with her own terminology now and then. It is this. The public thinks that the trance is important in securing messages because people suppose that all mental activity is suspended in the trance and that whatever comes in that state is the pure and unadulterated thought of the communicator. This is an illusion and the communicator is here correcting it. The subliminal is as active in the trance as the normal consciousness out of it, and may even be enhanced in its powers according to the communicator. As long as that is not in rapport with the spirit or transcendental world, we would get only products of the subliminal, even though it was actually stimulated from without. But put it in rapport with the spiritual world and transmit to the "dreaming consciousness," to use Mrs. Sidgwick's terms, the thoughts of the communicator, and you will have at least the mingled or interfused thoughts of communicator and subconscious. To purify the message the communicator must inhibit the subliminal stream of the medium or so saturate it with his own personality and thoughts as to get their expression in the writing or speech of the medium instead of its own current of thought. It seems also that it is necessary to eliminate the impressions left on the mind of the medium by some previous communicator. I have seen many evidences of this, but cannot quote them here. They are analogous to the changes of thought in a mind without knowing that a change of stimulus has taken place. That is, a line of thought in one direction serves to hamper a change of it to another line.

At the next sitting, February 13th, he mentioned his brother Benjamin by name and then referred first to Brooklyn as his New York home and immediately to the New Jersey home, using the expression "N. J. home, Mountain View," and explaining that it was the same as "Montclair," as I first read the word "Mountain." These were wholly unknown to Mrs. Chenoweth, as he spent only a few years there at the end of his life.

After a few general allusions to his long study of the subject, he said he had some manuscripts of value and many old photographs of friends and added that his "family was never much on having likenesses taken." Inquiry shows that he had some important manuscripts and that the mother was averse to having her picture taken, as the son thinks. He then went on in a confused message to say that he had "two places where he could keep things" and said he was not referring to his office. But he mentioned some "paraphernalia" which he described as relics of his experiments and the tricks that mediums tried to play on him. The son does not recall any such inner room, but I was once taken to an inner room in his office where he had kept a number of just such relics of mediumistic performances and we examined them quite carefully. He then referred to having seen Professor Muensterberg after his death. But the allusion was not evidential.

A curious and indirect piece of evidence was a communication from his mother on February 14th. It is valuable as representing things which it was impossible for the psychic to know, whatever we may suppose she did or might know about Dr. Funk. In the first place she spoke of him by his Christian name, just as a mother might naturally do, and evidently referred for him to an incident which was not made as clear the first time as was necessary. It was from her reference to it that I learned what the earlier allusion really meant. The following is the message.

I know that the idea of medals and medallions and all articles which suggest such form is a left over impression of his most striking evidence, and he is the receiver of so many suggestions of that nature from the living and the dead, because of his known interest in the ancient coin, and it always comes with force as he attempts to write.

When the "Widow's Mite" was referred to before as a "medallion," I did not even suspect at the time that he meant the coin. He had not used the technical term. Evidently the pictographic process had concealed from the control and the psychic what the intention was and the picture could be described and interpreted only from its external appearance. Here this is repeated, but fortunately the mother got the association between the "medallion" and the "ancient coin" established, so as to show what the meaning was in the earlier message. The mother was helping the son by acting as his intermediary, and though it is buried in subliminal coloring the import is unmistakable.

Immediately following this message, she referred to Martin Luther and the Wartburg and added some fragmentary communications that were evidently an attempt to show how different versions of the special message he planned to give might be caused by the difficulties of communication. There was an allusion to different translations of texts and evidently the reference to Luther and the Wartburg was to the translation of the Bible by Luther when there, and the incident was probably a part of a comparison to show that his message might take as various forms as translations of biblical texts. The value of the point, however, is that she, when living, was a Lutheran and naturally thought of associations of that kind. Mrs. Chenoweth knew nothing about his religious affiliations or hers. Even I only accidentally learned what they were, as he had long since been connected with Congregational associations, especially under Mr. Beecher.

It was March 28th, 1917, before he appeared again, other work having occupied my time and attention. When he came, he gave his attention to a ring, a pin, possibly breast pin, with hair in it, and an earring, saying that the ring was either that of his mother or wife. This message came by the indirect method and hence through the control. Consequently the doubt about the person to whom it belonged. They were said to be in a box. A ring is too common an object to make specially evidential, unless more is said of it. But the son had the mother's ring and a pin, not as here described, however, in a box for safe keeping. But he knew of no earring. Then came the following:

Has he ever referred to a family record of births and deaths?

(I think not.)

This looks like an old Bible of some size which was a part of the family life, and in which is a record of births, and I see 7, the figure 7, as if it were a count of some names recorded. It is not all that is there, but it is one branch which is so recorded, and there is a name which begins with R. That is all for this time.

On March 30th the same subject was taken up again by the indirect method, after a sort of humorous apology on the part of Jennie P. for showing unusual biblical knowledge which she disclaimed having.

There was something said about the family Bible. I think G. P. took that picture, did he not?

(Yes he did.)

Well, there is more to that; for in that Bible there have been no records kept for a long time, but there you will find a space between two groups of records, as if there were some things to be discovered and written in, but it was never done.

I mean by the discovery that some questions were to have been asked and it was not done, and the record remains incomplete. Mr. Wordman [Jennie P's name for Dr. Funk] says that there have been several attempts to get into communication with him at another place.

I of course knew nothing about this and neither did the son when I made the inquiry. He knew that there was an old family Bible, but had to make inquiries to find where it was. After some difficulty he located it and found that there were two groups of names there, as described, one of them with six or seven names, with a space between to put in names omitted. There was none with the initial R in the first group. But the incident is sufficiently specific to be an excellent one, in spite of the fact that it might be said that records of births and deaths are very frequently recorded in family Bibles. But the other details make it somewhat exceptional.

The collective import of these facts ought to be clear. We may find fault with any one or each incident by itself as measured against all knowledge of such phenomena in other cases. But it will not be easy to offer normal explanations for the complex and articulated whole. It happened that, in spite of his having been a public man, Mrs. Chenoweth knew little or nothing about him. She would not even have known his name but for the fact that his conversion to Spiritualism was bruited about as a conquest. Only casual information came to her and of that very little. The intimate and private things which I have quoted in the text were often wholly unknown to me and I very frequently saw the man and had long conversations with him. Hence when we take the group of private things unknown to Mrs. Chenoweth and to me, their collective significance is not to be despised, and it is synthetic or collective import that constitutes scientific evidence.

Now when you have eliminated fraud it does not take much evidence to prove the supernormal, and when you once get the supernormal, it is not much more difficult to exclude the alternatives to spirits. For intelligent readers telepathy will have no standing in the explanation of these phenomena, unless you ascribe powers too far beyond access to my own knowledge. That process applied to reading my mind is effectually excluded here, and the selectiveness of the incidents is so natural on the hypothesis that it is Dr. Funk who is the source of them, although they have to pass through even several minds before I get them, and is unescapable save by subterfuges which have no scientific standing whatever.

CHAPTER XVIII

CARROLL D. WRIGHT

MR. CARROLL D. WRIGHT was United States Labor Commissioner and afterward President of Clarke College in Worcester, Mass. This is all that I knew about him, save that he had studied his problems statistically. I found by inquiry that Mrs. Chenoweth knew nothing about him and apparently had never even heard of him. His name was given in sittings connected with Professor James and the claim made that he and Professor James were personal friends. This turned out to be erroneous and the confusion seems to have been due to the fact that Professor James did know Chauncy Wright, a colleague in Harvard University. During several sittings various incidents identifying Mr. Carroll D. Wright together with his full name came through, but they were not striking enough to emphasize here. Finally the following incidents came that had more weight. But some that might have been excellent were not verifiable and I resorted to an experiment described below that came to better results.

In one of my own experiments with the automatic writing the following incident was very pertinent.

C. W. places his hands on the table and says that he thought all the physical phenomena were easily explained by magnetic influence or simple fraud, but he has reversed that opinion. The subtle influence of spirit was not plain to him except as a factor in life. The communication with the dead was unsatisfactory in most instances, but he was not a psychologist, and so did not comprehend what was being done.

I learned from the family what I did not previously know, that Mr. Wright had witnessed physical phenomena in his early days, having seen table tipping, which is hinted at here by the reference to "his hands on the table." But he was not satisfied with the results and gave up the subject as one in which conclusions could not be assured. He was not a psychologist. He was a religious believer and accepted the existence of spirit, but not communication with the dead. All this was unknown to Mrs. Chenoweth.

He was stated to have carried a powder in his pocket as a simple remedy for stomach trouble and which he took at intervals before his death. This is not confirmed. On the contrary, it seems not to have been true. But it is possible that it is a distorted account of a later incident which also was not true in the form that it appears, but seems to have been a confused reference to what was true, namely, that he constantly used lithia tablets for stomach or other trouble. Then came the following.

I see also a great pile of papers, some printed, and some compiled for printing and all in a stack on a table, a matter in which he was engaged at the time of his last illness. It looks like some work which was left him to do as a sort of referee. There is a large number of cases cited and instances named and figures and estimates given, and it is all before him for final summing up.

Inquiry shows that Mr. Wright was engaged on the "Century Book of Facts" a short time before his death, having finished it in January and died in February. None of these facts were known by me or by Mrs. Chenoweth.

Immediately after this came a reference to agriculture, to a new building apparently connected with it and allusions to various interests in which he was engaged besides "his particular chair," and then a reference to statistics which were, in fact, a special line of work with him. The allusion to agriculture, however, seemed to the family to have no meaning but one of them happened to remark that he was a member of the Board of Trustees of the Agricultural College in Massachusetts, and it is possible that it was this he was trying to say or mention, a view born out by the reference to "varied interests." The statement that "in his school there was much to do with the soil, agriculture and the like" was not true of the college of which he was President, but it was true of the college of whose Board he was a member. An Aunt A was mentioned that no one recalls or recognizes, but the name Adams given almost immediately was that of one of his friends. He was said to have taken a trip to New York a short time before his death. Inquiry showed that this was true. A statement about the relative frequency of his going to Boston and New York was true but not evidential, as it might be expected. Reference to his preference for Harvard over Columbia has no evidential meaning if verifiable, as no one recognizes any special reason for the statement.

He was said to have had two rooms for his work. This was true of the college, not his home, and then a reference to a "glass of water as if he frequently kept one near him as he worked." He did keep a glass of water near for a lithia tablet when he wanted it. Some one by the name of S., said to have been near him, and for the name Sarah, might refer to his father's second wife whose name was Sarah. His deceased sister's name was Sophia.

Some of the most complex and detailed incidents were unrecognizable and so left the collective mass of evidence somewhat weak. I found from interrogation of the daughter, however, that some things were recognizable by her that Mrs. Wright did not recall or recognize. The consequence was that I resolved on an experiment that would be almost as good as cross reference. I found the daughter was willing to take some sittings. She was married and this shut off direct connections in the name. I arranged for sittings to be taken by a friend, not mentioning name, sex or relation to my work. I purposely arranged for the Starlight trance. Mrs. Chenoweth's regular work is done by this little control and it is oral, not automatic writing. I made the arrangements as if the sittings had no connection with this series of experiments and was to be away when the sittings were held. Mrs. Chenoweth had no hint of my interest in them. I arranged them as if they were for some stranger wholly unconnected with the present experiments and such was the impression that Mrs. Chenoweth had. The lady came on the appointed day, giving no name and conducting the sittings with as much care and prudence as any scientific man would desire. I had given directions on that point and indicated the method to be used in avoiding betrayal of identity or incidents by way of suggestion. The sequel showed that I hardly needed to give this advice, as she made an excellent sitter. The first two sittings show a repetition of some of the incidents which I received, reference was made to me in a way not usual with strangers at their sittings, Mr. Wright's name was almost given, and at a later sitting of my own the lady present was said to have been Carroll D. Wright's daughter, which was true, though this might have been inferred from statements of the sitter. The incidents, however, communicated at the daughter's sittings are, many of them, much better evidence of identity than any that I obtained.

In close and pertinent connection with the statement about his intellectual habits was a rather long passage about his spending time at the seashore for both work and rest and social intercourse with important friends. This was true, though the details are not given in a manner to impress the skeptic with their cogency. Then came the statement amid some general talk that he " loved humanity and was interested in the problem," and then the statement that his life was spent in the city rather than the country or the seaside and that he went back and forth from one to the other. This was recognized as accurate, though we can hardly make it evidential. In a few minutes came a more striking possibility.

I see him with his clothes on; whether he passed away with his outer clothes, like coat and vest and those things. (Yes.) Anyway I see something put on him, I can't tell you. I feel clothes on and I feel some one going into my pockets, as though there is an effort to see what is in my pockets, for something. Do you know anything about that?

(No.)

Did he pass away with his garments on?

(No.)

Well, I feel this, he was not taken sick was he, with his clothes on? (Well, he had them on when the doctor told him he had better go tc bed.)

This was followed up with a sort of explanation of the connection between the idea of dying in his clothes and what was admitted by the sitter which may be explained in any way you please as subliminal talk. But the medium came at least near to hitting the idea admitted by the sitter after the main facts had been stated.

The name Henry followed the reference and description of the child and it is not clear whether it has any important meaning or not. Certainly it was not evidentially related. It was indicated that he was outside the family and there was such a friend by that name outside the family, and there was good reason for mentioning him, but the record does not indicate with any assurance that he was meant. The next incident following some general statements about his interest in this subject that are not important has some specific interest.

Now do you know anything about a little thing that looks like a case? There are several little compartments in it. You know I see almost like wood and little compartments, and up in those compartments are things that I can take up. You know they are little grains of something, like round flat things that if I dropped them they would drop down like peas or things like that, like little pebbles, but they are in compartments, as though they are things that he had worked over and had them to use for something. Do you know anything about this?

(Why I don't seem to recall. You mean connected with his work?)

Yes, they look like grains, you know, as though they are all separate; they are larger than grains of sand and they look something like little pills, you know.

(Yes.)

Little pills, only dark colors. If they were white I would call them globules, but they seem to be dark and brown and different colors and none of them are disks. You know disks?

(Yes.)

Well, they are in different compartments, as though here's a few, there's a few and there's a few, and I take them up. I don't put them together. I look at them, as though they are for a different purpose, but they come in a different part of his work.

(His life?)

His life. Did he ever study anything where he would have some of those little things in it? He was not a doctor himself was he?

(No.)

Well do you know if he ever knew a doctor who had these little things?

(Yes, I think he was very fond of an uncle and studied with him.)

[A little later after some non-evidential talk about the same incidents allusion was made to] a wooden box where they were in compartments before they were put into other smaller things, given out to the people.

The very proximate character of this incident is clear in the daughter's note, which says: "He studied medicine with an uncle who was a physician and later was in a drug store for a time. There he was also called Doctor."

I think almost any one would recognize the description of a physician's case before it was admitted by the sitter and the coincidence would not naturally be guessed in the life of Carroll D. Wright, which the admission of the sitter makes characteristic of his early life. It refers as much to the identity of the uncle as to his own, though not adequate in either case to determine that identity.

This first sitting ended without any incident of more important note and in the second one, the next day, after the preliminary communications in getting adjustment, which were unevidential, and after an allusion to a lady who is recognizable as his mother-in-law, and the mention of an Elsie who was known, but without recognizable importance here, the following came at some length.

Do you know anything about music that he would be interested in? I see a big sheet of music and I see all the notes and everything on it as if it were all printed, and I see him hold that in his hand. I don't know whether he made music, but there is something like tones, you know. He does n't seem to do it with his hands so much as he does to sing. Do you know if he sang?

(Yes, he was very fond of singing.)

[Then followed considerable talk about his unfinished life with vague allusions to music before the ideas drifted into his general topic and then came the following.]

Well it seems as if he used to go somewhere where there was particular music sung. I can't tell you exactly, but I see people standing up several of them, more like a group of people who express together, you know, like a choir or a quartette or a group of people who express music, and I see him going where he was looking right up at them, you know, listening to them. Was he a church man? Did he go to church?

(Always.)

Well I see him as though looking at a choir where I hear them sing and that is one of the beautiful parts of the service, and he says, 'That is pretty good for me to say,' as though it meant something special when he said it, you understand.

(Yes that is very good.)

Of this the daughter says. "My father was very fond of music and sang in the church choir for eight years or more." He seems then to have had the retirement from the choir symbolically indicated in the picture of his looking at the choir while he is also represented first as in it.

Allusion to a child and its being in church with him was not accurate. He had a deceased grandchild but they were never in church together while living. There followed an allusion to a woman with general description that could not be definitely identified for the reason that, so far as the account goes, it might refer either to a sister-in-law or a mother-in-law, both of whom are dead and the person alluded to was definitely indicated as deceased.

After the long effort to get the name beginning with E and ending with Elsie the following perfectly definite incident came.

I see a chair and it has no rockers, but it is rather big and round and very comfortable, and it is a chair. It is not a Morris chair. It has got a round sort of a seat to it, and I see this man. I am trying to connect everything with him now.

(Yes that is nice.)

And I see him come in and sit down in this chair. It is so comfortable. He throws back his head and sits there and rests. It seems as though I want to sit down and just gather myself a little bit, and as though I would rest before I go on to do something else, and this chair I think is in his own house, because I come right in. About the first place I go I sit down in that chair. It is n't up stairs; it is down stairs. I come in and sit down in that chair and rest. He had the funniest little habit of coming in and sitting down where he was, as though he wanted to take a minute to get adjusted and then he goes on and it is what he wants to do.

(Do you see any color in it?)

Yes, brown, you know.

(That is very good.)

This was followed by reference to the associations of the chair and mention of the man's religious nature. The association would not be suggestive to those who did not know the man's habits. The daughter speaks of the incident in her note.

A brown velour chair — rocking slightly on a stationary base — was very big and round and fitted his length exactly. It stood last in the library beyond the wide hall, inside as one entered and when he came in he generally took off his hat and coat, hung them up in the big closet and then sat down to rest in his own chair. It was not a Morris chair, but the arms were solid and it came around at the side just as he liked. He would read and then put his head back and rest as though he were dreaming, but with every faculty alert and then after he would talk either of what he had been reading or of something suggested by it. His life was one of service to humanity and he was deeply spiritual and religious in the highest sense.

The following interesting passage came after the allusion to the chair which we have just described.

I wonder if yot know anything about some clothes. It looks to me like a black suit It is very, very dark and looks more like black than anything and I see him so — well I think it is fussy about handkerchiefs. I always want to be sure that I have some, some not one. You know what I mean.

(Yes.)

That I have got one here and one here. I want enough you know. And I see this suit, one that he had worn as if it were a suit for a special occasion, I can't tell you what, but it is one that he had worn in special ways and things he had done, as though he is put away in that. You know when his body is put away it is put away in a suit he had. It is n't like a new one or a robe or anything, but it is like a suit he had.

The daughter replies to inquiry that " he was not fussy about anything but liked plenty of fresh handkerchiefs and had extra ones. as I suppose all men do in their pockets." Of the coat incident she says: " He wore his frock coat down town the last time he went in January, as it was his warmest one and he felt cold. It was washed and made all clean and neat before it was put on after his death. It was the coat he wore, of course when he lectured or dressed a little more than in a sack coat."

The next incident is perhaps quite as definite and regards his watch which the details will explain.

Well, let me see. There is a little black silk thing with a bit of gold on it. It looks more like a watch chain of black, you know.

(Little fob?)

Yes with a little bit of gold on it. It is very simple, very plain, but it is black and I know it is soft like silk.

(Yes.)

And he puts that right down here, you know, and on the end of it a watch. Do you know if he had one like that?

(Yes.)

Well, do you know his watch?

(Yes, perfectly.)

Well, I see this watch as though it was a good one and that he had some time and I like very much. I don't know as that is already given away, but if it is n't, you know just where that is going, as though it is saved for somebody till they get big enough for it.

(That is quite true.)

The daughter's note is: " He had an old fashioned gold watch fob on a piece of silk ribbon. His watch was a special one he was very fond of. He carried it for many years and it was understood that it would go to his grandson named for him."

The next incident is a characteristic of more than usual interest, as it is one that it would be difficult to ascertain in any normal way.

I see another little way. It goes along with his not liking the ceremonial and all that, but anything he dislikes is these. You know white things that go over beds, pillow shams? Well, those things bother him.

(That is very good, very true.)

I never heard any spirit say it before, but suddenly I see a bed, I see something like all fussed up: sometimes when he had to go away and sleep in other people's beds and it would be as though I like my own bed. If I could be at home in my own bed, no nonsense about shams. The very name is distasteful to him and all this lace business. He is thoroughly a man. He likes comfortable things and pretty things and all that, but give me a bed with pillows.

The daughter's note on this incident is as follows. "He was impatient always of fuzzy things on beds and going about as much as he did, often spoke of lace spreads, etc., that bothered him."

The following incidents were evidently touched on in the automatic writing but not made clear enough for any possible recognition. Later still I brought the subject up for clearer identification and obtained some interesting data.

There is another thing. It looks to me more like a growing vine. There is something growing around a building. I am not in the same building where I was before where I saw the boys, but I am off here to another building that is a detached place, you know, detached house.

(Yes.)

And there is a little vine like woodbine or ivy something that grows up all over it. It is very pretty. There are two posts like a driveway, and two big tall posts. They are made of stone. It is a pretty place, you know, but it is gravel. I hear a carriage grind on the gravel and I step out just inside these posts, and here is a detached building, one that looks more like a home and I go in there and I am received in there. I call it inside grounds where there are posts and a driveway and there is somebody there. I don't know who it is, but it seems like a man as big as he is, as though they are equals.

(Yes.)

Perhaps doing the same thing he is, only at another point, you understand.

(Yes.)

Well he goes in here, but it is the funniest thing, as though this vine is all turned red like fall.

(Yes.)

As though the autumn and it is one of the last trips he made you know, with those autumn things around, pretty, beautiful but I feel a sense of the end. You know I don't know why I feel it, but I feel it at that place. Do you know anything about that?

(Would that be his own home?)

Did he have a house like that?

(Yes.)

Did he have some vines growing there just inside the drive, like a drive in, and anything like woodbine?

(I think it was on the veranda.)

No, this is not the place. It is n't his home. It is away. Where did he come from when he came home, some trip he made.

(He went to Washington.)

I see a drive in and I see this vine and it is fall, you know.

(Yes, it was.)

It is fall time, because the reason I see the vine is to show me the time, and it is all red, autumn colors, and I see him come home from there and die. Do you know what I mean?

(Yes.)

I come home weary. That is the end; that is the last trip. He is telling you he would do it all over again. That is what I see as though that was almost too much for him.

(That is true.)

Having found a possible clue to the incident about the vine clad building I resolved to ask that Mr. Wright be given a chance to communicate and throw light on the matter. I therefore expressed the desire to have him, having had it strongly in mind the day before I put it directly and during the beginning of the sitting of December 19th, 1911. Apparently my desire was already known as the response was so prompt. The following is the record of what occurred, after I had expressed my wish to hear from him again.

Well C. D. W. is here.

(All right. He will remember describing or referring to a vine covered house. The family does not recall it and I wish more about it. If he can tell where it is and what it is used for I may be able to verify it.)

Was it a brick or stone house.

(He did not say and I do not know, or if he said I do not recall.)

He shows me a house in the South where he went not long before his passing where there were vines all about and where the effect was of green growing things about the place. It was there he was entertained I think and as he was recalling the past that picture came in vividly before him and may have been interpolated as a part of the communication.

(I understand and can he say what use the house had?)

It looks more like a building in which a part of the curriculum of the work was carried on. Do you know if he went to the South to speak to some educational workers where there was a set of buildings devoted to work.

(No, but I shall inquire, though I know of a meeting not long before his death.)

In the South.

(That depends on the starting point and what . . .) [Writing began.]

South of here and South of Worcester. (Yes.) But not far South. (No.)

I go with him in a southerly direction and see these buildings, a group of them and among them this one with the vines. You know how much he was interested in all growing things and particularly in many kinds of vines. Do you know this.

(No, I do not, and perhaps he can tell about the country about that building.)

I will see. There are many trees and I see it is not a city like N. Y. [New York]. You did not have N. Y. in mind did you?

(No I did not.)

For it is not N. Y. which I mean but instantly when I made the comparison I became aware of his interest in several N. Y. people and institutions but the place to which I refer is not so large or thickly settled and is not a hilly country but rather pretty and has some special interest for him as he must have gone there with a specific work in mind. It has buildings of common interest. I mean like a community of interests but I do not know whether it is a university or not. I should rather think it something of that kind. Wait a little until I can see. Do you know anythink about a chapel where he went?

(No.)

I see a building which is like a church or chapel where there are many seats. I am inside and it is vacant, but it is a building used for audiences. Now he was entertained at a place. What is the W. for? Do you know?

(No, I do not but go on.) [Probably Washington.]

I see a large white house and it is so quiet and lovely about the place and there are people coming and going from other places but the house where he stays is quiet. It is strange that you do not know about this place in the South where he was entertained and where all this description has a bearing. It may be a place of which you are not aware now, but it is there that I find the vine covered house and I see some water and boats. It looks like fresh water more as if it were a lake of some size. It is all a very beautiful place and surroundings, but it is entirely on account of engagements that he goes there for he always could be at home.

(Tell more about that water and, if you can, the name of it.)

I will do all I can, but I see several kinds of boats on it which leads me to the conclusion that it is used for all kinds of pleasure craft and dotted around the shores are houses and cottages and there are trees and hills back from it. It is most beautiful. Do you know if he went to a lake and was entertained there?

(No I do not, but you would clear the whole thing up by an initial of the name of the water.)

Yes I suppose so and I have no idea why it does not come. It may be that he is not in working order this afternoon. He is talking with W. J. They are as usual most talkative and interested in each other. Just now I see a long bridge. It is rather more than the ordinary length and is of wood with some girders high on each side and the water is so clear and the reflections are as perfect as the things themselves.

When the vine clad house was mentioned in the automatic writing I had hoped that it would prove a good incident. But no member of the family recognized it as having any meaning at all. When it was thus repeated with more detail it still had no meaning for them. As he had lived in Washington a number of years I suspected the Smithsonian Institution, but found that he had no office in it and no associations with it. He had been entertained at the White House, but Ex-President Roosevelt did not recall any entertainment of the man in the fall of 1908 when Mr. Wright attended the meeting of the Carnegie Board of Trustees in Washington. I learned from the head of the Institution, however, that Mr. Wright had remained at the New Willard Hotel during that period and where the Board met, I believe in those days. The daughter, however, casually remarked that her father had been on the Board of the Hackley School at Tarrytown, New York. Inquiry immediately showed that it had vines over it and I then ascertained that Mr. Wright had attended the Board Meeting of this School in the fall of 1908 a few months before his death but did not attend the later meeting in January a few weeks before his death. I then visited the School and ascertained the truth of further incidents. The building is not covered with vines, as the communications might imply, but has a number of vines at different places on it and may some day be covered. There is a little chapel near it in which Mr. Wright, according to the statement of the Principal, had talked to the boys. There is a building back of the main School edifice which resembles a laboratory very much but is the infirmary. The wooden bridge spoken of I could not find in my personal investigations, but the Principal writes me that there was such a bridge near the building, but that it was recently removed. There are stone posts at the entrance to the grounds, but there are no vines near them or near the entrance. These are near and behind the chapel and are a very large collection of them, very noticeable to one driving in and up to the School. From points on or near the ground Haverstraw Bay which is an enlargement of the Hudson River, can be seen with the mountains beyond, making an extraordinarily fine view. Pleasure boats are numerous on the shores during the summer season.

The building is white stone and apparently the allusion to " W " had brought associations of Washington to Mr. Wright's mind and the White House where he had also been entertained by President Roosevelt. This also has vines on it. But the other incidents do not apply. The Hackley School stands in a fine wood of large trees on one of the high hills of the Hudson River. The indication that it was not hilly is therefore incorrect. But this is partly corrected when alluding to hills and trees in connection with the " lake," Haverstraw Bay. Whether the place should be described as hilly or not would depend on the amount and locality of the place gotten into the " mental picture " while communicating.

The place was southwest from Boston, not " South." He was entertained at the place, but the principal does not recall definitely whether he was entertained there at the time of the last Board meeting which he attended in the fall before his death in February, though he says: " A rather unreliable memory on my part suggests the likelihood that his visit *was* in the fall of 1908." He adds also: " I am sure that he did spend the night here at sometime within a year or two before his death."

The Board meetings were held in New York, and hence the pertinence of the immediate allusion to that city and friends there after saying that the building was not in New York but in the country.

After the long reference to the vine clad building and indication that it was associated with the end of his life, he turned to some incidents associated with the funeral and which are, of course, representative of posthumous, or what Mr. Myers called post-terrene knowledge.

There is another very sweet thing and it seems to be about his body. All over his casket, you know, everything is lovely there, but there is some thing all green, you know, like drapings of it. Funny thing but it is almost like laurel.

(Yes.)

Were you there?

(I was there.)

Do you know anything like some green that seems to be half draped. Whether it is laurel or smilax, it is something that is all green and it is draped in a way from his bier.

(Yes.)

And then I see a great big wreath, oh an immense one, that is so big, but it isn't green like the rest, it is red. (Yes.) Flowers in it but it is red, red, red, like red leaves and then here and there roses, I think.

(Yes.)

They look like roses to me. There is something else with that. You know they are mixed in little clusters here and there, I think. That is, from somebody special, this big wreath, you know.

(Yes.)

And then I see there was something of flowers, looks like a basket. Do they ever send baskets to funerals?

(Yes.)

Well this is a tall thing. I don't know whether it is a basket or what it is, but it is hanging from here and a ribbon on it. It really is a basket, a basket of flowers. It seems as though that is from one person. The wreath is from more. It is from several, and the basket is from one. Funniest thing: And you don't seem to remember it.

(There were many baskets, of course, many things.)

Of course. A man like that would have. Wait till I see something.

(Was there anything else over the casket that you see?)

Do you mean a banner? Was that what you meant?

(Anything like that.)

Yes, there is something. I don't mean a flag and I don't know whether you mean a flag or not. There are two or three things. There is something like a spearhead that this thing is on. It might be a cross, but it is silk or satin. It is shiny and is not red, white and blue flag. It is some other color, and I should think that is a thing that he belonged to, as though it came like you might have college colors or a banner that belonged to some particular organization that he was in.

(Yes.)

That is what I see; like there is something there with blue or purple: it is like that, but a little gold around it too, and this spearhead thing. Do you know anything about it? I think there was a flag there all right; but that is not what I see. I see these other things first. I think there is a flag, but it is off the other way. I am not looking at that at all. Then I see a man who is saying something, as though it is a eulogy. That is the thing you say about him.

(Yes.)

Well, do you know a tall, slim, oldish man with a quiet nice face and gray hair, but very quiet and dignified, who said something about him?

(Yes.)

Was n't that the man who stood up there. (Yes.) And he has a very beautiful quiet voice. This man was a friend of years. They did n't go into any extended eulogy. You know it was that came after, but this time it was a short one. You know that is what he would prefer.

The daughter's notes show that this passage contains very striking coincidences, perhaps of an unusually important kind.

" My mother's wreath of red calyx leaves was on the casket and all about were others, baskets, wreaths and flowers of all kinds and pieces. I think there was laurel and evergreen at the church.

" At the church, the four banners formed an unusual decoration. Over the casket was the silk flag. At either side of the pulpit stood these flags or banners, each on a stick with the end forming a spear-point. The flag of the Loyal Legion of Honor, the flag of the Commonwealth of Massachusetts, and I think the others. They were of silk and were most effective. These precious banners were in charge of some one sent by the Loyal Legion of Honor who never allowed them to leave his sight."

There followed this a reference to the name Charles which is that of one of his dearest friends, and then an attempt to give his own name. I shall not quote it in full as it is too long, but suffice to say that the " W " came easily enough and the last letter " t." He was referred to as Doctor, but distinguishing this from a physician by saying he " was not a pill doctor."

There were many other incidents of great evidential interest that were given. They would require too much space to present them, and it is hard to tell whether they are more or less cogent than such as I have given. One long set of messages evidently referred to Senator George F. Hoar who was the life long friend of Mr. Wright and who urgently advised him to go to Clark College. Mr. Wright's name was given in full and the pet name by which he called his daughter. A little bag which he had used in his early life was rather minutely described. Several names of relatives were given and more especially important were references to persons and incidents about which members of the family had to inquire among remote relatives for confirmation.

The facts that Clark College was not far — about 35 miles — from the home of Mrs. Chenoweth and that Mr. Wright was so well known to the general public enable doubters to raise the suspicion that at least some of the facts about him would either be public property or be easily acquired in various ways. This is true of the most general incidents connecting him with Clark College. But I have laid no stress on such facts and confined the interest to those little private incidents in his life that could not be obtained casually and many of them impossible without an elaborate detective system which Mrs. Chenoweth, even if she were disposed, which she is not, could not conduct with manifold times the means at her disposal. Readers need have no scruples on this point. But readers must remember that at the sittings of the daughter there was no opportunity to know who was present or that the same personality was wanted to communicate that came to me. You may very well assume a spontaneously worked up product for me, though there was no reason for doing so, as I had no personal relations with the man. In any case you can only speak of subconscious work as conscious fraud will be given no consideration by me.

The facts in many instances are especially good and absolutely all of them but his name and connection with Clark College were unknown to me, so that the toleration of anything supernormal in them excludes telepathy from my mind beyond question. I need not explain them here, however, as I am only concerned with the facts as they came from a man of national character.

CHAPTER XIX

EXPLANATIONS AND OBJECTIONS

IT has been clear in my treatment of the data that my own tendency is towards a spiritistic explanation. Indeed my attitude on the subject is so well known that I have not tried to conceal my bias when discussing explanations, nor to practice any obsequiousness when weighing evidence. I have been expounding a theory which has long appeared to me to be proved, and I have been trying to present the facts in a way to increase the difficulties of skepticism in rejecting that conclusion. It has been apparent throughout that I accept the spiritistic explanation of the facts, though I have endeavored to do justice to opposing views. But I have tried also to show that there are facts which the opposing theories cannot explain, and from these facts the argument gains its force.

But while I have presented the spiritistic hypothesis as the only one that even approximates an explanation, readers must not misunderstand the conditions under which I maintain such a doctrine. The prejudices and the ignorance of a century are organized against even the use of the term; and all the illusions which that century of progress in physical science has produced, together with the barriers of all sorts of orthodoxy, scientific, literary, and esthetic, are resorted to in defence of a hostile attitude toward the doctrine, though religions and philosophies pretend to believe the same thing under another name. Whoever accepts the belief in spirits from scientific evidence has to face this situation; and, if he has any regard for the good will of his neighbors, he will let the subject entirely alone. But cowardice is no safe refuge from facts, and there are people who know that truth and virtue are not under the dominion of fashion and good taste. They insist on ignoring mere orthodoxies as such and on penetrating the disguises of ignorance and custom to explore the despised territories of hard facts. They accept the leadership of truth whithersoever it takes them. Those who remain behind must accept the penalty; but those who go forward must meet hosts of illusions about their beliefs. No one has more trouble in this respect than the believer in spirits, though his enemies want to believe in everything that the doctrine means!

Most antagonists to spiritistic hypotheses, whether religious or skeptical, have much the same conception of what a spirit is. The only difference between the two classes is that one believes and the other does not believe in the reality of spirit so conceived. It is possible to show that both are under a delusion. The habits of thought prevailing in unscientific minds tend to make them trust in their imaginations, or in the interpretation of terms according to sense-experience. Hence most minds imagine spirits to be visible, tangible, audible beings, represented by apparitions, "materializations," ghosts that haunt houses and provoke unpleasant disturbances, or by angels with wings and flowing robes, with all the trappings of their physical state, including houses, occupations, clothes, and all the accessories of economic life.

This conception is so incredible from the point of view of traditional philosophy, with its complete dualism or antithesis between matter and spirit, that it is no wonder that it excites ridicule. I shall say frankly, however, that there may be more truth in it than I know. I do not know enough to deny the doctrine that the spiritual world is but the invisible side of the visible universe. For aught that I know it may be a complete ethereal replica of the physical universe, or if "ethereal" is too suggestive of something else than matter, for aught that I know, the spiritual world may be merely a sublimated condition of matter, effected by changes like those with which we are familiar in chemistry. We know that matter can be altered from the solid to the liquid and from the liquid to the gaseous condition, and that as a gas it may become wholly non-sensible and lose properties which it had in solid form. For aught that I know spirit may be some such sublimated condition of matter. But I do not contend for such a doctrine. I am indifferent to it at present. It is no part of our present problem to determine *what* spirit is, but *that* it is. All that we mean is that *something* survives death, whether we finally decide to call it matter, or spirit. The primary question is whether personal consciousness survives the body. So far as I am concerned here, spirit may be all that spiritualists claim, though it is hard to determine exactly what they claim. But when I defend the spiritistic hypothesis here, I am neither accepting popular spiritualism nor holding in reserve any system of metaphysics, material or spiritual.

What I contend for is, that there is satisfactory evidence for the survival of personal consciousness. But there is a tendency in academic circles to insist that we must have a theory of philosophy to discuss, some metaphysical explanation of facts, before we admit the facts themselves. This is a delusion of the first order. We can never tell *how* anything happens until we prove that it does happen. We are not required to have explanations before we are assured of the facts. Indeed, science may not seek to go beyond the establishment of facts and may suspend explanations altogether. It must at least subordinate theoretical considerations to the proof of its facts.

The only meaning that I give to the term " spirit " in the present stage of the work is, a stream of consciousness that may, in some way, subsist after the body has dissolved. How it subsists may be taken up in the later investigation of the subject, but it is not necessary to our problem that we shall define the nature of " spirit " in terms of its relation to matter. All that I contend for is, that certain facts are evidence of this continuity, not evidence of what it is. In other words our scientific problem is evidential rather than explanatory. When we have assured ourselves that personality survives, we may then take up the determination of the conditions under which it survives. At present we have only facts that indicate something supernormal, from which we infer the continuity of personal identity, though we do not know the conditions of that continued existence.

This ought to make clear all that I mean by spirit. Indeed I have emphasized the conception in the introductory chapter and in the definition of the problem, so that it is repeated here only for the sake of laying stress on the limitations of our knowledge.

The evidence I regard as scientifically proving survival, though it does not prove all that people believe under that name. There is no other rational explanation of the facts than the hypothesis of survival; and the cumulative evidence is so strong that I do not hesitate to say that the proof is even equal or superior to that for evolution. As a theory of the gradual as opposed to the catastrophic genesis of species, evolution is undoubtedly proved in every sense of the word scientific proof. To the same extent I think survival or the existence of spirit has been proved by the work of psychic research. The facts given in this volume are not sufficient evidence, and they are not given with the assumption that they constitute adequate proof. They are merely good illustrations of the nature of the evidence for supernormal knowledge of some kind. Indeed, the best evidence for survival can hardly be quoted, in many cases, without giving the entire record, with proper explanations of its psychological nature and its accuracy. The present volume is designed only to awaken interest; readers who are still doubtful must take the time and pains critically to study more elaborate reports. They will find it difficult to escape the conclusion that I have drawn.

They still may not feel satisfied, if they are under the delusion that their preconceived ideas of spirit and its behavior must be substantiated before they believe in its existence. But they are not entitled to draw from the facts any conclusion except what they indicate; and most, if not all, evidence for personal identity does not hold any hint of what the life is like or what spirits are like. Unless readers master that simple fact they are not qualified to study the subject. We are not upholding any preconceptions of spirit. We have to assume the materialistic point of view that there is no such thing, and then see whether our supernormal facts can be explained as functions of the brain. If we cannot give a materialistic explanation, which implies annihilation, we have to suppose that the phenomena imply the extension or continuance of the particular consciousness whose identity is established by the messages. All further questions as to the mode of existence must be determined by other methods and other evidence.

The phenomena do not establish survival or the existence of spirit because they are "wonderful." The popular idea is that, if a phenomenon is "wonderful" or inexplicable by ordinary causes, it must be evidence for spirits. It is not mystery that establishes the conclusion, but the perfect intelligibility of the facts. Supernormal experiences which do not indicate the continued personal identity of the dead might be explained by hypotheses as indefinite as the facts themselves; but when the circumstances are exactly what we should expect if a given person were communicating with us, the conclusion can hardly be escaped. The only circumstance that will give rise to resistance is prejudice based on the dogmatism of science about "matter" and on the lack of respectability among the advocates of spiritistic theories. These are, in reality, more powerful influences than any logic or proved facts. But the phenomena have so accumulated that it will soon be the mark of extreme ignorance to reject the conclusion.

When we consider objections to the spiritistic hypothesis, I think we may say to-day that none are valid. Twenty-five years ago we might have entertained objections, but the work done in the interim has effectively removed them. While chance coincidence and guessing may account for many occurrences advanced as evidence for the supernormal, they have long been thrown out of court as explanations of vast masses of phenomena, and those quoted in this volume as evidence of the supernormal exhibit their own exemption from such suspicion. Secondary personality fares no better. While it limits evidence and excludes spirits as the explanation of certain types of facts, the contents of its phenomena can be traced to normal experience, while genuinely supernormal knowledge can be explained only by a source external to the subconscious.

Telepathy is not a legitimate rival. I shall not discuss it here, after the exhaustive discussion given it in earlier chapters. I mention it as a whilom objection no longer cogent nor relevant. It has been eliminated for all who know anything about the facts and is pressed only by those who are too bewildered by the phenomena to make up their minds. It is noticeable, however, that telepathy, though probably a fact and a very limited fact, no longer plays its former rôle in the controversy, and represents an agency so little known that the burden of proof now rests on the believer in it rather than on the believer in spirits. The more rational theory must have the preference and telepathy has no rationality to commend it.

But if there are no longer any real objections to the spiritistic hypothesis, there are certain difficulties or perplexities for all of us. They are not objections to, but puzzles *in* the theory. They must be recognized despite the fact that the hypothesis has to be accepted. They may be summarized under two heads: (1) The mistakes and confusions in the communications and (2) the contradictions in the statements about the nature of the life after death. This latter question should be taken up in a later discussion of the nature of the spiritual life. Suffice it to say that no amount of contradiction in statement can be construed as an objection to a spiritistic theory. Spirits, like living people, may contradict each other, but the contradiction is no evidence against their existence.

The confusions and mistakes in the communications, though they no more than contradictory statements militate against the existence of spirits, do require explication if the phenomena are to be made intelligible. The difficulties which these mistakes involve are based solely on the assumption that, if spirits can communicate as they often appear to do, they ought not to make manifest errors in statement. This assumption, however, is wholly unwarranted and is founded on a superficial interpretation of the facts. The analogies of normal intercourse offer no standard for judging these phenomena. Careful students will detect the existence of conditions for communication between the spiritual and the physical worlds, very different from the conditions existing between living people. These conditions are so complex that the slightest knowledge of them will render intelligible the fragmentary nature of the messages and the mistakes and confusion. Indeed the wonder is that any communication whatever is possible.

If we know the conditions under which messages come, we cannot wonder at the confusions and mistakes. There is first the conscious mind of the psychic, whether normal or in a trance. This mind has to report the messages and must color them in the same way that any second person would color a message sent to a friend. Then there is the subconscious of the medium, which will also modify messages, with greater liability to confusion and mistake than exists in the normal consciousness. Add to this again the influence of the control's mind. All messages either come through the control's mind or are affected by it, in addition to the modifications which communications must undergo in the psychic's mind. An additional source of confusion is the fact that many messages are involuntary; that is, unintentional on the part of the communicator. There is also interfusion of the communicator's thoughts with those of others near by as well as with those of the medium and the control. All these are still further complicated by the pictographic process, which represents the communicator's thoughts to the control and the psychic in a panorama of mental imagery, subject to interpretation by either or both. If the pictures are symbolic they may represent in the mind of the communicator an association of ideas which are not connected in the mind of the living receiver or medium. Imagine what different accounts two persons would give of an ordinary panorama or procession! The psychic may hit upon incidents in the series of pictures, not intended by the communicator, and yet quite as good evidence, if verifiable, as any intentional picture. But the whole complex phantasmagoria exhibits incalculable opportunities for mistake.

Under such complex conditions mistakes and confusions enough are sure to occur. So far from expecting messages to be simple and clear, the intelligent man, when he knows such conditions to exist, will wonder that any intelligible communications at all should come. But mistakes thus made do not invalidate the spiritistic interpretation; and, when the mistakes are either spontaneously corrected or can be naturally explained they constitute evidence for the theory rather than against it.

The main difficulty raised is totally irrelevant. I refer to the trivialities of the facts advanced in proof of personal identity and the general vulgarity of an average spiritualistic performance. The offence taken at these is merely esthetic, not scientific, and hence is of no importance in a scientific investigation of the subject.

PART IV

MISCELLANEOUS QUESTIONS

CHAPTER XX

THE PHYSICAL PHENOMENA OF SPIRITUALISM

THE alleged physical phenomena of spiritualism consist of several types of real or apparent exception to the ordinary laws of matter. One of the most striking is telekinesis, the alleged movement of physical objects without visible normal contact, and without the intervention of any physical medium or agent. Raps, or the production of sounds without contact, is a second type. Levitation is another, but this is only a form of telekinesis. The production of lights is another. Alteration of weight by supernormal means is still another but infrequent type. Materialization is another type; but the term is so confusing that the alleged phenomena require separate treatment.

Stories of such events have been told from time immemorial and are plentiful, it seems, among all races. Familiarity with records not often mentioned by historians shows that among the Greeks and Romans there was as much of this sort of narrative as in modern times, awakening the same interest, though the resistance to belief was less obstinate then than now, because minds were not so saturated with the idea of fixed laws of nature as they are to-day. In modern times the interest broke out anew with the work of the Fox sisters. The missionary zeal of their movement centered attention on them and their phenomena; their spectacular career also helped greatly to emphasize the impression. But the phenomena were no different in kind from those known to the Greeks and Romans and to every race before and since their time. All this I have briefly touched upon in an earlier chapter. We are at present interested not in the history of such phenomena, but in their relation to the problem of psychic research.

The extravagant interest in physical phenomena supposedly caused by spirits or some unknown force, would be strange were it not the natural heir to the traditional interest in miracles. The scientific man cannot see why spiritualists attach so much value to physical phenomena as evidence for the existence of spirits. But the point of view is not difficult to understand. To the ordinary man all mental phenomena are equally mysterious, and he is slow to realize the exceptional character of any mental fact. Since all phases of mental life are inexplicable, telepathy or clairvoyance is no more to be wondered at than a funny dream. But these minds can easily perceive that certain physical phenomena are exceptions to their experience. They are familiar with the general laws of motion, especially with the law of contact; and, as they regard as a miracle anything that represents a violation of the law of contact as the cause of motion, they easily refer supernormal physical phenomena to spirits as a cause. This is the natural tendency of a mind brought up to believe in miracles. In the psychological field, telepathy and other instances of the supernormal are not to be specially wondered at, as they are no more exceptional than other idiosyncrasies of mind. But it is otherwise with physical phenomena. The rising of a table without contact at once appears inexplicable by any ordinary laws of experience. Common minds can see the unusual character of such phenomena, and, being accustomed to find in Christian doctrine physical miracles cited as proof of divinity, they easily resort to the spiritualistic interpretation of levitation. They are not often nice in their application of explanations, and make anything mysterious a signal for the appeal to spirits.

But they reckon ill with the problems of evidence. Levitation, raps, lights, and other physical phenomena are no more evidence for the existence of spirits than is the fall of a tree. The movement of a physical object through space without contact is in no way evidence for the existence and action of spirits. It may be accompanied by such evidence, but it is not itself this evidence. Proof of the existence of spirits requires not the mere occurrence of inexplicable phenomena, physical or mental, but facts of a supernormal character, evincing the continued personal identity of the dead. The phenomena must be explicable only as the acts of intelligence, indicating the presence and action of discarnate beings, as displayed in the transmission of messages or in the production of phenomena that show purpose. This indication of purposive intelligence, not the mechanical movement of objects, constitutes the evidence. There is no scientific excuse for the spiritualistic contention that physical phenomena prove the existence of spirits. Unaccompanied by mental phenomena they are useless. For telekinetic phenomena are among the most common in nature — magnetism, wireless telegraphy, and gravitation are illustrations. Intelligent scientific men will admit the possibility of telekinesis; it is merely a matter of evidence, not of *a priori* limitations to nature. But they can still maintain that, while the occurrence of supernormal physical phenomena may be entirely possible or even proved, these alone are not evidence for the existence of spirits.

The case might be very different if there appeared also mental phenomena, especially such as are unmistakably supernormal and reflect the personality of the dead. If the levitation of a table, for instance, were accompanied by mental phenomena involving the personal action of some one dead, it would have some interest for the skeptic asked to believe in the power of spirits to cause motion in physical objects. But if it occurred without indication of intelligence, incarnate or discarnate, it would be only a curious event.

It is in reality the *ensemble* of phenomena, the complex situation, that has impressed the spiritualist. This situation usually includes the presence of mental as well as physical phenomena: this association, not the physical phenomenon, justifies the suspicion of spiritistic agency. Unfortunately most people appeal to the physical "miracle" instead of to the mental phenomena, which appear to be less miraculous. Though, taken alone, physical phenomena have no evidential import whatever, we have to discuss them, partly because tradition has associated them with spiritism, and partly because mental phenomena of much significance have often occurred in connection with alleged physical events of an inexplicable nature.

If we should ever succeed in proving the existence of genuinely supernormal physical occurrences, definitely connected with supernormal mental occurrences, and so have reason to assign to both of them the same cause, we should have a result of very great cosmic interest. To find that extra-organic intelligence can move matter without the intervention of normal human agency, even though mediumship be usually associated with the movement, would be to raise the question of the relation of intelligence to all mechanical action. If we once establish the fact of telekinesis by intelligence alone — that is, the movement of inorganic objects by discarnate agencies, without contact, we open the way for considering the question of the priority of intelligence to all mechanical movement in the universe. The materialistic theory has so long accustomed us to think of physical movement as mechanically caused, and not as possibly caused directly by intelligence that we are not prepared to admit any but mechanical causes in the physical universe. This has been the tendency of philosophic thought from the time of the earliest thinkers of Greece. They sought to remove intelligence from cosmic action; and, though they sometimes admitted the existence of spirit or spirits, they relegated them to the *intermundia,* where they could exercise no influence on the course of physical events. But once let it be proved that the discarnate can be efficient to produce motion in inorganic objects, materialism will be forever dislodged from its stronghold. Consciousness will have been proved capable, in an extra-organic existence, of producing more or less direct effects on inorganic matter; and no one will be able to assign to this ability any limits save such as experience may define.

This larger aspect of the question is the phase of real interest in the problem of telekinesis as associated with intelligence. But the prospect of accomplishing results that will illustrate or prove this larger view is very remote. We have hardly started on the way. We are still too doubtful of the occurrence of the phenomena in any form to begin drawing inferences from them. However, in the mental field, facts to prove the existence of spirits are multiplying; and, their existence once conceded, there will be more probability of our discovering that they are influential in determining events. We may therefore soon be on the road to solving the larger questions of telekinesis.

The historical records in support of supernormal physical phenomena are not very impressive, unless we except those of Robert Hare and Sir William Crookes. Robert Hare was professor of chemistry in the University of Pennsylvania. His volume on his experiments and inquiries has been quoted by spiritualists as more or less conclusive in their favor. But his mere academic authority is all that spiritualists have emphasized; they have not been able to reproduce his alleged results. Moreover, examination of his work reveals the justice of Mr. Podmore's criticising it, at least of his accusation of defectiveness in the account of experiments and inquiries. Mr. Podmore, however, was so obsessed with his belief in fraud that he could recognize neither its limits nor the significance of hysteria and other abnormal mental states in honest subjects. No doubt Professor Hare erred in the opposite direction, though this error may be more apparent in his writings than in his actual investigations. Unfortunately the latter are so imperfectly described that the critic is free to make all sorts of accusations that cannot be refuted if false, nor proved if true. Some of the apparatus he invented was good, but we know far too little about the exact conditions of his experiments. He merely states in a description of his apparatus that he succeeded in registering a pressure of eighteen pounds under conditions, as he thought, that do not permit of normal explanation; but he does not describe insufficient detail the manner of experimenting. Like all investigators of that period — 1850 to 1860 — as soon as he was convinced of his theory he accepted all sorts of phenomena and mediumistic statements without any criticism. He went elaborately into the revelations of another life, as if the mere fact that these revelations came from spirits attested their credibility. But he shows us no reason to be assured that many of the statements had any transcendental source whatever. We may urge in his defence that at that time nothing was known about the subconscious. The most natural thing in the world, after being personally convinced of the honesty and veracity of the medium, was to take the communications at their face value, even though they might be unprovable and perplexing. He seems not to have thought of such a thing as careful sifting and criticism of the evidence for spirit existence, much less to have established any criteria for determining the validity of statements about the spiritual world. He cannot be quoted by any scientific or intelligent man in support either of the existence of spirits or, if they exist, of the truth of their communications.

One circumstance, however, which Mr. Podmore quotes with an

apparent sneer, is not indefensible. Professor Hare invented an apparatus for spelling out messages, in which the dial and hand were so concealed that the observer, but not the medium, could see where the index pointed. He records that results were more difficult to obtain, and failures more frequent under these conditions. When the spirits were taken to task for these failures, they replied that, since the medium could not see the face of the dial and the index, the spirits had to see them through Dr. Hare's eyes. This reply Mr. Podmore evidently thought a preposterous subterfuge. But it is quite conceivable that the spirits must see what they are doing. It may be that they cannot always or easily see physical objects without the use of sensory organs.

Strange as it may seem, I have some evidence that this claim is more or less justified. I have not proved it even to my own satisfaction. I have been too busy trying to get more important questions solved and to secure evidence of survival rather than evidence of the character of intercommunication between the physical and spiritual worlds. But I have noted some important facts bearing on this very question. Their significance is determined entirely by the fact that supernormal information justifying the spiritistic hypothesis was obtained in connection with the phenomena which I shall here detail.

(1) At one time in my experiments with Mrs. Chenoweth I used a head-rest to support her head when she was in the trance. Her eyes were buried in the pillow. Once, when the automatic writing was going on and Dr. Hodgson was purporting to communicate, she turned her face over so that her eyes, though closed, were exposed to the light. The communicator, apparently not knowing what had happened, remarked that he could almost see. Supposedly the light penetrating the eye-lids had affected the communicator so that he could use the sense-organs. This incident, of course, is not conclusive, as we may explain it by supposing that the light passing through the eye-lids was appreciated by the subconscious impersonating the communicator. I do not dispute that explanation; it is probably correct enough. But it does not stand in the way of supposing that the discarnate, if it exists and is capable of using the nervous organism of a living person may have perceptions as

claimed. At any rate, the incident quoted is of a character to support that claim, if it were otherwise justified.

(2) I have often noticed that one of the controls in the work of Mrs. Chenoweth, Jennie P., can always avoid superposing when communicating for herself; but, when she is trying to get messages from others, she has to be watched for this mistake, and I have to regulate the sheet of paper to prevent it. All the while, Mrs. Chenoweth is in the trance and her eyes are not only closed, but are often turned away from the paper. Superposition would probably occur if any normal person tried to write at the same time that he had his head turned away in order to listen to some one talking. If communication involves the visual interpretation of symbols used by the communicator to transmit his thoughts or messages to the control, we can realize how Jennie P. has to act under the circumstances.

(3) More directly in support of the statement recorded by Dr. Hare is the following fact. Since the development of Mrs. Chenoweth's trance into what we may call either a deeper state or a further dissociation of the subconscious, I have frequently noticed that I must keep my eyes on the sheet of paper to prevent superposition. If I turn away to reach a new pad or to make notes, superposition is sure to begin; I may prevent it by keeping my eyes on the paper, even when I do not have to move the pad in order to prevent the occurrence. Apparently my own visual picture of the paper is immediately transferred to the control and he or she can regulate the writing accordingly.

To prove this contention will require much more evidence than I have adduced. It is my purpose here only to state a problem and to note that Dr. Hare has recorded a statement of some interest, at which we need not sneer, though I should have done so myself if I had been in the same position as Mr. Podmore and thousands of others during the earlier stage of the investigations. With the practice of restraint and tolerance, we may some day find a satisfactory explanation of apparent absurdities in many statements that have long passed as genuine communications from a transcendental world, even though we do not accept the revelations at their superficial value.

The work of Sir William Crookes is more impressive. He was not himself responsible for the form in which it was published in this country. He wrote only brief accounts in the "Quarterly Journal of Science," in which he was conducting a controversy with critics of his paper, read before the British Association for the Advancement of Science, and these brief accounts were reprinted in this country without his revision or authority. Enough, however, was included to give a fairly clear idea of part of his experiments; those connected with the movement of physical objects without contact and with increase of weight have never been satisfactorily explained. William Huggins, a scientist of no mean repute, witnessed some of the phenomena and attests them; but scientific men generally refused to accept the challenge to investigate with him. The reception of his report led Sir William Crookes to abandon the subject, though he has maintained the convictions which his work established, and reiterated them after more than thirty years.

Strange to say, the incidents which spiritualists and the public love to quote most frequently, almost ignoring his best experiments, are those connected with alleged materialization. These, however, are poorly reported and their import depends solely on the authority of Sir William Crookes. While that must have weight, we should have had a detailed account of the experiments and results.

The report on materialization is the least impressive in the whole work; but to the public it is interesting precisely in proportion to its incredibility. If emphasis had been laid on the experiments with D. D. Home, though suspension of judgment has to be applied to some of them, the work would have received a more respectful hearing. It is significant in this connection that many years afterward, Sir William Crookes in his presidential address before the Society for Psychical Research, confessed to the wish that he had studied the mental phenomena before he announced his conclusions. If he had done so, he might have found the clue to his materialization phenomena.

This discussion offers the opportunity to explain the confusion connected with this term. When we say "materialization," meaning the alleged appearance of a spirit, the scientific man understands us to assert that a physical body has been created apparently out of nothing, or, as some spiritualists maintain, out of the surrounding matter. In either case the hypothesis is, that a physical body is formed without any apparent source for the substance and properties manifested. This conception is incredible. We have no precedent in scientific work for the sudden and apparently miraculous production of organic beings and their disappearance in a few moments like the "baseless fabric of a dream." The spiritualist may just as well admit the difficulties and not try to explain them by suppositions more far-fetched than the main theory.

But I have observed many times that people in reporting materializations do not mean the creation of physical organisms. They even speak of apparitions as "materializations"; this usage shows what they really mean by the term. Apparitions are phantasms, not physical substance. They may be veridical, and prove quite as much as any materialization would prove, without the intellectual difficulties attaching to the materialization theory. If they are called phantasms or apparitions, though the description may be incomplete, it expresses a proved fact. Whatever other elements are present can then be the subject of further investigation. We should not ask the mind, especially the scientific mind, accustomed to employ its terms with great accuracy and clear definition, to believe in so improbable an event as the creation of matter out of nothing, or the formation of inorganic matter into organic and its disintegration, independent of the usual process of dissolution. I have known instances of apparitions thus appearing in the presence of mediums. They occurred during the presence of Mrs. Catherine Paine Sutton with Mrs. Piper. They occasionally occur with considerable vividness to Mrs. Chenoweth. They are a constant phenomenon with Mrs. Chenoweth when the pictographic process is employed for communication. But the phenomena are either mere mental pictures or veridical phantasms. The simplest course is to treat them as apparitions, acknowledging the possibility both of collective phantasms and of synesthetic apparitions. These, of course, are also hard to accept, but they conform to what we know of phantasms.

When Sir William Crookes said that he wished that he had investigated the mental phenomena first, he admitted the possibility that the phenomena of Katie King might possibly be brought under that classification, and if so, would be more easily credible. But incredibility apparently attracts the average spiritualist, who, instead of fixing his attention on the best attested accounts of Sir William Crookes, concentrates his interest on the least probable of the phenomena. We may well admit that something unusual happened, without accepting the first explanation that comes to hand. We have a right to pause before accepting so incredible an occurrence as that described, especially as no detailed account of the facts accompanies the statement and as Sir William Crookes has himself publicly stated that he is not responsible for the book as published in this country.

It is to be hoped that Sir William Crookes has recorded the facts in full, and that they may some day see the light. Meanwhile we have only the letters to the "Quarterly Journal of Science." We can describe only one of his experiments here, and even that cannot be made as clear as the printed account, because the complex apparatus employed cannot be here represented. The purpose of this experiment was to get evidence of the existence of raps and of their objective nature, whatever their source. Raps are often said to occur without contact of the hands or other physical object. Sir William Crookes sought to demonstrate that they do occur in this manner and are really objective physical phenomena.

The apparatus contained an elastic membrane on which was placed a small piece of graphite, which would be thrown upward by the slightest jar to the membrane. The psychic was brought into the room without having the nature or object of the experiment explained, and was asked to place her hands on a board, that contact with the elastic membranes might be prevented. Sir William Crookes held his hands on those of the medium, in order to detect any conscious or unconscious movement of her hands. Soon sharp, percussive raps occurred, and the piece of graphite was projected upward from the membrane about one-fiftieth of an inch. The apparatus contained also a lever so arranged that its point would register in curves the amount of mechanical energy employed.

Perhaps physicists would find flaws in this experiment, and we should certainly want to be assured that tension of the lady's hands under those of Sir William Crookes on the board could not produce the effect. But this objection could not be urged against his experiment in adding to the weight of an object, which we cannot detail here. An experiment with D. D. Home and an accordion, even Dr. Hodgson found no means of explaining away. The accordion was held in one hand inside a wire basket, so that neither the hand nor foot of Home could touch the other end of the instrument, which moved and played music. There were other experiments equally puzzling.

But I do not cite them as absolute proof. They are of a type to challenge attention and to require further investigation. The scientific man is entirely within his rights in demanding that they shall be repeated, and Sir William Crookes himself recognized this need. The fundamental condition of scientific proof is not merely a crucial experiment, but a large number of experiments, conducted by different people in different parts of the world. Hence we quote Sir William Crookes's experiences, not as final proof, but as a challenge to experiment on the subject, and not to reject phenomena as impossible because they are unusual and apparently inconsistent with ordinary experience. Copernican astronomy was inconsistent with preceding theories and with ordinary observation. The motion of the earth round the sun contradicts the most natural inference from sense-perception. Telekinesis, especially since it has analogues in magnetism, wireless telegraphy, and gravitation, should not be regarded as *a priori* impossible. At any rate Sir William Crookes has challenged the scientific world; and, as similar phenomena have been produced since his experiments, we are not in a position to ridicule his conclusions.

Dr. W. J. Crawford, a man of some scientific standing and a lecturer in mechanical engineering in Queen's University at Belfast, Ireland, has performed a more recent series of experiments in levitation, under conditions and with results that make them of unusual interest. The description of his work has been published and is readily accessible. A family of spiritualists were conducting experiments in the levitation of a table and in communication with the dead by raps. Dr. Crawford learned of their efforts and was admitted to the circle. The room was sufficiently light for all persons sitting about the table to be seen, at least after a little time when the eyes had become accustomed to the dimness. The sitters held hands; all were at least eighteen inches away from the table. Without any contact, the table rose into the air and remained poised there for some time, often as high as one or two feet. The suspicion that some of the party, consciously or unconsciously, might have raised it by hands or feet was set aside by the following facts. (1) While the table was in the air, Dr. Crawford could walk all round it, except between it and the psychic. (2) He observed that she was not touching the table. Sir William Barrett, Fellow of the Royal Society and was professor of physics in the Royal College of Science in Dublin, reports his own observations on one occasion when he was permitted to be present. His statement is taken from his work on "The Threshold of the Unseen":

"I was permitted to have an evening sitting with the family, Dr. Crawford accompanying me. We sat outside the small family circle; the room was illuminated with a bright gas flame burning in a lantern with a large red glass window, on the mantelpiece. The room was small, and, as our eyes got accustomed to the light, we could see all the sitters clearly. They sat round a small table with hands joined together, but no one touching the table. Very soon knocks came and messages were spelt out as one of us repeated the alphabet aloud. Suddenly the knocks increased in violence, and, being encouraged, a tremendous bang came which shook the room and resembled the blow of a sledge hammer on an anvil. A tin trumpet which had been placed below the table now poked out its smaller end close under the top of the table where I was sitting. I was allowed to try to catch it, but it dodged all my attempts in the most amusing way; the medium on the opposite side sat perfectly still, while at my request all held up their hands so that I could see no one was touching the trumpet, as it played peep-bo with me. Sounds like the sawing of wood, the bouncing of a ball and other noises occurred, which were inexplicable.

"Then the table began to rise from the floor some eighteen inches and remained so suspended and quite level. I was allowed to go up to the table and saw clearly no one was touching it, a clear space separating the sitters from the table. I tried to press the table down, and though I exerted all my strength could not do so; then I climbed up on the table and sat on it, my feet off the floor, when I was swayed to and fro and finally tipped off. The table of its own accord now turned upside down, no one touching it, and I tried to lift it off the ground, but it could not be stirred, it appeared screwed down to the floor. At my request all the sitters' clasped hands had been kept raised above their heads, and I could see that no one was touching the table — when I desisted from trying to lift the inverted table from the floor, it righted itself again of its own accord, no one helping it."

I am not concerned with any explanation of these facts. Let each reader apply his own hypothesis. But Dr. Crawford performed further important experiments which help to show the genuineness of the phenomena. He weighed the table and also the medium. Then he placed the medium on scales while the experiment with levitation was made. While the table was in the air, all of its weight, except two ounces, was transferred to the medium on the scales, though she was not touching the table. He then placed one of the other sitters, slightly psychic, on the scales, and accounted for the remaining two ounces. He then placed scales under the table; when they were under the center of the floating table, the scales registered appreciable weight, though the table was not touching them. He noted also that, when a light cloth was placed under the scales, hardly any levitation occurred. He put a dark cloth under the scales, and the levitation became normal. He found that he could throw light from a bull's-eye electric lamp upon the top of the table without disturbing the levitation; but, if he threw it under the table, the latter immediately fell to the floor. Hence in these experiments he found that light prevented the occurrence of the phenomena. I found this to be true also of the phenomena of Miss Burton. The most obvious explanation is, that the light prevented playing the trick; but the observer was able to see that no hands nor feet were in contact with the table.

The transfer of the weight of the table to the medium would be quite in accord with well-known laws of mechanics if any visible energy extruded itself from the body of the medium and raised the table. This is the theory that Dr. Crawford, being convinced that there was no physical contact, advanced. The experiment should be repeated, before the scientific world can be impressed, but the authority for the facts is not to be summarily dismissed.

A later and very important experiment was performed by Dr. Crawford. He made a table with four small wings attached by a hinge to a central piece and resting on springs which, when the hands of four persons pressed as much as *two* pounds upon them, would cause metallic contacts and the ringing of a bell. The whole was suspended three or four inches from the floor to scales attached to the ceiling. Under these conditions the scales registered as much as 26½ pounds more than the weight of the table without the ringing of the bell. That is without a pressure of two pounds by the hands the table registered 26½ pounds more than its own weight.

The experiment is important as showing that unconscious muscular action will not account for the whole result. We may explain it as we please. The fact establishes limits to the explanation by unconscious muscular action in such cases, though it neither excludes it nor prevents the hypothesis that external influences may even affect unconscious muscular action.

My own experience with physical phenomena has been limited to raps and lights. I had a very striking series of experiments with a young lady some years ago. She was not a professional. All that she could do at that time was to produce raps and spell out messages by means of raps, and, by the same means, answer "Yes" and "No" to questions.

Her physician brought her to me at a city club where she had never been before. I first asked for raps on different sides of her chair; these were produced. Then I took her to a very large table, on which I had her place her hands. Very distinct raps were heard on the table, though no motion of her hands or fingers was observable. When I put my ear to the table, while still watching her hands, I could feel the vibration of the table as well as hear the raps. I then had her move her hands, one at a time, from the table, and saw that her feet did not touch it. The raps continued as before and the vibration in the table was perceptible. Having heard that she had made a piano-string ring, I took her to the piano. The piano was closed; she sat down near it as if to play, and in a few minutes loud raps were audible in the piano, making the string or wire ring. I then asked her to remove her hands one at a time and to put her feet back from the piano. She did so, having her feet as much as eight inches distant from the piano and her hands more than a foot. The raps and ringing of the string went on as before. All this was in broad daylight. There was nothing to hinder observation.

I arranged to meet her again at her uncle's house, in order to try some further experiments. After getting raps under her feet, I had her stand on a very thick cushion. When she was standing on the cushion, which was at least six or eight inches thick, the raps occurred exactly as before, with the same quality of sound. If made by the joints, the raps would have been muffled when the feet were on the cushion. I then had her stand with a foot on each of my hands, which rested on the cushion, and the raps occurred apparently on the floor, with the same quality of sound as when her feet were on the floor. I then tried the steam radiator some distance away, and the rap had a metallic ring, as if on iron. I then tried the piano experiment again. This time I had her hold her hands on a large book of music, on which were a dozen or two dozen sheets of music. The piano was closed. The raps were very loud, and made the string ring so that the sound could be heard perhaps a hundred feet away. I again had her remove a hand at a time and stand away from the piano. Though not quite so loud, the raps continued as before.

Though we might suppose that there was some apparatus on the body for making raps like those on the floor, we cannot so easily explain the ringing of the piano strings without any contact. I had no means of applying mechanical tests to the case. I needed apparatus for excluding the hypothesis of mechanical means concealed on the body. But in the absence of opportunity for such tests, I had to vary the experiment so that whatever hypothesis applied to one instance would not apply to another. The results favored the acceptance of the genuineness of the raps.

I got raps with Miss Burton also, while she was holding both hands and feet away from the table. Moreover, some of the raps under these conditions were not on the table, but on the window-sills ten feet distant. On one occasion the raps sounded on the window-sill, which was about eight feet distant and in the light. I then stood near the window, within a foot, and the raps were repeated many times, while Miss Burton, in a trance, was six or eight feet distant, in the light, not moving her hands. Questions were intelligently answered by these raps; by them we were even directed how to manage the girl in the trance when one of the personalities accidentally got "locked up," as it were.

I have given elsewhere a detailed account of the production of independent lights by Miss Burton. It is too long to here quote in full. After taking every precaution against her having apparatus about her person for making lights, and while holding her hands, I saw very large lights. They were of a kind that cannot be made by either phosphorus or electricity. The conditions excluded artificial methods. It is very probable that some, but not all of them occurred on the tips of her fingers. Some were six feet distant, as the illumination of a phonograph showed.

Later I received messages by means of these lights. The messages were written in letters of fire on the air in pitch darkness and gave cross-references with other psychics. They had to be read sometimes a letter at a time, and repeated until I could be certain of them.

Professor James reported an instance of physical phenomena in an article published in the "Journal" of the American Society (Vol. III, pp. 109–113). He witnessed, in a private circle of people, a brass ring moved without the contact of any hand. The details cannot be given here. The case rests on the authority of Professor James.

I have said nothing of the Palladino case and shall not quote it, as the public has long accepted the verdict of some investigators in this country, among them Professor Muensterberg, who condemned the case as fraud. I think they had no evidence of fraud; but I hold this opinion because I should treat the case from the standpoint of hysteria, which, though it furnishes a normal explanation, excludes fraud. Palladino should have been studied, as Miss Burton was, from the point of view of abnormal psychology. In contradiction of the verdict in this country, the English Society obtained striking results in levitation, and other investigators found mental phenomena of some interest, with, in one or two cases, significant apparitions. Continental investigators also vouch for genuine physical phenomena in her case, though admitting that she sometimes practised fraud. I shall not defend the case here, in as much as public opinion generally accepts the verdict of trickery. I may say, however, that one of the men who signed the negative report did so under protest; another confessed to me that he had witnessed phenomena in the experiments not so easily explained; and one distinguished scientific man stated privately his personal conviction that some of the phenomena were genuine. The case, however, is too debatable to be used in evidence of supernormal physical phenomena.

I can only repeat in conclusion that physical phenomena taken alone are not evidence for the existence or the action of spirits. At best, when taken alone, they only *disprove* certain claims about the limitations of nature, or prove the possibility of motion without normal contact. The association of mental phenomena or intelligence with them, supernormal knowledge evidential of transcendental agencies, would give them value as evidence for spiritism, and would also suggest radical modification of our conception of the relation of intelligence to the physical world. But this is not the place to dwell longer on that aspect of the problem. We were obliged to consider physical phenomena because of their traditional connection with psychic phenomena and research. They have still to receive as much confirmation as the mental phenomena have obtained, and this confirmation will probably not be forthcoming until laboratory methods can be applied to them.

CHAPTER XXI

MODE OF LIFE AFTER DEATH

THE general public has been led by psychic research to hope that we all survive death, and it has tolerated our laborious and tedious investigations with the expectation that we should soon announce our conclusions about the nature of another life. But no word has come from investigators to give assurance of anything except that we survive. It is the character of the future life, however, that interests most people far more than evidence of continued existence without any information as to what it is like. When the assertion is made that we live after death, the average man wants to know what that life offers in the way of enjoyment.

But those who look at the subject in this way understand neither the scientific problem nor the difficulties in the way of satisfying their desires. The evidence which proves the fact may not reveal a single feature of its nature. We simply observe facts which cannot be accounted for by ordinary explanations. Supernormal knowledge obtainable only by the continued activity of deceased persons justifies the inference that consciousness continues, but does not reveal the nature of the life thus implied. The problem of determining this nature is very complex, and no hasty demands can be made upon the scientific man to satisfy the natural desire to know what the transcendental world really is.

It is sense-perception that gives us a clear idea of what reality is or appears to be in normal experience. We react to physical stimuli affecting the sensory end-organs. These experiences attest for us the existence of an external physical world, even when they may not reveal its true nature. Whatever theories we may hold about sense-perception, it is the means of learning that we have to reckon with something else than ourselves and is the only means of intercommunication with one another. For all practical purposes, it serves to define the nature of reality, though by that nature we may mean no more than uniformity of effect on the sense-organs. Its constancy and our dependence on it for our adjustments in life make sense-perception the standard of our ideas, especially of such as can be communicated to other men. All conceptions that have no such reference are considered subjective or abstract. Ideas not expressible in terms of sense-perception are vague and not communicable to others. Most people, when listening to statements about a future life, must naturally try to conceive or picture it by means of sensory images, which make it intelligible to them. The Book of Revelation, for instance, which gives at least one form of the Christian conception, describes the spiritual world in terms of sensory pictures of physical realities. Even though we try to interpret the representation as symbolic, the details of the description are dependent on material analogies. The doctrine of the physical resurrection assumes that the spiritual world is like the physical. But the philosophic mind can never be made to believe this. To it the spiritual is the antithesis of the material. It even goes so far as to deprive spirit of every attribute of matter, leaving it a spaceless point of force. This theory is neither intelligible nor interesting to the average man, who conceives all reality by means of sensory images. A spiritual world that is not a "world" at all, but the absence of everything that constitutes what we call a world, does not appeal to him as worth either proving or having. That is to say, the tendency is to conceive the spiritual world as resembling the physical, even when we acknowledge that it is different in certain fundamental aspects.

The paradox of the ordinary view of a spiritual world lies in definition of spirit as opposed to matter, while at the same time the spiritual world is described in terms of that very matter which has been excluded. Such a view offers a good butt for ridicule; often the accounts of life in a spiritual world include so complete a duplication of all that goes on in the physical world, when we are supposed to have been divested of the conditions that made such aids necessary, that the skeptic may be excused for his contempt. He takes the antithesis between matter and spirit in earnest, while the believer does not. When we are told that spirits wear clothes, partake of banquets, have the same vocations there as here, are teachers, artists, manufacturers, merchants, and perhaps farmers, we are listening only to the logical consequences of making the spiritual world exactly like our own. But such economic arrangements are superfluous when we are rid of the body. Why all the useless machinery of an earthly life when it serves no imaginable purpose in a "spiritual" world? The accounts on these points are not always consistent. Some deny the existence of any conditions such as I have mentioned, and others tell us that we can form no conception of the future life.

We may say, however, that it is much easier to defend the physical view of the spiritual world from the standpoint of physical science than is at first apparent. Physical science with all its boasted dependence on sense-perception for its standard of reality pays no attention to this standard when it seeks explanations. It deals with supersensible realities quite as extensively as does theology or religion or spiritualism. Its atoms, ions, electrons, corpuscles, ether, X-rays, N-rays, and even the vibrations supposed to cause light, are as unrepresentable in sense-perception as spirit can possibly be to any one who refuses to conceive it in terms of sensory properties. The *real* physical world of the scientists, though it is called "matter." is quite as truly beyond sense-perception as spirit is. The original notion of matter is of a substance which affects the senses. Atoms, ions, and electrons are not sensible objects of knowledge. Why, then, are they called matter?

The fact is that very soon in its development physical science extended its conception of matter to include supersensible forms. The atomists set up the atoms, the earlier thinkers set up elements which were only adumbration of the atoms. Though the atoms were no more the objects of sense than are spirits, yet because they were supposed to comprise complex sensible wholes, organic or inorganic, bcause they were regarded as the material cause of what we can see or feel, the "stuff" out of which these things were made, the term "physical" or "material" was applied to them. From that time on science had the ineradicable habit of including the supersensible in the conception of matter as well as of spirit, though it continued its hostility to the latter!

Now if there can be a supersensible world of matter why may there not also be a supersensible world of spirit? The very philosophers who thus extended the conception of matter held that spirit was itself a fine form of matter; they simply regarded it as a supersensible type of matter. It was much later that the difference between matter and spirit was developed into a complete antithesis.

This antithesis was probably occasioned by the change in the definition of matter. The extension of the term to cover supersensible realities at the basis of the sensible made it necessary to abandon sensible qualities as part of the definition, for all but practical purposes. Hence to the modern physicist matter is that which manifests inertia, gravity and impenetrability. These properties are supposed to apply to its supersensible as well as its sensible forms. After this conception of matter was accepted, spirit lost its ancient meaning of a fine form of matter and was described by qualities that bear no resemblance to those of matter. In the conceptions of Leibnitz and Boscovitch it is spaceless and characterized only by intelligence or consciousness. This radical dualism, not characteristic of ancient thought, is what has made incredible the statements in which a spiritual world is given material characteristics and habits of action. The advocate of spirit is perhaps as much to blame as his opponents for this predicament. At any rate it arose, and involved the difficulty of believing any description of a transcendental world that is only matter disguised and yet is called "spiritual," when the spiritual supposedly has none of the qualities of the material. The mere acknowledgment of supersensible reality, therefore, does not imply the spiritual, if so extreme a conception of it be taken. Yet it opens such a vista of possibilities that scientific and materialistic dogmatism has no ground for assurance on its side. When matter can assume supersensible forms — that is, lose such properties as make it accessible to sense-perception — may it not further change its form so as to lose even those properties by which science now recognizes it even in its supersensible forms? May there not exist either a kind or a condition of matter in which it may lose inertia, gravity and impenetrability, or any one or two of these properties, and may manifest consciousness? I am far from believing this theory, as there is neither evidence for it nor justification in the mere desire to save spiritistic philosophies. But I am not so dogmatic as to say that it is impossible. We merely know that analogies to this transformation exist in physics and chemistry, and we may keep our minds open to such possibilities, if qualitative unity in nature be required. The fact is, however, that we do not require any such unity. We do not know the limits of the multiplicity of nature. It is only the desire for what is called monism that leads men to eliminate spirit from nature. But there is multiplicity enough within every system of monism, materialistic or otherwise, to include all that goes by the name of spirit.

The conception of spirit by radical dualism as the opposite of matter, tends to make us think that matter and spirit cannot exist side by side nor interact. Even the ancients took this position, though perhaps for other reasons. The Epicureans, though materialists, admitted the existence of the gods, but placed them in the *intermundia* where they could exercise no influence nor causal action on the course of nature. The Epicurean theory of "material causes" eliminated mind as a cause of anything, cosmic or individual. Other philosophers placed mind back of the cosmic order, but postulated an eternal substance besides mind. The materialists who admitted the existence of mind or soul, gave it neither causal action on the body nor survival after death. How they could compass its destruction consistently with their theory of the permanence of other things is not easy to understand.

Modern materialism cut the Gordian knot by abandoning the existence of soul and explaining its apparent activities as functions of the brain. But it gives no further definition of consciousness; it does nothing to reduce it to physical types; it leaves its nature as mysterious as before. There are, then, at least two and perhaps three considerations which may be urged upon physical science to show the possibility of a spiritual world like the physical world we know, though not wholly described in terms of our sensory life.

There is, first, the concession of a supersensible world even of matter.

There is, second, the fact that even materialism has to admit the existence of consciousness as an irreducible phenomenon, though only as a function of matter, and thus assumes that something different from matter can exist side by side with it. It concedes that matter can be known by consciousness and yet not participate in its nature; that is, not have the properties by which matter is known.

A third and more important point of view is the following: If we have evidence enough to justify the belief that consciousness survives death, we prove at the same time that consciousness or the soul existed side by side with matter before death. That is, the physical world is not incompatible with the presence of a soul whether defined as a fine form of matter or as the absolute antithesis to matter.

Now in the present discussion the existence and survival of a soul is taken as scientifically proved. We need not determine its nature in relation to matter. The fact remains that consciousness is not a function of the brain, that spiritual realities exist in the present physical order. Death then may be only the separation of the spiritual form from the sensory form of the physical, or the sensory manifestation of the physical, and the soul's environment after death may be the same physical world in its supersensible aspects. That is, the spiritual world may be like the physical without being any more accessible to sense-perception than the supersensible world of physical science is now.

Now we come to the experiences which at least appear to point in just this direction. These are of two types: (1) apparitions, and (2) mediumistic communications. Apparitions represent spirit in the spatial form of physical reality. They probably gave rise to the Epicurean doctrine of the "ethereal organism" and the Pauline "spiritual body," and the "astral body" of the theosophists, though this last term is sometimes given a more technical meaning. But they imply a reality in certain respects like matter, though not visible to normal sense-perception. The natural interpretation is, that we see spirits when we see apparitions. If we accept that interpretation, there at least seems to be a decided resemblance of the spiritual world to the physical, even in the very nature and form of spirit itself. In support of this theory are frequent statements through mediums, which may not be conclusive, but have weight and make it imperative that we should investigate their meaning fully. Both of these sources imply that the spiritual world is like the physical, at least in its form and appearance, though it may differ from the physical world as known to the senses, as much as the supersensible physical world differs from the sensible. It may thus be a world in which the supersensible is without inertia, gravity and impenetrability, and yet has the apparent form of matter.

The only difficulty in urging this view is that many apparitions are simply phantasms produced either by telepathy between the living or by telepathy between the dead and the living. Mediumistic communications, whether conclusive or not, are more cogent as evidence. But when we consider that a pictographic process is the frequent or constant method of communication from a transcendental world, and that the interpretation of the mental pictures by the subconscious minds of the mediums may distort their significance as representations of spiritual realities, we may have to suspend judgment.

But phantasms and appearances represented in mediumistic messages, regardless of supposed distortion in their transmission to us, may still correctly represent the nature of a spiritual world, as the image on a photograph plate or the retina represents the object producing it.

I am far from regarding all this argument as proof of the doctrine, but it clears away the perplexities which attend the radically dualistic theory. If apparitions and mediumistic communications attest the existence of spirit, and if we are willing to recognize the possibility that the apparitions correctly represent reality, we may then have recourse to other methods for ascertaining how far the resemblance to the physical world extends. We raise no questions whether spirit is material or immaterial. We decide first that it can exist independently of matter as we know it sensibly, or even supersensibly, and then investigate in other ways its further nature. For all that we know, therefore, the next world or life may be very like the present one, despite apparently very radical differences. No man is in a position scientifically to deny such a possibility. The scientific evidence for the existence of spirit establishes such a world, whether we chose to regard it as objectively similar or dissimilar to our physical world.

We may conceive the next life, then, as having the same physical cosmos to deal with, but as not perceiving it in the same way. The spiritual world may be simply the supersensible side of what is now sensible to us. How we may be related to it as we are to matter in our physical embodiment is not conjecturable, as facts to indicate the relation have not yet been discovered. But it is entirely conceivable that it should be the same world and yet not appear to be the same, since the stimulus on spirit after death may be very different from present stimuli on the physical sense-organs. It may be the same world even without our directly knowing it at all, though existing in it; for only one aspect of it appears to us now. The soul's activities may be more active or creative in the spiritual than in the terrestrial life. But we do not know. There are many possibilities which await further investigation.

But there is one more important objection or difficulty with which we have to deal: the contradictions in the messages descriptive of the future life. Though they speak of it as if it were the same physical world as that known to sense, hardly any two writers or communicators represent it in the same way. One may tell us that spirits wear clothes and another may modify this statement by saying that the clothes are "creations of thought." One represents the dead as living in houses, and others deny that they do so, while still others mediate between these two extremes by making the houses products of thought or purely imaginary. Some tell us that we could not understand any statement about the spiritual world. All these contradictions imply either differences of opinion about the other life or the distortion of messages by the subconscious of the medium, or perhaps both combined. In any case, the statements are so different and apparently so contradictory that we cannot unreservedly trust any communication as correctly describing the nature of that life.

But there is a way to establish unity in this apparent chaos of inconsistencies. We have found by experience that subconscious states produce a far more distinct appearance of reality than does normal imagination. The subconscious, in dreams, delirium, hallucinations, and hypnosis, gives apparent physical reality to its objects. Mental creations appear to be physical or objective realities. Now as such creations are often independent of normal physical stimuli, we may suppose that these functions are those that survive bodily death; and, if this be true, they would often produce apparent physical realities, just as they do in our subconscious. If they did so, and we could not introspect nor analyze any more than we can in sleep or hypnosis, we should take them for reality. If some spirits should continue the exercise of subconscious activities, whatever the cause, temporary or permanent, they might take the result to be real; but, even if they did not, the transmission of pictures to the living through subconscious functions might stimulate reality. We should then find the statements about the spiritual world as various as the experiences and opinions of the communicators. At least a part of the after life may be *mental,* a subjective creation, though taken as physically real either by the spirit or by the medium through which the messages come.

Perhaps the matter can be somewhat clarified by approaching it through what every one knows of normal mental action. Our knowledge or experience is divided into two types, both perfectly familiar to every one. The first is sensation, the response to physical stimuli. The second is reflection or self-consciousness, the inner mental states, so to speak. These may not be representable in terms of external things, but are as clearly known as sensations. Their peculiarity is that they have a degree of independence of sensory states and of external stimuli or physical objects. We can think when we are not having sensations and we can always think *about* sensations. These acts of mind go on whether we are responding to external physical impressions or not. In fact these inner states, especially the emotions, are the representatives of *value* in experience, and appear to us to be the most important. Sensory phenomena are important only as signals in our relation to the physical world. If we could free ourselves from this relation, we might go on with the inner life without reference to an external world. When death destroys the sensory functions it may leave the reflective functions to continue their action; that is, it may simply make them more independent of matter than they are in the bodily life.

A further support of this view comes from study of the subconscious activities of the mind. These are manifestly more nearly independent of normal stimuli than is ordinary self-consciousness. They are going on all the time. We have evidence that sleep does not suspend them in the least and that the dreams we know are but fragments of the images produced in sleep. In healthy conditions they are concealed from us altogether, and only when some derangement is present do they invade normal activities and cause all sorts of hysterias and dissociations. They produce images that are taken for realities — for instance, hallucinations. Often a dream is so vivid that the subject can easily and clearly distinguish between it and ordinary dreams, which are more like the products of imagination, known to be unreal. Assuming, as did Mr. Myers, that the subconscious functions, freed from sense domination, adumbrate the nature of the future life and themselves survive in independence of sensory stimuli, we have a theory that explains all the contradictions in the revelations of the next life. Different persons have different interests and tastes, and these interests are preserved with their personal identity. If they continue to use the functions represented in subliminal activities, creating apparent reality as in dreams, somnambulism, hallucinations, and hypnosis, they will differ as much as men differ now in their thoughts and ideals. When in contact with living psychics, these states will be transferred as pictographic images, consciously or unconsciously, by the communicator and accepted by the psychic as representing at least a quasi-physical reality. In such a situation all sorts of confusion might arise. The earth-bound, who are those mostly interested in the memories and experiences of a physical life, would reflect states that belonged to their past sensory lives, and, in the course of communication by the pictographic process, create the impression that the spiritual life simply duplicates the physical.

A life of mere thinking and dreaming may not appear very inviting to most people, but I am not concerned with what we like or dislike. Science has to accept the universe as it is, and to find out what it is doing, not necessarily to gratify human desires. If the next life consists of day-dreaming, we shall have to accept it whether we like it or not. But I am not sure that this conception rightly represents the facts. We have not evidence enough to show what the transcendental world is in its entirety. I have already said that it may be only the other side of our own world, with a little more subjective or creative independence than normal consciousness now has. We discover in the confused statements about it, especially the paradoxical assertions of the earth-bound and the occasional explanation of their mental states as illusions and hallucinations; in the frequent admission that thought and creative influences are more dominant there than here; in the views of Swedenborg, which anticipated all that the pictographic process reveals — in all these we discover traces of a mental world which has much more freedom for activity than when it is hampered by bodily wants and subjected to physical influences. It is certain, if a future life has been proved or rendered probable at all, that, at least in the first period of life after death for many people, the creative functions of consciousness play a part in the representation of the spiritual world. Only the knowledge that subconscious influences in the living media of transmission may distort the message or make it fragmentary will induce us to state the conditions cautiously and with the reservation that the point of view above taken is at most a tentative and partial account of the facts.

To quote the evidence in support of this contention would require a volume or two. Much of the material could not be regarded as satisfactory evidence. Only sporadic and unconscious remarks in the course of discussion of other problems indicate to us a mental world analogous to that of dreams, except that it is more rational and systematic. Even on the other side, irrationality may be met with often enough in those unadjusted to their environment or obsessed with sensory memories and desire.

I am willing to admit that the expression "mental world" will not convey much information or be clear to most people, and I do not pretend that it indicates very much even to me. It is a barren phrase to most people and hardly less so to myself. But it affords a point of contact with philosophic idealism, and it also enables us to make a psychological approach to the problem through the subliminal processes and the inner life of reflection, which do not wholly depend upon sense-experience for their meaning. That is, those functions of mind that exhibit activities other than sensory may be the basis for conceiving the initial stages of a transcendental world independent of sense-perception. Hence "mental world" expresses the group of activities that may constitute a life a little more independent of stimuli than is life in our physical embodiment.

As I have already indicated, the next world may only be the supersensible form of the physical world, and we may react to it as we do to the present, with something corresponding to sensation. But the conception of spirit as independent of the senses, is better represented by the subjective functions of the mind. The severance of our connection with the physical world as known to sense, may leave us nothing to start with except the inner functions of the mind, memories and subliminal faculties, which will have to create their own realities or apparent realities, as in dreams, poetizing, reverie, and day-dreaming, at least until some power at present unknown may enable us to respond to the new environment. This response may come sooner or later in our development on the other side. With some it may be instantaneous or not even interrupted by death, and with others much intervening time may elapse. The failure to have any but terrestrial memories to live upon, with their attachment to sensuous interests, gives rise to what is called the earth-bound condition, a state in which, as in delirium and dreams, we take our own mental states for physical realities. We may have to pass beyond this stage in order to become adjusted to our environment; the eradication of purely terrestrial memories may be necessary before we can feel and appreciate the nature of a spiritual world just as purely sensuous activities here have to be restrained, if we are to realize what is called spiritual life within us.

The various contradictions about the next life make scientific and intelligent people doubt the assertions so frequently made about it. It is human nature to suppose that, if we accept messages as proof of continued personal identity, we should also accept the statements made about the future life. It is not, however, the veracity of communicators that secures the belief in their existence, but the evidence we have among the living that their statements are true.

No message is accepted because it claims a transcendental origin, but only because we have proof that the psychic through whom it came was ignorant of the facts announced, and because we can verify it on the testimony of the living. We do not assume the veracity of a spirit until it has been proved by the same methods as those used among the living to justify trust in their statements. Even if proved to be honestly meant, the communications may not be true. They may be the result of mistaken judgment. More than honesty is required to guarantee truth. Intelligence is quite as important as veracity. The consequence is that we can accept nothing purporting to come from spirits except what we can prove. This statement is especially important in this connection because the conditions for communicating are not the same as those between the living. They are much more complex, so complex that we have to reckon with liabilities of error, even though both the veracity and the intelligence of the communicator have been established. The distortion of messages in transmission is an important factor in the result; and when we recognize also the likelihood of error in the impersonations, we may well doubt statements concerning the nature of the next life.

The contradictions are so numerous that it is hopeless to try to accept a superficial interpretation of the phenomena. One set of communicators — it makes no difference whether they are real or merely subconscious personalities — tells us that life in the spiritual world duplicates the physical life exactly, including food, dress, trade, art, " cigar manufactories," " whiskey sodas," and the whole gamut of objects and employments that we indulge in. Another set totally denies this and tells us that we cannot conceive what the world is like. Some tell us that reincarnation is true; others deny it. Some teach orthodox religious views, others the opposite. Some believe in God and some do not. Some claim to live in houses and others do not. There is no sort of unity in such claims except on the theory that the after life, as Swedenborg maintained, is one of *mental states*. Every one is free to think as he desires; and, if he can create his own world, as is constantly asserted in communications, that world will take as many forms as there are variant minds to create it, just as the subjective existences of living people differ. Landing in the spiritual world with personal identity and the memories of a terrestrial life, most of them sensory, and with the inherent tendency of the subliminal functions to produce the appearance of physical reality, spirits might well give discrepant accounts of the life. The conception of a world of mental states brings a certain consistency into the phenomena, to which we may hold while we pursue investigations, until we have positive evidence of the nature of the environment that constitutes objective life in the spiritual world.

CHAPTER XXII

REVELATIONS OF THE OTHER WORLD

THE discussion in the previous chapter prepares the way for what is to be said on this present subject. If it be difficult to tell what the nature of a transcendental life is, it will be equally different to say what the spiritual world itself is. But there have been bold enough attempts to describe it. St. John's Book of Revelation was perhaps the first after Greek mythology. In modern times, the works of Emanuel Swedenborg and later of Andrew Jackson Davis, have perhaps exercised more influence than any others. Swedenborg described the spiritual world rather minutely, but his symbolic diction was not always understood and his theory of mental states was never appreciated as highly by the laity as by scholars. The laity too often interpreted it literally, though he specifically corrected this misconception. Andrew Jackson Davis frankly described the spiritual world in sensory terms and developed no theory of mental states nor any doctrine of idealism.

Before saying anything about the value of revelations I should perhaps give examples of them. They intermingle descriptive accounts of the spiritual world and its life with philosophy and admonitions or precepts.

I am not going to raise or decide the question whether the mediums through whom the revelations came are honest or fraudulent. For our purpose here it makes no difference. We are discussing not the *source,* but the *validity* of the messages. The conditions determining the source of messages are one thing and the conditions determining validity are another, even though ultimately we must know something of the source when considering the validity of messages purporting to describe a transcendental world. But even then their validity will depend not upon the *fact* that they are spiritistic, but upon the articulation and correlation of the total mass of material into a consistent whole and perhaps upon some relation to the known in the physical world. I do not care at present to decide this question of source. The authors from whom I quote the statements *believed* the messages to come from a spiritual world. We are studying the relation of these accounts to existing knowledge and to each other. It makes no difference whether they came from frauds or from honest people. If we knew enough of the transcendental world to accept statements upon the proved veracity of the communicators it might suffice to be assured of the honesty of the source. But veracity is only one requirement when we have to learn from spirit sources the nature of the next world and its life. *Competency* to report is just as necessary as veracity. If there are degrees of intelligence and different planes of existence, the testimonies of various communicators will not have the same value, and a given communication may not represent the whole of transcendental existence. Furthermore, with competency proved, we have to reckon with the limitations of the medium, which may so modify and color the messages as wholly transform them on the way. All these, and perhaps more, considerations enter into the evaluation of the messages; but we have no space to detail them. We are only illustrating the "revelations" purporting to give accounts of the spiritual world, disregarding their source and the influence of the living mind upon their transmission. We have here to deal with them superficially as they come to us.

I shall first quote a passage from Dr. Hare's work. It purports to come from a spirit that died as a very little child and now reports what it had much later learned.

"My life here has been a charmed one, enrapturing scenes of beauty being constantly presented to view, like the ever varying landscapes delineated on the canvas by a skilful artist. Now is seen a beautiful silvery lake on whose translucent bosom floats the graceful swan, bending his pliant neck, as if proudly conscious of his surpassing beauty; and anon, among the hills of this lake, which appear like gems on a virgin brow, shoots a tiny barque, freighted with angelic children. Then is presented a bolder view, of towering mountains and wide-extended plains, with the accompanying characteristics of hill and dell.

"There are gardens there of inconceivable beauty, filled with the choicest and most aromatic herbs and flowers, and birds with every conceivable variety of plumage. The parks are of great magnitude, and abound with the most beautiful animals. The swift antelope, the wild gazelle, and the graceful deer are seen ranging over the flowery plains. There the lion and the lamb lie down together in peaceful innocence. There are congregated millions of spirits, who are associated together like a harmonious and happy family. The vales are vocal with celestial melody, and the air is redolent with the perfume of flowers."

Men may differ as to the spirituality of this heaven. Some would regard it as purely materialistic, but I am sure that most of them would enjoy it nevertheless.

In regard to the employments of spirits the following passage is of especial interest, particularly as one statement in it may throw light upon the whole subject of the transcendental life.

"Our scientific researches and investigations are extended to all that pertains to the phenomena of universal nature; to all the wonders of the heavens and the earth, and to whatever the mind of man is capable of conceiving: all of which exercise our faculties, and form a considerable part of our enjoyments. The noble and sublime sciences of astronomy, chemistry, and mathematics, engage a considerable portion of our attention, and afford us an inexhaustible subject for study and reflection.

"We do not study those practical arts, which are so essential to the earth-life, such as mechanics, etc.; for we do not stand in need of their applications; our studies being wholly of a mental character, we attend to the fundamental principles only. All the more intellectual branches of the arts and sciences are cultivated in a much more perfect manner than that to which we have been accustomed upon earth."

Like the previous passage, this regards the spiritual world as a perfect replica of the physical universe, with certain exceptions which the careful reader will note. The thing to be specially remarked is the denial of the existence of the practical arts and the emphasis upon "mental" occupations. Either this is evidence of a subconscious revolt against the complete reproduction of a physical existence, or it is a tacit admission of radical differences between that world and this. The allusion to mental occupations implies Swedenborg's view; namely, that the spiritual world is mental and creative, and that the appearance of the physical is therefore an illusion. If we accept the pictographic process of intercommunication between minds, we can interpret the above descriptions as pertaining to a dream life of some kind, whether rational or otherwise. But I am not concerned here with deciding such a question. The main point is to notice that we have either to reckon with subconscious imaginings of the medium or with a conception very different from the literal meaning of the report. After being taught by the Cartesian philosophy and much Christian speculation that the spiritual world is not material and that it can have no resemblance to the present life, we are confronted with a description of it as exactly like our own, except for the absence of evil. Only a careful scrutiny of the accounts reveals sporadic but significant statements completely altering the conception that hasty reading creates.

I shall next quote a passage from the work of Judge Edmunds. But I must first remind the reader that he must be on the lookout for symbolic meaning in the description. The tone of the account is realistic, and we should not ordinarily suspect that it had any other import. Before the experiment the persons present had been told that a vision would come to Dr. Dexter, the medium in the case. After following instructions, the party waited, and there came the following vision. It is descriptive of some features of the next life.

"Away off in the regions of space, as if in the midst of the starry firmament, I saw a bright and majestic spirit sitting in a sort of throne, which was placed on a fleecy, white cloud. A few feet above his head reposed a wreath of flowers, from whence flowed rays of light to his head, forming, as it were, a crown of light and flowers. He had on a loose garment, beautifully variegated with blue and pink, and ornamented with purple velvet, which sparkled as with diamonds. His left hand rested on a globe, on the arm of his seat, from which radiated a golden light, indicative of affection. On the right arm of his chair was a similar globe radiating a silver light, indicating wisdom. His right arm was raised, and he pointed me to a distant view. He was evidently of a higher command in the execution of God's laws than I had yet seen. Far beneath him were innumerable stars of all sizes careering through space, and apparently gamboling in the exuberance of their joy. At first the scene seemed to me one of great disorder; but as I gazed I saw how all was order and harmony. I saw many spirits coming to and going from him, as if with messages — coming as from distant stars, and vanishing in space with inconceivable rapidity.

"While I gazed, I saw a very bright light, most gorgeous, like a blazing sun, approaching him from behind, and forming a background to him. The rays of it were ever shooting out from its center various hues, yet it seemed formed of numberless concentric rings of different colors. I can convey no idea of its glorious splendor.

"That light was the central sun of all these systems of worlds I saw beneath his feet, and he was the high and holy intelligence that governed their action in obedience to the laws of God.

"He arose from his seat, and leaning on it with one arm, he pointed me with the other off to his right. There I saw a bright and dazzling spirit, with no clothing upon him, but shining like burnished silver. He was floating in the blue ethereal, and seemed a great storehouse of dazzling light, which he was scattering from him in all directions.

"I saw that he was superior to the other spirit, yet I felt as if there was a sense of solitude about him, and that he had no companions. He replied to my thought by spreading out his hands and saying, 'These worlds are my companions; my solitude is peopled by myriads of shining intelligences.'

"He pointed me to other systems of worlds far off in the illimitable distance, and immense in number. He seemed to be the apex of a cone; spreading out and beneath him were the worlds which he governed, whose guide and director he was. He pointed me to one still higher than himself, his superior in power and wisdom. Of that one I saw only the head."

Now we have only to look carefully at this description to see that it is symbolical. The figures said to represent affection and wisdom are the first clear intimation of the way the vision is to be interpreted. The latter part carries its own suggestion. But as if suggestion were not enough, the author adds the following as a part of the message conveyed by the vision:

"The great lesson taught by these scenes is the occupation of spirits, one above another, in their career of progression — each greater than the other, and executing God's laws on a larger scale and in a higher sphere."

The whole elaborate imagery is therefore symbolic, as those familiar with the pictographic process will readily recognize, while we have also to reckon with the fact that the language of the description is Dr. Dexter's. The picture does not carry with it its own language nor its own interpretation. Whether this last comes from the mind of Dr. Dexter, or from the transcendental world, makes no difference. The narrative continues with the following passage by automatic writing through Dr. Dexter's hand:

"This is one process of development. Watch and see his form rising from that brilliant cloud of lambent flame. This personifies truth as developed to minds prepared to receive it. You never, perhaps, may see anything so brilliant and gorgeous again. Let the circle be particularly silent and let their minds turn to this subject."

Note that this passage is explanatory of the meaning of the vision up to this point. The phrase, "Personifying truth," for "minds prepared to receive it" is an indication that the apparently sensuous description is really concerned with abstract ideas. The vision continues:

"There arose up from beneath this bodiless spirit a beautiful rose-colored light. It was indeed a glorious sight, which language is inadequate to describe.

"The temple was surrounded by a great number of spirits, with musical instruments in their hands, and from them arose a flood of music, far surpassing anything ever heard by mortal ears. The building had a Doric roof, and stood high up from its base. It was ascended by a flight of many steps, extending across the whole front. There were three rows of columns on each side, of infinite variety of colors; they were not Doric in form, but tall and slender, and somewhat of the Ionic order. This temple was open at its sides, and its pavement and columns shone with a brilliant sparkling gleam amid that rose-colored atmosphere.

"On each side of the building was a glorious garden, variegated with water, shrubbery, and flowers, equally dazzling in their brilliancy. The leaves of the flowers and plants were transparent, yet shone with a glitter like the ice-plant, or as if covered with frost in the morning sun. The water was now a calm and placid pool, now a bubbling stream, now a jet, and anon a tumbling fall. The flowers were of all possible colors, and I could see their perfume arise from them and mingle with the atmosphere. At the same time I could see the plants drinking in, through their leaves, the life-principle from the atmosphere, and giving it out sublimated and refined as a perfume. Those plants were in all stages of development, so that it seemed as if spring and summer, conjoined, reigned there forever. There was every variety of foliage and shady trees, now dense, dark and cool, and now sparse and transparent. The water was full of fishes. gamboling in the joyousness of life in such pure waters and the air was full of birds, rendering it beautiful with their plumage, and vocal with their song. One bird I noticed in particular: he was brown and plain in look, and as he reposed on a limb of one of the trees, he sent up his joyous song, ringing clear over all other sounds — its notes like the softest flute, expressive of happiness, and imparting a feeling of gladness to all around."

We must not forget that the description is Dr. Dexter's own, and that he has before him a panorama of pictures, pictographic imagery, with here and there a note of symbolism. Such phrases as *seeing* the perfume rising, and the plants "drinking in the life-principle and giving it out subliminated and refined as a perfume," are natural symbolic expressions for speculative truth, represented as apparent fact. All this will become clearer in some later comments. The narrative goes on:

> "The basement of the temple, I saw, was prepared and fitted up for a room in which public meetings were to be held. At one end of it was the seat of the presiding spirit. It was the precise, tomb-like monument of myself that I had seen once before, on which was recorded my age when I died. Back of that, on the wall, was a picture of that cross in the sky, which I had seen with its attendant spirit and its scrolls. Beneath that picture was my new seal painted, and on each side two other seals; they consisted of shields and emblazonry. One had a cross-bar running diagonally, above which was the scene of the good Samaritan; and below a bright spirit, who was lifting a slave from the ground and knocking off his chains. The scroll beneath the shield contained these words: 'Love conquers all things.'"

This was Dr. Dexter's coat of arms; the other was Mr. Warren's. It was quartered by bars crossing each other at right angles. In one quarter was a shepherd surrounded by his flock; he was reclining under a tree, and examining the starry firmament. In the second quarter was a man far down in a deep pit, examining the formation of the rock and earth. In the third, was a man reading; and in the fourth, one with crucibles and other chemical apparatus. The inscription was, "Knowledge is Progressive."

The description continues for nearly two pages, but we have seen enough to understand the character of the whole. We are concerned here only with that part which contains internal evidence of being symbolic. The symbolic meaning is unconsciously revealed in the very contents of the message. For instance, Dr. Dexter's monument, inscribed with his epitaph, is not a vision of present reality, but a premonition. The shield and other figures are also symbolic. More especially we note a prediction of the downfall of slavery, which was not an established fact at the time of this vision, in 1853. The vision, therefore, was not of actual facts, but consisted of images signifying future events. It matters not what the source of these pictures may be; we are assuming their spiritistic origin here only to indicate that the symbolic character of the pictures is not affected thereby, while it is taken for granted on any other theory of their source. That part which is obviously symbolic suggests the same interpretation for the rest.

We could go through the literature of spiritualism and find many examples of symbolic vision. As the pictographic process of communication is so common, even when the personal identity of the discarnate is being proved, when we cannot for a moment suppose that real things are seen, we have to bear in mind in considering such narratives, the conditions of that process with its inherent symbolism. This point can be brought out in another way.

Strictly scientific language is inadequate to interpret art. We cannot directly convey the impressions and emotions we experience in the enjoyment of works of art. We have to describe the product in terms that carry with them certain emotional values; and, unless the recipient has had experience enough to read into the language what the communicator has in mind, he fails to get the meaning. The descriptions contain words signifying certain emotional effects; and, as we can communicate with each other only in terms of sense-perception, of pictorial imagery of some kind, a criticism may often enough seem absurd to the stickler for scientific accuracy, though perfectly intelligible to the man who appreciates art and the emotional reactions to beauty.

We can apply the psychology of art to our present problem. If the spiritual world be dominantly a world to be described appreciatively, not scientifically, we may well understand how descriptive accounts have a symbolic meaning which should be interpreted in terms of emotion. Many of the revelations of the spiritual world characterize it as dominantly emotional and affectional. Mere knowledge is secondary among its interests. Just as we use sensuous imagery in interpreting any work of art, so the pictographic process, recognizing the difficulties of describing a spiritual world, uses such pictures as will carry with them emotions characteristic of the spiritual life wherever found. In the attempt to describe a piece of music, the critic or artist endeavors to make a body of sound intelligible in terms of visual imagery. A musician may call his composition " A Rose," meaning that his musical work gives rise to the same emotion as that produced by a rose. The writer who speaks of "a symphony of color" is using musical terms to describe a visual effect. The language cannot be taken literally; the appreciative mind must construe the meaning in terms of emotional reactions. The same principle may apply to the accounts of the spiritual world. The pictographic process must represent it in pictorial images, but the mind must see in them the emotional meaning of the representations, and ignore the literal import.

The work of Andrew Jackson Davis has proved attractive to most people because it contains more description and philosophy than most similar productions, and because the author maintains that he had read little or nothing on the subject. His "Summer Land" is as complete a description as was ever given of the other world in terms of sense. This characteristic arouses at once the skepticism of the more intelligent and the enthusiasm of the ignorant. There can be no doubt that his work is remarkable as a case for the psychologist; but its literal truth is another matter.

Since we have had no experience of the transcendental world it requires scrutiny and discrimination to determine what reports are acceptable and what are not. The veracity of the communicator does not guarantee the truth of his statements. We need to know two things in addition to his veracity. (1) We must know his competency or the intelligence of his judgment in making his observations. (2) We must know that he is reporting more than his individual impressions. When these two conditions are fulfilled we may be able to accept reports about the next world.

Now when we add to the difficulties just mentioned the further complications (1) that the accounts of the spiritual world do not agree in their details, and (2) that the reactions of different spirits may vary as widely as do the esthetic judgments of the living, we shall have abundant reason to exercise caution before accepting accounts of the spiritual world at their face value. If the descriptions are highly symbolic and if they are determined by the degree of development of the individual spirit, we could hardly expect them to be identical or even consistent. The differences between the spiritual and the physical world make it difficult to give a satisfactory account of the former. Just in proportion as it is different from this life, spirits must be unable to describe it in the only terms by which it can be made intelligible to most people. Just in proportion as it is like the physical world the stories about it will be credible to the ordinary person and at the same time will excite the skepticism of the man who does not think altogether in terms of sensory images. The contradictions in the accounts make it easy to understand why the intelligent man hesitates to accept the revelations, though the average man simply selects what pleases him and ignores the rest. The conflict lies between different criteria of truth, the untrained mind accepting at its face value every narrative couched in sensory terms, and the scientific mind doubting everything that pretends to describe a spiritual world in physical terms. The reconciliation lies in the belief in a supersensible physical universe saturated with spirit, whatever view of spirit we take, and in the belief in spiritual activities of a dominantly emotional type, which have to be translated into sensory terms when they are described to the living. But we have still to prove the existence of such a state of affairs.

Contradictions in the statements are due partly to the same causes which make the living differ in their opinions, and partly to differences in the conditions under which spirits exist. There are what we call the earth-bound spirits who live in their sensory memories and desires. Their communications must reflect their own mental condition and would naturally contain just such stories as those which offend the scientific intelligence. Then there is the crank, who still insists on teaching us his doctrine whenever he can find a channel through which to express it. It is probable that the earth-bound and the cranks can communicate more easily than can the more highly developed, and that they would be more persistent in their efforts. Death does not make radical changes in our natures. We retain the same characters; if we have resisted progress here we may do so in the spiritual world. Moreover, many messages are compounds formed by two or more minds acting at the same time. It is probable that this condition exercises a more distorting influence on results than do the messages of the earth-bound. But we have to reckon with so many obstacles to the intelligibility of the messages, including their frequently symbolic nature, that we have to be exceedingly wary in the acceptance of any revelation.

The manifold difficulties which I have discussed above will always stare us in the face, though we may be forced to admit that there is some basis of truth in the revelations. Only the common elements in the total mass of conflicting accounts can be accepted, and even these only on the assurance that they are not reflections of normal ideas and imaginings. We must be sure that the mind which delivers them has not known any of the ideas and theories of spiritualism, if we are to exclude the influence of conscious and subconscious knowledge on the statements. To secure an adequate conception of the spiritual world by such a process of sifting will require many years of investigation and study. We are in no position at present to provide the scientific mind with a clear conception of the transcendental world nor with any simple criterion of validity for the communications concerning that world.

CHAPTER XXIII

REINCARNATION

THE doctrine of reincarnation is one form of belief in survival after death. We meet with it in early Buddhism, in early Greek philosophy, among the physicists or so-called materialists of the Pre-Socratic period and again in Plato. The early materialists are represented as believers in survival in any form only by the more exhaustive historians of the period; and even they mention the belief merely for the sake of completeness, as if it were an irrelevant detail of the system. But it was too important an element in the philosophy of Plato to be ignored. He seems to have been the only prominent philosopher of Greece in the intellectual period who had the hardihood to defend it. The theosophists of modern times have advocated it: most of them derive their belief from Buddhism. The idea prevailed in other religious and philosophic sects of India, either growing out of Buddhism or out of the systems that preceded Buddhism.

I do not intend here to go into the history of the doctrine. I mention its antiquity primarily to show that it is not the result of modern scientific progress. But its value must rest on facts and not on antiquity or authority. I have discussed it in another work, "The Border-land of Psychic Research." I shall here take up only additional matters, which have become important through the revival of interest in the doctrine by the theosophists.

In general, reincarnation means that the soul after death comes back again to the earthly life in another physical body. It assumes that the materialistic theory of consciousness is not true; either taking the existence of a soul for granted, or adducing the facts of normal consciousness and experience as sufficient to justify the belief in the existence of a soul. Its doctrine of re-embodiment or transmigration as a form of survival, differs in certain details from the Christian and other similar views. It does not accept the bodily resurrection; perhaps advanced Christianity does not do so any longer, though many Christians still cling to it. This theory implies that the soul retains its identity when it re-occupies a body, either the old one resurrected or a new one created for the purpose. But reincarnation does not assume any resurrection. It assumes that the soul, without memory of the past, comes back and occupies a body created by ordinary sexual union. This denial of memory is the fundamental characteristic of the doctrine, as held by most theosophists to-day and in the past. If faced with the disadvantages of the loss of memory, theosophists maintain that after various reincarnations this memory of all past experiences is recovered. It is lost as a consequence of the individual's mistake and sins, and is restored when his "karma" or probationary discipline is complete; after his various transmigrations.

Now it must be said that this belief rests on metaphysics alone. It has no scientific foundation whatever. Some venture to adduce facts to support it, but these will not bear the slightest examination as evidence. For instance, some will tell us that they can remember a previous existence. But they do not reckon with illusions of memory. We sometimes recall something which we locate in a certain time and place, but find later that this location was wrong. When the total experience is recalled we find that we are dealing with two events connected only by similarity. We confused them because of the imperfection of the recall. This imperfect recall will explain most of the alleged instances of recollection of a prenatal past.

Other facts adduced in support of reincarnation can be explained as mediumistic phenomena. That is, discarnate personalities may produce in the minds of psychics the feeling of long past time or of previous existence by the transmission, telepathically perhaps, of their own feelings and states of mind. These would naturally enough be interpreted as evidence of reincarnation. But when we find that they are memories transmitted from the discarnate to the living mind, their claims as evidence are nullified. The sense of recognizing a place which we are seeing for the first time is another type of fact like the one just considered, except that it involves space instead of time. It too can be explained either as an illusion of memory or as clairvoyance. Either hypothesis nullifies the value of the facts as evidence for reincarnation.

I allude thus briefly to the alleged evidence for transmigration, in order to show that it has no scientific standing. Its metaphysical character is another matter; I have eliminated its scientific claims in order to show that it is only a metaphysical theory. It may be true or false, but it cannot be assumed to be true without evidence: for metaphysical theories are to-day discredited unless they can produce evidence in their support. They are legitimate enough as imaginary possibilities, but woe unto the man who asserts them to be facts. What it is that can recommend the doctrine of reincarnation to its believers is difficult to understand. It contains nothing desirable and nothing ethical. To be sure, its desirability or undesirability has nothing to do with its truth or falsity. It might be true, though very undesirable, and it might be false, though very desirable. But as it is a metaphysical theory, we have a right to test its relation to practical life and the native instincts of man, when we cannot find scientific evidence to prove it.

Reincarnation is not desirable, because it does not satisfy the only instinct that makes survival of any kind interesting, namely, the instinct to preserve the consciousness of personal identity. This is denied to the process until its end and that is never in sight! Moreover, assertion of even this return of memory is purely arbitrary. Man's only interest in survival is for the persistence of his personal identity. It is a form of the impulse towards self-preservation, which is fundamental to all the acquisitions of experience and character in this life. A future life must be the continuity of this consciousness or it is not a life to us at all.

Moreover, there is nothing ethical in the doctrine. The absolutely fundamental condition of all ethics is *memory* and the retention of personal identity, and memory and personal identity are excluded from the process of reincarnation. That you cannot maintain a theory of responsibility in any existence without memory is a truism in ethics and even in our civil courts. If our personal identity were changed, we could not be held responsible for anything we did. If we lost our memory every five minutes we should be regarded as insane, and crime could not be ascribed to us. In cases of alternating personality, punishment might be meted out to the personality performing the act, but this restraint could not apply to the other personality. The result is that cases of dissociation and change of personality are subjects for the physician and not the police.

The doctrine of reincarnation has to face this large question. We cannot apply to any future life the categories of the present, unless personal identity be assumed. Memory from one stage to another is necessary to the continuance of existence. "Karma" without memory is retribution minus all grounds for it, abstracting everything that makes it rational.

How then did such a doctrine originate? What could have given rise to such a theory? Plato may be forgiven because we know his poetic and literary instincts. But there was some reason for the maintenance of the belief, and we may well ask what this reason was. Even fantastic views, when persistently and seriously held, have some reason for their existence; and the doctrine of reincarnation is too old and too insistent not to have had some reason for its origin.

If the doctrine could be defined as meaning the survival of consciousness in the spiritual body, it would be consistent not only with some forms of spiritualism, but also with Christianity. But usually its advocates deny this view. Some of them are as much opposed to spiritistic theories as are the skeptics, though many regard psychic research as a stepping stone to their own philosophy. They often admit the existence of a spiritual body, but do not conceive the relation of personality or consciousness to it as one of transmigration. If they could conceive that relation as the transfer of the present consciousness to a spiritual body there would be no logical, no ethical, and no scientific difficulties in the way of that conception. But this would be giving up their denial that memory endures throughout the process of reincarnation; and few, if any, theosophists will admit the conception just defined.

It was this idea with which Professor James was playing when he tried to defend the possibility of immortality by the doctrine of *transmissive* functions of the brain. He did not call his theory reincarnation, for to do so would at once have discredited his view in the minds of scientists, if only because of associations and implications which he did not admit and which the theosophists hold. Professor James, instead of using the results of psychic research to prove survival after death, confined himself to physiological and psychological arguments, maintaining the materialistic view of the nature of consciousness. He admitted, with the materialist, that consciousness is a function of the brain. But, in order to avoid the materialist's conclusion he tried to distinguish between what he called *transmissive* and *productive* functions of the brain. He did not make the distinction very clear or tenable in relation to facts, but he used the idea consistently enough. By productive functions of the brain he meant such as are so organically connected with it that they perish when the body dies. He imagined that consciousness, however, might be a function that could be transmitted from the brain to some other structure, whether the transmission be conceived as reincarnation with or without the retention of personal identity. He said nothing about transmigration of the soul to other human bodies, and he probably would not have tolerated the idea. Neither did he say anything about the question whether any "spiritual," "astral," or ethereal organisms existed without any connection with a body. He left us to infer that they might be formed or created for the transmitted consciousness after death. But the notion of transmission is not necessary to spiritism. Consciousness either is now a function of the "spiritual body," whether spatial or spaceless, or is so closely associated with such an organism that it goes with it at death, without the need of "transmission." But to assume "transmission," as Professor James did, is to assume that the "ethereal organism" is not now associated with consciousness, but awaits the reception of it when it has left the brain.

This view has the merit of forcing the materialist to argue the case from his own premises, but it is totally without evidence. It is quite as *a priori* as any mediaeval theology, and therefore is inconsistent with the "radical empiricism" which was the fundamental belief of Professor James.

When, in the light of psychic research, we examine the early theories of animism and the doctrine of reincarnation as held among the early Greek philosophers, even the materialists Empedocles and Democritus, we may discover how the theory of reincarnation originated. Primitive animism was bound up with the belief in reincarnation, but it was not clearly worked out into a logical and consistent philosophy. We find in animism only the seeds of the doctrine, in the naïve ideas of ignorant people with a penchant for explaining things. But when we recognize undeveloped spiritualism in this primitive animism, we find a clue to the origin of the theory of reincarnation.

Spiritualism based upon communication with the dead assumes the return of the discarnate spirit to the earthly life; and its temporary occupation of a human body in order to effect the communication. This return might be called an incarnation. Communicators have often said that their return is like getting into the living body and living over again in that organism. Unphilosophic ages might develop this circumstance into a theory of reincarnation, after they had forgotten the conditions which gave rise to the original meaning of the term. Such development is very frequent in the history of religious and philosophic beliefs. For instance, we cannot read the New Testament in the light of psychic research and the meaning of Greek and Hebrew words, without noting that the resurrection was originally only a theory of survival based upon apparitions. Long before Christianity arose, *anastasis,* the Greek word for resurrection, in one of its meanings, signified the appearance of apparitions. The doctrine had been discussed between the Sadducees and the Pharisees before Christ was said to have risen. The Greeks had been long familiar with the idea, which developed into the doctrine of the bodily resurrection only after the facts on which it was based were discarded or forgotten, perhaps partly because of the confusion attending, on the one hand, the conceptions of matter and spirit, and, on the other, the real meaning of the " spiritual body " of St. Paul. A similar development is apparent in the doctrine of the Trinity. It meant something intelligible with reference to the Greek conception of *personality* as simply a representation of characteristics in a subject, not the subject itself. When this meaning was lost and the terminology retained as a dogma, philosophers and theologians felt the necessity of trying to explain it by concocting preposterous arguments to bolster up a phrase that had lost its primitive significance.

In some such way we can conceive the origin of the doctrine of reincarnation, without supposing that it was fabricated by the imagination without any facts whatever upon which to work. Both mediumistic phenomena and the statements of communicators suggest something like reincarnation, though they do not support the developed system. They show that returning to communicate involves something like the old relation of the soul to the body, which for them might be called "reincarnation," though not as a mode of "karma" or punishment.

This latter doctrine, a concomitant of reincarnation, may have arisen from certain phenomena associated with what are called earth-bound spirits. These are persons so obsessed with their earthly life that it is often difficult for them to get away from their former interests. It is represented in some communications that this condition may be remedied by bringing earth-bound spirits into contact with living organisms, especially psychics, in order to remove the fixed ideas and the attachment to earthly memories and experiences. In this way they work out their salvation, so to speak; and any mention of this state of affairs in communications would call to mind the doctrine of expiation and punishment.

But until reincarnation can adduce scientific facts in its support, it cannot rival psychic research. Scientific doctrines always produce evidence, and do not extend their theories or explanations beyond facts. Metaphysical speculations are possible; and are the delight of certain types of mind, but they are not substitutes for facts. All that scientific men ask of the reincarnationist is that he produce satisfactory evidence for transmigration; until he does so, the theory cannot claim to be based on fact. It is only fair to give it a hearing in this connection and to eliminate all suspicion of prejudice against it, I can only say that, if proper evidence be adduced for it, I shall admit it, though I should have to regard the cosmos as irrational. The probable origin of the theory of reincarnation explains the element of truth which it contains. But the survival of personal identity, adequately supported by facts, contradicts the main doctrine of the reincarnationist.

It is true that communications, or what purport to be communications, from the dead assert the doctrine of reincarnation. But we must remember that there is no agreement in communications of the dead about their life. The disagreement is as great as it is about philosophic views among the living. Perhaps there is no literature in which contradictory conceptions of spiritual existence are more numerous than in the real or alleged descriptions in spiritualistic records. This inconsistency prevents our uncritical acceptance of these records as final on any point. It goes to prove that we are receiving only statements of opinion, not facts, from communicators, if we accept the statements as communications from a transcendental world. Some communicators deny the reincarnation. Consequently, when we consider that the retention of personal identity includes retention of the views that we held when living, especially if we remain earth-bound and unadjusted to the new environment for a time; when we consider subconscious distortion and coloring of messages by the medium, especially if he normally believes in reincarnation; when we allow for misinterpretation of both facts and messages; and when we recognize the fragmentary character of all messages and the limitations of the medium, we shall quite understand that communications from the dead, whether for or against reincarnation, are not to be accepted at their superficial value. The contradictions require us either to distrust all communications on this subject or to reconstruct the messages in the light of an extensive study of all the recorded statements.

CHAPTER XXIV

OBSESSION

THE Christian church should be as familiar with obsession as it is with the divinity of Christ, miracles, the immaculate conception, inspiration, baptism, and other doctrines: for the existence of evil spirits affecting the living is as clearly taught in the New Testament, and implied in the Old Testament, as any doctrine there expounded. But the church has repudiated belief in " witchcraft," which it cannot escape save by accepting the verdict of science instead of revelation. It has reduced the Biblical cases of obsession to hysteria, epilepsy, paranoia and similar maladies, thus disposing of facts which we might easily believe by its own doctrine of the " communion of the saints ": for we can hardly admit that evil spirits do not know the method of communication which the " saints " practice. So we should have no difficulty in forcing all believers in the New Testament to believe in obsession and to set about mastering what it implies.

Nevertheless, obsession is not lightly to be believed. It is quite as conceivable as ordinary communication with the dead, but it is not so easily proved. In our search for scientific proof of survival we have been dealing with honest personalities, ready to make concessions and to supply evidence of their identity. But experience has shown that mischievous personalities are desirous of concealing instead of revealing their identity. In default of evidence to the contrary, we should have to accept the orthodox verdict of medicine and psychiatry, which explain obsessions as cases of dual or multiple personality, hysteria, or some form of insanity. It required ten years of investigation, after I had admitted the existence of spirits is credible, to convince me of the possibility of obsession; then followed some years of work to accumulate the facts which make it scientifically probable.

Most people are familiar with the campaign of the church and the law against belief in witchcraft throughout the Western world; the medical explanation was sufficient, if not to eliminate the phenomena, at least to eradicate the belief in obsession. But, in reporting on some of the investigations in the Piper case, Professor James said that, though hesitating to accept the spiritistic theory, he was certain that belief in demoniac possession would have its innings again. He lived long enough to see the report on the Thompson-Gifford case published in the American Proceedings; it was that case which overcame my resistance to the idea of obsession, though I felt and said that it alone was hardly adequate evidence.

There can be no *a priori* argument against obsession after the existence of discarnate spirits in any form has been proved or even shown to be possible or probable. The process employed to establish the personal identity of spirits may well be used by mischievous or ignorant personalities in order to disturb the normal life of the living. It is not at all likely that sane and intelligent spirits are the only ones to exert influence from a transcendental world. If they can act on the living there is no reason why others cannot do so as well. The process in either case would be the same; we should have to possess adequate proof that nature puts more restrictions upon ignorance and evil in the next life than in this, in order to establish the certainty that mischievous personalities do not or cannot perform nefarious deeds. The objection that such a doctrine makes the world seem evil applies equally to the situation in the present life.

Obsession, a term used by psychiatry to denote *fixed ideas,* is employed by psychic researchers to denote the abnormal influence of spirits on the living. It does not mean ordinary mediumship, which either may occur without disturbing normal life or may be a merely temporary interruption of that normal life. It represents a dissociation of functions, varying from the slightest disturbance of normal personality to complete displacement. But in all cases it represents an influence foreign to the organism instead of within it, due to the action of a discarnate spirit or spirits, whether the influence be voluntary or involuntary. The process by which this influence is exercised may be the same as that which is employed to communicate desirable messages, but it is conducted either with a very different purpose or as the result of laws which happen to involve ignorant spirits in toils from which they sometimes cannot easily escape.

The phenomena which I have ultimately come to think are due to foreign action, do not appear to be evidence of any such invasions. They are not like the facts which we have been accustomed to regard as evidence of the existence of spirits or of supernormal knowledge. They appear to be morbid states of the subject afflicted. Many cases of hysteria, of dementia precox, of paranoia, of manic depressive insanity, and of dual or multiple personality do not show any superficial indications of spirit invasion. The psychiatrist has been quite right in refusing to diagnose them as obsessions. Cases of dual and multiple personality immediately suggest obsessions, because of the dissociation between the personalities. But the lack of evidence of supernormal knowledge and of the identity of the spirits in some, if not in all, of these cases, at first prevented the application of a spiritistic explanation to them.

But I found a way to supply this evidence by the method of cross-reference. I take the patient to a psychic under conditions that exclude from the psychic all normal knowledge of the situation, and see what happens. If the same phenomena that occur in the patient are repeated through the medium: if I am able to establish the identity of the personalities affecting the patient: or if I can obtain indubitably supernormal information connecting the patient with the statements made through the psychic, I have reason to regard the mental phenomena observed in the patient as of external origin. While the experiences of the patient may not in themselves be evidence of the supernormal or of foreign invasion, the repetition of the same experiences through the psychic, who is ignorant of them, establishes their supernormal character without question. In a number of cases, persons whose condition would ordinarily be described as due to hysteria, dual, or multiple personality, dementia precox, paranoia, or some other form of mental disturbance, showed unmistakable indications of invasion by foreign and discarnate agencies.

It is not necessary to suppose that these invasions were the primary cause of the trouble. Organic lesions sometimes open the way to all sorts of other disorders. Functional disturbances may be due to invasions of the discarnate, but in some instances these influences were preceded by organic derangements or by accidents. The hypothesis of obsession does not set aside physiological causes. It designates only a concomitant cause or disturbance in the situation, unless in certain types of purely functional trouble the discarnate be primary and sufficient cause. Obsession is not incompatible with hysteria, dual or multiple personality, and the like. It only adds to the complications of the phenomena and may lead to the consideration of more causes than have hitherto been recognized.

We do not need accept the spiritistic hypothesis in order to admit the possibility of obsession. If we believe in telepathy, we believe in a process which makes possible the invasion of personality by some one at a distance. Telepathy not only involves the transmission of thoughts from one person to another, but very distinctly implies that these thoughts can exercise a causal influence on the percipient. Psychology assumes that only physical stimuli, through the intermediation of the body, can affect the mind. But telepathy assumes that one mind affects another. This very supposition contains the possibility of all that we observe in obsession, if it be proved to exist. Consequently there is no need of insisting that spirits are the sole agents in obsession. We might point out that there would be no hope for a cure if telepathy caused the obsession, as we might never be able to find the personality guilty of producing the effect on the patient, and so would not be in a position to exorcize him or to teach him to avoid using his influence. Telepathy thus used would be Mrs. Eddy's "malicious animal magnetism," which is only obsession disguised so as not to imply the spiritistic theory, which she once believed and later rejected. But such an explanation represents the malady as incurable, since on this hypothesis we cannot get at the causes. On the spiritistic theory it is possible to find the causes and to deal with them.

But examination of the actual facts will show not only that telepathy is wholly irrelevant to the problem, but also that only spiritistic agencies rationally explain the phenomena, while the admission of the existence of spirits on other evidence prepares the way, more definitely than does telepathy, for acceptance of the possibility of obsession. The whole case will rest upon the special nature of the facts obtainable in support of the hypothesis.

If we could interpret every case of psychic invasion as obsession, the case would be won in all instances where the supernormal is discoverable. It would make the term synonymous with mediumship; perhaps in principle they really are the same. But the term has usually been confined to those cases which do not show the usual type of evidence for spirit invasion. The term denominates abnormal cases, in which the dissociation and disintegration of normal life has been so great as thoroughly to demoralize it. This is not true of what may be called normal mediumship. There is no hard and fast line between the two types, except the application of the term obsession to cases that do not in themselves contain evidence for the supernormal and that are characterized by clear and distinct evidence of the abnormal.

Now as the supernormal is not superficially apparent in these cases, we cannot assume them to be instances of obsession unless we can produce evidence that the ordinary medical diagnosis is either incorrect or imperfect. Mrs. Piper, Mrs. Smead, Mrs. Chenoweth, Mrs. Verrall, Mrs. Holland and others gave unmistakable evidence for the supernormal, which could be proved by very simple methods. All we had to do was to take strangers to them and record the subsequent events. But cases of hysteria and of dual or multiple personality furnished no such revelations of the personal identity of the dead. Hence we had either to contrive a new method of experiment or to surrender the diagnosis to psychiatry.

The method of experiment adopted, when the influence of discarnate spirits was suspected, was that of cross-reference. If the same phenomena that had occurred in the patient were repeated through the psychic, and if this repetition was accompanied by unmistakable evidence of supernormal knowledge relevant to the case, there would be reason at least to raise the question of obsession. If the same personalities as those constituting the dual or multiple personalities were manifest in a trained psychic, we should have strong evidence that they were not in the first instance merely subjective creations. This sort of experiment was tried for the purpose of seeing whether we could secure evidence of external personality in what seemed to be merely an abnormal state in the patient. We have tried this experiment in a number of cases with the same result; a similar result never manifested itself when normal persons were the sitters or subjects of experiment.

The case which first suggested obsession to me was that of Mr. Thompson. The invading agent was Mr. Gifford. Mr. Thompson, after a period in which he felt compelled to paint in Gifford's style, was unable to resume his profession as a silversmith. It nauseated him. This indicated to me that the invasion had brought about some sort of organic alteration in his interests and physiological habits. The persistent invasion of Gifford to accomplish his purpose and the organic alteration of the man's habits and tastes suggested, though it did not prove, obsession. It made me resolve to investigate similar cases until I should have ascertained what was going on. In the experiences of Mr. Thompson there was no evidence that would convince the scientific man, especially the student of abnormal psychology, that he was the subject of discarnate invasion. Indeed two physicians diagnosed the case as paranoia, and one of them, without offering to cure it, expressed a desire to watch the progress of the malady. But cross-reference proved very clearly that the spirit of Mr. Gifford, whatever the motive, was behind the phenomena; and the abnormality of the effect on the profession of Mr. Thompson suggested that something more than mediumship was manifested.

Soon afterwards I came across three other cases which every psychiatrist would diagnose as hysteria, two of them perhaps as incipient paranoia. One of these persons was writing stories purporting to come from a well-known author who had died some years before and about whom the automatist knew very little. Another was engaged in musical composition both for the piano and the opera. There were decided symptoms of hysteria in her case. The third case showed no disagreeable indications of dissociation, but was doing automatic writing purporting to come from Emma Abbott and was singing under the same inspiration. All three were taken to Mrs. Chenoweth under conditions that excluded all normal knowledge of the persons and the facts. The personalities purporting to direct the subjects claimed to communicate through Mrs. Chenoweth and so to be the instigators of the phenomena observed. None of the three cases was the victim of serious dissociation save the first, who was rendered incapable of earning her living. When the work with the psychic had been done, however, she recovered her balance. None of them had reached a stage in which physicians would have assigned them to an asylum. They were not cases that would pass for victims of obsession, in the sense of constant persecution by transcendental agencies. Such persecution is the distinguishing characteristic of cases that demand special treatment.

Another case, that of a young girl just entering womanhood, was diagnosed by two physicians as dementia precox or paranoia. There were no apparent symptoms of physical degeneration: but she became perfectly stupid, so that she could not always rationally answer questions of the simplest kind. When a narrative of the child's experiences came to my attention I at once saw possibilities that I should not have suspected until I had observed and proved what was happening in the several cases outlined above; and I resolved to try the experiment of investigation with the child. I soon found that the phenomena were instigated from without and got into contact with a personality whose influence on the child can be discussed only in a medical work. I tried two psychics, with the same general result. We had not the means to continue the work until we obtained a perfect cure. But there was unmistakable evidence that the phenomena were of foreign instigation, though affected by the subconsciousness of the child. There was no superficial evidence of foreign stimuli until cross-reference was applied to the case.

The next case, that of Doris Fischer, is most important; but the summary of it must be preceded by a brief account of the celebrated case of Sally Beauchamp, treated by Dr. Morton Prince of Boston. Doris Fischer had one personality so like the mischievous personality of Sally Beauchamp that a comparison between the two is necessary.

Sally Beauchamp manifested four chief personalities; that is, there appeared to be four different persons inhabiting the one body. These were designated as B. I, B. II, B. III or Sally, and B. IV.

None of them knew anything about the others, except that Sally knew the other three, knowing B. IV only partly. There was no connection of memory between them except that Sally knew and remembered what the others thought and did as well as what she herself knew and did; she knew what B. IV *thought* but not what B. IV *did*. These are the complications; but the important point is that she was mischievous, like one of the main personalities in Doris Fischer. The Beauchamp case was never tested for evidence of spirit agencies. All that we can say is that Sally showed four characteristics that we find in controls of mediums: (1) she claimed to be a spirit; (2) she did automatic writing; (3) she was always conscious; (4) she had no perception of time. These characteristics seem not to have marked the chief secondary personality in the case of Doris Fischer.

When a child of three and a half years, Doris Fischer was picked up by her drunken father and thrown down on the floor so violently that her head was injured; from that time on she suffered from dissociation or dual personality until the death of her mother when Doris was seventeen years of age. Until the death of her mother there were but two personalities manifested, the normal Doris and a secondary personality who called herself Margaret. The shock of her mother's death increased the number of personalities to five. The addition to the family, so to speak, consisted of personalities called Sick Doris, Sick Real Doris and Sleeping Margaret. This last never appeared except in sleep. Margaret might appear at any time and stayed for a short or a long time apparently according to caprice. She was mischievous, like Sally Beauchamp. Sally would play all sorts of pranks on the other personalities. B. I was the especial object of her enmity. Sally would take control and go out to the country on the last street car and then leave the girl; that is, let the normal self come in, and the girl would have to walk back home, arriving exhausted. Or Sally would put into a box spiders, toads, or other animals of which the normal self had a horror, and leave them on the bureau so that when the normal self opened the box she would have a severe fright. She would take or lose money belonging to the normal self and thus embarrass the girl when she found that her money was gone. Margaret in the Doris Fischer case would play similar tricks on Doris, the normal self. She would steal aprons or candies from places where Doris was working, so that Doris would be blamed for the theft. That is, Margaret would come — she was not discoverable by strangers, since the child would go on with her work as if normal — and steal and hide what she wanted. The normal self, knowing nothing about it, had to take the blame. Margaret would hide the child's books at school so that the normal self could not study her lessons. She had a bureau drawer at home into which Doris, the normal self, was not allowed to look. There Margaret would keep things she wanted or had stolen, and if Doris accidentally went to it and found something of her own or Margaret's, Margaret would scratch the body until it bled all over, and the normal self would have to endure the pains and sores. Margaret would come in and eat the candy that Doris had bought for herself. Margaret would take horses from the livery stable and ride them into the country, but would return them after her ride. She would rush down to the river and take swims with all the child's clothes on; the river was very dirty at its best, with much of the filth of a large city floating on its surface. The normal self had no memory of the acts, and could not understand the effects.

Margaret did not claim to be a spirit, as did Sally in the Beauchamp case; neither did she manifest other qualities of a control, such as ignorance of time, continuous consciousness, and automatic writing. She seemed to be only a dissociated group of the mental states of Doris. Sleeping Margaret, however, after claiming not to be a spirit, at last came to believe and to insist that she was. But she could give no evidence of her claim. Sick Doris was very stupid; when she was in control the girl seemed to be very ill, but when the personality changed she would be instantly perfectly well without a feeling or appearance of illness. The transformation was astonishing.

In all these manifestations there was not the slightest trace of spirits. Margaret occasionally exhibited telepathic powers; but as soon as Dr. Walter H. Prince, who had adopted her to effect a cure, began to experiment with the telepathy, Margaret ceased to show what she could do. Sleeping Margaret directed the cure of the child and the removal of Margaret in a manner that suggested supernormal knowledge. Her knowledge usually, however, was limited to the normal memories and knowledge of Doris, and, when you tested her on matters that spirits ought to know, she wholly disappointed you. She could not tell what spirits should tell. Consequently there was no apparent reason to classify Doris Fischer with the mediumistic type or to treat her personalities as anything but dissociated groups of memories of the girl herself. Whatever the explanation, each personality had to be treated as a group or series of mental states separated from the other group or series by amnesia. There was no evidence of such personal identity as we have to insist upon finding when we test the claims of communicating spirits. Whether the "split" was between different groups of mental states or between different brain cells, the phenomena showed slight indication of being due to foreign personalities. They were just mysteriously separated groups of mental states simulating real individuals in their memories and behavior.

I had resolved on experiment with the case as soon as Dr. Walter H. Prince had succeeded in his treatment of the girl sufficiently for me to bring her from California to Boston. Nothing had ever been published about the case and even the community in which he lived did not know that the girl was an invalid of the type above described. I brought her all the way from California and had her stay in the country some eighteen or twenty miles from Boston, coming in each morning for the experiments for a few weeks; I then kept her for a time at my own home in New York while the experiments continued, and then took her again to Boston for more immediate contact with the psychic; finally I allowed her to return to California, while I continued experiments for some months more. As usual, I did not allow Mrs. Chenoweth to see the patient at any time. The detailed record shows for itself the results, of which we can give only a very brief summary here.

The mother of Doris, who had been dead eight years, first communicated. She did excellent work to prove her identity, by trivial incidents which were unusually good for the purpose. It is not necessary to summarize them here; but they, together with the evidence of supernormal knowledge, establish the presumption that what she said about the condition of Doris at least has to be reckoned with in the solution of the problem. The mother, however, seems not to have suspected that her daughter was obsessed by mischievous discarnate personalities. The first hint of obsession came from Dr. Hodgson, who came to communicate; he compared the case to that of Sally Beauchamp and remarked that it was as "important as any that Morton Prince ever had." Dr. Hodgson had seen and experimented with Miss Beauchamp when he was living and knew Dr. Morton Prince personally. I had undertaken the experiments partly to see if any comparison with the Beauchamp case could be made; but when he had made the comparison he went on to indicate that Doris's malady was a case of obsession, saying that we should have to reckon with a little Indian in connection with the case. After her cure, Doris developed automatic writing with the planchette. The personality instigating this writing purported to be a guide for the girl and told a few things that had happened in the development of the case, which I was able to verify in California. Then came the little Indian personality to whom Dr. Hodgson had referred; she gave the name Minnehaha or Laughing Water. This name is too well known to be significant, and her identity could not be proved. But the record shows that she was well acquainted with incidents in Doris Fischer's life. She described what had gone on and defined the nature of obsession very well in what she said of the vicious personalities associated with it.

As Sleeping Margaret had claimed to be a spirit, I tried to verify her statement. Margaret made no such claims. But in my first series of experiments no trace of either of them appeared. I then took Doris to New York and had a séance with Sleeping Margaret to know why she had not communicated in Boston. Her answer was that she did not get a chance, as there were so many others there. I then asked her to come to Boston while Doris remained in New York, and to communicate with me. She said that she could not do it; that she could not go so far away from Doris. But she promised to try, if I took her back to Boston. I did so, but I received no trace of Sleeping Margaret as a communicator. I then resolved on a new experiment. Dr. Hodgson had said that

Starlight, a little Indian control of Mrs. Chenoweth, had discovered Minnehaha, and I thought I might find out whether she could get into contact with Sleeping Margaret, if the latter was a spirit at all. I arranged the experiment so that Mrs. Chenoweth would not know that I was dealing with the same case and so that she would seem to be sitting for some stranger. Again I did not allow Mrs. Chenoweth to see Doris. As the experiment had to be carried out when Doris was asleep I had her go to bed and be asleep when I admitted Mrs. Chenoweth. I had the face, hands and body of Doris covered up so that she could not be seen. As soon as Mrs. Chenoweth went into the trance, Starlight saw Minnehaha and tried to give her name, but did not succeed. She got "water lily" and then said, in accordance with the pictographic process: "I see, like a waterfall, just like water falling over and whether it is Water Fall or — something like that." Then she remarked: "She laughs after she shows me the water." Readers will remark that the name was actually given in this description; but it is strange that the subliminal could not do better when the name had been given before clearly enough, and was presumably already known, according to skeptical theories, by the subliminal. But Starlight saw no one else except the mother and "the spirit of the girl herself," partly out of the body and partly in, as she stated, remarking that, if she would go out farther she could communicate with the dead. Sleeping Margaret had not shown herself able to do this; I had thus been unable to prove her a spirit. On the contrary Starlight insisted that she was "the spirit of the girl" herself, and later the work made this interpretation clearer. When I resumed my regular work at the next sitting, Minnehaha came; she named both the Margarets and indicated that Sleeping Margaret was what Starlight had said. Then Margaret was put to work to "confess" what she had done to the child. Margaret told a number of the tricks and pranks she had played on the girl and then followed a number of other personalities said to have been concerned in the phenomena observed and reported by Dr. Walter F. Prince. Various events in the life of Doris which thus came out indicated that Margaret was a spirit, though there was no evidence to that effect in the experiences of Doris. Minnehaha terminated the experiments by recounting a large number of facts which had occurred in California after Doris returned home. They do not directly bear upon the subject of obsession, but in so far as evidence of supernormal knowledge enables us to assign limits to subliminal influence, they are consonant with the evidence for obsession.

I have known three other instances, none of which have been reported. which show the same kind of evidence that foreign agencies can perform a great deal of mischief, when they get access to the mind or body of a living person. I cannot summarize these cases here. Suffice it to say that they add to the number of cases in which we have to reckon with an influence that has not yet been admitted to the archives of psychiatry.

It is important to remark at the outset of the explanation of obsession that I do not mean this idea to be a substitute for hysteria, dementia precox, paranoia or other maladies, nor is it a rival explanation. Even the controls stated through Mrs. Chenoweth that obsession might itself be caused by disease or accident, thus conceding that lesions might give rise to it and hence that we are not to set aside organic and functional troubles in body and mind when acknowledging that obsession by spirits is an accompaniment of the trouble. It is quite conceivable that any disturbance to healthy functions, bodily or mental, might create conditions in which accidental connections with the discarnate would be established and would open the way to all sorts of voluntary and involuntary invasions. At least that is the theory of the spirits themselves, and the facts tend to support the contention.

It must therefore be thoroughly understood that we are not controverting physiological or psychiatrical explanations. The only revolution that we wish to introduce into medicine is the denial of the limits ordinarily assigned to causes of disease and methods of treatment. The terms hysteria, dementia precox, paranoia, manic depressive insanity, and epilepsy are largely descriptive; the causes are revealed only by the autopsy and other such methods. Obsession does not displace other causes, but adds to them another factor. It is a cause, not a mere description, because it implies that an external agency produces the phenomena. A foreign influence is added to the subjective conditions.

We cannot as yet say exactly how these foreign influences act. All that we contend is, that the facts are evidence that they do act; it remains for the future to determine how. This will be no easy task. We have but touched the surface in this problem, and we may have to experiment with a thousand cases in order to fix upon any generalization about the results or to determine rules of procedure and therapeutics. At any rate, we cannot generalize from the few cases that have yielded to investigation. We have still to experiment and to develop methods of healing.

As to how obsession takes place, we can resort only to speculation. We have little data to go upon at present in this limitless field. I have alluded to telepathy as making possible the influence of mind upon mind independently of normal methods of causation, and said that we need not adopt a spiritistic hypothesis to explain the facts. But one cannot examine these facts and be impressed with telepathic explanations. When the existence of discarnate spirits is once admitted, we have to assume some sort of transcendental process as the method of obsession. Whatever the process is in telepathy, it is conceivably applicable to obsession. But the means are not the first thing to be determined. The frequency of occurrence is more important at present than the cause. We can hope to understand obsession if we can get at the reason for its frequency.

Many features in the ordinary communications between the dead and the living suggest where we must look if we are to understand the phenomena, even though we have not as yet brought them under experimental control. In the first place, even in cases of mediumship, in which the process of communication is probably the same as in obsession, though under the control of more intelligent personalities, it is clear that many messages are involuntary. The communicator cannot always determine what he shall send. If the spirit present does not know his business, he may cause evils of all sorts without knowing what he is doing. If he knows what he is doing, the result will depend on his character. In addition to these factors, proximity of a spirit to an impressionable subject may expose the latter to either intentional or unintentional influences from the transcendental world. Obsession may be accidental rather than purposive; but, when once invaded, the subject is an open door for the transmission of anything that comes his way.

For all that we know consciousness is a form of energy with its own laws of transmission and inhibition. If it be such, we can well surmise how the way might often be accidentally opened to the reception of foreign influences which may lead to disastrous results. But these influences are as often purposive and malicious as accidental; the problem is to ascertain how we may practically deal with such cases. The orderly or disorderly impingement of the spiritual world upon the embodied soul in the physical world depends on a combination of circumstances which we have not yet exactly determined. The influence may be found to have analogies with mechanical forces; its benevolent or malevolent operation may depend on our ability to regulate the conditions that make the influence possible, or to guide the agencies into a course of action that will not interfere with the normal life of men. That is no easy task. The cures effected have required much time and patience, the use of psychotherapeutics of an unusual kind, and the employment of psychics to get into contact with the obsessing agents and thus to release the hold which such agents have, or to educate them to voluntary abandonment of their persecutions.

This is not the place for details of this question. All that I desire to do in this discussion is to suggest the wide application of the hypothesis in the treatment of cases regarded as incurably insane. It is the consequence to the theories and therapeutics of insanity that is important here. Dr. Meyer Solomon of Chicago, when reviewing the case of Doris Fischer, said that if our explanation of that case be true, we should have "to apply it to all hysteria, dementia precox, paranoia, manic-depressive insanity, and genius." I am not yet prepared to generalize or to determine extensions of the hypothesis. But we have proved enough to suggest the possibilities; and any physician who recognizes them and the facts will open his mind to revolutionary possibilities in the diagnosis and cure of cases usually regarded as hopelessly insane. Doris Fischer was so regarded by the physicians who saw her. Dr. Walter Prince, however, cured her by care and suggestion; until she became so healthy and rational that she was able to manage a chicken farm of large dimensions, to serve as Vice President of the Poultry Association in her home county, and to preside at meetings with tact and control. One case that I myself cured by hypnotic suggestion in three days has been perfectly well for five or six years, earning his living with his violin on the stage. He was sent to Bellevue Hospital in the belief that he was incurable.

I repeat that I am not prepared to make generalizations on the subject, either with reference to diagnosis or cure. But I do know that every single case of dissociation and paranoia to which I have applied cross-reference has yielded to the method and proved the existence of foreign agencies complicated with the symptoms of mental or physical deterioration. It is high time to prosecute experiments on a large scale in a field that promises to have as much practical value as any application of the scalpel and the microscope.

CHAPTER XXV

MEDIUMSHIP

MANY people would like to know what mediumship is, or by what marks we can discover and recognize it. The briefest answer to such a query is, either that we do not know what the marks are; or that they are phenomena which can be proved to be genuinely supernormal, representing a communication between different minds. But we can hardly dismiss the subject with so summary an account.

Usually in telling what a thing *is*, we have to give it a place in a known class, with some distinguishing mark that defines it as a special type in that class. There is also a descriptive definition which names the various marks or properties by which the term defined may be known. There are no distinguishing marks of the physical kind to describe mediums, or to mark them off from other people; the only mark is the ability to give supernormal information about the discarnate world, though the term is loosely applied to a person who can give any supernormal manifestation, since spiritualists explain all such phenomena due to the intervention of spirits. Etymologically the term is derived from the Latin word "medium," which denotes the "middle" or the intermediary between two things, the way to reach them, the means of communication. It was hence adopted to denote the agency which intervenes between the physical and the transcendental world. The ordinary analogy is to an electric wire, which is the "medium" of communication in telegraphy, whereby the agent transmits messages from one point to another. But the analogy is not exact, as the processes involve no known resemblances to electrical action. The only means of communicating with the dead has been found to be a living organism capable of connecting the two worlds.

But this definition of mediumship depends wholly upon the phenomena in question and does not enable us to point out any marks or characteristics other than the very facts to be proved; whereas what every one desires to know is what particular characteristic enables the medium to do what is claimed. I do not know of any physical characteristics whatever that might lead us to designate a medium without testing her for supernormal phenomena. One Frenchman thought he had discovered a spot in the eye that indicated mediumship. But I see no evidence of the truth of this discovery and find nothing in my experience to confirm it. So far as I know, the only mental characteristic is hysteria. But the application of the term "hysteria," apart from a consideration of the circumstances, cannot be indiscriminately made. All depends on the definition of hysteria. In the older meaning of the term, which described a nervous and excitable person who could not exercise self-control, hysteria is certainly no mark of mediumship. That type is seldom or never marked by psychic abilities. But in later times the term "hysteria" has come to mean more technically, and at the same time more inclusively, the presence of automatism or subconscious action, in the form of *dissociation.* The terms "hysteria" and "dissociation" are largely synonymous, or at least denote the same general phenomena. Liability to what is called *automatism* is in many, if not all, cases a symptom of hysteria.

Now it is probable that dissociation and automatism characterize all mediums, though there are types that betray no evidence of these conditions, except the production of certain results. There are instances within my own observation in which the subject himself discovered the mediumship or psychic abilities only by the occurrence of supernormal coincidences in his experience, without any apparent alteration of the normal conditions of body or mind. But it is true that automatism is characteristic of all well-developed mediumship that has come within my own observation. This means that automatic writing, automatic visions, or automatic voices occur, and may be regarded as a fundamental characteristic of mediumship. It is true that automatism and dissociation often occur without any traces of the supernormal or of mediumship in its narrower import of communication with the dead. But their presence in developed mediums suggests that the instances which exhibit no supernormal capacities are simply undeveloped cases; that perhaps the automatism and dissociation are absolutely necessary to mediumship, but that the development of them into sources of supernormal knowledge depends on the establishing of rapport with the transcendental world instead of confining it to the physical world. That has been largely my own experience, and only the fact that this experience has not been extensive enough to justify generalization prevents me from stating that as a law. It is a good hypothesis on which to work, and we may ultimately find that the instances of supernormal coincidence which do not superficially betray dissociation nevertheless contain it in a latent form so adjusted to the normal life that its existence is not easily detected.

At any rate it is fairly certain that cases of dissociation and automatism are worth investigating for the development of mediumship or psychic powers of some kind. This means that we may regard automatism and dissociation as fundamental marks of mediumship, though they do not constitute all that is necessary to achieve the desired result. Rapport with a transcendental world either of other living minds or of discarnate personalities, may be the further characteristic necessary to make the mediumship complete.

It will probably require a long time accurately to determine the nature and limits of mediumship. There has been, so far, no effort to define it save by the presence of the supernormal. Critics and skeptics, especially in the fields of medicine and psychology, have tried often enough to discredit mediumship by calling it hysteria or dissociation. Hysteria at best is but a descriptive term. It is not in the least explanatory, and does not carry with it any clear implications of the cause. The skeptic wants us to conceive hysteria and dissociation as explanations of phenomena which at least superficially appear to be supernormal. But I am going here to insist that hysteria, dissociation, and automatism are in no respect rivals or contradictories of mediumship. They are conditions of its existence, at least apparently and in most cases. The only legitimate factor of the skeptic's contention is, that if nothing more than automatism is present, we are without *evidence* of actual mediumship, in so far as mediumship implies the supernormal. We have neither explained the automatism nor succeeded in setting up a conception that displaces genuine mediumship, whose distinguishing mark is facts *exhibiting* evidence of supernormal knowledge, no matter what the physiological and psychological condition of the subject. The question is, whether there is a connection between the mental phenomena of the hysteric, automatist, insane patient, or other person, and some event foreign to this subject's knowledge. The psychic researcher can admit, if the facts require it, that all supernormal phenomena are accompanied by abnormal mental states in the subject. The crucial question is, *first,* whether the phenomena are referable to subjective causes or to causes external to the mind affected; and *second,* whether the external cause, if it exist, is an ordinary physical stimulus or is independent of normal sense-perception. We are insisting only that supernormal phenomena cannot be classified under hysteria, automatism, dissociation, secondary personality, or insanity as phenomena of a purely subjective nature.

The first question as to the nature of mediumship is not its *cause* in the sense of its initiation or production, but its *occurrence* and classification. If certain phenomena bear no *evidence* of the supernormal, but are accompanied by hysteria, automatism, etc., we may well describe them by these latter terms and admit that their cause is either functional derangement of the mind or some ordinary physical stimulus. But if the phenomena show an undoubted relation to some external event not known to the subject and thus outside the range of normal sense-perception, we can safely refuse to classify them with phenomena that are provably connected with normal causes. We can seek for causes other than physical stimuli, when we have determined whether the facts are included in the normal and abnormal field or are excluded from it. We name them supernormal when they are thus excluded.

There is overwhelming evidence for the existence of supernormal experience, whether manifested in telepathy, clairvoyance, or communication with the dead. It is certain that there is a vast field of facts not explained by hysteria, automatism, dissociation, secondary personality, or insanity. These facts suffice to indicate some acceptable meaning for mediumship.

So much for the existence and the nature of mediumship. The

explanation of it may await the future. What most people wish to know is some practical criterion for telling when it is present and what to do with it. This is perhaps the most important aspect of the present question.

From what I have said about its nature and the marks which distinguish it, it is perhaps clear that we have no final assurance of its presence until we actually prove the presence of supernormal phenomena. Prior to that stage of its development we may have to be content with hysteria, automatism, dissociation, and secondary personality, which are limiting ideas, so to speak, or terms indicating that *evidence* of the supernormal is lacking. No doubt there are many supernormal experiences besides those that are evidential; but, in the present stage of the investigation, we have to be careful about accepting these. The nature of evidence of the supernormal has been fully explained in the chapter on "Problems of Evidence"; it includes both the negative characteristic of excluding fraud, the subconscious, chance coincidence and guessing, and the positive characteristic of a connection with some event not known by the subject. The criterion just defined applies to *individual* cases of mediumship. It requires that each incident shall at least be explicable by a foreign and transcendental stimulus; the multiplication of these individual test cases will prove the existence of the supernormal. But there are many non-evidential incidents and statements. They may refer to alleged events in a transcendental world, which no living person can verify. The primary test of genuine supernormality cannot apply to them. But if we can make a large number of records of similar statements issuing from real or alleged mediums who were not in communication with each other, their collective unity will have some value. If they all agree as to the nature of the transcendental world, and we can prove that the mediums had never read about the subject and were not familiar with any of the ideas expressed, the consistency of such records would have at least some suggestive value.

Further than these suggestions, we know little of the conditions for mediumship, and there are at present no facilities for investigating them. The remaining question is how to cultivate the faculty. On this point also we can give very few definite instructions and certainly no dogmatic rules. We as yet know too little to do more than ask for adequate investigation, which will require the careful study of all possible cases that may come to us. This is not possible as yet; the cases have been too few to justify wide and confident generalizations. At one time, from my experience with a dozen instances, I felt secure in saying that there is no danger in the cultivation of mediumship; but, after the discovery of obsession, I felt more cautious in giving assurance that there are no risks. I do not mean to assert or imply that it is generally dangerous, for it seems not to be; often even in the cases which seem most alarming. But we know too little to say that it is either dangerous or not dangerous. I am only certain that in many cases it has not only not been dangerous but has been beneficial, physically and mentally, to the subjects. There are also cases where the reverse is true. Hence it remains to determine the risks in each individual instance.

The circumstances under which mediumship develops are various. It appears not to be the consequence of weak-mindedness, but may be induced by illness or accident. It is probable that the main condition of its development is *passivity* of will. This is compatible with any degree of intelligence, even of strong will. If the individual can voluntarily suppress his will, he may develop mediumistic qualities, though they are less likely to occur under these circumstances than in cases of natural passivity. It is probable that the relation of illness and accident to mediumship is due to the effect of such conditions in making the will passive at least until the mediumship has developed; it may then become a fixed feature of the constitution. If it be due to natural passivity of will, the prevention of its harmful forms may be more difficult; but if the passivity is voluntary, the prevention of danger lies largely with the subject.

The first thing to keep in mind regarding incipient mediumship is that it cannot easily be prevented. One cannot kill it by disregarding it. It betokens the existence of physiological and psychological conditions which the will did not produce; whether the psychic power is a casual product of temperament or the effect of outside agencies, it cannot be created at will. If desired, the condition might develop in time, but it will not come at command. One who finds that it suddenly manifests itself when he becomes interested in the subject may rest assured that it was latent all the while. I have seen many cases in which the subject was wholly unaware of his power until either the ouija board or automatic writing was tried, when the faculty was at once manifest, though perhaps not developed to the point of doing systematic scientific work. On the other hand I have seen it in an incipient stage, with automatic writing quite fluent and easy; and yet years of practice did not improve it. We cannot tell beforehand what will take place in any given instance.

The proper manner of dealing with mediumship when observed is to treat it seriously. If it is not fully developed, treating it as a joke or using it for mere amusement exposes the subject to various kinds of danger. If spiritistic agencies are concerned, treating mediumship as a joke will only attract those on the other side whose temperaments make them look at it in the same way, and the subject will be exposed to the risk of unwelcome obsessions. I do not mean that it need be treated too solemnly, but that its phenomena should be seriously investigated, and not made an occasion for horse-fun. Intelligent spirits will not waste time in producing phenomena with fools.

High motives and the persistent purpose to make good use of the faculty will protect the subject, at least in most cases, from the dangers of which I spoke. Probably the power can be protected by those on the other side; and, if the medium insists on making a serious use of the ability, he will soon be under the protection of the better type of personality, and unpleasant obsessions will not occur. Unpleasant phenomena may occur even under the best of protection, but they do not last long and are less likely to occur at all.

In the early stages of development often there will appear wandering personalities, persons who have recently died and are seeking expression or communication through the psychic, or are put there to help in the preliminary development of the medium. The law involved in this occurrence we do not yet know, but it is frequent enough to be reckoned with, and to justify the stopping of such intrusions only when experience shows that their presence is neither normal nor helpful in the development of the psychic.

Those chance comers seldom appear in fully developed psychics and then usually with the express permission of the guides or controls for various purposes. Among them the most frequent is the purpose to help some spirit from an earth-bound condition, or to help some living friend of the wanderer. If the situation is rightly managed, there is apparently no risk in admitting such a person. But one must firmly insist that the reason for his presence be known, and while the correctness of the reason given cannot be proved, if it is clearly possible or not unreasonable, it is advisable to experiment until the effect is proved to be good or bad.

The only danger, so far as I can see, is that of obsession. This can usually be prevented either by the use of a strong will against any disposition to disturb one's normal life, or by insisting that nothing but serious objects in the work shall be admitted. Weakness of will is dangerous, and the individual must learn to cultivate his own individuality and to insist that this shall not be invaded except for good purposes. The good person does not always prevent the bad spirit from coming nor does the bad person prevent the good spirit from coming. The attitude of will has more to do with the result than anything else. If the subject is intellectually and morally passive, or does not insist on evidence that any special presence is good, then any kind of determined foreign will can take control. The subject should be as critical as the unconvinced sitter. In this way obsessions can be prevented.

The first thing to demand is that the alleged spirit either prove his own identity or help in proving that of others. The proof of identity will be most satisfactory when the facts are wholly unknown to the medium; indeed it would require an immense number of coördinated facts, if known by the medium, to constitute adequate evidence. The proper thing to do is patiently and tolerantly to insist that incidents be given which the psychic does not know, preferably facts which the sitter also does not know but can verify.

The greatest patience should be exercised. Often the personalities will leave if roughly addressed. The subconscious of the psychic must be made to feel that the sitter is serious and patient with the difficulties; the coöperation of the subconscious is a necessary condition in securing evidence. If distrust be aroused in the medium, no matter how genuine he may be, good evidence cannot be obtained. The very first condition of success is to keep on good terms with the subconscious, by being serious and by exercising patience and tact. Opinions of the phenomena may be formed afterwards, but unfavorable judgments should not be revealed at the time.

The real or alleged communicators should have as much time as may be necessary for their expression. The sitter may calmly and firmly insist that he cannot believe until the proper evidence is forthcoming, but he should be a spectator rather than a director of the phenomena, though judgment may be exercised as to the amount of time granted. The appearance of a mischievous personality should be received tolerantly and the nature of the work explained, with the insistence that he conform to that aim. If he does not, the sitter can insist as firmly upon his leaving, and the best way to accomplish this is to stop the work. When the work becomes systematically developed, such invaders either will not appear or can be controlled by the guides.

No matter what the sitter may think of the phenomena, he should treat them as if they were really spiritistic and keep his opinions to himself when experimenting. The conditions for successful communication with others, living or dead, by supernormal means are very delicate. Everything must be done to encourage favorable states of mind in both medium and communicator. For this reason laymen often get better results than scientific men. At any rate the above method should be tried before any other.

These are only general suggestions and not at all hard and fast rules. Much depends on the experience and good judgment of the experimenter. There may be further important conditions to be learned, either subordinate or in addition to these. But they will have to be ascertained by investigation in the future. My own experience is not large enough to enable me to dictate to others, or to say that such directions need not be revised. They are tentative rules, whose application should be determined in the individual case by intelligent experience. They at least show the complexity of the situation, which is the first and most important fact to be learned by experimenters. The phenomena appear, superficially, to be very simple, but no greater delusion can be harbored. Superficially the circumstances seem to resemble the conversation of one person with another, with nothing intervening to hinder. This notion, however, is a mistake. Not only may there be two or more personalities between the communicator and the experimenter, but there may be a dozen spirits coöperating. The conditions for obtaining messages are not what they are usually assumed to be. The laws regulating conversation between the living do not apply. All that we perceive is the automatic writing, or the automatic voice, or other phenomenon; we do not see the complex machinery which makes the manifestation possible. Inter-mundane and intra-organic difficulties, perhaps of very large dimensions, may be present. We do not know their extent, but we have abundant reason to believe that they are there, and the intelligent experimenter will reckon with their existence.

The medium herself, when possible, and certainly those surrounding her, should make, so far as possible, a verbatim record of what occurs, with as much stress on what those present say, as on what the alleged communicator says. Only in this way can we learn to understand and to regulate the phenomena. Everything should be recorded in chronological order and reported to some scientific body that will preserve the record for comparison with similar cases. In the past history of mankind everything of the sort, if not recorded, has died with the persons who knew the facts; and nearly as often the record, when made, finds its way into the waste-basket, either during the life of the persons interested or very soon after they have died. This should not be. In every other department of activity, whether of business or science, we keep careful records; any other course means that each generation has to begin afresh. Most of our science, however, is concerned with the physical world; and the spiritual side of man receives scant recognition. But it is the whole of nature that concerns us and affects the larger interests of personality, and we have no excuse for the evasion of these larger interests.

CHAPTER XXVI

THE SUBCONSCIOUS

THE explanation of certain experiences as due to the action of the subconscious plays a very prominent part in modern psychological discussions, and in none more than in discussions of psychic research. For only a little more than a century has anything been definitely known about subconsciousness. Leibnitz seems to have been the first who distinctly recognized it, though he gave it no technical name beyond that of "insensible perceptions." Sir William Hamilton first called attention to it in England in his doctrine of "latent mental modifications." He was followed by Carpenter with the theory of "unconscious cerebration." In Germany, Schopenhauer gave the idea currency as an important influence on human actions; he was followed by Hartmann, who was inclined to explain everything by the action of the unconscious. But the term was not accurately defined, though there could be no doubt of the existence of mental processes below the threshold of normal consciousness.

I shall not go at length into a very large and complex problem. Indeed I should not have to allude to the subconscious, but for the use which has been made of it as an alternative explanation to the spiritistic interpretation of certain phenomena.

There are three terms more or less synonymous in this connection. They are the "unconscious," the "subconscious," and the "subliminal." For the general purposes of psychical research they all denote the same thing. There is sometimes need of a distinction between the "unconscious" and the "subconscious," but there is no real difference between the "subliminal" and the "subconscious," and for our present purpose there is no need to insist upon technical differences. Occurrences whose cause lies within the subject of the experiences, and which show no satisfactory evidence of the activity of spirits, may be said to be caused by the subconscious mind of the subject.

Though the three terms are practically synonymous, they are more or less equivocal. In their relation to normal consciousness the terms indicate every function of the mind and body that is excluded from the ken of normal consciousness. In a positive sense they denote certain mental states for which we have indirect evidence, and which may have characteristics much like those of conscious processes. Normal consciousness includes those mental states of which we have direct knowledge, such as sensation, self-consciousness, reasoning, emotion, pleasure and pain, and volition. Hence, in a negative sense, the terms "subliminal," "subconsciousness" and often the "unconscious" refer merely to experiences that are not subject to direct introspection. In the widest import of such a negative meaning, intelligence would be wholly excluded from subconscious phenomena. Harmoniously with this view many persons actually maintained for a long time that such phenomena were wholly mechanical or non-intelligent. But they were confronted by the fact that certain phenomena not within the ken of normal introspection show all the characteristics of intelligent ability except that of being directly known. In other words, there is overwhelming evidence of intelligent action beyond the compass of introspection. That sufficed to give standing to the use of such terms as "subconscious" and "subliminal" mentality.

While we may regard them as purely negative terms — that is, as denoting the mental states of which we are not conscious, we cannot deny that the processes thus included have the characteristics of intelligent action, which is so fundamental an element in self-consciousness. Hence it becomes necessary in the discussion of the psychological problem to define the term more accurately than by its purely negative import.

Some people regard the subconscious as equivalent to a "secondary personality," something apart from and independent of the subject. These people suppose that secondary personality is like a spirit foreign to the body in which the phenomena manifest themselves. This is a natural view for those who think of it as excluded from the normal personality and yet as having an intelligence of its own. But only untrained minds take this view. For psychologists the subconscious or subliminal comprises mental processes occurring in the same organism with those normally introspected, but not within the ken of consciousness. That is, they are *dissociated* from normal consciousness. "Split consciousness," "dissociation," "alternating personality," "secondary or multiple personality," and similar terms denote that portion of the mental life that is not directly known to the subject. But these states are mental functions like the normal in all respects save that of accessibility to introspection.

The subconscious, therefore, is a name for mental phenomena dissociated from those directly or introspectively known. It does not denote separate or new functions of the mind, but the same functions or activities as those of normal consciousness. That is to say, the mind is *one,* though its processes are *many.* We have not yet distinctly defined the area of this subconscious. We know that it extends beyond the scope of normal action, but where it ceases we do not know. I do not mean by this that it is unlimited, for there is evidence enough to the contrary. In fact, it shows evidence of being at least as limited as normal consciousness in its reach, though it performs feats impossible to the normal mind.

That the subconscious or subliminal exists is clearly proved by somnambulism and hypnosis. In these conditions a man acts exactly as if normal; but, in his normal state, he remembers nothing that he has done while asleep, unless the somnambulism or hypnosis is very light. This state is probably similar to that of dreaming. We are aware of our ordinary dreams, which evidently occur in a transitional state between normal consciousness and true sleep or total unconsciousness. But we have evidence through the study both of somnambulism and hypnosis and of instances of dissociation that some mental activities do not emerge either in dreams or in normal consciousness. They are true subliminal activities.

In the margin of normal consciousness we may find traces of the subconsciousness, for example in abstraction and reverie. In these states we narrow the field of direct attention so that, though the mind may be distinctly aware of some objects or events in the narrower field of attention, it may not notice other incidents, even while it acts on the supposition of their presence and influence. Here the fields of normal and subliminal consciousness interpenetrate. If we read a book and become absorbed in it, any excitement of the mind will produce effects in the hand holding a pencil, though the reader may be unaware of any motion in the hand. Freud has shown that our dreams may reflect long-lost memories in symbolic forms, though we cannot ourselves explain their meaning or recall the facts until the psycho-analyst deciphers them and reminds us of them. In cases of secondary personality, like those of Ansel Bourne, Charles Brewin, and Doris Fischer, there is a perfect simulation of real and distinct personalities, of which the normal self knows nothing. They may be caused by foreign influences, but there is no internal evidence of such a source.

The recognition of the subconscious is important as a limitation to the application of spiritistic explanations. Before the discovery of subliminal activities, philosophers and laymen alike sought the explanation of phenomena not known to normal consciousness in causes outside the mind. The Cartesian philosophy regarded consciousness as the necessary property or function of the mind, and any fact not known by it was regarded as caused by something else than the mind. Hence this system offered good excuse for appealing to the spiritistic explanation wherever intelligent activity was manifested, which could not be referred to the normal consciousness of the subject. But the discovery of subconscious mental activities made it necessary to limit the number of cases in which the hypothesis of foreign influences was needed to explain the phenomena. The theory of the subconscious was, therefore, a very useful and convenient means for restraining hasty speculation. It explained phenomena which the untrained mind had been accustomed either to make more mysterious than they were or to refer to foreign intelligences, when their meaning or content was to be found within the experience of the organism in which they appeared.

But having once found a way to avoid resorting to explanation of the facts as due to spirits, many minds began unduly to extend the meaning of the subconscious. It was endowed with powers for which there was either very inadequate evidence or no evidence at all. The term lost much of its definiteness in the extension and became a catch-all of explanation for people who refused to believe in the existence of spirits. It is not a universal explanation. There is one thing about it on which all scientific psychologists are agreed — its content is acquired either through the normal channels of sense or through stimuli that act in the same way as known stimuli, though they may not be immediately known. Only a few writers like Mr. Myers ascribe supernormal "faculties" to the subconscious, and regard it is in rapport with a transcendental world by virtue of those faculties. While this theory contains a germ of truth, it involves what the psychologist does not admit; namely, new and transcendent "faculties" which are conceived as wholly independent of any stimulus. For the orthodox psychologist, the subconscious is simply the mind acting without awareness of the stimulus, and supernormal "faculties" or functions are denied or ignored. But those who wished to limit or eliminate the appeal to spirits ascribe supernormal functions to the subconscious, by which it is endowed with ability directly to perceive the transcendental.

As a result of the discussion, we shall probably find that the subconscious or subliminal includes the same functions of the mind as those of normal consciousness, acting in response to a different kind of stimulus. For instance, Mr. Myers ascribed telæsthesia and telepathy to supernormal functions of the mind. But the psychologist will probably come to believe that the functions are normal, although the stimuli are different. He will then discriminate among the facts with reference to their evidential or non-evidential value in support of any special explanation. This view can be taken, perhaps, without setting aside what Mr. Myers and his colleagues really had in mind. The term "faculties" may be more elastic than at first appears; but it is an unfortunate term. In order to avoid confusion, the present writer thinks that it might be cast aside in favor of the theory that the subconscious is identical with normal consciousness in function, though its contents may not be identical with those of the normal mind. This theory conceives it as having definite limits, such as we now apply to normal intelligence. We have now only to ascertain what stimuli affect the normal consciousness and what stimuli affect the subliminal. In this way the whole problem of estimating the supernormal becomes one of *rapport,* and not of new "*faculties.*" That is, normal rapport with the physical world gives us purely physical knowledge, while rapport with a transcendental world gives us transcendental knowledge. The difference between the two is merely that between kinds of stimulus and not between endowments of the mind, though the two points of view may ultimately be unified or reconciled. What I want here to emphasize is the importance of the living mind in determining the *form* of the knowledge which is derived from either type of stimulus.

The value of this conception of the subconscious is, that it reconciles subconscious activity with spirit agencies while it admits that the evidence for the action of spirits is limited. The ordinary view of the subliminal is that it is necessarily a substitute for spirits as an explanation. The two hypotheses are supposed to be mutually exclusive, though, in the opinion of the present writer, both may be applicable to the phenomena. The subliminal functions of the mind may be absolutely necessary for securing messages from spirits, instead of vitiating the reality of such messages. That, at least, is the view taken by the present writer. He fully recognizes that many phenomena by the subconscious are not evidence of the influence of spirits, but may be traced to subjective sources, or to ordinary physical stimuli not normally perceived; but he also insists that the subconscious may be the instrument for the receipt and transmission of foreign, transcendental stimuli. That is to say, the hypothesis of the subconscious does not deny the reality of spirits, but only limits the kind of facts which may be taken as evidence of their action.

This theory assumes a closer relation with a transcendental world than the orthodox view of the subconscious implies, and at the same time provides the means for distinguishing between the *functions* of the subconscious and its *contents.* In the first place, I have explained that its functions are those of the normal mind; in my conception of its relation to the transcendental world, I assume that its *functions* remain the same, and that its *objects* of knowledge differ only as the stimulus differs from that of normal impressions. Our normal isolation from a transcendental world is only the inability to be stimulated by it; and a psychic is simply a person who can overcome that isolation and come into rapport with a transcendental stimulus. Then, in accordance with well-known laws of normal experience, this transcendental stimulus will be represented in the reaction of the living mind according to its nature and habits. Hence the influence of the subconscious on the form of the messages. We do not yet know the nature of that foreign stimulus. If it be instigative, it is like any physical stimulus which merely sets mental functions in operation, and the result will be determined by the nature or experience of the subject affected. For instance, a blow on the head will make us *see* "stars." Normally visual reactions take the form of responses to luminous stimuli; but when the stimulus is tactual and the reaction or response is visual, there is an abnormal phenomenon or a reaction, as we would say, inappropriate to the stimulus. An overloaded stomach produces nightmare or hallucinations in sleep. In these cases the stimulus is only *instigative*. But a *transmissive* stimulus produces results less symbolical. The thought of the foreign agent seems to be transferred intact and literally. In some cases the form may be symbolical, but the transmission may nevertheless be direct. At any rate the transmission often seems to be exactly like that of the telephone or telegraph, in which the very language of the communicator is reported. In such cases the subconscious seems to have no part in the process.

But the fact is, that the subconscious is still the vehicle of transmission. Its *functions* are employed, while its *contents*, normal knowledge and expression, are suppressed or inhibited. It becomes a more or less passive instrument for the conveyance of knowledge rather than an agent for the interpretation of stimuli or the expression of its own reaction aroused by an instigative stimulus. In this way we keep the subliminal as a necessary means of intercommunication between the two worlds, while we provide an explanation for the variety in the products of the connection.

This conception is not simple. The part played by the subliminal should be consistent with the actual complexity of the phenomena, and the view just taken of it provides that very desideratum. It shows the complexities to consist in the variety of connections made between the two worlds, and at the same time relates these realms in a manner suggested by the law of continuity in evolution, which shows that many things are more closely related than is at first apparent. The slightest examination of the facts will show that the dividing line between normal and supernormal experience is often hard to draw; it is in that border-land that we should seek to discover the causes which will explain the experiences, though we must demand a radically different type of phenomena as definitive *evidence* of those agencies. Thus, for instance, the *evidence* to prove the existence of telepathy must be facts clearly exceptional in their nature; that is, obviously inexplicable by ordinary causes. But the *explanation* of such facts must be found in processes that will at least articulate with known causes. These known causes will be such as lie on the border-land of the totally new, and the totally new must find some point of contact with the old, before it can be satisfactorily explained. Hence while evidence must be found in the new, explanation must be found in the already known.

Now the subconscious lies on the border between the normal and the supernormal realms, and may serve to bridge what seems to many people to be an impassable chasm; namely, that between normal and supernormal experience. Its functions, so far as a transcendental world is concerned, are latent, like the body and mind of the infant before it is born, developed in a prenatal condition for action in a postnatal life. With powers of appreciating stimuli that the grosser senses do not perceive, it may, on favorable occasions, be percipient of stimuli from a spiritual world, whether that world be constituted by individual minds or by a general reality capable of making impressions, like matter, on delicate sense-organs. The subconscious is thus intermediate between a purely physical and a purely spiritual existence.

We must not suppose that the recognition of the subliminal deprives us of the right to consider the spiritistic hypothesis in its proper place. The concept of the subconscious legitimately enough limits the nature of the evidence for the activity of spirits; but, like telepathy, it does not define the character of the explanation to be accepted. Indeed, if we regard the subconscious after the analogy above mentioned — namely, as latent functions waiting for expression after the dissolution of the body, we may find in it a clue to what the spiritual life after death may be. The functions of the body are foreshadowed by conditions latent before birth; so the subconscious, with its present activities in dreams, delirium, hallucinations, and even normal imagination, may forecast the larger exercise of the same functions after death in the creation of apparent reality.

But it is not necessary to introduce speculation into a purely scientific discussion of the place of the subliminal. All that we require for the present is a clear recognition that the subconscious is not a rival explanation of facts, except in a limited field, and that it may be the connecting link between the transcendental and the physical worlds. The recognition of this connection will remove half the objections commonly raised against belief in a spiritual existence. We can believe that the subconscious is such a medium without fully understanding its nature, while the attempt to make of it an explanation excluding the influence of spirits makes it necessary to enlarge the conception of its powers to such stupendous proportions that it becomes more difficult to believe in it than in the spirits themselves. The conception of subliminal activity cannot supplant the spiritistic hypothesis, in cases which furnish undoubted proof of the supernormal.

CHAPTER XXVII

SPIRITUALISM, RELIGION AND SCIENCE

MANY people of the last generation had the extraordinary notion that spiritualism began with the performances of the Fox sisters at Hydeville, N. Y. But we should bear in mind, as earlier discussion showed, that every aspect of it can be traced to the belief of savages and is found in the folk-lore of most nations. The extraordinary impetus which spiritualism received at the hands of the Fox sisters, and perhaps of Judge Edmunds and Andrew Jackson Davis, between 1848 and 1860, has only given it a prominence which otherwise it might not have had. Probably the new interest in the subject was due less to the Fox sisters than to the outbreak among the common people of skepticism regarding the Christian doctrine of immortality. Most intelligent people had come to feel that Christian beliefs required proof, and they were ready for any evidence of survival after death, whose attractiveness to mankind had probably been a stronger influence in creating belief than had the testimony of traditional Christianity.

The form of the Fox phenomena was calculated to appeal to untrained minds, under the influence of the Christian apologists. For generations, upholders of Christianity had defended miracles; one could hardly pick up a volume of "Evidences of Christianity" without being impressed by the stress laid upon the physical phenomena of the New Testament as the most conclusive evidence in favor of Christian teaching. The force of the argument rested on the assurance that the stories of such miracles were true. The average Christian believer was not skeptical nor critical; but when science began to discredit the narratives of the New Testament, public opinion, in so far as it was affected by science, also began to question such miracles. Laymen generally were not disposed to deny miracles which they personally saw, having been inoculated for ages with the conviction that they were possible; they only applied the teaching of orthodox Christianity when they attached great value to the raps and knockings of the Fox sisters. These were not evidence for the conclusions drawn, but neither are the physical miracles of the New Testament evidence of the divine. The occurrences might, if true, transcend the accepted limitations of natural action, but they are not indicative of any great intelligence. This circumstance, apparent in the Fox phenomena, together with the rising influence of scientific discrimination, evoked skepticism of spiritualism; various other objections were due sometimes to prejudice, scientific or religious, more often to the offense to esthetic and refinement given by the people and phenomena concerned.

The effect of the public performances accompanied by an organized effort to substitute demonstrations for the worship and services of the orthodox churches, was to perpetuate the method known as spiritualism. As the term had been dropped from philosophic usage since the time of Immanuel Kant, it assumed the implications and associations which the vulgarity of the performances often justified. An illiterate person talking twaddle for gospel, without any of the intellectual and esthetic equipment of the educated man, only presented an unfavorable contrast to the accepted methods of teaching and preaching. The sect did too little to expose fraud, and indeed often tolerated it, when the utmost intolerance should have been practiced. It upheld performances without discrimination between frauds and honest people; and it showed none of the ethical or religious interest of those who make immortality the key to a spiritual life. Spiritualism endeavored to protect its work by claiming to be a religion when it got into trouble with the police, although it failed to exhibit the religious qualities of reverence and spiritual seriousness.

It is true that Christianity had a humble origin in the same kind of phenomena, and the record shows that it had its contest with frauds and sorcerers. It was not a religion of intellectual snobs and esthetes. Christians have no reason to look down on humble origins. But in the course of time they imbibed the tastes and habits of the intellectual and esthetic classes and could not recognize their own cousins among the spiritualists. There is no sin in good taste and the cultivation of refinement, but to frown upon alleged evidence for survival because its appearance is not esthetically inviting is a mistake, if not a sin. Respectability has much in its favor, but neither esthetics nor respectability can be a substitute for ethics or truth.

The spiritualists were right in their general conception of what would prove existence after death. They did not use a scientific method, but they realized that dogma and authority could not retain their influence in an age of freedom of thought, and that we require facts, not philosophical or theological theories, to support doctrines. They at least dimly saw the problem as scientific. But they did not organize their investigations. They were bent on satisfying curiosity and on calling their performances religion. Consequently they brought their facts and their methods into contempt among people of intelligence and good taste.

On the other hand, the orthodox religious bodies, whatever faults they had, did have respect for decency and culture and were inclined to insist upon suitable methods of investigation. They demanded the practical application of belief to the spiritual habits of the individual, while many spiritualists lent a receptive ear to the teaching and practice of men like Moses Hull, who should have been cast out of their society. They assumed an attitude of hostility towards Christianity, although claiming that it had originated in spiritualism. If they had realized the strength of the religious mind, whatever its foibles, they might have made their peace with it and conquered it. But they persisted in warfare, manifesting none of its virtues while asking for a hearing from it.

Enthusiasm, on the one hand, and the need of protection against the police, on the other, impelled spiritualists to claim that their performances constituted a religion. They thus invited comparison with the other religious bodies of the world, especially Christianity, as the central doctrine of both is immortality. But the people first attracted to spiritualism were free-thinkers, usually of the type that is either opposed to Christianity and religion altogether or wants its comforts and consolations without its dogmas. In the concentration of interest on the experimental evidence for existence after death, the ethical and spiritual achievements of religion in the life of the individual were disregarded. Interest was centered on communication with another world, and the larger ethical meaning of the cosmos and the personal duties of the individual were ignored. The whole emphasis of Christianity was so evidently reversed that the system made an excellent target for Christian attack. The opportunity was not lost. Neither side could see that both were right. Religion had lost the realization that evidence was necessary for its dogmas, and spiritualism had no interest in the ethical and spiritual aims of religion. Christianity had forgotten that its system primarily emphasized conduct and our mental attitude towards our neighbors. It stressed philosophical beliefs and dogmas, not, it is true, without some attention to humanitarianism, but with the tacit acknowledgment that this was incidental. The spiritualists forgot that Christ had deplored the interest of the people in his miracles or psychic phenomena, and had urged the promulgation of the ethics of the Sermon on the Mount as the object of his coming. They insisted on miracles and mediumistic performances to the neglect of the spiritual life. No wonder they came into conflict with the rising tendency of religion to reform its attitude on dogmas and to restore the emphasis to life and conduct.

The one hope of the church lies in the revision of its creeds and the concentration of its interest on practical life. This was its original mission, which was later supplemented by its emphasis on the belief in immortality. It has met with such hostility from science and reason, and has lost so many battles for its dogmas, that it is beginning to realize that it can save itself only by reverting to its primitive impulse. It must make its peace with science. Many of the institutions which arose from Christian impulses have assumed secular form and have even forgotten their origin. Charities, hospitals, protection of children, chivalry, and the rights of women have all been derived from Christian ideas. The spiritualists did not realize this. They were intent on "miracles," most of them exhibitions of vulgarity which the developed refinement of most people could not endure. Their performances might be very suggestive to those interested in facts, but not to those who considered good taste important. The ethical and spiritual impulses of religion were discarded in behalf of "demonstrations" of communication with the dead, many of them either pure conjuring and fraud, or incapable of being distinguished from these. No confidence could be established in their alleged facts. The practical application of belief in a future life had no interest for them; and there is no reason for concerning ourselves with immortality unless it has an influence on ethical life. Spiritualism shows no interest in either science or religion. Unless it reforms its methods it is doomed to extinction. Its first duty is to take part in the world's ethical redemption. If it will organize charities and hospital work, young men's and young women's social and ethical institutions, and in general reproduce the practical services of the church, it can expect to survive. If it had done these things from the start, instead of conducting demonstrations which should have been left to scientists, it might have conquered the church and the world fifty years ago.

Science, however, is beginning to take up the subject. It will conduct the proof or demonstrations with decency and order and will enter into sympathy with the primary and most important impulses of religion. The best indication of the doom which awaits spiritualism is seen in the final results to some of its best credited representatives. The confession of one of the Fox sisters made it impossible to have confidence in their performances, even though some or many of the phenomena may have been genuine. The last days of Slade show what comes to those who cannot preserve moral character while proving the supernormal. He is said to have made and spent two fortunes, and then to have ended his days in poverty, giving sittings at ten cents each. His methods and conduct were such that not only was his private life impeached, but no one can defend any of his claims or those of his supporters. He is almost totally forgotten. Even Zoellner's experiments with him have been discredited; and whatever of the genuine may have been included in some of his performances is nullified by proved fraud. The same is true of hundreds of similar but less conspicuous mediums and deceivers. Spiritualism, with such a history, can never attract intelligent people; the growing demand that scientific method with its discriminating procedure shall take up the subject will leave the spiritualists without either religious or scientific support.

Men usually form their conception of a religion, a sect, or a society by its most manifest characteristics. If it is ethical and practical, they respect it. If it is a mere show, they regard it with amusement, as most people regard spiritualism. All that most people can see in it is a vaudeville performance, and one not well conducted at that. Illiterate mediums talk platitudes or twaddle to the audience, deliver messages which either are not understood or are without evidential value and are so trivial and vulgar as to carry no inspiration to intelligent minds. They should not then expect the intellectual world to admire and wonder.

It is possible to charge the other side, however, with the opposite faults. Many of the religious type are too much influenced by esthetics, and many skeptics are too dogmatic in their denials to deserve any tolerance from really scientific minds. Having followed science in the judgment that spiritualism is either fraud or delusion, religious minds are content with forms and consolatory faith and pass by on the other side, though facts have stared them in the face ever since the time of the apostles. On the other hand, science, content, without thorough inquiry, to confine its investigations to the physical world in which it has achieved so much, will not open its eyes to anomalies in the realm of mind and nature, and so degenerates into a dogmatism exactly like that of theology. Spiritualism is thus ground to pieces between the upper and nether millstones of these two points of view. It can redeem itself only by making its peace with both, by submitting its claims to the judgment of science and returning to the ethical work of the church.

Science, in its contrast to theology, resorts to *present experience,* or facts immediately verifiable, instead of to faith in authority and tradition. It may insist that this was also the original attitude of religion, and that Christianity was a scientific movement which appealed to *facts* instead of authority for its belief in survival. This is indeed true; and for this reason science may well demand the use of its method to verify or to refute the claims of the past. In its relation to spiritualism, science insists not only on strict determination of conditions, but also on cumulative and collective, not merely individual, results. The scientific man knows full well that the honesty of the subject is not a sufficient guarantee of results, though it is important. Any one is likely to make false observations and mistakes of judgment, which can be eliminated only by the collection of a sufficiently large number of genuine and thoroughly accredited facts to eliminate unconscious error. This condition the spiritualists have wholly neglected. They have no scientific records, and their " demonstrations " depend on faith for even so much interest as would suggest investigation. They prove nothing scientifically. Their work is often striking enough to arouse attention and challenge investigation, and has perhaps served to keep interest in the subject alive. But science must work by laboratory methods, which can control the conditions and produce trustworthy results. It must multiply the facts indefinitely and be able to offer some rational explanation of their complications in order to obtain any consensus of opinion in favor of the supernormal. If spiritualists would only recognize this necessity and then devote themselves to the natural correlate of immortality, namely, the ethical regeneration of a world saturated with materialism, they not only would bring their cause into better repute, but also would refute most of the objections directed against them.

Psychic researchers have had to coin the term " spiritism " in order to avoid the bad associations of the term " spiritualism." Both words refer to the same type of facts; but spiritism implies that these facts have been examined more carefully than spiritualism demands. If there is any difference at all between spiritism and spiritualism it lies only in this: that spiritism is supported by facts much better accredited than most of the data of the spiritualists.

I make this statement because I am well aware of both the advantages and disadvantages of names. Most people think only in words, in the meaning which ordinary experience gives them. If they are spectators of a public spiritualistic performance and find it an offense against good taste and intelligence, they form their entire conception of the term " spiritualism " from the appearance of that performance. Hence it is often necessary to coin new words, since it is hard to divest the traditional terms of their associations. To avoid misunderstanding from those who are inclined to ridicule instead of to argue, it may be necessary to indicate a distinction by a new word and then to force men to recognize the real identity of the new and the old terms. But the facts are the same, whatever the words used to express them. The intelligent man will concentrate his attention on judging these facts, and will not allow critics to discredit them by the mere use of names.

CHAPTER XXVIII

PSYCHOLOGY, RELIGION AND MEDICINE

VERY few would deny the eclipse of religion in this age, especially when measured by the conception of it which the past has afforded. They might save a discouraging view by changing their conception of it, as most people have done and perhaps always will do with any force so perennial as that which has embodied itself under that term. It would seem far more doubtful to affirm the eclipse of medicine in the age when it seems to be in the very midst of its triumphs and to promise still more wonderful achievements. Medicine would be claimed by the physician as the very last department of human endeavor to be overshadowed. The university man devoted to psychology also would not accept the intimation that his subject is under a shadow. But his contention would not be so clear as the physician's. He cannot point to any such achievements as the physiologist can summon in his defence. Besides, one indisputable fact shows its subordinate place among the successful sciences. Once it was much like philosophy, the queen of the sciences. Indeed it was itself the very basis of philosophy. But with the partition of that great dominion it was reduced in rank and the physical usurped the place of the mental in the reflective world. "Philosophy," says Lotze, "is a mother wounded by the ingratitude of her children. Once she was all in all. Mathematics and Astronomy, Physics and Physiology, no less than Ethics and Politics, sprang from her loins. But the offspring soon set up establishments of their own, each the earlier as it made vigorous progress under the influence of parental authority. Then conscious of what they had created by their own endeavors they turned against the comprehensive scope of philosophy, which could not follow them into the details of this new life, and became weary of the everlasting repetitions without progress which had characterized the parental career. At last, when each suckling had attained its independence, it left philosophy in undisputed possession of the insoluble problems of the universe. With this ancient portion she still sits reflecting on the old riddles with the hope of holding fast to the central interest of human knowledge."

Psychology has had to share in the decline, partly because she sought independence and partly because she had no general mission for the world, and to-day she depends mainly on the traditional place she has had in the curriculum of human knowledge. Psychology has divested itself of all interest in the existence of a soul and, to save an open defence of materialism, employs the term "mind" to denote mental states whose basis it will not discuss. It is a technical study for neophytes and idlers; unless, perchance, it can detect crime or claim importance in pedagogy, for which it has done little or nothing up to date. It has no message for common life, as had the doctrines of Plato and Christianity. It is a kind of learned amusement, or a *Brodwissenschaft* for those who cannot otherwise earn bread. It lives on the momentum of its traditional importance, and would have been cast out of education long ago but for fear of the consequences of materialism, which all hold but will not avow. It is not a propædeutic to other knowledge but the refuge of those who either get their wisdom by looking into their navels or escape a dirt-philosophy only by refusing to soil their hands.

Medicine, however, will claim exemption from this verdict. As already remarked, its practical achievements are second only to those of physics and chemistry. It will vehemently deny any accusation of retrogression. It will passionately resent the charge that the shadows are falling on its course. But in spite of all this I shall insist that it is under an eclipse. We do not see it because we have become accustomed to the darkness. The achievements it has effected, no one will dispute; but their importance is to be measured solely according to our standards of value. If our philosophy, whether intuitive or reasoned, conscious or unconscious, be materialistic we shall see no eclipse. We shall rejoice in the darkness and not be aware of the light. We shall be living like the blind fish in Mammoth Cave. We deny the existence of light because we refuse to look at it. It is man's satisfaction with existence as he finds it that prevents his looking for anything further, especially if he feels the weight of evidence to be against the existence of more than presents itself to superficial vision. When we insist on remaining at the surface we do not see below it. This is what materialism does. It confines man to the external plane of existence. And we are materialists when we take physical science as our measure of reality.

Men, individually and collectively, are governed by their conceptions of the cosmos. They may not always be clearly aware of these conceptions, or at least of their origin in tradition or environment. But however they have acquired it, all have some conception of a relation to things in general, and this conception determines their conduct. If man adopts the doctrine that matter is the prius and limit of reality he makes himself the subject of what he must forever estimate as inferior to himself. Matter he regards as inert and unintelligent, though he admits that in the fortuitous combinations of its elements intelligence escapes as an accident. But he regards matter as the womb and the grave of all that he prizes. He will not worship what he has to conquer in order to live. A universe that offers no permanent development for intelligence and morality in the individual must encourage pessimism and despair. We may conceal all this from ourselves in the pleasures of outwitting the power that will extinguish us if we do not conquer it. Material satisfactions — the freedom that wealth may bring from the hardship of toil and suffering — may hide from us for a while the ugly Medusa-head of nature, but when we come to pay our bonds we are confronted with the terrific oracle of Œdipus: "May'st thou ne'er know the truth of what thou art." Only a spiritual conception of reality will rescue idealism from the clutches of a dark fate. The stability of nature and the preservation of peaceful societies hide the gulfs over which we live. But when nature reverts to chaos, in tornado or earthquake, we discover the frailty of all human power. "The earth, green as she looks, rests everywhere on dread foundations were we further down, and Pan to whose music the nymphs dance has a cry in him that can drive all men distracted." Famine and disease will make the stoutest hearts quail unless education and courage have trained them to accept the issue in defiance. No religious faith teaches the worship of impersonal forces. Reverence is reserved for something else than matter. Unless the divine can be found somewhere in the mysterious labyrinths of nature, man accepts battle with nature's forces with the assurance only of death and with no hope of salvation. He grits his teeth and plunges into the war without expectation of either giving or receiving quarter. While obedience to the laws of nature may bring him much, it is the obedience of prudence, not of reverence. It requires another philosophy to subdue the hostility of the mind to forces that have the power to crush, but neither the intelligence nor the mercy to save. Materialism can only exalt the remorseless sway of force, the pitiless Juggernaut of Time crushing its own worshipers. Wise men, of course, will not whine over tasks that cannot be done or hopes that cannot be realized, but they would be happier if the cosmos offered something for idealism to cherish. Materialism is a good antidote for superstition and ignorance, and it is the philosophy which forces attention to the fixed uniformity of nature; but personality can find no ideals in impersonality, and it is here that this philosophy fails to satisfy the desires of man. Hence he is impelled to penetrate the veil into the inner sanctuary of nature in the hope of finding a satisfaction that materialism cannot give.

Among savages, religion and medicine were the same thing. When Greece shook off the incubus of polytheism, medicine was frankly materialistic, having discarded religion. It was left to Plato to revive interest in the mind and in such religion as philosophy could support at that time. In Christianity all three joined hands. Psychology offered a philosophic defence for the existence and immortality of the soul, and medicine took care of the body in the interest of the soul. After the revival of science, each went its own way, medicine into materialism and psychology into idealism or spiritualism. But materialism triumphed and even subjugated psychology to its own services, and left religion without sympathy or protection. The great ethical ideals that made the mind more important than the body have now retired into the limbo of illusion, and a full stomach is considered a greater desideratum than any amount of penance or piety. Materialism, whether avowed or denied, has absorbed every form of activity and has extended its influence over every institution. Religion lives only upon traditions. The great belief in a soul and in its survival of bodily death has crumbled into ashes, except for that faithful class which either stops thinking or turns to science for its hopes. Medicine has taken charge of all that is worth living for, and those who have money and leisure may worship in soft pews and listen to the ritual, or to desperate efforts to adjust worn-out creeds to a philosophy which is incompatible with them.

But the last twenty-five years have developed a movement which is now like only a small cloud on the horizon but which bids fair soon to change the whole scientific and philosophic tendency of the age. Just at the moment when religion seemed to be dying the new movement came into sight, and yet religion turned away its face. It, too, has become saturated with materialism and goes stumbling about, blindly groping for light and protection, while its erstwhile enemy, medicine, wears the crown of victory. The primary object of religion was to save the soul; that of medicine to save the body. As long as psychology could maintain that there was a soul and that its preservation was more important than that of the body, religion reigned supreme and medicine occupied a secondary place. The coffers of mankind were poured into the church. Money and salvation went together. But materialism has turned the tables. Medicine is now more lucrative than priestcraft. We do not believe we have any souls, but we are sure of our bodies, *pace* the good Bishop Berkeley and the Christian Scientists. Medical science is organized to save the body and does not care what becomes of the soul, if there be any. Its business is not with another world. It has a business syndicate's grip on the passion to live. It has availed itself of this advantage and but for competition and a code of ethics not yet extinct would have no better reputation than Shylock. Christianity has always taught that salvation is free; it supported the priest by wages paid collectively, and thus socialized religion. Salvation was not individually paid for until the sale of indulgences, and this terminated the abuses associated with the more mercenary tendencies of religion.

In all this period, however, medicine was not socialized. The individual paid for his services. Saving the body was not free, it had to be paid for. As soon as materialism triumphed it decreased the interest in another life and intensified the passion for this one. This situation has yielded a harvest for medicine, and medicine has availed itself of its opportunities. In fact, medicine is not wholly exempt from the charge of extortion. The salvation of the body is the primary thing. Indeed there is nothing else to save. Psychology offers us no soul in which to be interested, and physiology has undertaken to correct or prevent the ravages of disease and the brutalities of accident. In the meantime discovery and invention have multiplied the comforts of life and justified materialism of her children. Our wealth goes into saving the body; and such attention as the soul gets, where it is assumed at all, is perfunctory and ritualistic. In the Middle Ages men built cathedrals and worshipped God, living like Simeon Stylites; in the present age we build hospitals and worship our bellies, living like princes. Materialism has commercialized everything, and medicine, despite its charities, has not escaped the general tendency. The university was founded to defend religion and has developed into a forum for science. Only the denominational college remains to protect religion. The non-sectarian institution has to cultivate Laodiceanism in order to attract students and Mr. Carnegie's pensions in order to save paying its teachers duly for their services. Psychology, which might have saved the soul for ethics and religion, has gone off into "empiricism" or materialism; and medicine, no longer having to cope with mental phenomena, has a free field for materialistic therapeutics. Mind no longer counts either as a cause or a prize. The body is everything, and the resources of civilization are employed in protecting private property from the hungry maws of the masses, who were once taught by Christianity that they were our brothers and were deserving of the right to live When medicine cannot exploit the poor, it refers them to the almshouse and buries them in Potter's Field. The physician may not save the epicure's body, but he may get his money. No religion comes in to make it imperative to consider man's soul. Only his body deserves or receives attention, and that only when he can pay for it or when we wish to evade the appearance of inhumanity.

Charity is the remnant of the religion which materialism has displaced, and, in the light of evolution, with its struggle for existence and the survival of the fittest or strongest, even charity threatens to become an extinct virtue.

Religion managed to get into a hostile attitude towards science. At the inception of Christianity they were allied except for the contest with the Epicureans and their materialism. Even there the argument was *ad hominem*. The Epicurean admitted the existence of a soul but denied its immortality; and when confronted with alleged evidence of survival, instead of acknowledging defeat, he changed his ground and continued in his denial. He gave up the existence of the soul rather than admit its mortality and accept a reconciliation with religion. Otherwise religion quickly seized upon philosophy and science for its support and directed its hostility to art. Idolatry, as the embodiment of art and of a purely esthetic conception of the divine, was the *bête noir* of Christianity. The early Christian could not distinguish between the symbolism and the reality of polytheism, and, taking offense, rightly I think, at the sensuous conception of the divine as nothing but sublimated matter, established a conflict with art and an alliance with science. Science, at least when it based its explanations on atoms and similar realities, rested as much on the supersensible as religion had done, and hence had in that respect a natural affinity with religion. So long as religion could enlist philosophy and science in its defense it was assured of protection. But as soon as it began a dalliance with art its decay began, with the rise of materialism in the church. When pictures and cathedrals became necessary for religion, the protection of philosophy was no longer necessary, or it required too strenuous use of the intellect to justify the labor. So physical science began a career independnt of religion and soon attacked its fundamental claims. Physical science won in all its battles until religion now crouches in terror before the loss of all its traditions. Psychology and philosophy are no longer its handmaids, but have gone off into the service of the intellectual curiosity shop. Medicine has appropriated all that had belonged to its rival or master and has assumed a determined hostility to everything spiritual.

Psychic research. with its facts to suggest or to prove the existence of a soul and its survival, had neither a scientific nor a therapeutic interest for medicine. Professing to be devoted to a scientific view of man, the moment that any promise of sustaining the value of personality appeared on the horizon, medicine and academic psychology began either to take to cover or to ridicule what had been the real object of psychological science in the beginning. Medicine had founded its claims on materialism, and psychology dared not oppose medicine for fear of losing its bread. Both ridiculed what they had not the courage to face nor the knowledge to understand.

But medicine did yield to the influence of Christian Science! It pretended to investigate it, but there was nothing scientific in the verdict, though it was correct enough in all probability. It laughed at mesmerism until mesmerism was revived under the term hypnotism and then, accepted the facts and their utility; but the moment that hypnotism approached the confines of the supernormal it was to be neglected. Christian Science followed. The system was one half spiritualism and one half a scheme to make money. Neuropathic patients whom the regular physicians could not cure went in multitudes to the new "Science" and were cured. The demonstration that drugs were not always necessary for successful cures was a challenge to the whole system of medicine, which rested on chemistry alone. Mind was not a factor in the pharmacopœia. Psychology made no such claim as Christian Science did, and if it had done so, materialistic medicine would have laughed the claim out of court. It was content simply to attack the cures of Christian Science on the evidential side. It was an easy victory to show that Christian Science was not scientific. But the fact remained that sufferers sought and found relief or health in a system which did its work in defiance of physiological orthodoxy. This fact would not down, and it was not the exclusive property of Christian Science. Mental healing had been successful long before Mrs. Eddy gave it notoriety. Hypnotic suggestion had been scientifically applied by Charcot, Bernheim, Janet, Baron von Schrenck-Notzing and a host of predecessors. But its methods were too esoteric for the average practitioner to use or to learn and the confidence in drugs rose in proportion to the assurance that materialism was the true philosophy.

What medicine should have done was to seize the first indication of any unusual mental phenomena and investigate them scientifically, and then, by a just verdict, make an end of the matter. But what did it do with mesmerism? It appointed a committee which reported much charlatanry and some important facts in the claims of Mesmer and his followers; and then refused to accept this verdict, packed a committee to condemn it, and published the later report, shelving the first. Orthodoxy and dogmatism, bigotry and intolerance are not confined to religion and their results are not felt there alone. Science can destroy its own authority as easily as did religion. Why science should have neglected the investigation of hypnotism and taken alarm at Christian Science is explainable only by the ease with which it could divest the latter of its claims; but even there "McClure's Magazine" did more and better work than the medical profession.

There is no escaping the fact that mind as well as matter is a causal factor in the world. But materialism, though it might have conceded this fact, has stubbornly refused to recognize it. Though the physician knew that the mental condition of his patient was a factor in therapeutics, he refused to give it the place in practice that it merited. He was too much absorbed in brain centers, about which there has been written as much unprovable metaphysics as about the unseen. Matter was the prius of everything and that was the end of investigation. However, the slow and steady accumulation of facts by psychic research, if it has not been able scientifically to establish the causal influence of mind on matter, has opened the densest materialistic mind to something besides brain centers. To introduce a soul into the investigations of biology and physiology is to revolutionize them. Psychology might have shared the honors of this result, but it chose to run away, preferring either materialism or intellectual snobbery. But psychology and medicine have only postponed the day of judgment which is coming to rob the old authorities of their prestige and power. The stone which was despised of the builders is to become the head of the corner. Mind will take a place among the causal agencies of nature. This position will be won either by the study of suggestion and mental healing or by the evidence for survival after death. Medicine will have to give up the exclusive use of drugs and admit the influence of mental states on the condition of the body. The more gracefully it does this the better for its own influence. Its hostility to Christian Science was at least excusable, and the writer thinks justified, by the equally one-sided views which that system takes. Mind is one of the causal agents in the world, but it is not the only one. However, the writer freely concedes that without the evidence of psychic research, the materialist has the best of the case. The facts and the argument are on his side, if the supernormal is to be debarred from consideration.

The cowardice about this question is astonishing when we consider how alert the scientific mind is in other provinces. The most useless inquiries in physics or chemistry, will engage hundreds of men and unlimited resources, if only fame or curiosity can be satisfied. North Pole expeditions are organized at enormous expense with nothing of importance as a result, and the public goes wild about them. But when one offers to prove that man has a soul or that the mind may be a factor in therapeutics, he meets only ridicule. The momentum of materialistic science is so great that the most important of all problems has to wait for half a century to win attention.

The present writer thinks that the main contention in this field has been sustained and that it is only stupidity and prejudice that stand in the way of its wider acceptance. He will no longer make any concession to a skepticism that refuses to investigate.

The one great change which the proof of the causal influence of mind will bring to medicine will be the placing of ethics in a more important position in therapeutics. Materialism with its drug methods was based upon the assumption that medicine could cure the effects of vice and sin. Physicians knew better, but the patient wanted to believe this and it was not always convenient or profitable to disillusion him on this point. The achievements in the use of *materia medica* in lieu of *spiritus medicus* tended to sustain confidence in the possibility of escaping the consequences of sin, and man went to his physician instead of the priest for relief. The time was when he went to the priest first and afterward to the doctor. But this procedure has been reversed. Materialism taught us to believe that, if we only had good enough doctors, we could sin as we pleased. We consulted the physician and took his drugs instead of buying indulgences. The fact is that the one is no better than the other for buying release from moral responsibility. If chemistry can relieve us from the consequences of sin, why give ethics any place at all? So thought materialism in its attempt to evade the facts of morality. But to put mind among the therapeutic agents is to turn the tide the other way. It will not set aside the achievements of the *materia medica,* but it will add a new force to healing. The physician will have to become a psychologist and a moralist. He has already found, in spite of his materialism, that drugs will not do everything, and he squints cautiously towards mind-cure without realizing the extent of the changes that must come from any dalliance with it. But to it he must come, if he is to be scientific at all, instead of resting in traditions and dogmatism no less fatal to progress than mediæval theology. But physician and patient alike must learn that ethics are the best and the cheapest therapeutic, and that mind is the primary factor in healing. We cannot substitute drugs for conscience, except to secure more fees and fewer cures. What is needed is the organization of the medical profession on the same basis as the priesthood. Disinterestedness and humanity must be the primary motives of its work, or at least the mercenary interest must be minimized. As it is to-day, the clergyman receives on the average scarcely a living wage, and this is right enough if there be no soul to save. The rewards should all go to the physician if the body is all in all. But when we are assured that there is a soul and that it survives in another and invisible environment, the physician must either adjust his practice to the demands of ethics or retire from the field.

The physician may endeavor to heal without raising the question of ultimate causes, but he cannot effect a permanent cure until his patient is spiritually sound. The individual is not always the sinner and hence the physician cannot always throw the blame on the victim. He must cure, if he can, regardless of the relation between individual and social sin. No doubt each man must accept responsibility for his error, but too often the sin is that of society and the individual has to bear the suffering vicariously. The happiness of the successful is often more or less at the expense of the unsuccessful. Hospitals and asylums are embodiments of this idea, and the only question is, how far the principle shall be applied. The passion to live is so strong that if man is without any belief that better times are reserved for him beyond the grave, he will give all he has, to prolong consciousness. The physician's advantage in the situation is tremendous. If he does not possess character he may make the suffering of the patient a thumbscrew for extorting good fees.

Half the applause heaped on medicine is from those who rejoice at the ability to escape the results of sin and to outwit nature or Providence. Since medicine is so near religion, it must be socialized and brought to recognize that the morality of patients is more important than life. That condition can be secured only by changing the relative position assigned the body in the scheme of values that we cherish. Materialism, on its own premises, of course, is justified in its estimate, but only because it does not recognize the existence and the superior importance of the soul. The consequences, however, of the estimate, like all those of materialism, are proving disastrous. If the materialist wants to debauch either in philosophy or life he can get it; for nature will not interfere with our choice. It will silently weave about it a set of consequences which ultimately correct the error, and we can escape only by retracing our steps.

Therapeutics, no less than ethics, require a soul and the physician will never effect the best results until he accepts that point of view. He cannot do it, of course, with the methods of normal psychology. It is the residual phenomena of nature that establish the widest conclusions. They have to be unified with the whole, and in doing this we discover new agents. Forced by the facts to recognize mental states as causal agents in therapeutic processes, however limited the field of their activity, medicine admits an entering wedge into its scheme of things and sooner or later it must submit to the restoration of the ethical and religious point of view, divested of the mass of illusions and errors that have gathered about it like barnacles. Curing diseases without curing sin only multiplies the cases with which we have to deal, and present-day medicine is no help in the ethical regeneration of man. We seek at enormous expense the means for escaping pain, but we will not give a cent to ascertain whether we have a soul and what its duties are. Liberty and irresponsibility are what we desire, and not an ideal that looks beyond an Epicurean paradise.

And yet there is always progress. We take present satisfaction as an index of the right condition of things. It is this that makes all conservatism. But nature never rests. She will have change at all costs. If we resist it we pay the heavier penalty. We may cry as much as we please over the crumbling of the past into ashes, with all those institutions which we have learned to prize, but we would not do so could we see in the change a sure harbinger of a greater paradise. It is the darkness of the future that makes us lament the loss of the past. Give us a beacon light into the future and we can endure much. Ethical ideals beyond sense can find their justification only in a non-sensuous philosophy; and ethical ideals point to the future. They are ideals for that reason. Psychology does nothing for us unless it supplies them, and medicine can effect no permanent cures without accepting as imperative and primary the need of ethical adjustments. It will have to make mind the cause and effect, to speak paradoxically, of all that it does accomplish, if it expects to achieve its best conquests. Indeed religion and medicine will have to join partnership again and they can do this only by one of them abandoning materialism and the other accepting science as its guide. The one should be no more a commercial business than the other, but commercial they must both be, when materialism is our only philosophy.

Public opinion has accepted materialism without knowing what it means, and it pays its servants according to their power and willingness to pander to its wants. Education and religion are organized for catering to materialism and no scientific truth is sought, except such as may come from the accidents of that organization or from the necessity of supplying material wants. Respectability is on the side of materialism, and spiritualism, which had ruled eighteen centuries of civilization, badly enough, it is true, but with more success than either Greece or Rome achieved, is forsaken and forlorn and left to foster its faith without evidence. Fortunately it is rapidly gaining a position from which it may issue with "grim fire-eyed defiance" to challenge any dispute of its claims. It will then dictate terms to religion and medicine, to the one without disturbing its faith and to the other without disturbing its science, and psychology will come again to serve them both, recovering its rightful domain in cultivating the wider interests of man.

Man first placed the golden age in the dim vistas of the past, but philosophy and science soon showed that it was only mythological. Christian idealism, accepting the legend of paradise and man's fallen estate, making the present carnal life one of sin and suffering, placed its golden age in the future where it seemed safer from attack. Legend may be assaulted by history, but imagination can only be ignored or ridiculed. Faith proved a stronger fortress than tradition, which dissolves in the light of science like a morning mist before the sun. Yet science with its materialism and redoubtable energies came again to conquer the world from illusion and in doing so left nothing but darkness. But mariners will not sail the seas without a harbor in which to anchor and something to requite their toil. There is no commerce with the unknown, and hence it will devolve upon science either to submit to some other source of knowledge and governance or to give us a religion that shall be stronger than faith and more adventurous than doubt. "Science," says Lord Morley, who was saturated with the philosophy of the Encyclopedists, "when she has accomplished all her triumphs in her own order, will still have to go back, when the time comes, to assist in building up a new creed by which man may live." That time has come, and recreant or cowardly is the man who does not seize the opportunity to shield the ideals that may bring a "little sheen of inspiration out of the surrounding eternity to color with its own hues man's little islet of time." All action has its fruition in the future and we must see the prospect before we can act rationally. Only he who has hope can be moved to any ventures that have idealism for their motive or progress for their rational end.

For my purpose holds
To sail beyond the sunset and the baths
Of all the western stars, until I die.

> It may be that the gulfs will wash us down:
> It may be we shall touch the Happy Isles
> And see the great Achilles whom we knew.

But in the travail of that voyage the light of science and hope may reveal, in the cross section of evolution which we study, some vision of eternal life, and the final moments which the gloomy fears instigated by materialism have saddened, may be cheered by a greater outlook, and man, chastened by toil and pain, may be happy yet.

CHAPTER XXIX

PSYCHIC RESEARCH AND THE WAR

THIS age is so practical that men engaged in any work are expected to defend it by showing its relation to the problems with which the world is immediately concerned. We cannot get a hearing unless we satisfy the public that we can contribute to its ends. Each science tries to vindicate itself by declaring what it does for the general welfare or for the solution of the problems confronting civilization. Most of the sciences have a direct relation to practical problems. Many, therefore, will ask whether psychic research can help to solve the world problems of the day. Those who are interested in the question whether we live after death will have no difficulty in answering the question. But those who are absorbed in material affairs may ridicule or neglect the remote issues of a problem like psychic research. To most people it seems a vain endeavor to lift the veil of existence. Their assumption is that Isis must always remain veiled and that man's business is only with the world of sense. Like the ancient Greeks, who thought that the gods lived in an intermundane world where they could exercise no influence on terrestrial events, they disconnect spirit from earthly affairs and await in sullen or happy indifference the end of life and the world.

But the psychic researcher has a problem of more immediate interest than the skeptic and the Philistine dream of. We are not seeking to establish remote relationships when we assert that psychic research bears directly on the problems of war. People easily see that wheat, turnips, and pig iron affect the issues of civilization, but they less clearly realize the place of psychic phenomena in determining history.

If psychic research were occupied merely with a few oddities of mental experience it might well be said to have no connection with the war. If it were exclusively concerned with phenomena like telepathy or mind-reading, or with coincidental dreams, or with the mysteries of the diving-rod, a man would be foolhardy who essayed to speak of its importance in the problems of war, unless he could show its direct connection with the one consideration that makes war a nightmare to the better members of the human race. We may explore the marginal phenomena of the mind all we please and find no practical interest in them, until we find their relation to the one pivotal interest of human reflection; namely, the immortality of the soul. We may criticize human nature, justly or unjustly, for its obsession with this idea. We may contend that man is too much concerned with the other world and too little concerned with his daily duties in this world. But this criticism does not alter the facts. The practical problem is to deal with facts as they are and to consider what effect a belief has, whether or not it is justifiable. Hence in any preliminary discussion of this problem we are concerned not with what is ideally preferable, but with the actual state of mind that determines human conduct. Psychic research would have little interest for most people, if it did not bear upon this large question of the nature and destiny of the human mind. Its subsidiary phenomena might otherwise interest only men who seek to amuse themselves with abnormalities. But the scientific study of the relation between matter and mind shows many of the phenomena of psychic research to be crucial in determining the meaning of all mental facts. There are marginal phenomena which suggest that consciousness and personality are not bubbles on the ocean, soon lost in its engulfing embrace. Apparitions, mediumistic communications with the dead, and suggestions of a transcendental world that reveal an infinite scope for the mind give the subject an interest and importance scarcely equaled since the speculations of Plato and the teachings of Christ.

How does the belief in immortality affect the problems of war? What are the problems of war? The answers to these questions are not simple. But the one element that enters into both answers is the problem of death. If war were a pugilistic encounter, in which both combatants come out alive, psychic research would have nothing to do with the issue. But the central interests in war are human ideals and death. In war death comes to the strongest of the race and comes without the ordinary calculations and risks of life. In the normal conditions of existence, the healthy man has no time or interest to spend in thinking about death. The attainment of our ideals is the object of action and when these preoccupy attention the prospect of death fades into the margin of consciousness. If we cannot achieve our aims and are attacked by disease, we lose interest in life and calmly await the end. It is true that human kind cannot be classified in this hard and fast way. For there are large numbers that can never lose sight of the grave in their thought and action. But the majority of men are Stoics, if not in virtue, in the habit of taking things as they come and wasting as little energy as possible on the fear of death. Lack of time, or fear of losing the game, keeps the dread spectre below the horizon. But when war confronts us, it brings certainties and risks that we do not have to meet in the regular course of normal life. The one thing that hovers always in the field of consciousness is the prospect of losing life and ideals at one stroke; the question for the man who values his present existence is whether the sacrifice is worth while. Death or maiming for life confronts the soldier every day of his career, and he will feel the tragedy of the situation in proportion to the value which he places on life.

If we asserted that a belief in immortality is essential to the making of good soldiers, that unqualified statement would meet with instant denial. There are instances in which the belief has favorably affected the character and the courage of soldiers. All will agree that the courage of the Japanese in the war against Russia was increased by their belief in survival and a future meeting with their ancestors. The Crusaders also were influenced by their belief in immortality. And we could perhaps find many races profoundly influenced in their martial life and ideals by this belief. But it is far from universal. Whole races in the past either did not have the belief at all, or held it in a form that did not connect it with martial valor. Savages are usually little influenced by it. The Greeks and Romans, especially the latter, were not primarily affected in military affairs by the belief in immortality. Other motives were substituted for it. The Roman race was essentially Stoic in temperament, long before the philosophy of that name organized reasons for its view of life. Roman citizens died for the state and did not expect to reap a reward in another world for their heroism, though we can find among them individual exceptions. It was Christianity that gave the doctrine of the immortality of the soul an important place in the philosophy of conduct. Christianity emphasized the belief so strongly and merged other interests in it in such a manner that it became the pivotal doctrine of the system. The belief in immortality is certainly not essential to the formation of the heroic virtues of the soldier, and it would be folly for any man to insist that it always has this effect on life and character. All depends on the place it occupies in the social and individual scheme of life. Its importance will depend entirely on its relation to the rest of our beliefs.

I said above that the influence of the belief on conduct will depend on the value which we attach to the present life. If we do not value this life, we are not likely to place any high value on life after death. Emphasis on the importance of death is proportionate to interest in present living. When it is not mere desire of living that determines our actions, but some principle, such as patriotism, the family, science, literature, or success, we are apt to put the idea of survival in a secondary place among motives. But if we regard the joys of physical life either as above all others or as the only joys we are sure of, we thus emphasize the importance of death as the termination of them. Now the materialistic philosophy emphasizes the idea that death is the end of all things and assures us that we are not certain of any other happiness than what we can attain in the present. It thus cuts off the unsuccessful from any hope of realizing natural ambitions and assures all persons that the shortening of life is so much unrequited sacrifice. In an age of little comfort and hard living, the passions of luxury and avarice have no place; and when happiness is hardly attainable on any terms, the sacrifice of life is easy. The comforts and luxuries which science and invention have brought to modern life make life so attractive that death, if not feared, is at least hated. When in doubt about a future life man tries to prolong consciousness in present conditions and endeavors to stave off the fatal day of death, because he feels no assurance that there is anything for his personality beyond the grave. What he can achieve here he is certain of. What the future holds in store for him is unknown, and the unknown is no incentive to action. But if he is sure that death is not the end of all things and that it only brings a change of environment; that it only continues life, and that it brings a reward for deeds well done, he meets it cheerfully and giving up this life is no sacrifice to him.

Lucretius, the Roman materialist, regarded the fear of death as the greatest evil man has to face, and St. Paul accepted the same view of it. But each had a different solution of the problem. Lucretius thought to overcome this fear by teaching man the doctrine of annihilation. St. Paul endeavored to overcome it by teaching immortality. But in the present state of human opinion no man can expect to dispel this evil by denying immortality. Survival after death may not be a fact; but annihilation is none the less dreaded. If the existence and prolongation of consciousness can be proved to be evil, men may logically be taught that it should be destroyed. But the average healthy man will not be influenced by the doctrine that suicide is his duty or his salvation!

The view of life after death as somewhat like the Hades of ancient superstitions or the sulphurous hell of some later ages, makes the fear of death natural. It was possibly such a conception that aroused the hostility of Epicurus and Lucretius. A life after death which only brought more suffering might well suggest the desirability of annihilation. The materialism of Lucretius was a moral protest against an absurd and unjust hell rather than against the prolongation of consciousness. St. Paul saw the problem in a clearer light, and distinguished between survival and suffering. Christianity emphasized *salvation* quite as much as immortality. St. Paul saw that the fear of death could not be eradicated from the normal man by a doctrine of eternal sleep. If man looks on consciousness as a good, he is not likely to ask for its termination as the great desideratum. He will want to prolong it.

Now in opposition to materialism Christianity taught the infinite value of the soul and of consciousness. It emphasized life and not death as the highest good. It regarded suffering as a punishment for immoral conduct, not as the caprices of fortune, and so kept a possibility of permanent happiness before the imagination. In this way it established a love of life which, owing to the precarious fortunes of war and the suffering prevalent in some ancient civilizations, hitherto had little opportunity for expression and cultivation. Then with its assurance of life after death, it could face the future with hope; and hope is always the foundation of rational endeavor. It organized civilization on this basis for many centuries and fixed in the human mind expectations which the materialist could not support. When modern materialism came forward with a doctrine of annihilation, it opposed the established ideals of man. It does not degrade or impeach the pleasures of living. It places all man's hopes in the prudent and intelligent pursuit of material good. It places a value on life and yet has to admit that death ends it. It discourages the soldier by asking him to make all the sacrifices while the survivors of war enjoy all the rewards. It laughs at the vicarious atonement taught by religion and yet asks the soldier to perform it. It expects a man to give up all that is dear to him without hope of reward, though it estimates value only in terms of wages and profits. On the theory of materialism man can act only on self-interest in peace and only on self-sacrifice in war. A philosophy which cannot observe the same maxims in peace as in war is destined to easy refutation. But when the doctrine of self-interest is adopted, it dominates the whole attitude towards death. Good soldiers cannot be made from men who measure life by its rewards and yet are asked to relinquish all reward in facing a death that offers them only annihilation.

In this age, therefore, a belief in immortality will help to produce soldierly qualities. I shall agree at the outset, however, that many persons are not influenced by such a faith. Their sense of right and justice is sufficient to make them disregard desire of reward in another life, and, like the Roman Stoics, they sacrifice life without thinking of any future. Their willingness to act without hope or expectation of reward shows a character which is perhaps more highly respected by the community than if they sought a reward for their action. Some will serve the right, though the heavens fall, and ask no rewards here or hereafter. Even the man who acts from passion may disregard consequences. The old Roman Stoic philosophers took a very uncompromising attitude toward all emotional considerations in conduct, and thought a man a sentimentalist, a weakling, who allowed undue grief, or even any grief, to affect him under the loss of friends or loved ones. They demanded the complete sacrifice of emotion as the sign of virtue or manliness. But, as Mr. Lecky finely remarks, this philosophy will not successfully lead men who are not Stoics. The majority of men and women act from motives very different from those enjoined by philosophers. Whether weak or strong, these men have to be reckoned with in the problems of life, individual and social. Most men are governed by some expectation of reward in their lives; indeed in all ordinary affairs any other course is irrational. The man who has amassed a large fortune may work for nothing, but he has already satisfied his ambition for independence. Like all others he expected profits as the wages and reward for action, often wholly disproportionate to the amount of labor performed. In such a world we can not afford to disregard the practical consideration of rewards or consequences. With this consideration dominating most men, whether it be the highest motive of action or not, a belief in survival may be reckoned with as an incentive. It can be used to influence those who would otherwise be cowards in the struggle for right. Much cowardice comes from the love of life. Many of our pacifists are too cowardly to admit that it is want of moral courage that determines their pacifism. They disguise it under the name of conscientious scruples against war. Conscientiousness is regarded as a virtue, and if the coward can deceive the public by assuming the garb of conscientiousness, and thus disguising his cowardice, he may keep the respect of the public or at least ward off its contempt.

The resentment against the draft was probably in large measure due to exaltation of the love of life above devotion to the principle of sacrifice for justice and for posterity. Under a volunteer system the belief in immortality has less influence than under a draft system. The volunteer has moral character to start with, whether due to a belief in survival or not. He sees his duty and will make any sacrifice to perform it. But the man who will not volunteer, must see some reward in view beyond this life, to make him a good soldier. He has become so habituated to the utilitarian view of life that he must be made to see that he loses nothing by giving his life for an unpersonal ideal of country, family, or justice. If men are convinced that death brings no cessation of their development, they will be good soldiers in peace or war. For soldierly qualities are as important in peace as in war. Courage is not exclusively the virtue of the fighter. It is as necessary in social as in martial life.

The pragmatist in philosophy cannot escape the view here defended. He measures all truth, especially ethical truth, by consequences. He cannot be a Stoic on the subject of a future life. He must estimate the truth and value of the doctrine by its consequences on the will of men. In this age, saturated as it is with materialistic ideals, he must recognize that immortality is calculated to reclaim the coward. If we are to sacrifice life without regard to consequences, we can reject pragmatism in favor of another philosophy.

Christ made an interesting statement which seems paradoxical, when he said that he who would have his life must lose it. No saying was ever better justified than this. But it is true only when we understand the spiritual sense in which it is to be taken. No doubt there is a verbal contradiction if we take the term "life" in the same sense in both parts of the sentence. But if the teaching means that the man who voluntarily gives up his life for an ideal loses nothing in the economy of the cosmos, it furnishes an effective basis for the ethics of both peace and war. In fact, no man ever attains salvation in any other way. The mother and father who are tormented by the fear that a son will be killed in the war, forget that his sacrifice, if voluntary, *is* his salvation. His life in peace might have been anything but his salvation. But when he resolves to be a man and to stand for right in the world, and is willing to give up his life for that service, he is saved. Most Christians worship their Savior because he sacrificed his life on the cross for their redemption, but they do not want their sons to follow his example! They accept the vicarious atonement, but are not willing to make it.

If psychic research can assure men of a life beyond death, it will put the materialistic love of physical life to shame. There can be no doubt that the materialist is right, if he can show that no life after death is possible. Man must then make the most of the present and perform as few sacrifices as possible to attain his ends. But if it is certain that consciousness and personality continue beyond the grave, it will be much easier to surrender the present and to live the heroic virtues. Indeed they will even be less "heroic." We admire the hero for the sacrifice he makes; but if losing one's life is gaining it, nature requires no such sacrifices of us as the Stoic demands. Sacrifice is not ultimately sacrifice. We make it such only by our false theories. In fact, we might say that our admiration is directly proportioned to our unwillingness to be heroes ourselves. It is the coward who most admires courage. The soldier does not think of his virtues nor of his right to the respect of his fellows. He is not actuated by the desire to be thought heroic; so much the more, then, he needs to be led away from the temptation to value his life according to the pleasures he can secure if he refuses sacrifice in behalf of his country or justice. Psychic research, at least as a part of its service, can administer a benefit to the world, if it can remove all temptation to disregard the appeal to duty and to higher ideals.

Selfishness is the only sin. It has many ramifications; but all other sins can be interpreted as forms of selfishness and all virtues as self-sacrifice. This maxim once seized, the path of duty is clear to every man. The soldier may commit mistakes of judgment; he may fight on the wrong side; but if his will is right he will not suffer the consequences of bad character. He will have made self-sacrifice the center to which all other forms of virtue gravitate. Any maxim, once adopted, determines of the place of all others in the system of conduct, and serves as the test for their adoption or rejection. Supreme devotion to duty at the sacrifice of life is the one revolutionary decision for every man to make; his life then conforms to the order of the cosmos and his salvation is assured. It is assured because his life goes on, and his compensation is the permanent consciousness of having done the right thing and paid the price. In such a system the continuity of life assures the compensation and shows just what estimate nature puts upon the present life. Materialistic systems make present advantage only standard of value. But ideals can be realized only in the future. No act of will takes place without having future consequences as the determinant of its moral value. That is why belief in survival is a condition of the highest ethical life, even though humanity has not always made the best use of it as a motive.

Salvation is a state of mind, not any external achievement. We may fail in business or in any other effort to which we devote life; but if we have the right state of mind, we gain a success worth more than the accumulation of material goods. This state of mind will constitute the source of happiness in another world and will serve as the condition for proper adjustment to the future life, as it is also in the present existence, if we would only see it. Hence the sacrifices that the soldier makes help to fix his character and to save him from the epicurean temptations of ordinary life.

Peace may be a worse state of civilization than war. It often gives an opportunity for the vice and revelry that affect character more harmfully than war can do. To be sure, war is not always good; it is never right on the part of the deliberate aggressor, though it is right on the part of the defender against wanton aggression. Its value is determined by the motives and ideals of the parties involved. War is better than peace when it is waged for ideals better than those of peace. The argument against war is its unnecessary waste and loss in promoting civilization. Devotion to the cause of human brotherhood and reason might effect the same result without the destruction involved in war. Peace, however, may cultivate vices and sins worse than those of war, and fatal to the spiritual development of man. If peace bred the sacrifices and virtues of war, then war would not be necessary. But war is only the natural consequence of the vices which we mistake for civilization. In peace we lie and cheat, in war we kill; and salvation can be obtained by neither course.

If we can scientifically guarantee a future life we shall have shown that nature values personality or consciousness more highly than physical life, and we shall be in a position to urge the realization of human brotherhood with tenfold force. If any message from the spiritual world can be accepted because of its frequent repetition, it is that human brotherhood, human love, alone guarantees salvation. If that attitude, the conduct inspired by it, were established as the basis of social life, wars would cease and peace would not breed the sins that inevitably lead to war.

Many of the psychic phenomena of interest to the public in connection with the present war have not been sufficiently accredited to be valuable as evidence. The stories of the apparitions at Mons have not been scientifically verified. The newspaper story of Mr. Machen, which innocently gave rise to one of the most important legends, though written with no intention of misleading readers, was believed by thousands. When the author saw how it was being taken, he publicly announced that it was fiction. Probably "The White Comrade" is genuine, and possibly there have been many apparitions seen by individual soldiers, as we might expect in any case. But intelligent men will be cautious about using these for evidence of survival or of spirit intervention. Even when they occur and are more than ordinary hallucinations, they may not be what the popular mind supposes. Visions of Joan of Arc or of Napoleon might be veridical without actually representing these personalities. Veridical hallucinations are not representative, but symbolic. They may be externally and spiritually instigated, but subjectively formed. Our own memories and ideals may give form to the apparition even when it is caused by a spirit. There is overwhelming evidence that messages from a transcendental world are modified by the mind that receives them. Our organic habits give them their shape, so that the utmost that we can affirm is that they indicate foreign causes, subjectively interpreted. Hence the whole subject of the apparitions recorded in current stories, must be left to much more careful investigation than has yet been possible. The evidence of survival and of spirit intervention must be of a different kind. What these psychic experiences show is the place that psychic research may have in helping to solve world problems. It transfigures life, or at least the possibilities of life, in a way impossible to materialistic science.

CHAPTER XXX

PSYCHICS AND POLITICS

WALTER BAGEHOT chose "Physics and Politics" as the title of one of his books, though he did not discuss in it the influence of physical science upon social and political life. What he did consider was the influence of heredity on the body politic. This study might have led him to look much deeper and to see the far larger, though latent, influence of the modern interest in physical science upon the tendencies of politics. At any rate, Mr. Bagehot's juxtaposition of the two terms suggests a contrast between the physical and the spiritual conceptions of life and their ultimate influence on ethical, social, and political affairs. The clearly developed opposition between mind and matter, which finally issued in the definite dualism of Descartes, gathered about each term the appropriate associations. Under different auspices the development might have taken another course, but the antithesis between the Epicurean conception of nature and life and the sternly moralistic Christian idea of the soul created opposing centers of gravity for men's beliefs. History records the varying fortunes of their warfare.

Physical science is occupied with the observation and study of the material world, and teaches that the external forces of the universe move relentlessly over every aspiration cherished by the religious mind. Psychology, or the study of the soul, has always sought in the inner life some justification of the belief in another life when the grave has closed over all we know, a hope that would at least set aside the apparent indifference of the universe to the ideals which arise in the creatures of its own activity. At one stage of human reflection the opposition between the two points of view was not so marked; but the predisposition to uncompromising separation of interests and to the organization of these interests into opposing groups, has given matter and mind, physics and psychics, opposite meanings. Ideas once accepted by large bodies of men are not easily set aside. They either become identified with the institutions that serve as their defence, or habit gives them a force which they might not have. Consequently, regardless of their intrinsic merits, they give rise to parties and prejudices which cannot be overthrown except by the prolonged efforts of criticism and the gradual adjustment of the mind to new ideas.

I have said, or implied, that physical science has exercised a profound influence upon modern social and political life. This influence may be illustrated in a thousand ways. I need not call attention at present to the initial impulse of the movement, which began with the renaissance as a reaction against the excessive occupation of men's minds with the other world. To contrast the civilizations of the Middle Ages and the present would be to bring out into strong relief the two different tendencies and would clearly exhibit the influences which have gradually resulted in the domination of physical science over the life of man. If we compare the meager comforts and enjoyments of the first fifteen centuries of the Christian era with the multiplied resources for pleasure which we now possess, and consider the reluctance of the material universe to concede any favors not extorted from it, we shall form some conception of the power of physical science. The railway, the telegraph, the telephone, ocean travel, the mechanical inventions that cheapen labor and multiply products, cheap printing, and a thousand forms of satisfaction and comfort that ancient and mediæval societies would not have dreamed of, are now the commonplaces of the poor. They are all due to physical science, which had to win its way against the stubborn opposition of more conservative beliefs and habits. They are all indications of the effect of physics on our institutions.

The economic ideal, which is only another term for the physical conception of society and human action, is now dominant, and wealth is the standard of success and social recognition. This standard has been accepted even by the religious institutions of the age; and we have so far departed from the spiritual conception of life as to neglect all features of it except intellectual culture, which is valued more for its efficiency in the economic and social world than for the development of the soul. Such are the triumphs of physical science and the ideals fostered by it. Its utility is demonstrated by its success in supplying the comforts which seem to us both a pleasure in themselves and a protection against the cruelties of nature. The older religious ideals, which despised these comforts as " carnal " and turned the imagination toward another world, the " Elysian fields where joy forever reigns," as contrasted with this life of pain and suffering, have lost the basis on which they rested. We have found physical and economic salvation in the conquest of nature, instead of despising its power and living in penury and contemplative asceticism. Physics has determined and dominated all the ideals of our life and must affect our ethics in proportion as it has supplanted the spiritual conceptions of another philosophy. How far this influence will extend depends upon the degree to which it takes possession of the lower strata of society.

The rejuvenation of the social order and of civilization fell to Christianity after the decline and fall of the Roman Empire. The one central tenet of Christianity is its association of the immortality of the soul with the brotherhood of man. It did not begin in a system of philosophy or theology. A reasoned theism was no part of its primary impulse, however closely it might be related to such a system. The divine supervision of the world was not its fundamental belief, though it might be accepted as a corollary of the primary doctrine. The belief in a future life was its initial doctrine, and received its credentials from an appeal to real or alleged facts. The view that immortality can be accepted as the corollary of a theistic interpretation of nature was a later conception, arising when Christianity was so far removed from its origin that its miracles and traditions were objects of suspicion. This first inspiration was received from the direct observation of facts, or alleged facts, which directly challenged the prevailing materialism. The Epicureans had denied the possibility of survival after death, and their philosophy dominated Rome in its declining days and the most important political sect in Palestine, the Sadducees. Judaism was no longer under the direction of its older religious conceptions, which had indeed never made belief in the immortality of the soul a social influence. Such a belief could not become important to social institutions until it was used to enforce certain ethical maxims. What gave the immortality of the soul its ethical and political value was its association with the brotherhood of man in the doctrine of salvation. Neither Judaistic nor Greek civilization attached any special importance to the doctrine as a means of enjoining the virtues that would lead to happiness beyond the grave. The doctrine of probation for a future life had not yet developed. It was latent in the religions of Greece and Rome and was perhaps an unconscious factor in the ethical position of some Hebrews, though it was not sufficiently active in that religious system to obtain any definite recognition. In Greco-Roman literature a doctrine of probation as an encouragement of virtue is apparent. We all know it in the works of Plato and Vergil, and they but reflected, in this respect, the popular religion, so that the doctrine of the immortality of the soul as held by them already foreshadowed the later view of salvation. It did not, however, take on the fire and enthusiasm of a religion until social and political life began to break up and men felt that there was no hope of realizing their ideals in a world that offered so much resistance to their struggles. Physics and politics were against them, the one making creature comforts, the other social freedom impossible to obtain. In this condition of things it was natural to turn the eyes to some future world either as a reward for following duty or as a punishment for transgression. In this way the thought of immortality began to encourage the performance of duties hitherto sanctioned only by society; and the happiness which a decaying world could not grant in this life was hoped for in another. The organization of virtue and happiness around the concept of a future life gave it the power to influence ethics and politics. The assertion of the persistence of personality was important to the individual, and the association of the idea with human brotherhood gave it an influence on political institutions.

In the present age, which represents a reaction against the extreme other-worldliness of the mediæval period, there are many who will question the value of belief in immortality. They will point to the superior civilization which has been the result of the conquests of physical science. While I shall not gainsay much that is urged in support of this contention, I may call attention to two facts. The first is, that all this conquest of nature was rendered possible by the firm establishment in men's minds of the virtues which gave stability to the social order and so made possible the continuity of scientific progress. The second is, that we are too closely attached to a materialistic order as yet to see its tendencies and consequences, except as they are beginning to reveal themselves in the decadence of the virtues that protected the advance of physical science itself. Moreover the materialist may not be in a position to estimate rightly the nature of the order which he denies. His victories over the physical world, in subordinating it to his desires, may blind him to the value of what he lost by turning his view from the spiritual conception of man and life. The distortion of this conception in the past has concealed from us the better aspects of the spiritual ideal; and, while we are forced by our nature to make concessions to the demands of the physical world, it is just as easy to overestimate the value of the physical as of the spiritual. We may therefore turn a scrutinizing and skeptical eye toward the confident worship of physical science which is trying to supplant the conceptions that have made us rise above nature while we conquered it.

However, we may disregard the question of ethical value and limit our consideration to the efficacy of the spiritual view as an agent in the determination of human institutions. The Middle Ages are proof of the power of belief in a future life to affect civil institutions. That influence may have been good or bad. But its effectiveness as a motive is well authenticated by twenty centuries of history. What I wish to show is that all general ideas inevitably affect ethical and political institutions in proportion to their success in organizing about them the various customs and duties which they are made to protect. If other general ideas are thus effective, we may establish a presumption that the belief of immortality is of similar character. This conception, with its relation to important ethical ideas, will hardly fall short of others in the power to mold human life and institutions. Let us illustrate by reference to beliefs which have no ethical implications.

The effect of a general conception on human conduct may be illustrated by the influence of monotheism in religion and monism in philosophy on the tendencies of Greek politics. In the earlier stages of her development Greece was under the domination of polytheism in religion and of provincialism in politics. Indeed they were one and the same thing. The influence of local divinities was as noticeable as it was during the struggle of Judaism for Jehovah against foreign gods. Polytheism was itself the expression of local independence, and nothing could incite the Grecian states to any unity of action except threatened invasion by Persia. The warfare of the gods both expressed or perpetuated the same state of affairs in the Achæan peninsula. In the colder region of philosophy the same idea was expressed in the conception of Chaos followed by a multiple of elements always in the process of union and disruption. The religious and philosophic ideas ran parallel and had their influence on political action, which consisted of perpetual war and preparation for war. Brotherhood and the arts of peace were hardly possible when the gods set no ethical example and when nature was conceived as a chaos of elements struggling into a casual and transient order.

But Xenophanes, the philosopher, came forward to express in one conception the unity of nature and of the Divine. He insisted, against both anthropomorphism and polytheism, that there was but one God and that he was not human in character. The philosophers, who were the educators of the statesmen, urged this view; and, with the rise of skepticism concerning the character of the gods, it gained possession of all thinking minds. Instead of a chaos of warring elements, the world was conceived as a cosmos, an orderly arrangement of harmonious elements. Hardly had philosophy achieved this triumph when Alexander the Great undertook to extend the area of empire. We must not forget that he was educated by Aristotle, the greatest of philosophers, and, as Dante called him, the " master of those who know." Aristotle may not have approved of the military conquests of his ward; but that conception of unity and order expressed in the Demiourgos of Plato, the Nous of Anaxagoras, and the *primum mobile* of Aristotle, was the precursor of the empires of Alexander the Great and of Julius Cæsar. It brought forth directly in the Stoics the anticipation of Christianity expressed in their conception of the brotherhood of man. Whether because of indolence or social corruption and decay, they did not put their doctrine into practical effect, and the traditions of war kept back human redemption until another civilization could revive it under the wings of theism and the belief of immortality, when the " wars and commotions that had revolved through long tracts of time had terminated in one immense dominion and the troubled elements of human society sank into universal calm. The spirit of war, wearied by perpetual carnage, had seemed willing to enjoy a moment's slumber or was hushed into silence by the advent of the Prince of Peace."

The brotherhood of man came first as the ideal of a philosophy unable to contend against the decadence of the social system that Plato had tried to preserve. But belief in the unity of nature extended the conception of government and left to all posterity the ideal of a state that shall realize universal empire without conquest, an ideal that arbitration and the Court of The Hague are now attempting to bring about.

Let me take, as another instance of the influence of a concept on conduct and politics, Copernican astronomy. Until the sixteenth century it was the universal belief that the sun went around the earth. The earth was conceived as the center of the universe toward which all heavy matter moved unless sustained by some mysterious power. There was no theory of gravity to explain this motion. The earth was supposed to be flat, and, without adequate means of navigation, there was no way to refute this hypothesis. The ignorance and superstition of the age prevented the exercise of that adventurous spirit which later surmounted so many obstacles. The known limits of the earth were very narrow, and, with no unifying conception like gravitation to explain the cosmos and the relations of its parts, the mind was left free to believe in all sorts of capricious powers or beings as explanation of such unity as was actually found.

But the Ptolemaic system had its anomalies which appeared confusing to Copernicus. He simply asked whether the hypothesis that the earth moves about the sun would not satisfy all the demands of an explanation and eliminate the perplexities which had to be solved in the Ptolemaic system by suppositions as disturbing as the primary assumption. Copernicus saw that this new theory fitted, and so clear were its consequences that the priests thought to overthrow it by asserting that, if it were true, the planets would show phases as does the moon. Galileo accepted the challenge and pointed out the phases of Venus. From that time on the triumph of Copernican astronomy was assured. This discovery may be said to have given the initial impulse to the Protestant Reformation. It was not so felt, nor was it a part of any conscious revolt against the political and ecclesiastical institutions of the Middle Ages, but it was a decisive triumph over accepted ideas. The stupidity of the church had given the incipient scientific spirit an opportunity to display its power. That stupidity consisted in having linked religious beliefs too closely with the fortunes of a cosmic theory that was not true. At first Christianity was concerned only with the immortality of the soul and the brotherhood of man and the worship of God, without concern for any speculations about the nature of the world. But in becoming the heir to the Roman Empire as an agent for the reorganization of society, the church appropriated the domain of physical knowledge and associated it so closely with its scheme of salvation that the least break in its wall would threaten it with destruction. Its power frightened every inquirer away from the study of nature, and kept men respectfully silent concerning everything but the prevailing conceptions in politics and religion, and in these fields expression had to be obsequious and flattering. The church had complete control of knowledge and behavior.

This coalition of science and religion was both a strength and a weakness. If religious belief had been placed upon a basis unaffected by the vicissitudes of physical science, no change in the constitution of that knowledge would have affected the fortunes of the church. It might have gone on in blissful peace, unharmed by physical discoveries. But the tendency was to associate religion with science, to identify it with cosmic views. The ancient toleration of all religions, the result of the politician's indifference to them and his exclusive interest in economic questions, had kept religion more or less free from concern with physical knowledge. Religious people were taxed, not educated. But Christianity set a new example. Man was to be saved, and taxation became a secondary interest. The church set about the unifying of human opinion. With the machinery of the Roman Empire in its hands, it could use force as well as reason to achieve this unity; and it used these resources with relentless energy. It was impossible to avoid appropriating physical science, such as it was, to this end, and after Paul had set the example of conceiving man's salvation as a part of the cosmic system, it was only natural that the church, which was at the same time the state, should monopolize all knowledge and determine the right to believe or not to believe. From the tolerance of all religious beliefs which had characterized Pagan policy it went to the opposite extreme of tolerating none but its own, and thus claimed the keys to all knowledge physical and spiritual, holding the scepter of political power to enforce its claims.

It will be apparent that the whole system was thus delicately balanced. The effectual disturbance of any part of it involved the whole in ruin, though it would take as many ages to effect the dissolution as it would take to educate the whole mass of believers. Copernican astronomy established the falsity of one of the fundamental tenets of the church. Confidence in its authority and wisdom was irretrievably shaken by the proof that the Ptolemaic conception of celestial action was false. To yield without resistance and to reconstruct its position in accordance with the new point of view was as much the policy of wisdom as it was of allegiance to the truth. But the church would have none of this policy. It forced Copernicus to recant and threatened Galileo with the stake. It clearly saw the consequences of the new knowledge and thought to controvert its influence. No doubt there were sporadic and perhaps frequent cases of skepticism throughout this period, but the skeptic is not usually a missionary and is adept in the prudences which center about self-preservation; besides, the power of those in authority was so great as to make any other course than prudence appear foolhardy. Only when a man had the courage of a martyr would he venture to question the integrity of the system under which he lived.

It is to be remarked that those who sought to correct the scientific beliefs of the time still sincerely adhered to the religious doctrines of the church. But the ecclesiastical tribunal insisted that physical science was intimately bound up with its scheme of salvation and spiritual philosophy. It was determined that the new view of the cosmos should not prevail, and thus exposed itself to the tremendous consequences of Galileo's telescope, which gave actual sensible proof of what the priests themselves had said should follow from the claims of Copernicus. No more effective mode of silencing opposition could have been devised. It took time to effect the final overthrow of ecclesiastical domination, but the coming destruction was evident in this one incident in the career of scholasticism. There followed Kepler's theory that the planetary orbits were ellipses, and both Galileo and Kepler prepared the way for Newton's theory of universal gravitation. Then came the theory of evolution, which did for time what Newton and Copernicus had done for space, unifying cosmic causal action in both spheres, in direct antagonism to the dogmas of the church.

On its practical side, this new astronomy gave impetus to the curiosity which led to the theory of Columbus that land should be found on the opposite side of the earth. The next inevitable step was to penetrate beyond the limitations of vision which the sea placed upon human knowledge. To establish a reason for undertaking such a journey, Columbus had to use the difference between the specific gravity of water and of solid matter to prove that there must be land at the antipodes to balance the protrusion of the European continent from the ocean. Step by step the whole system of knowledge and economic interest led to this issue. America opened up to the imagination and cupidity of Europe such a field of adventure and exploitation as made the Crusades appear worthless in comparison. But all was done in the name and under the protection of religion. Neither an avowed nor a concealed attack on that system was involved. The new opportunity for adventure and for the acquisition of wealth could easily claim and receive the patronage of the church. The ultimate influence of the new discoveries on religious belief was not apparent. But the discovery of the new world was only another result of the initial conception of Copernicus.

The next step was a direct assault on the authority of the Pope and an attack on the church in its central position. The Protestant Reformation simply marked the growth of the skepticism which had been encouraged by the triumph of Galileo when he exhibited to every human eye the phases of Venus. Physical science had by this time established its claim to a hearing, more or less regardless of the consequences to traditional dogma. Its votaries, however, still claimed allegiance to the church and tried to enlist the new knowledge in its defence. But the Reformation emancipated thought sufficiently to free it from any need of defending itself by obsequiousness, and physical science soon took a course which placed it in antagonism to religion. The freedom of conscience was only a corollary to the freedom of the intellect, which was established beyond the right of cavil by the death-blow dealt by Copernicus to the Ptolemaic system of astronomy.

No better illustration of the influence of an idea, worked out into its logical consequences, on the common conceptions of mankind could be imagined. If astronomy had been a matter of interest to only a small clique of philosophers, its influence would have extended no farther. But the sense-perception of men was so identified with the Ptolemaic system that a direct and intelligent assault upon it was necessary to show the senses their error. Proof of the fallibility of those who had been the depositors of all knowledge disturbed the general confidence and established a new source of knowledge and a new standard for scientific discovery and advancement. The supremacy of the church was doomed from that moment, though it took many centuries to complete its downfall, aided by the inventions that, under the direction of physical science, have so cheapened the spread of knowledge that it comes within the reach of the multitude. The printing press and the invention of paper made this dissemination possible; but they would hardly have had permission so to extend knowledge but for the weakness of the church after the enforced surrender of its old authority as the protector of all human beliefs. The keystone of its arch was its cosmogony; and, when Copernicus removed this, it fell into ruins, though it took time to relax the cohesiveness of its parts. The whole of modern history was determined by this one revolution in thought. The same development might indeed have occurred without these specific discoveries of Copernicus and Galileo; but these were crucial events in the actual series that constitute history. It is certain that the break in the wall was actually accomplished by Copernicus, no matter how many before him may have seen or felt its weakness. The initial impulse to revolution was given by his conception of the cosmos, though it might not have proved effective but for the sympathy and aid that he received from the intellectual preparation prevalent among his contemporaries. This one idea was the rallying point for reconstruction, and must have the credit of starting human knowledge upon the course of its subsequent development.

No one can directly trace the effect of this scientific revolution upon politics, but it is nevertheless a remote consequence of Copernican astronomy that our political institutions are what they are. No political freedom is possible until men have obtained intellectual freedom, and no one had this intellectual freedom until the progress of physical science and discovery had shown that the church held false views of the universe. Church and state were so closely associated that the slightest disturbance of their union was sure to make itself felt throughout the whole organism. The Reformation recognized this relation, and, after trying to obtain its freedom without a break with the papal system, Germany obtained it only by the use of political power. England soon followed under Henry VIII, and the papal power began to weaken. Gradually Europe threw off the shackles and the papal supremacy remained intact only in Italy and Spain, until at last Italy confined the political dominion of the papacy to the Vatican. But states could not throw off the yoke of the church without teaching their subjects the same rebellious spirit. Men had already learned to distrust the authority of the priest, first in science and finally in religion. But gradually the spirit which had led men to resist authority on scientific questions expressed itself in opposition to the arbitrary powers of government, and representative institutions were the consequence. Political freedom is thus traceable to the work of Copernicus in disputing the Ptolemaic astronomy. I shall not venture to assert that this one early astronomic discovery was the only force leading to the final result, but it is entitled to precedence in the estimation of causes.

We see, therefore, in the history of conceptions, those of the unity of the world and of the Copernican astronomy, the ultimate influence of ideas on social and political institutions. Both were scientific doctrines, yet they affected such remote concerns as constitutions and governments.

We are all familiar with the influence of the theory of evolution on modern ideas of nature and man, and with its destructive effect on the older ethical ideas and institutions. It has given impetus to the materialistic tendencies of the age, initiated by the physical discoveries of the past, and its influence has not yet reached its climax. But I shall not work out the details of this last agency in modifying our conceptions of nature and man. It suffices to have shown the social and political effects of two great physical doctrines, and then to ask whether any special conception of man and his destiny can have a similar effect on human institutions.

One does not have to go beyond Gibbon to know what influence on history the doctrine of man's immortality has exercised. It produced this effect without applying the brotherhood of man in connection with the doctrine of immortality, as it had been taught by the founder of Christianity. The concept of human brotherhood was as much a reaction against the narrow policy of Judaism as it was the logical consequence of Greek monism in philosophy. Judaism had drawn very sharply the distinction between the "stranger" or Gentile and its own race, and the former was almost entirely outside the pale of the law and the sanctuary. But when the better spirits of that race saw the defects of this narrow conception of God and man, even in the time of the prophets, they, like the Stoics, recognized the wider duties of human relationship, though without expressing them in civil institutions. The subjugation of Palestine by the Roman legions, however, brought home the lesson. In the dissolution of the ancient religion and the political institutions of the Jews, the utter desolation of both their sanctuary and their law, there came the sense of human brotherhood that never had appealed to the national consciousness in the days of its triumphs. The mind was prepared by its afflictions and the loss of its national hopes to listen to another gospel that suddenly appeared on the horizon — a belief that had not been characteristic of Judaism, namely, the doctrine of the immortality of the soul. It arose in opposition to the materialism of the Epicureans that had dominated the later periods of Greco-Roman history and that had come to infect the sects of Judaism. It established a new point of view for the interpretation of the world and of man. With its spiritual conception of God, this new doctrine availed to give the spiritual conception of things the primary place in determining the meaning of the cosmos and human institutions. The ultimate reality of matter was denied, and spirit was regarded as the cause instead of the effect of matter. The whole of mediæval philosophy and theology was based upon this conception. The whole material universe was supposed to have been created by spirit and subordinated to the interests of man and his salvation.

Apart from comparison and contrast of the Greek with the Judaistic movement, the important point is the place which the idea of the immortality of the soul held in the reconstruction of political institutions that had crumbled into ruin on account of the ravages of materialism. What it kept in the forefront of human thought was the value of the individual man, the permanent importance of his personality, showing that it was this and not the glories of the state that survived the ravages of time. Ancient civilization had no such conception of the relation between the state and the individual citizen as we hold. Man existed for the institutions, political and religious, that prevailed. He was a servant, not a master, of the social order. He paid his tribute and gave his life to it without being able to exact any but the most meager service from it. The state had all the rights and the citizen none, and on critical examination the state turned out to be embodied in certain favored individuals with irresponsible power to rule the citizen as they pleased. But to adopt the immortality of the soul as the center of human interest and to conceive the cosmos as an order subordinate to man's development and salvation wrought a profound change. It brought forward, not only the value of the individual, but also a conception of his relation to things which opposed his subordination to political masters and made even nature a servant to his ends. In this way the immortality of the soul involved human brotherhood; and this latter idea attained a practical importance, instead of a purely speculative interest.

When the attempt to put into practice the brotherhood of man by its early communistic system had failed, Christianity concentrated its interest on the realization of its kingdom of God in a life beyond the grave; and, with an ascetic view of life and a pessimistic view of nature, it set about reorganizing ethical and religious institutions around the idea of personal salvation. The radical character of its theistic conception, which made no concessions to materialism, and the enthusiasm for a future life resulted in fifteen centuries of uninterrupted triumph for the Christian view of life and social relations. The traditions of government, combined with other influences, made it impossible or inconvenient to carry out the communism implied in the notion of human brotherhood, and the mediæval period had to be content with charity as the embodiment of its social feeling; and even this was regarded as a means of personal salvation rather than as the expression of altruistic feeling. But two ideas remained dominant in the minds of men: the immortality of the soul and the attainment of that immortality by human service. These ideas implied the subordination of the state to the welfare of the subject, even though government continued to use its power for arbitrary and selfish ends. Alexander the Great and Julius Cæsar sought to establish universal dominion for the sake of the glories of political power and conquest; Christianity in the Middle Ages sought the same end, at least nominally and ostensibly, for the salvation of the citizen. The early Christian's "Kingdom of God," Augustine's "Civitas Dei," and the "Utopia" of Sir Thomas More could not have been conceived on any other basis, and they lacked only the will of men in order to become effective.

The placing of man's hopes in another life tempted him to buy his salvation with perfunctory works. He also showed a contempt for physical nature hardly compatible with his view of the relation of Providence to its creation. The reaction against the debaucheries of Epicurean materialism carried him into an "otherworldliness" scarcely less objectionable than the previous worldliness. The belief that matter is essentially evil in its nature led only to the fixing of human vision on an imaginary world that was less carnal only because it could not be made the subject of personal experience here and now. Such a statement, of course, is qualified by the presence, in many minds, of purer conceptions of duty and of the hereafter. But even Dante's and Milton's works were founded on a more literal interpretation of Christianity than the idealistic theories that came after. The very necessity of adapting its ideals to the understanding of the multitude for whose salvation every individual was responsible was an influence to keep religious conceptions upon the plane of the sensory imagination. Protestantism, with its vindication of individual judgment, put the priest at the mercy of those whom he had previously been privileged to direct, and inevitably the standard of sense-perception again became the measure of truth even in the strongholds of the church. With the revival of this point of view, the ascetic conception of life was sure to meet criticism. The renaissance, on the one hand, with its revival of interest in Greek ideals, and the reinstatement of the study of nature in astronomy, physics, and chemistry, on the other, brought into being the materialistic attitude that has dominated the subsequent centuries.

But, if the priority of spiritual interests resulted only in their overthrow by physical science, we shall be asked why we attempt to reinstate an idea that has been tried and found wanting. When so much progress has been effected by modern science, why endeavor to turn its wheel backward?

The first answer is that we have only been stating history, not adopting an ideal. I have been mainly interested in the efficacy of the spiritual ideal to produce a civilization and to sustain it much longer than Greece and Rome were able to maintain their institutions. If duration of success is a measure of value, the Christian conception of life has won the approval of time, and it yet remains for physical science to accomplish a similar result.

A second reply is simply to call attention to the consequences of the materialism in which we live. One need not question the importance of the revival of physical science; and this concession is not grudgingly made. The religious mind had forfeited the confidence of most intelligent men by its departure from fact, as well as by its alliance with corrupt political institutions, and it had become so petrified in external works and ceremonies that the really ethical mind could not accept its hypocrisies, even when it conceded the value of ritualism to some temperaments. When physical science had once proved its ability to explain the universe, or at least to show that the order of nature had not been accurately described by the theologians, the way was opened for the system which could make the world appear reasonable. The confidence in priestcraft was impaired and in its place came the enthusiasm for nature and for those who could understand its processes and use its agencies in the service of human comfort.

The triumph of physical science has given us what may be called the economic age, an age in which the accumulation of wealth is greater than at any other period of history. We enjoy advantages which antiquity never dreamed of. We have multiplied the forces of invention and machinery, which increase production a hundredfold and, in thus increasing the supply of goods, similarly increase the demand. The production due to machinery has far outstripped the actual needs of even the larger population; but it has been matched by a similarly greater consumption. This satisfaction of an increased number of desires leads directly to the estimation of life by physical instead of intellectual and spiritual standards. Political freedom followed the emancipation of the intellect by science and created preconceptions on which the average mind measures the claims of any belief, while the reign of comfort compared with the struggle for existence in the Middle Ages makes most minds inaccessible to spiritual appeals. Ethics has to wait on economics, for when the latter gets the first hearing there is no time nor inclination for the former. The theater is preferred to the church. We doubt the reality of any life hereafter to make sacrifices for, and we "make hay while the sun shines," that is, we expend all our labor in the accumulation of the means for physical enjoyment. Travel and amusement offer more pleasure than does worship, and, as nature is not to be feared but appropriated to the making of money, there are no terrors to blast our hopes. If we can make our satisfactions of the sensuous sort sufficiently intense, we may be so spiritually benumbed as not to fear death any more. We face it, not as Stoics, whose maxims pay an involuntary tribute to hopes that they do not share, but as Epicureans, who have got all they want until their satiated senses no longer feel the love of life. We expect the sacrifices we make to be repaid with interest, and we place our political power in the hands of the "business" man who knows how to play the part of a sophist while he rifles our pockets. The standards of success are those of the money maker, not those of the moralist. The measure of social standing is wealth, not intellect nor conscience. We are unable to accomplish anything without money, and common labor is a disgrace. All the duties of the world rest on the poor and all the liberties are with the rich.

It is scarcely possible to overestimate the influence of this materialism. We all know its power, but ignore its tendencies. Our philosophy does not protect us against the insidious encroachments of this materialism, which is as triumphant in speculation as in practice. We think Idealism is no protection against it, for in fact there is no difference between them in their practical working, except that one prizes intellectual accomplishments and the other financial success and sensuous enjoyments; neither acts on the supposition that we have a soul that survives death. The first great philosophical assault on Christian theology was the doctrine of the indestructibility of matter. Christianity affirmed the secondary and created nature of matter in all its forms, both sensible and supersensible. Plato had maintained that the function of Providence was only to arrange the cosmic elements in their order. Anaxagoras had held the same view of his Reason or Nous. Aristotle had his *primum mobile* start the universe and then sit back in contemplative bliss to watch it go. The Epicureans had taught that chance coincidence brought together the eternal elements or atoms and that the whole creation was brought about by these chance combinations of imperishable atoms. But Christianity assaulted this central position of the indestructibility of matter and took spirit to be the permanent reality. But the scientific proof of the indestructibility of matter and later of the conservation of energy exposed the error of this position, and the main philosophic fortress of Christianity was captured. The inevitable effect was to give matter the priority in speculative interest and to subordinate spirit to it. Spirit, from being the substance of reality, became its phenomenon, a transient accompaniment of it in some of its manifold organic forms. This view was soon supported by the discoveries of physiology, in which consciousness seemed to be the victimized creature of brain functions, not the ruler of a material organism. All the phenomena which the older view had regarded as proving the existence of a soul came to be regarded as mere incidents in the casual development of material bodies. Materialism became triumphant and the human mind, liberated from the speculative and political shackles of the mediæval period, began to enjoy its freedom in gradually breaking away from all the restraints that had developed and sustained the social, political, and religious conscience for so many centuries. We are still living in the period of rapid decline of the ethical impulse, and nothing but the possibility of reinstating a spiritual view of nature and life can restrain the progress of that retrograde movement.

The effect upon politics was felt as soon as the spiritual view of nature and life had lost the confidence of the public. Materialism relaxed the force of conscience while it opened the physical world to unlimited exploitation. All our laws are judged by those in power according to their relation to " business " or the accumulation of wealth, and the politician is as conscienceless as was the tax-gatherer in the Roman Empire. He has no ideals of human welfare, but only the desire to make the citizen pay tribute to his avaricious ambitions. If he can manipulate the laws he will save himself the trouble of work. The common citizen becomes saturated with the same ideals, and society is a struggle for wealth instead of for character. Science is on the side of materialism and all intelligence is against the church. But on all the issues that concern the correction of materialism the church itself is divided and is hopelessly implicated in the same ideals as our political system. In order to hold itself together the church has been obliged to resort to everything except the appeal to intelligence and may soon be reduced to mumbling a ritual over the cerements of its past. Materialism governs the thought and action of the common laborer, who was once under the influence of religion, and of the highest officers of state, who were once proud to serve the public, but now have only a predatory interest in the service which they can extort from the helpless citizens. We are following the path of Greco-Roman civilization in the days of its decadence, because the same economic and social forces are operative now as then, under the loss of the ethical ideals and beliefs of the preceding religious period. The laboring classes have abandoned their religion, and are struggling with the capitalists for a share in the profits of production. Their philosophy and ideals are the same as those of the capitalist; they too are straining their efforts only to secure a larger share of materialistic reward.

I am not questioning the right to insist on economic justice nor even the importance of more nearly equal distribution of the world's goods. But the value of this larger share will depend wholly upon the use to which it is put when it has been acquired. Money is power, and like all power it should receive respect only in proportion to its furtherance of ethical ideals. Materialism offers no ideals but those of sense to the majority of men; the few who follow the intellectual life make it an otiose escape from toil. The ultimate value of this culture and of the inner life is not indicated. It is to end in the grave and nothing is to be left to our children but the short memory of it. The redemption that we seek is from poverty, not from sin. The joys of life are those of the table, the holiday, and the theater.

This is a dark picture, and there are not wanting exceptions to whom such a judgment does not apply. I have no doubt that more than five can be found to save our modern Sodom and Gomorrah. There is always a sufficient leaven to protect the whole from final destruction; but it is the part of a discussion like this to point out the tendencies that might reduce the saving influences to impotency. We need above all to revive the spiritual meaning of existence. I do not mean that we shall return to the beliefs of the past, nor that we have to subordinate the material universe to spirit in the same sense as before. Certain discoveries of physical science with their implications must remain a permanent acquisition of knowledge and practice. They have taught us to acknowledge that inflexible order of nature which is quite as important to our ethics as any revelation of its limitations. A part of man's salvation lies in the humility which a fixed order makes necessary; only false pride can come from feeling that he has nature always at his command. A limitation on the will is quite as important as freedom, and a materialism which imposes inexorable limits to human arrogance is quite as ethical an influence as any view which makes man despise nature. But materialism may be as onesided as spiritualism; we need to restore the importance of consciousness and duty in the world, and this restoration depends on the proof that there is a soul and a future life instead of mental phenomena that are mere incidental functions of the brain.

If psychic research promises anything to the world it holds out hope of throwing light upon the nature and destiny of the soul, and of doing this by the scientific method instead of by pure speculation or faith. If belief in immortality carries the same assurance that we have of Copernican astronomy, Newtonian gravitation, and Darwinian evolution, it will have an efficacy that can never attach to a belief not so assured.

The revival of the importance of spirit in nature will have the same power to uphold moral agencies in the world that it had in the past. The value that the doctrine gives to human personality enables the teacher of mankind to enforce his ideals of morality. We have seen what a subordinate place the individual had in the politics of antiquity, when the social system took no account of the importance of personality and of our duty to save it. No sense of responsibility for the salvation of our neighbor was inculcated in the ancient religion or politics. Those in power were at liberty to exploit the rest of mankind as they pleased. But Christianity created a new social standard, based upon the importance of the individual soul and our responsibility for its salvation. The materialistic reaction has threatened this conception with extinction, as is apparent in the new imperialism that has arisen and in the contempt for other races that has followed. We no longer feel the racial sympathy that the missionary felt or the sense of the unity of the human race created by the obligation to extend the influence of Christianity. We have adopted morals that threaten our own race with extinction and then despise or fear those races that promise to take our place. That our social conduct might injure a soul's life after death does not enter into our calculations. But if we can prove that the materialistic theory of consciousness is false and that man has a more important end than the satisfaction of his bodily wants and his merely earthly happiness we shall have established a new fulcrum for the moralist.

It is not the mere fact that we survive death that will affect the conduct of individuals and societies, but its place in the organic system of ideas of the body politic. It was not the mere belief in immortality that gave Christianity its efficacy, but its doctrine of limited probation that enabled it to carry out both its ecclesiastical and political policies. But that doctrine of probation would have had no meaning at all without belief in a future life. It is clear that belief in a future life is the best fortification for all the duties which have a relation to an existence beyond the present. If we can organize in association with that belief a stronger sense of human brotherhood it must ultimately influence our political institutions as profoundly as did the fifteen centuries of Christian supremacy, though it may take as long to attain that end. But this time it has scientific method and authority instead of mere faith and opinion to support it. If science can furnish men a creed by which they are to live for some end other than the present life, the reconciliation between science and religion, which has been so long sought, may easily be attained.

I have not appealed to the sentimental value of the belief in anything that I have said of its importance. I have emphasized only the intellectual place which it may hold in supporting or reconstructing the foundations of ethics and moral idealism. Its influence on the griefs and sufferings of mankind is scarcely less great than the influence of medicine, and is capable of being made greater. On that feature of its value I shall not dwell. If the theory of evolution can modify all the maxims which prevented men from modelling their attitude toward their neighbors after the standards of nature, we may well imagine what a defence of humanitarianism may be based upon the proof of survival after death, especially if we find, as we may, that the destiny of every man is affected by the character of his physical life quite as much as by the habits of his soul. It is at least certain that a new measure of human value will come into use if we find nature to be as careful of personality as she is of the elements. The certainty of the survival of personality will put a stop to all those skeptical discussions which postpone the acceptance of ethical standards founded on immortality until the proof of survival is presented. It will give the idealists a chance to reanimate that estimate of life from which spring both poetry and religion, and with these that sense of human relationship which may do more to reconstruct politics than all other intellectual forces.

CHAPTER XXXI

SUMMARY AND REFLECTIONS

THE facts reported in this volume are but samples from a thousandfold larger mass, whose meaning is apparent. Whatever skepticism prevails regarding them is due to various influences. Sometimes it is mere prejudice, sometimes it is ignorance both of the problem and of the facts; and there is much opposition that is based on neither prejudice nor ignorance, but on mere intellectual obstinacy and pride. It is easy to oppose any belief if you are so disposed. Reasons can always be given, whether rational or not, against a theory, if one chooses to give them. The "will to disbelieve" is quite as prevalent as the "will to believe," and is no more creditable. Much prejudice and ignorance are excusable, when we consider how powerfully environment acts on our beliefs. Unanimity of opinion is essential to any social order. We keep out of perpetual war only by agreeing on something. Our interests are so bound up with the opinion of the community that it is not safe for us to take the part of rebels. Hence we accept the ideas in which we are born and bred. Childhood trusts, and our beliefs are largely made in childhood. The line of least resistance is to follow the ideas of the community. Prejudice is, therefore, more or less unavoidable, at least on matters about which we have little or no opportunity to work out systematic beliefs. Ignorance is but an accompaniment of these influences and is more excusable than prejudice, because the latter has a tendency to include influences from the desire and the will.

Hostility, however, based upon intellectual pride and obstinacy has no such excuse. It is irrefutable except by ridicule and the resistance of public opinion. It infects all minds sophisticated by knowledge and tending to defend preëxisting ideas. It causes a sort of obsession which has become fixed partly by personal interests and partly by the extent to which this knowledge represents accepted scientific truth. Nevertheless, all intelligent people are called upon to keep preconceptions in abeyance in the presence of new facts. No doubt the discoverer of new truth may exhibit too much haste to revolutionize things, but this fault is not any worse than an inflexible conservatism in a changing and progressing world. Truth is always dependent on facts enough to make it clear that it represents some sort of law in the world. Even if facts are exceptional, they must be compatible with the unity in nature. Frequency of occurrence is the evidence of law and of articulation with the cosmic order. This fact explains, and at least half justifies, the cautiousness of the average man in weighing every claim that comes along for the supernormal. But history has shown us that caution has its limits. Such an influence might be invoked, as it was by the church, against any change of our ideas whatever. But no such habit should characterize the scientific mind. The very essence of science is the understanding of change as well as of the constancies of nature. The scientist has always insisted that we relax religious obstinacy and prejudice in the consideration of hypotheses that might seem to conflict with preëstablished ideas. It therefore becomes obligatory upon him to practice his own preaching in the consideration of supernormal phenomena.

The course suggested, however, has not often been taken. From no one has psychic research met more opposition than from the scientific man. His attitude is explicable, but not always excusable. The conquests of physical science are supposed to have eliminated the "supernatural" from human belief, and most scientific men think that psychic research threatens to restore that beast to power. But there is no danger that past conceptions will again find currency, and no serious consequences can happen from giving the term "supernatural" as clear a meaning as that of "nature."' Those who reduce everything to "nature" can hardly give an intelligible account of what they mean by the term save as the order of frequently observed facts. And yet this is made an idol for a worship as extravagant as that of a savage for his fetish.

The emphasis, however, upon regularity is important. The systematic and rational behavior of life depends upon the constancies of the cosmos. If it were as changeable as the supernaturalist assumes it to be, there would be little opportunity for any ethical development and perhaps none for the slow evolution of human life and its functions. It is the constancy of "nature" that makes possible human character and development. The scientific skeptic of the "supernatural" has in his hands the answer to the question *cui bono,* if only he will use it instead of merely making the concept of nature serve as the basis of a new dogmatism and a new intolerance. But in order to defend regularity, he sacrifices all the benefits that come from a spiritual conception of the world's order. His opponent insists as strenuously on a conception that invokes caprice against law. Why are not both law and caprice as reconcilable with nature as with the supernatural? Why should either of them be regarded either as necessary or as antagonistic to one or the other of these conceptions? It is certain that both exist, whatever view we take of either nature or the supernatural. What we want is *facts;* we can then decide whether they are natural or supernatural.

It is wearisome to insist on the meaning of such facts as I have cited in this volume. Their import is clear. They certainly make a spiritistic hypothesis acceptable. The illustrations quoted may not suffice to demonstrate the existence of a future life, if taken alone or regarded as the total evidence in favor of such a theory, and I do not quote them with the expectation that they alone will settle the issue. They are but examples of phenomena as old as history and as extensive and constant as any other phenomenon of nature. But they are better accredited than most instances and so make it imperative for them to be investigated.

The only difficulty the spiritistic hypothesis faces is the ignorance and prejudice of the public. That ignorance and prejudice may be excusable; but they are obstacles, and the only obstacles, to the belief in immortality. The objections based upon the triviality of the facts, the fragmentary and confused nature of the communications, and the absurdity of the revelations are beside the mark. They betray total ignorance of the problem and of the process involved in getting the data. The problem of the proof of personal identity is crucial, and nothing but trivial facts will satisfy the conditions of such proof. The fragmentary nature of the messages and the apparent absurdities of revelations about the other world are caused by the process of communicating and by the difficulties of representing a different world in terms of our own. Untrained readers assume too readily that the conditions of intercourse between the two worlds are either like our own or so nearly like them as not to affect the contents of the messages. The spiritistic hypothesis is not itself a revelation, but an explanation. Its development and ramifications await future work. At present it is necessary as a means of making the main facts intelligible. It maintains only that there is scientific evidence of the survival of personal consciousness, and not that we know all about the nature and conditions of a transcendental world. It establishes the main point, and leaves the accessories of the hypothesis to be determined.

Personally I regard the fact of survival after death as scientifically proved. I agree that this opinion is not upheld in scientific quarters. But this is neither our fault nor that of the facts. Evolution was not believed until long after it was proved. The fault lay with those who were too ignorant or too stubborn to accept the facts. History shows that every intelligent man who has gone into this investigation, if he gave it adequate examination at all, has come out believing in spirits; this circumstance places the burden of proof on the shoulders of the skeptic.

The present war and the manner in which it is making multitudes think of the meaning of life and death will do more than a hundred years of academic talk to awaken interest in the problem. Thousands who suffer losses and ask what they mean, would not think of the matter so keenly in the ordinary vicissitudes of life. The person suffering the pangs of grief or asking for a solution of the enigma of existence, and not afraid of his neighbors, will think for himself; and, even if he does appear to have an emotional bias, he will see facts more clearly than the man who boasts of his exemption from the influence of personal interest, but who, in reality, is only under the domination of another interest equally strong and more dangerous because the man has the illusion that he is free from it. Those who have to face the realities, both economical and moral, will not trust their salvation to sophists or to men who do not enter into the real problems of the world. They will go straight to the solution that fits the facts, and as usual the academic sophist will lose his hold on the forces of civilization. Insight has more to do with the problem and its solution than much learning. The public will go straight to the heart of the matter, and those who assume academic authority without scientific knowledge of the facts will find themselves shorn of power. Those who should have led will have to follow. If they do not see their opportunity, we can only repeat the warning of the prophet: Israel is joined to his idols, let him alone.

The circumstance that gives so much power to skepticism is the uninterrupted triumph of physical science, based on the easy observation and reproduction of its phenomena. It has relied upon sense-perception for its data and especially for such data as it can easily verify in human experience. The more elusive phenomena of nature it either ignores or questions, and thus has established a criterion of reality that makes the claims of supersensible facts difficult to establish. Very early it excluded spiritual reality from the causes of the world, even when it admitted its existence. The earlier and later materialists in Greek philosophy were at one on this point. They all agreed that the gods existed, but they gave them no causal influence in the world. They were assigned to a place in the intermundia where they were harmless and inefficient, where they were equally unable to cause evil or to do good. Their position might be envied by those who suffer from the pains of unremitting toil, but it would offer no delightful prospect to those who abhor idleness. They could not assuage grief and pain nor exercise any benevolent force in the universe. They could only live in an idleness that is as irksome to the ethical man as it is envied by the unethical. They are

> The Gods who haunt
> The lucid interspace of world and world,
> Where never creeps a cloud, or moves a wind,
> Nor ever falls the least white star of snow,
> Nor ever lowest roll of thunder moans,
> Nor sound of human sorrow mounts to mar
> Their sacred everlasting calm.

Beings that only watch things go will never be objects either of fear or reverence, nor appear as ideals for moral character.

But whatever we believe about immortality to-day, we cannot question the causal influence of consciousness on the stream of physical phenomena. If we once grant the existence of spirit, incarnate or discarnate, we must admit it to a place among the causes in nature; indeed we shall hardly discover its existence save through its effects. But we do not question its causal power in the series of physical and mental phenomena that come to our attention, and we do not accept the *a priori* theories that defined the nature and limits of mind in the Epicurean and other forms of materialism. All that we do is to insist on evidence; and only the prejudices for a theory that relies as much on tradition as do the orthodoxies of religion, now stand in the way of a ready belief in the existence of discarnate spirit. The evidences of its causal influence in the physical world are so plentiful that they are almost self-evident. We have therefore only to prove that it survives death, to prove that its causal action extends beyond the grave, as there is no proof of survival which does not carry with it the implication of some influence on the living as the condition of that proof.

The phenomena of spiritual healing and of obsession well illustrate the extent of the causal action of discarnate consciousness. The symptoms of hysteria, of secondary personality, of some maladies diagnosed as dementia precox and paranoia, and perhaps others, assure us of an immense field for the practical application of psychic research, which will be recognized as soon as the world accepts the fact of survival. In the recurrence of spiritual healing, primitive Christianity will be revived. A new meaning will be put into the New Testament and the work of Christ.

Moreover, the ethical value of the belief in survival can hardly be measured. An age that has had to give it up because of materialism and the lack of evidence pretends not to be interested in it. It assumes the garb of courage and of Stoicism, parading in self-righteousness what is but the virtue of necessity. It is hardly to be blamed. Our duty always is to make the best of a bad bargain. But why insist that life is a bad bargain? "All is well that ends well," even if we have spilled the milk. Nature may not be a Medusa-head after all. Many of her rougher actions and inflictions of pain are but the just discipline for our own vices. The great fog-bank into which materialism sails is more easily penetrated than it surmises. It conceals a beautiful sun-lit sea and the happy isles, and psychic research ventures on embarking where the philosophy of Immanuel Kant only warned the sailor against rocky shoals and disaster. Mythology was sound in its psychology and its ethics when, after allowing the escape of all the evils in the world, it left Hope at the bottom of Pandora's box.

No one can act rationally in life without hope. It is essential to every desire we have and to every volition we exercise. There is no rationality in any act save as we can hope for its fruition as the fulfillment of our wishes. If personality has any value in nature, we must appraise it as nature does. If consciousness perishes at death it is clear that hope has no application beyond the grave. If personality extends beyond the grave, hope has a wider sphere of meaning, and so has life. Personality takes the chief place in the estimation of values and both our individual and our social ethics may be based upon it. The disposition to prolong consciousness and to value the higher intellectual and emotional expressions of it above the lower is so much testimony to that evaluation.

It is not necessary to take an optimistic view of the world in dealing with the question. The scientific problem is to guarantee survival, whether it is desirable or not, whether the next world is ideal or unpleasantly real. In saying a word for hope in the scheme of things, we may not offer assurance of satisfaction for every specific desire we cultivate or indulge. It will be enough to show that nature ensures the survival of personal identity; and then, whatever curtailment of our selfish expectations may follow, we still have the opportunity of correction. Annihilation will allow neither progress nor correction of the past. Desire and volition have no meaning except with reference to a future; and, with no prospect of attainment of our aims, we can have little reverence for an order that allows no genuine achievement, and only keeps us at the eternal task of Sisyphus.

I do not forget that the belief in immortality may be abused. It is as easy to be too "other-worldly" as to be too worldly. The truth is beneficial or harmful according to the character of the man who accepts it. Guns and gunpowder are exceedingly useful in the hands of the right man, but a dangerous evil in the wrong hands. We prize liberty, but there is no conception which cannot be abused more than this. There is probably not a single truth which human nature cannot pervert. A belief in a future life is no exception. But the fact that it was abused in the Middle Ages, or that it may be too much stressed by some minds, is no reason for ignoring the doctrine. Some tell us that nature or Providence does not intend for us to know about a future life. But the same type of mind told us that we should not inquire into the processes of nature. While maintaining that nature is a product of the Divine and while enjoying the fruit of scientific conquests over it, they counselled neglecting its revelations! There is no truth that can be made more helpful to man than a belief in survival. It will all depend on his balance of mind. Disregarding it leads to emphasis on the materialism that has nearly wrecked civilization in the greatest war of history. We do not want the belief established in order to concentrate interest again on the hereafter, but to fix a balance in human endeavor. If nature values the inner life, what man has called the "spiritual" life, the virtues of reflection, gentility, unselfishness and all the attitudes of mind and will that take him away from an exclusively sensuous life, it is time that we have a philosophy and an outlook that helps to sustain the higher ideals of consciousness. It is for its reflex influence on the ethics of the present life that it is important, not for its power to make us ignore the imperative duties of the present.

We are told that the interest in immortality is a selfish one. It is probable that the belief can be used as selfishly as any other, but he who lays too much stress on this aspect of it does not know human nature. While I see many that have only a personal interest in it and only desire to gain a further surplus from nature after having an undue share of this world's goods, the most important feeling, in my experience and observation, is the altruism which lies at the basis of the most poignant grief. I find that those who suffer most from the doubt of immortality, do not care so much for survival for themselves as they do for their departed friends. They desire that their loved ones shall "still hae a stake" in the clash of the world's forces. With them it is an altruistic, not an egoistic hope, an unselfish, not a selfish desire. The bitterest pain and perplexity come where the affection is the strongest. In such situations it is quite as important to assuage grief as it is to satisfy appetites. When a man has lived the properly ethical life it is natural for him to feel disturbed at the thought of the interruption of life. He must seek in some belief a means of interpreting nature consistently with his moral ideals. He must find the clue to her purposes that he may be reconciled to the temporary appearance of inharmony in the world's ethical order. He wants to see far beyond in the future the trend of events which may sustain his faith in an ethical order while it keeps the torch of hope before him.

'Tis not for self we feel the glow
Of passion for continued life,
But love for those whose passage mars
The growth of soul and all its aims.
For death, in his remorseless path,
Leaves here no evidence for hope,
And we must seek its guerdon there
Where chance may bring a cheering word
From out the gates of grief and pain.
But when we bridge the sombre gulf
Twixt life and death, and learn that love
Still waits upon the shining shores
Of time and fate to meet us there,
We watch forever and forever
The distant purposes of God,

We may say that this is an emotional attitude of mind, and I do not question the statement. I only say that emotion has quite as legitimate a place in the world as intellect. It is the basis of all the ethics we possess, and intelligence is only a secondary acquirement in the cosmos. Science shows us that the chief function of intelligence is to enable us to occupy a better place in the struggle for existence; it is usually a thousandfold more egoistic than emotions.

The neglect or hostility which the subject receives is one of the curious problems of psychology. If a new engine for an aeroplane is announced the inventor is acclaimed a benefactor of the world. If some new substance to take the place of gasoline is discovered, all the capitalists in the country tumble over each other to get the control of it. A new element in chemistry is announced with all the fervor of a miracle. Anything that will fill the human belly with the husks that the swine do eat, is considered the greatest thing in the world. But if a man offers evidence that he has a soul and that he may expect to live after death, he is called insane, though he may prove the prolongation of consciousness, which is the one aspiration of every effort a man makes in life! No better indication of the utter materialism of the age could be adduced. But at last the consequences of war, bearing the fruits of materialism in the ugly spectacle of death and grief, are forcing attention on the subject.

The belief in immortality is the keystone to the arch of history, or the pivotal point about which move the intellectual, the ethical, and the political forces of all time. If science cannot protect our ethical ideals it will have to succumb to the same corrosion that has worn away the church. Something must put an end to doubt. There are many situations in life that call for heroic measures, and skepticism on the outcome of life offers no inducement to the heroic virtues.

Poetry has probably done more than philosophy to redeem the human race. It sees more than naked facts. These last we must see and respect, with all the clearness that will prevent their discoloration from interest and emotion. But if we suppose that knowledge achieves its ends without feeling, we shall miss the main opportunities of life. Neither one nor the other is the whole object of existence. They supplement each other. Plato's myth of the chariot drawn by the two steeds of passion and impulse, without the guidance of reason, illustrate the consequences of unadjusted energies.

Wisdom and passion
Playing for place,
Whichever winneth
Loses its grace.

When the two, peaceful,
Mingle and kiss,
Then cometh sweetly
Power and bliss.

The Stoic, on the one hand, and the Epicurean, on the other, equally miss the meaning of life. The *via media* has always been the path of sanity and common sense, and neither knowledge nor emotion alone will give intellectual and moral health. Their functions must be adjusted to each other; only on that condition will a man be saved the ravages of skepticism and the consequences of libertinism.

The age is in the throes of a search for certitude, and it is not limited, in that search, to the problem of immortality. The belief in immortality, which had been made important for many centuries, was doomed to decay unless assurance could be given the human mind regarding it. It had been so closely related to ethics that its decay threatened the destruction of all ethical and spiritual endeavor. We take what is certain, if it is only the sensuous life, but if we find that nature assigns this a secondary place and means to preserve the inner spiritual life for further cultivation the sacrifice of the physical and the sensuous is rendered more easy and even when it has a place in our spiritual development, it will not have the intensity of interest that it possesses when we have the prospect of nothing else.

It is easy for the man who has the comforts of life and who has stored up much goods, who has been successful in the struggle of existence, to congratulate himself on this security and to neglect Lazarus lying at his gates. He may thank God that he is not as other men are. But he should not blame the unsuccessful for taking a less optimistic view of nature. If the world has any claims to be regarded as good to its creatures, we should find the evidence of it in its outcome. We may endure temporary inequalities and suffering, if all ends well. But when the misfortunes of life are not equally distributed, we must not wonder that the victims of pain and disappointment are rebels. We may become reconciled to pain, if it results in a healing discipline, but if the chance for redemption and amelioration be forever cut off, the ugly spectre of death will give the final touch of despair to human ideals and hopes. We need to be in a position to see beyond the horizon, if the conflicts of the present life are to be met with patience and endurance. The wider outlook will soothe many a pain or give it a spiritual significance.

The sadder moments of a wearied hope
Find on their fringe a dream of better days,
And while their aura holds the leash of pain,
That keenly throbs about one's passing joys,
The bitter sweet will fuse its mingled shades
Into the calm majestic life of God.

Were we mere animals without ideals or hopes, we might be indifferent to the course of nature. We might live in the present moment without doing any violence to the moral laws. But if ideals encourage in us a life above the sensual we need assurance that nature will compensate us for the present loss; and if we find that survival is a part of her scheme, the bitterness that would haunt us if we were without hope will be less poignant. I do not emphasize the joys of such a hope or of its fruition. But we need an interpretation of the world which will do something to mitigate suffering, if we cannot escape it, or to excuse it, if we find it a means to an end. The sadness of sunset is only sublime pathos when we are assured of another dawn.

INDEX